PENGUIN

MEMOIRS FROM BEYOND THE TOMB

FRANÇOIS-RENÉ, VICOMTE DE CHATEAUBRIAND, was a brilliant representative of the reaction against the ideas of the French Revolution, and the most celebrated figure in French literature during the First Empire. He was born in Saint-Malo in 1768, and received a commission in the army in 1786. While living in Paris, he met the men of letters of whom he left remarkable portraits in his memoirs. Though not opposed to the Revolution in its first stages, Chateaubriand was disturbed by its excesses, and his restlessness caused him to depart for America in the spring of 1791. In 1792, after news of the arrest of Louis XVI brought him back to France, he married Céleste Buisson de Lavigne. His first publication, *Essai historique, politique et moral sur les révolutions*, in 1797, was written during his exile in England. His next work, *Atala, ou les amours de deux sauvages dans le désert*, appeared in 1801, and immediately made his reputation, thanks to its exquisite style, impassioned eloquence and glowing descriptions of nature. His *Génie du christianisme*, a defence of the Catholic faith, then appeared in 1802, on the eve of Napoleon's re-establishment of the Catholic religion in France. His influence in French literature, on authors such as Alfred de Vigny, Alphonse de Lamartine and Victor Hugo, was incalculable. Chateaubriand died on the 4th of July 1848, after spending the last fifteen years of his life writing his controversial and celebrated *Mémoires d'outre-tombe*, which were published shortly after his death.

ROBERT BALDICK was a Fellow of Pembroke College, Oxford and of the Royal College of Literature, and joint editor of Penguin Classics (1964–72). He translated the works of a wide range of French authors, from Chateaubriand, Flaubert, Huysmans and Verne to Montherlant, Sartre, Salacrou and Simenon. He also wrote a history of duelling, a study of the Siege of Paris, and biographies of Huysmans, the Goncourts, Frédérick Lemaître and Murger. He was married to the American writer and translator, Jacqueline Baldick. Robert Baldick died in 1972.

PHILIP MANSEL is a historian of France and the Middle East. His books on French history include *Louis XVIII* (1981), *The Court of France 1789–1830* (1989), and *Paris Between Empires* (2001). Six have been translated into French. In 2012 he won the London Library Life in Literature award. He is currently writing a life of Louis XIV and is editor of *The Court Historian*, journal of the Society for Court Studies (www.courtstudies.org).

FRANÇOIS-RENÉ DE CHATEAUBRIAND

Memoirs From Beyond the Tomb

Selected and translated by
ROBERT BALDICK

Introduction by
PHILIP MANSEL

PENGUIN BOOKS

PENGUIN CLASSICS

Published by the Penguin Group
Penguin Books Ltd, 80 Strand, London WC2R ORL, England
Penguin Group (USA) Inc., 375 Hudson Street, New York, New York 10014, USA
Penguin Group (Canada), 90 Eglinton Avenue East, Suite 700, Toronto, Ontario, Canada M4P 2Y3
(a division of Pearson Penguin Canada Inc.)
Penguin Ireland, 25 St Stephen's Green, Dublin 2, Ireland (a division of Penguin Books Ltd)
Penguin Group (Australia), 707 Collins Street, Melbourne, Victoria 3008, Australia
(a division of Pearson Australia Group Pty Ltd)
Penguin Books India Pvt Ltd, 11 Community Centre, Panchsheel Park, New Delhi – 110 017, India
Penguin Group (NZ), 67 Apollo Drive, Rosedale, Auckland 0632, New Zealand
(a division of Pearson New Zealand Ltd)
Penguin Books (South Africa) (Pty) Ltd, Block D, Rosebank Office Park,
181 Jan Smuts Avenue, Parktown North, Gauteng 2193, South Africa

Penguin Books Ltd, Registered Offices: 80 Strand, London WC2R ORL, England

www.penguin.com

This edition first published by Hamish Hamilton Ltd 1961
Published in Penguin Books 1965
Published, with a new introduction, in Penguin Classics 2014
010

Translation © Hamish Hamilton Ltd, 1961
Introduction © Philip Mansel, 2014
All rights reserved

The moral right of the translator and the author of the introduction has been asserted

Set in 10.25/12.25pt Postscript Adobe Sabon
Typeset by Jouve (UK), Milton Keynes
Printed in Great Britain by Clays Ltd, Elcograf S.p.A.

ISBN: 978-0-141-39312-4

www.greenpenguin.co.uk

MIX
Paper from
responsible sources
FSC
www.fsc.org   FSC® C018179

Penguin Books is committed to a sustainable
future for our business, our readers and our planet.
This book is made from Forest Stewardship
Council™ certified paper.

Contents

Introduction   vii

Testamentary Preface   xiii

MEMOIRS FROM
BEYOND THE TOMB

PART ONE
Monarchy and Revolution
1768–1800

1 Ancestors   5

2 Childhood   16

3 Youth   31

4 Manhood   54

5 Soldier and Courtier   75

6 The French Revolution   94

7 To America   114

8 With the Savages   135

9 With the Emigrant Army   160

10 Exile in England   181

PART TWO
Consulate and Empire
1800–1814

1 Madame de Beaumont   205
2 The Execution of the Duc
   d'Enghien   217
3 The Death of Lucile   223
4 Bonaparte and the
   Chateaubriands   228
5 Napoleon in Russia   236
6 The Fall of Napoleon   257
7 The Hundred Days   270
8 St Helena   291

PART THREE
Restoration and Revolution
1814–1841

1 Triumph and Disgrace   327
2 Madame Récamier   335
3 Rome   349
4 The July Revolution   359
5 The Plague in Paris   369

   Conclusion   373
   Index   379

Introduction

Memoirs From Beyond the Tomb combines the autobiography of a great Romantic with the history of a great revolution. The result is a masterpiece.

François-René de Chateaubriand was born in 1768 and grew up in a large turreted château called Combourg, in north-east Brittany, between Rennes and Saint-Malo. His father's passion to improve the family fortunes encouraged him to engage in the slave trade, among others. Chateaubriand himself considered that noble birth gave him a passion for liberty. He served as an officer in the French army, was presented at Versailles, travelled in 1791 for six months in America, emigrated in 1792, and fought in the Armée des Princes against the French republic. Between 1793 and 1800 he lived in London, where, in 1797, he published his first book, *Essai historique, politique et moral sur les révolutions*.

When Chateaubriand returned to Paris in 1800, he was, as he wrote, 'English in manner, in taste and up to a certain point in thoughts'. Other French émigrés who were half-English in attitude, and wrote brilliant memoirs (which deserve republication), include Madame de La Tour du Pin and Madame de Boigne. Chateaubriand contributed to the popularity of English Romantic literature in France, wrote on the Stuarts and helped translate Milton. For him the sight of thousands of ships moored in the port of London surpassed 'all images of power'.

He soon became one of the most famous writers in Europe, with a string of best-selling works, which contributed to the Catholic revival: *Le Génie du christianisme* (1802: begun in London, finished in Paris); *Les Martyrs* (1809), about Christian martyrs under the Roman Empire; *Itinéraire de Paris à Jérusalem et de Jérusalem à Paris* (1811), about his pilgrimage to the Holy Land.

Royalism, as well as Catholicism, shaped his life. He resigned from government service in 1804, when Bonaparte kidnapped and executed an exiled Bourbon prince, the Duc d'Enghien. His best-selling pamphlet attacking Napoleon I, *De Buonaparte et des Bourbons*, contributed to the restoration of the Bourbons in 1814. Thereafter, he was one of the leading protagonists in the attempt to establish a constitutional monarchy in France – under the brothers of Louis XVI, Louis XVIII (1814–24) and Charles X (1824–30) – as a political journalist; a peer of France; ambassador to Berlin (1821) and London (1822); Minister of Foreign Affairs (1823–4); and ambassador again, to Rome (1828–9).

Chateaubriand was liberal as well as Royalist. He resigned in 1829 on receiving news of Charles X's appointment of Jules de Polignac as President of the Council, because of his 'fatal and unpopular name ... in revolutions a name has more effect than an army' (Polignac was the reactionary son of a favourite of Marie Antoinette). On 7 August 1830, after Parisians fighting in the July Revolution had overthrown Charles X and placed his cousin, Louis-Philippe, on the throne, Chateaubriand made a speech in the Chamber of Peers, calling himself a 'useless Cassandra': 'all I have left to do is to seat myself on the debris which I have so many times predicted. I acknowledge that misfortune has every kind of power, except that of releasing me from my oaths of loyalty.' Leaving these memoirs to be published after his death – hence the title 'd'outre-tombe' – he died in Paris in 1848.

Memoirs From Beyond the Tomb is part of the flood of memoirs – over 1, 000 in all – in which, after the event, Frenchmen and -women tried to make sense of the Revolution and the Empire. It is distinguished from the others by the originality of its construction and the seduction of its style. Chateaubriand includes physical details of the events and people he witnessed, such as the smile on the face of Marie Antoinette, the sheets used by his wife as white Royalist flags in 1814, and the appearance and manners of Louis XVIII.

In addition, more than other autobiographers, he supports

his own narrative with excerpts from others. He includes extracts from the official account of the trial of the Duc d'Enghien; from the diary of his servant Julien during their journey in the Levant in 1806; and letters from friends and diplomatic despatches from his time as ambassador and minister. A poet with a sense of history, he also includes quotations from the Bible, from the Greek and Latin classics, and, for comparison with contemporary revolutions, from a sixteenth-century chronicle of the wars of religion by Pierre de l'Estoile. Thus readers enjoy a constant change of perspective, and narrator, which enlivens and authenticates the memoirs. Even Chateaubriand's own perspective changes, both in time and space, in the course of his memoirs: some parts were written outside Paris in 1811, others in London in 1821 and Prague in 1833.

Another change in tone occurs when Chateaubriand breaks his narrative to provide detailed portraits of, among others, the famous beauty Madame Récamier, who became his muse, although not his mistress; and Napoleon, whose genius he admired but whose despotism he detested. He saw that the Empire led to exile for the Bonapartes and diminution for France. Bringing a second European invasion and poisoning French politics, the Hundred Days – during which Chateaubriand served as Louis XVIII's Minister of the Interior in exile in Ghent – was Napoleon's 'unredeemable crime and capital error'. France never recovered the place it had held in Europe before 1789, due to the hecatombs caused by the wars of the revolution and the Empire, and its failure to keep its 'natural frontiers' of the Rhine.

Memoirs From Beyond the Tomb is distinguished by its royalism. Chateaubriand was Royalist by birth, by conviction and by revulsion. In July 1789 he had seen paraded on pikes the heads of some of the revolution's earlier victims: two royal officials called Foulon and Bertier (whose murders, like almost all others, went unpunished). He never varied in his feelings of disgust and fear – which were more widely shared than is generally realized. He claims that, after the restoration of order by Bonaparte in 1799, the people of Paris shunned those who had

participated in massacres. He could have said of French revolutionaries what Ivan Bunin would say of Russian ones a hundred
years later: 'what a bunch of criminals!' When Lamartine wrote
a defence of the Girondins, Chateaubriand commented: 'he is
gilding the guillotine'.

His political creed was: 'legitimate, constitutional monarchy
has always seemed to me the gentlest and surest path to complete liberty'. Helping to give him a critical distance from his
own epoch, royalism defined his life. He spent part of his old
age looking after aged priests and other victims of the revolution, with his unloved wife, in the Infirmerie Marie-Thérèse,
which she had founded and named after the daughter of Louis
XVI (today it is still a home for retired priests). After 1830
he visited the exiled Bourbons in Prague, London and Venice,
wrote pamphlets in their favour, and received financial help
from them.

His royalism did not, however, blind him to their faults. He
admired Louis XVIII's 'veritable empire'; he was 'king everywhere, as God is God everywhere'. Yet he also half despised the
king, who, despite his promise to die in the defence of his constitution, bolted from Paris on 19 March 1815, a few hours
before the arrival of Napoleon. Opposing Louis XVIII's liberal
ministries in 1816–20, he supported the reactionary policies of
the Comte d'Artois, the future Charles X; but he also admitted
that some of this king's decisions were 'enough to make one
despair of the race'. The July Revolution was the fault of the
king, who had issued ordonnances restricting the freedoms
granted by Louis XVIII, not that of the institutions of France.
Similarly, the revolution of 1789, in Chateaubriand's opinion,
was due to the weakness of Louis XVI.

Chateaubriand detested Talleyrand, in part because of Talleyrand's revolutionary past as an apostate bishop who supported
the execution of the Duc d'Enghien. Hence his celebrated
description – confirmed by the recently published memoirs of
another eye-witness, the Marquis de La Maisonfort – of seeing
Talleyrand and Fouché (a mass murderer who had become
Minister of Police). They are on their way to an audience with

Louis XVIII at Saint-Denis in July 1815, as the king returns to
Paris after the allied victory at Waterloo:

> Suddenly a door is opened: vice leaning on the arm of crime silently
> enters, M. de Talleyrand supported by M. Fouché; the infernal
> vision passes slowly before me, enters the King's study and disap-
> pears. Fouché had come to swear allegiance and fidelity to his
> lord. The loyal regicide on his knees put the hands which con-
> demned Louis XVI's head to fall between the hands of the brother
> of the martyr king. The apostate bishop stood surety for the oath.

Chateaubriand proves that, in France, Royalists could be at least
as liberal and dynamic as revolutionaries. He was the best-selling
author of his day, and had a world view, thinking that France
should help install liberal Bourbon monarchies in Spain's former
colonies in South America. He warned the daughter of Louis
XVI of the instability of thrones, and the unreliability of using
guards and gendarmes to protect them from ideas. He deplored
'the too great disproportion of fortunes and conditions', and
predicted 'the old European order is expiring; society is dying'.
Christianity, in his opinion, was the future of the world.

Memoirs From Beyond the Tomb is a case for the defence –
of himself and the Bourbons. Eager to present himself as an
innocent victim, he does not admit the driving ambition which
made him such a successful writer and politician – and a
ruthless negotiator with publishers. As his magnificent correspondence, now being published, makes clear, in his eagerness
for office he would write to different female admirers on the
same day, often using similar phrases: to Madame Récamier,
Madame de Montcalm, Madame de Pisieux, the Duchesse de
Duras. In his memoirs he writes at length about Madame
Récamier, but does not mention more carnal mistresses, such as
Madame Lafont or Hortense Allart.

This pious Catholic does, however, admit: 'I do not possess
evangelical perfection' – he refused to turn the other cheek, and
demanded revenge, even or especially on fellow Royalists. The
book is full of embittered asides. Marriage is called 'the high

road to all misfortunes'. Money is 'the source of freedom. With you one is young, beautiful, adored'. 'Is life anything but a lie?'

Many of his contemporaries loathed him. Charles X's adviser, the Duc de Blacas, called him 'capable of everything except of repairing the harm he has done' – in reference to his support of liberals duing their campaign, against the Royalist government of 1827, for freedom of the press. For Baron d'Eckstein and others, Chateaubriand, devoured by love of 'the great chimaera' success, and 'the demon of publicity', was one of the unhappiest men he knew (Balzac also found him 'bien maussade, bien chagrin' at Madame Récamier's). We know Chateaubriand's views of the Bourbons; unfortunately, due to the dispersion of their archives, we know little of their attitude to him. The French public, while loving his books, smiled at his pretensions to be a national leader.

Even if Chateaubriand could arouse smiles or envy, if Charles X had followed his advice, in an age when the press was, as Chateaubrinad wrote, 'social electricity' – and political dynamite – he could have protected the throne better than Polignac and Jean-Baptiste de Villèle. The interdependence of rulers and writers (Louis XIV and Racine, Louis XV and Voltaire, de Gaulle and Malraux) is a characteristic of French history and one of the themes of *Memoirs From Beyond the Tomb*.

As Chateaubriand minimizes his ambition and success, so he does that of his class. Far from 'the last hour' sounding for the French nobility, as he wrote, the nineteenth century was one of its golden ages. It was more ambitious after than before the revolution, since it had family fortunes and properties to restore. It provided France with prime ministers, marshals and geniuses, such as Chateaubriand himself (and Lamartine, de Tocqueville, de Vigny, de Maupassant, among many others). A French noble, Baron Pierre de Coubertin, would re-found the Olympics in 1896. Today the château of Combourg, where Chateaubriand spent his isolated youth, is still owned by descendants of his brother. And Chateaubriand's work is still taught in French schools as a model of literary style.

Philip Mansel, 2014

TESTAMENTARY PREFACE

Sicut nubes ... quasi naves ... velut umbra (JOB)
Paris, 1 December 1833

As it is impossible for me to foresee the date of my death, and as at my age the days granted to man are only days of grace, or rather of hardship, I intend, for fear of being taken by surprise, to explain the nature of a work destined to beguile for me the boredom of those last, lonely hours which nobody wants and which one does not know how to employ.

The *Memoirs* at whose head this preface is to be placed span or will span the entire course of my life; they were begun as far back as 1811 and have been continued down to the present day. I recount in what has been completed, and will recount in what has so far only been sketched out, my childhood, my education, my youth, my entry into the service, my arrival in Paris, my presentation to Louis XVI, the initial scenes of the Revolution, my travels in America, my return to Europe, my emigration to Germany and England, my return to France under the Consulate, my pursuits and works under the Restoration, and finally the complete history of that Restoration and its fall.

I have met nearly all the men who in my time have played a great or small part in my own or other countries, from Washington to Napoleon, from Louis XVIII to Alexander, from Pius VII to Gregory XVI, from Fox, Burke, Pitt, Sheridan, Londonderry, and Capo-d'Istrias to Malesherbes, Mirabeau, etc; from Nelson, Bolivar, and Mehemet Ali, Pasha of Egypt, to Suffren, Bougainville, La Pérouse, Moreau, etc. I have formed part of a triumvirate without precedent: three poets of different interests and nationalities who, almost at the same time, found themselves Foreign Ministers, myself of France, Mr Canning of England, and Señor Martinez de la Rosa of Spain. I have traversed in succession the empty years of my youth and the full years of the Republican era, of the splendours of Bonaparte and of the reign of the Legitimacy.

I have explored the seas of the Old World and the New, and trodden the soil of the four quarters of the globe. After sleeping in the cabins of Iroquois and the tents of Arabs, in the wigwams of Hurons and the remains of Athens, Jerusalem, Memphis, Carthage, and Granada, in the homes of Greeks, Turks, and Moors and among forests and ruins; after wearing the bearskin cloak of the savage and the silk caftan of the Mameluke, and after enduring poverty, hunger, thirst, and exile, I have taken my place, as a minister and ambassador, trimmed with gold lace and plastered with ribbons and decorations, at the table of kings, at the festivities of princes and princesses, only to fall once more into indigence and to taste prison life.

I have had dealings with hundreds of notabilities in the armed services, the Church, politics, the judiciary, the sciences, and the arts. I possess enormous quantities of material, over four thousand private letters, the diplomatic correspondences of my various embassies and those of my period at the Ministry of Foreign Affairs, including documents which are my private concern, unique and unknown to others. I have carried the soldier's musket, the traveller's stick, the pilgrim's staff: as a sailor, my destinies have had the inconstancy of the winds, and like a kingfisher I have made my nest on the waves.

I have had a hand in the making of peace and war; I have signed treaties and conventions and in the meantime published numerous works of my own. I have been initiated in the secrets of parties, court, and state; I have seen from close at hand the rarest misfortunes, the greatest successes, the highest reputations. I have been present at sieges, at congresses, at conclaves, at the restoration and demolition of thrones. I have made history and had the opportunity to write it. And my lonely, reflective, poetic life passed through this world of realities, catastrophes, noise, and tumult, with the sons of my dreams, Chactas, René, Eudore, Aben-Hamet, and the daughters of my reveries, Atala, Amélie, Blanca, Velléda, Cymodocée. Living within and beside my times, I may have exerted upon them, without wishing or trying to do so, a triple influence: religious, political, and literary.

I have now only four or five contemporaries of long-standing fame around me. Alfieri, Canova, and Monti have disappeared; of its great days, Italy retains only Pindemonte and Manzoni; Pellico has spent his best years in the dungeons of the Spielberg; the talents of Dante's homeland are condemned to silence or forced to languish on foreign soil. Lord Byron and Mr Canning have died young; Walter Scott has gone; Goethe has left us, loaded with glory and years. France has almost nothing left of her rich past and is entering on a new era; I remain to bury my times, like the old priest who, in the sack of Béziers, had to go on ringing the bell until he himself fell, after the last citizen had died.

When death rings down the curtain between me and the world, it will be found that my life's drama is divided into three acts.

From my early youth until 1800, I was a soldier and traveller; from 1800 until 1814, under the Consulate and the Empire, my life was devoted to literature; from the Restoration down to the present day, my life has been political.

In each of my three successive careers I have set myself a great task: as a traveller, I have endeavoured to open up the polar regions; as a writer, I have tried to rebuild religion on its own ruins; as a statesman, I have striven to give the nations the true system of constitutional monarchy with its various freedoms: I have at least helped to win that freedom which is equal to all others, can take their place, and can stand instead of any constitution – the freedom of the Press. If I have often failed in my enterprises that has been the fault of destiny. Foreigners who have succeeded in their projects have been helped by good fortune: they had powerful friends behind them and a peaceful homeland. I have not had that advantage.

Of the modern French writers of my time, I am almost the only one whose life resembles his works: a traveller, soldier, poet, and publicist, it was in the forest that I sang of the forests, on board ship that I depicted the sea, in camp that I spoke of war, in exile that I learnt the lessons of exile, at court, in assemblies, or in public affairs that I studied princes, politics, law, and history. The orators of Greece and Rome were implicated in public life and shared its destiny. In the Italy and Spain of the late Middle Ages and the Renaissance, the great geniuses of literature and the arts took part in the evolution of society. How stormy and beautiful were the lives of Dante, Tasso, Camoëns, Ercilla, and Cervantes!

In France our ancient poets and historians sang and wrote in the midst of pilgrimages and battles; Thibault, Comte de Champagne, Villehardouin, and Joinville owe the felicities of their style to the adventures they lived through; Froissart went looking for history on the high road, and learnt it from the knights and priests whom he encountered and with whom he rode along. But as from the reign of François I, our writers have been isolated individuals whose talents might be the expression of the spirit, but not the events, of their period. If I were destined to survive, I should represent in my person, as depicted in my memoirs, the principles, the ideas, the events, the catastrophes, the epic of my time, all the more so in that I have seen the beginning and the end of a world, and that the opposite characteristics of that end and that beginning are combined in my opinions. I have found myself between two centuries as at the junction between two rivers; I have plunged into their troubled waters, regretfully leaving behind the ancient strand where I was born and swimming hopefully towards the unknown shores where the new generations will land.

The *Memoirs*, divided into books and chapters, have been written at different times and in different places: these divisions naturally give rise to kinds of prologue which recall the incidents which have occurred since the last dates, and depict the places where I pick up the thread of my story. The varied events and the changing forms of my life thus enter into one another: at moments of personal prosperity I may talk of times when I was poor, and in days of tribulation I may recall days of happiness. The various feelings of my various times of life, my youth encroaching on my old age, the gravity of my years of maturity saddening my green years; the rays of my sun, from its rising to its setting, crossing and merging like the separate reflections of

my existence, impart a sort of indefinable unity to my work:
my cradle has something of my grave about it, my grave something of my cradle, my suffering becomes pleasure, my pleasure
pain, and one cannot tell whether these *Memoirs* are the work
of a young head or an old.

I am not saying this to justify myself, for I do not know
whether this is a good thing: I am relating the facts, recounting
what has happened, without my thinking about it, through the
very inconstancy of the storms unleashed against my craft,
storms that have often left me with nothing on which to write
about certain episodes of my life but the rock on which I have
come to grief.

I have lavished a positively fatherly care on the preparation of
these *Memoirs*, and I wish that it were possible for me to come
to life again at the witching hour in order to correct the proofs
of the finished work: the dead, so they say, waste no time.

Several of my friends have urged me to publish part of my
story now, but I have been unable to agree to this. If I did so, in
the first place I would be bound, despite myself, to be less frank
and truthful, and secondly I have always imagined that I was
writing these *Memoirs* in my coffin. This has lent the work a
certain religious quality which I could not subtract from it
without seriously impairing it; I would find it painful to stifle
this far-off voice from beyond the grave which can be heard
throughout my story. I trust it will not be considered strange
that I should be preoccupied with the fate of the poor orphan
destined to survive me. If I have suffered enough in this world
to be a happy shade in the next, a little light from the Elysian
Fields, falling on my last picture, may help to make the painter's failings less obvious. Life becomes me ill; perhaps death
will suit me better.

Memoirs From
Beyond the Tomb

PART ONE

MONARCHY AND REVOLUTION
1768–1800

ONE

Ancestors

It is four years now since, on my return from the Holy Land, I bought a gardener's house, hidden among the wooded hills near the hamlet of Aulnay, close to Sceaux and Châtenay. The sandy and uneven ground attached to this house was just a wild orchard with a ravine and a clump of chestnut trees at the far end. This narrow space seemed to me well suited to the containment of my far-ranging hopes; *spatio brevi spem longam reseces*. The trees which I have planted here are thriving; they are still so small that I provide them with shade when I stand between them and the sun. One day, giving this shade back to me, they will protect my old age as I have protected their youth. I have chosen them as far as possible from the various climes in which I have wandered; they remind me of my travels and nourish other illusions in the depths of my heart.

If ever the Bourbons return to the throne, all that I shall ask of them as a reward for my loyalty is to make me rich enough to join to my property the skirt of the surrounding woods: ambition has taken hold of me; I should like to extend the range of my walks by a few acres: knight-errant though I am, I have the sedentary tastes of a monk: since living in this retreat, I do not believe I have set foot outside my close as many as three times. If my pines, firs, larches, and cedars keep their promises, the Vallée-aux-Loups will become a veritable charterhouse. When Voltaire was born at Châtenay, on 20 February

1694, what did the hillside look like to which, in 1807, the author of *Le Génie du christianisme* was to retire?

Here I have written *Les Martyrs, Les Abencerages, L'Itinéraire,* and *Moïse*; what shall I do now in these autumn evenings? This 4 October 1811, my birthday and the anniversary of my entry into Jerusalem, tempts me to embark on the story of my life. The man who today gives the mastery of the world to France only to trample her underfoot, the man whose genius I admire and whose despotism I abhor, envelops me in his tyranny as in another solitude; but though he dominates the present, the past defies him, and I retain my liberty in all that has preceded his glory.

Most of my feelings have remained in the depths of my soul, or have been revealed in my works only as applied to imaginary beings. Now that I hanker after my chimeras without pursuing them, I want to revive the inclinations of my best years: these *Memoirs* will be a mortuary temple erected by the light of my memories.

My father's birth and the trials he endured in his first situation endowed him with one of the most sombre characters there have ever been. This character influenced my ideas by terrifying my childhood, saddening my youth, and determining the nature of my upbringing.

I was born a gentleman. In my opinion, I have profited by this accident of the cradle, keeping that steadfast love of liberty which is the special characteristic of an aristocracy whose last hour has struck. The aristocracy has three successive ages: the age of superiority, the age of privilege, the age of vanity; once it has left the first behind, it degenerates in the second and expires in the last.

Anybody may discover the facts about my family, if the fancy takes him, in Moréri's dictionary, in the various histories of Brittany by D'Argentré, Dom Lobineau, and Dom Morice, in the *Histoire généalogique de plusieurs maisons illustres de Bretagne* by Père Du Paz, in Toussaint Saint-Luc, Le Borgne, and finally in the *Histoire des grands officiers de la Couronne* by Père Anselme.

The proofs of my lineage were established by Chérin for the

admission of my sister Lucile as a canoness to the Chapter of L'Argentière, whence she was to pass to that of Remiremont; they were produced for my presentation to Louis XVI, reproduced once again for my affiliation to the Order of Malta, and reproduced for the last time when my brother was presented to the same unfortunate Louis XVI.

My name was first written as *Brien*, then as *Briant* and *Briand*, as the result of the invasion of French orthography. Guillaume le Breton gives it as *Castrum-Briani*. There is not a single name in France that does not present similar variations. What is the correct spelling of Du Guesclin?

About the beginning of the eleventh century, the *Briens* gave their name to an important château in Brittany, and this château became the seat of the barony of Chateaubriand. The Chateaubriand arms were originally some pine-cones with the motto: *Je sème l'or*. Geoffroy, Baron de Chateaubriand, travelled to the Holy Land with St Louis, was taken prisoner at the Battle of the Massorah, but returned to France, where his wife Sibylle died of joy and surprise on seeing him again. As a reward for his services, St Louis granted him and his heirs, in exchange for their old coat of arms, a shield of gules powdered with golden fleur-de-lis: *Cui et ejus haeredibus*, states a cartulary in Bérée Priory, *sanctus Ludovicus tum Francorum rex, propter ejus probitatem in armis, flores liliis auri, loco pomorum pini auri, contulit.*

The Chateaubriands divided from the very beginning into three branches: the first, known as the *Barons de Chateaubriand*, the stock of the other two, begun in the year 1000 in the person of Thiern, son of Brien, grandson of Alain III, Count of Brittany; the second, called the *Seigneurs des Roches Baritaut* or the *Seigneurs du Lion d'Angers*; and the third, going under the name of the *Sires de Beaufort*.

After my presentation to Louis XVI, my brother thought of increasing my inheritance as the younger son of the family by providing me with some of those ecclesiastical allowances known as *simples bénéfices*. There was only one practical way of achieving this object, seeing that I was a layman and a soldier, and that was to incorporate me in the Order of Malta.

My brother sent my proofs to Malta, and shortly afterwards presented a petition in my name to the Chapter of the Grand Priory of Aquitaine, in session at Poitiers, asking it to appoint commissioners who could adjudicate upon the question as a matter of urgency. M. Pontois was at that time archivist, genealogist, and Vice-Chancellor of the Order of Malta at the Priory.

The President of the Chapter was Louis-Joseph des Escotais, Bailiff and Grand Prior of Aquitaine, and he was assisted by the Bailiff of Freslon, the Chevalier de la Laurencie, the Chevalier de Murat, the Chevalier de Lanjamet, the Chevalier de la Bourdonnaye-Montluc, and the Chevalier du Bouëtiez. The petition was granted on 9, 10, and 11 September 1789. It was said, in the terms of the *Mémorial*, that I deserved *on more than one ground* the favour I was soliciting, and that *considerations of the greatest weight* made me worthy of the honour to which I aspired.

And all this took place after the fall of the Bastille, on the eve of the scenes of 6 October 1789 and the transfer of the royal family to Paris! And, at the sitting of 7 August of the same year 1789, the National Assembly had abolished titles! How, too, could the Chevaliers who examined my proofs find that I deserved *on more than one ground the favour I was soliciting*, etc, when I was nothing more than a wretched little second lieutenant in the infantry, completely unknown, with no reputation, no influence, and no fortune?

I would never finish if I recounted everything of which I have chosen to give only a brief summary. I hold these trifles of little account, but even so I find that today people go rather too far in the opposite direction; it has become fashionable to boast that one is of peasant stock, that one has the honour of being the son of a man of the soil. Are these boasts as disinterested as they are philosophical? Are they not a means of siding with the stronger party? The marquesses, counts, and barons of our times, possessing neither land nor privileges, three-quarters of them dying of hunger, running one another down, refusing to recognize one another, challenging one another's titles; these nobles, whose own names are denied them or are granted only

with reservations, are they capable of inspiring any fear whatever? I must beg my readers' indulgence for having been obliged
to descend to these puerile recitations, in order to explain my
father's ruling passion, a passion which formed the crux of the
drama of my youth. For my part, I neither boast nor complain of
the old or the new social order. If, in the first, I was the Chevalier
or the Vicomte de Chateaubriand, in the second I am François de
Chateaubriand; I prefer my name to my title.

My father would have been quite capable of calling God *the
Gentleman up there*, after the fashion of the great medieval
landowners, and describing Nicodemus (the Nicodemus of the
Gospels) as a *holy gentleman*. Now, passing by way of my
begetter, let us go from Christophe, sovereign Lord of La Guerrande, directly descended from the Barons of Chateaubriand,
down to myself, François, vassal-less, penniless Lord of the
Vallée-aux-Loups.

Going back up the line of the Chateaubriands, we find that
two of the three branches of the family died out, while the third,
that of the Sires of Beaufort, extended by a minor branch (the
Chateaubriands of La Guerrande), grew steadily poorer, as an
inevitable result of the law of the land: the elder son appropri-
ated two thirds of the estate; the younger sons divided among all
the rest of them a mere third of the patrimonial inheritance. The
decomposition of the latter's paltry inheritance went all the more
quickly in that they married; and as the same division in the pro-
portion two to one applied to their children, these younger sons
of younger sons were soon reduced to dividing up a pigeon, a
rabbit, a duck-pond, and a hunting dog, although they still
remained *noble knights and powerful lords* of a dove-cote, a
toad-hole, and a rabbit-warren. In the old aristocratic families
one can discover a considerable number of younger sons; one
can follow their traces for two or three generations; then they
disappear, having gradually descended to the plough or been
absorbed by the working classes, without anybody knowing
what has become of them.

The head of the family, in both name and arms, at the beginning of the eighteenth century was Alexis de Chateaubriand,

Lord of La Guerrande, and the son of Michel, which Michel had a brother called Amaury.

At the same time as this head of the family in name and arms, there lived his cousin François, the son of Amaury, Michel's younger brother. François, born on 19 February 1683, possessed the little estates of Les Touches and La Villeneuve. He had married, on 27 August 1713, Pétronille-Claude Lamour, Dame of Lanjégu, by whom he had four sons: François-Henri, René (my father), Pierre, Lord of Le Plessis, and Joseph, Lord of Le Parc. My grandfather, François, died on 28 March 1729; my grandmother, whom I knew in my childhood, still had beautiful eyes which smiled in the shadow of her years. At the time of her husband's death she was living in the manor of La Villeneuve, in the neighbourhood of Dinan. My grandmother's entire fortune did not bring in more than 5,000 francs a year, of which her eldest son took two thirds, 3,333 francs: there remained an annual income of 1,666 francs for the three younger sons, from which sum the eldest once more deducted the major portion.

As a crowning misfortune, my grandmother's plans were thwarted by her sons' temperaments. The eldest, François-Henri, who had inherited the magnificent estate of La Villeneuve, refused to marry and became a priest; but instead of applying for the benefices which his name could have obtained for him, he asked for nothing out of pride or indifference. He buried himself in a country living and was successively rector of Saint-Launeuc and of Merdrignac, in the diocese of Saint-Malo. He had a passion for poetry; I have seen a fair amount of his verse. The jovial character of this sort of aristocratic Rabelais and the cult of the Muses which this Christian priest practised in a presbytery excited people's curiosity. He gave away all that he possessed and died insolvent.

The last of the four sons, Joseph, went to Paris and shut himself up in a library: every year he was sent the 416 francs which were his portion as a younger son. He went unnoticed in the world of books; he devoted himself to historical research. During his lifetime, which was brief, he wrote every New Year's Day to his mother, the only sign of life he ever gave. What a strange fate! There were my two uncles, the one a scholar and

the other a poet; my elder brother wrote quite pleasant verse;
one of my sisters, Mme de Farcy, had a real gift for poetry;
another sister of mine, the Comtesse Lucile, a canoness, deserves
to be remembered for a few admirable pages; I myself have
covered a great deal of paper. My brother died on the scaffold;
my two sisters departed from a life of suffering after languishing
in prison; my two uncles did not leave enough to pay for the
four planks of their coffin; while literature has caused me joy
and anguish, and, with God's help, I can still look forward to
dying in the workhouse.

My grandmother, after wearing herself out trying to make
something out of her eldest and youngest sons, could do nothing for the other two, René, my father, and Pierre, my uncle.
This family, which had *scattered gold*, in accordance with its
motto, could see from its country seat the rich abbeys which it
had founded and which contained the remains of its forebears.
It had presided over the States of Brittany, as possessing one of
the nine baronies; it had given its signature to a treaty between
sovereigns and served as surety for Clisson, yet it had not
enough influence to obtain a second-lieutenant's commission
for the heir to its name.

There remained one course open to the poverty-stricken
aristocracy of Brittany: the Royal Navy. The family decided to
adopt it in the case of my father, but first of all he would have
to go to Brest, live there, pay his instructors, buy his uniform,
his arms, his books, and his mathematical instruments: how
was he to meet these expenses? The commission for which the
Minister for the Navy had been petitioned failed to arrive, for
want of a protector to demand its despatch: the lady of the
manor of Villeneuve fell ill with grief.

It was then that my father showed the first sign of that determined character of which I later had personal experience. He
was about fifteen years old: becoming aware of his mother's
anxiety, he went up to the bed where she was lying and said
to her:

'I do not wish to be a burden upon you any longer.'

At this, my grandmother started to cry (I have heard my
father describe this scene to me a score of times).

'René,' she replied, 'what do you want to do? You must till your field.'

'It cannot provide us all with food; let me go.'

She kissed the boy, sobbing bitterly. That very evening, my father left his mother's farm and went to Dinan, where one of our relations gave him a letter of recommendation for a citizen of Saint-Malo. The orphan adventurer was signed on as a volunteer on an armed schooner which set sail a few days later.

The little republic of Saint-Malo was at that time alone in upholding the honour of the French flag on the high seas. The schooner joined the fleet which Cardinal Fleury was sending to help Stanislas, besieged in Danzig by the Russians. My father stepped ashore and found himself involved in the memorable battle which fifteen hundred Frenchmen, led by the valiant Breton De Bréhan, Comte de Plélo, waged on 29 May 1734 against forty thousand Muscovites under the command of Munich. De Bréhan, diplomat, warrior and poet, was killed and my father twice wounded. He returned to France and signed on again. Shipwrecked on the Spanish coast, he was attacked and stripped of all he possessed by robbers in Galicia; he worked his passage on a boat to Bayonne and appeared once more at home. His courage and his methodical nature had won him a certain reputation. He went over to the West Indies, made money in the colonies, and laid the foundations of a new fortune for his family.

My grandmother entrusted to her son René her son Pierre, M. de Chateaubriand du Plessis, whose son, Armand de Chateaubriand, was shot on Bonaparte's orders on Good Friday of the year 1809. He was one of the last French nobles to die for the monarchy. My father undertook to look after his brother, although he had contracted, from the habit of suffering, a certain rigidity of character which he kept all his life; the idea that suffering teaches kindness – Virgil's *Non ignara mali* – is not always true: unhappiness can engender hardness as well as tenderness.

M. de Chateaubriand was a tall, gaunt figure; he had a Roman nose, thin, pale lips, and small, deep-set eyes which were sea-green or blue-grey, like the eyes of lions or barbarians of old. I have never seen eyes like his: when anger entered into them, the gleaming pupils seemed to detach themselves and strike one like bullets.

My father was dominated by a single passion, that of his name. His habitual condition was a profound melancholy which old age increased and a silence from which he emerged only to give vent to violent outbursts of anger. Miserly in the hope of restoring its original splendour to his family, haughty with his fellow nobles at the States of Brittany, autocratic with his vassals at Combourg, silent, despotic, and menacing at home, the very sight of him inspired fear. If he had lived to see the Revolution, and if he had been younger, he would have played an important part in history or he would have died in the defence of his château. He most certainly had genius: I have no doubt that in a high administrative or army post he would have shown extraordinary brilliance.

It was on his return from America that he decided to take a wife. Born on 23 September 1718, he married at thirty-five, on 3 July 1753, Apolline-Jeanne-Suzanne de Bedée, born on 7 April 1726, the daughter of M. Ange-Annibal, Comte de Bedée, Lord of La Bouëtardais. He established himself with her at Saint-Malo, which was some twenty miles from where both of them had been born, so that from their house they could see the skyline beneath which they had come into the world. My maternal grandmother, Marie-Anne de Ravenel du Boisteilleul, Mme de Bedée, born at Rennes on 16 October 1698, had received her schooling at Saint-Cyr during the last years of Mme de Maintenon: her education had been handed on to her daughters.

My mother, who was endowed by nature with considerable intelligence and a prodigious imagination, was brought up on Fénelon, Racine, and Mme de Sévigné, and fed with anecdotes about the court of Louis XIV; she knew the whole of *Cyrus* by heart. Apolline de Bedée had large features and was dark, dainty and ugly; her elegant manners and lively temperament contrasted with my father's stiffness and equanimity. As fond of society as he was of solitude, and as high-spirited and cheerful as he was cold and unemotional, she did not have a single taste which was not at variance with those of her husband. The constraint to which she was submitted made a melancholy creature of a woman who had been gay and light-hearted. Obliged to keep silent when she would have liked to speak, she found consolation in a kind of noisy sadness broken by sighs which formed the only interruption to the mute sadness of my father. In matters of piety, my mother was an angel.

My mother gave birth at Saint-Malo to a boy who died in infancy and who was called Geoffroy, like nearly all the eldest sons of my family. This son was followed by another and by two daughters who lived only a few months.

These four children died of a rush of blood to the brain. Finally my mother brought into the world a third boy who was called Jean-Baptiste: it was he who later became the grandson-in-law of M. de Malesherbes. After Jean-Baptiste four daughters were born: Marie-Anne, Bénigne, Julie, and Lucile, all four of rare beauty, and of whom only the two eldest survived the storms of the Revolution. Beauty, that serious frivolity, remains when all the others have gone. I was the last of these ten children. It seems probable that my four sisters owed their existence to my father's desire to see his name made secure by the arrival of a second boy; I tarried, having an aversion for life.

This is my baptismal certificate:

Extract from the archives of the registry office of the Commune of Saint-Malo for the year 1768.

François-René de Chateaubriand, son of René de Chateaubriand and of Pauline-Jeanne-Suzanne de Bedée, his wife, born on 4 September 1768, baptized the following day by ourselves, Pierre-Henri Nouail, Vicar-General to the Bishop of Saint-Malo. The godfather was Jean-Baptiste de Chateaubriand, his brother, and the godmother Françoise-Gertrude de Contades, who signs this register with the father. Signed: Contades de Plouër, Jean-Baptiste de Chateaubriand, Brignon de Chateaubriand, De Chateaubriand and Nouail, Vicar-General.

The house which my parents occupied at that time stands in a dark, narrow street in Saint-Malo called the Rue des Juifs; it has now been converted into an inn. The bedroom in which my mother was confined overlooks an empty stretch of the city walls, and from the windows of this room one can see the sea extending into the distance and breaking on the reefs. My godfather, as can be seen from my baptismal certificate, was my brother, and my godmother the Comtesse de Plouër, the daughter of the Maréchal de Contades. I was almost dead when I came into the world. The roar of the waves whipped up by a squall heralding the autumnal equinox drowned my cries: these details have often been recounted to me; the sadness of them has never left my memory. Not a day passes but, thinking of what I have been, I picture once more the rock on which I was born, the bedroom in which my mother inflicted life upon me, the storm which accompanied my first sleep, and the unhappy brother who gave me a name which I have nearly always dragged through misfortune. Heaven seemed to have gathered together these various circumstances in order to place in my cradle an image of my destiny.

TWO

Childhood

I had scarcely left my mother's womb when I suffered my first exile; I was relegated to Plancoët, a pretty little village situated between Dinan, Saint-Malo, and Lamballe. My mother's only brother, the Comte de Bedée, had built the Château of Monchoix close to the village. My maternal grandmother's property in this region stretched as far as the little town of Corseul, the Curiosolites of Caesar's *Commentaries*. My grandmother, who had been a widow for a long time, lived with her sister, Mlle de Boisteilleul, in a hamlet separated from Plancoët by a bridge and called L'Abbaye, on account of a Benedictine abbey dedicated to Our Lady of Nazareth.

My wet-nurse turned out to be sterile; another poor Christian took me to her bosom. She dedicated me to the patroness of the hamlet, Our Lady of Nazareth, and promised her that I should wear white and blue in her honour until I reached the age of seven. I was only a few hours old, and the burden of time had already marked my brow. Why was I not allowed to die? It entered into the counsels of God to grant, in return for the vow of obscurity and innocence, the preservation of a life which a vain reputation threatened to extinguish.

After three years I was brought back to Saint-Malo; it was already seven years since my father had regained possession of the estate of Combourg. He wished to retrieve the lands where his ancestors had lived; unable to negotiate either for the seigneury of Beaufort, which had gone to the Goyon family, or for the barony of Chateaubriand, which had passed to the house of Condé, he turned his eyes towards Combourg, which Froissart calls Combour: several branches of my family had possessed it by means of marriages with the Coëtquens. Combourg defended Brittany against the Normans and the English: Junken, the Bishop of Dol, built it in 1016; the great tower dates from 1100. Marshal de Duras, who had Combourg from his wife, Maclovie de Coëtquen, the daughter of a Chateaubriand, came to an agreement with my father. The Marquis du Hallay, an officer in the mounted grenadiers of the Royal Guard who is almost too well known for his courage, is the last of the Coëtquen-Chateaubriands: M. du Hallay has a brother. The same Marshal de Duras, acting as our relation by marriage, later presented my brother and myself to Louis XVI.

I was destined for the Royal Navy: disdain for Court life came naturally to a Breton, and especially to my father. The aristocracy of our States fortified him in this feeling.

When I was brought back to Saint-Malo, my father was at Combourg and my brother at the school of Saint-Brieuc; my four sisters were living with my mother.

All the latter's affection was concentrated on her elder son; not that she was not fond of her other children, but she showed a blind preference for the young Comte de Combourg. It is true that as a boy, as the last-comer, as the Chevalier (for so I was called), I enjoyed certain privileges over my sisters; but in the final analysis I was left in the care of the servants. Moreover my mother, being a woman of wit and virtue, was preoccupied by the cares of society and the duties of religion. Orderly as she was, she allowed her children to run wild; generous as she was, she gave an impression of avarice; gentle as she was, she was for ever scolding: my father was the terror of the servants, my mother the scourge.

These characteristics of my parents gave rise to the first feelings I can remember. I became extremely attached to the woman who looked after me, an excellent creature called La Ville-neuve, whose name I write with gratitude in my heart and tears in my eyes. La Villeneuve was a sort of chief lady-in-waiting, carrying me in her arms, secretly giving me anything she could find, wiping away my tears, kissing me, throwing me in a cor-ner, picking me up again, and all the time muttering: 'This little fellow won't grow up high-and-mighty! He has a good heart, he has! He isn't hard on poor folk! Here, my love' – and she would fill me with wine and sugar.

My childish affection for La Villeneuve was soon eclipsed by a worthier friendship.

Lucile, the fourth of my sisters, was two years older than I. The neglected youngest daughter, she was dressed in nothing but her sisters' cast-offs. Imagine a thin little girl, too tall for her age, with ungainly arms and a timid expression, who found it difficult to talk and impossible to learn anything; give her a borrowed dress of a different size from her own; imprison her chest in a boned bodice whose points chafed her sides; encircle her neck in an iron collar trimmed with brown velvet; draw back her hair on to the crown of her head and enclose it in a black toque; and you will see the wretched creature who met my gaze when I returned home. Nobody would have suspected the existence in this pitiful Lucile of the talents and the beauty which would shine in her one day.

She was handed over to me like a toy; I did not take advantage of my power over her; instead of submitting her to my wishes, I became her defender. I was taken with her every morning to the house of the Couppart sisters, two old hunchbacks dressed in black who taught children to read. Lucile read very badly; I read even worse. She was scolded; I scratched the sisters: complaints were made to my mother. I began to acquire the reputation of a waster, a rebel, a lazy scamp, and a donkey. These ideas became firmly fixed in my parents' minds: my father used to say that all the Chevaliers of Chateaubriand had been idle, tipsy, and quarrelsome. My mother would sigh and grumble at the state of my jacket. Though I was only a child, my father's remark roused me to indignation; when my mother crowned her remonstrances with praise for my brother, whom she called a Cato and a hero, I felt prepared to commit all the mischief that seemed to be expected of me.

Saint-Malo is nothing but a rock. Standing in former times in the middle of a salt-marsh, it became an island as a result of the tidal wave which, in 709, hollowed out the bay and placed Mont Saint-Michel in the midst of the waves. Today, the rock of Saint-Malo is connected to the mainland only by a causeway with the poetic name of Le Sillon, or the Furrow. Le Sillon is assailed on one side by the open sea and washed on the other side by the tide which turns round Saint-Malo to enter the port. A storm almost entirely destroyed it in 1730. At low tide, the port is dry for several hours, and on the north and east a beach of the finest sand is revealed. It is then possible to walk right round my father's home. Close at hand and in the distance are scattered rocks, forts, and uninhabited islets: Fort Royal, La Conchée, Cézembre, and Le Grand-Bé, where I am to be buried; without knowing, I chose well, for *bé*, in Breton, means *grave*.

At the end of Le Sillon, on which a calvary has been set up, there is a mound of sand at the edge of the open sea. This mound is called La Hoguette and is surmounted by an old gibbet: we contended with the birds for possession of the uprights, on which we used to play puss in the corner. But it was never without a kind of fear that we lingered in this spot.

There too are the Miels, dunes where sheep used to graze; on the right there are some meadows, lying at the foot of Paramé, the road to Saint-Servan, the new cemetery, a calvary, and some windmills on hillocks, like those which stand on Achilles's grave at the entrance to the Hellespont.

When I had almost attained the age of seven, my mother took me to Plancoët to be released from my wet-nurse's vow; we stayed with my grandmother. If I have ever known happiness, it was certainly in that house.

My grandmother lived in the Rue du Hameau-de-l'Abbaye, in a house with terraced gardens leading down to the bottom of a little valley where there was a spring surrounded by willows. Mme de Bedée could no longer walk, but apart from that she suffered from none of the disadvantages of her age: she was a charming old lady, plump, white, and neat, with a distinguished appearance and fine aristocratic manners, who wore old-fashioned pleated dresses and a black lace cap tied under the chin. Her wit was mannered, her conversation solemn, her temperament serious. She was looked after by her sister, Mlle de Boisteilleul, who resembled her in nothing but her kindness.

The latter was a thin little creature, sprightly, gay, and talkative. She had been in love with a certain Comte de Trémignon who had promised to marry her but had broken his promise. My aunt had found consolation in singing of her love, for she was a poet. I remember often seeing her embroidering double cuffs for her sister, with her spectacles perched on her nose, and singing in a nasal voice an apologia about a sparrow-hawk which loved a warbler, which has always struck me as a strange thing for a sparrow-hawk to do.

My grandmother relied upon her sister to run the house. She had dinner at eleven o'clock in the morning, followed by her siesta; at one o'clock she would wake up; she would then be carried to the bottom of the garden terraces and installed under the willows by the spring, where she would sit knitting, surrounded by her sister, her children, and her grandchildren. In those days, old age was a dignity; today it is a burden. At four o'clock my grandmother was carried back into her drawing-room; Pierre, the servant, put out a card-table; Mlle de Boisteilleul knocked with the tongs on the fire-back, and a few minutes later there entered three other old maids who came from the house next-door in answer to my aunt's summons. These three sisters were called the Demoiselles Villedeneu; the daughters of an impoverished noble, instead of dividing up his meagre fortune, they had enjoyed it in common, had never separated, and had never left their native village. Closely acquainted with my grandmother since childhood, they lived next-door and came every day, at the agreed signal on the fire-back, to play quadrille with their friend. The game began; the good ladies quarrelled; this was the only event in their lives, the only moment when the evenness of their tempers was altered. At eight o'clock supper restored peace. Often my uncle De Bedée, with his son and his three daughters, would join my grandmother at supper. The latter told countless stories of the old days; my uncle in his turn recounted the Battle of Fontenoy, in which he had taken part, and topped off his boasting with some rather outspoken anecdotes which made the good ladies almost die with laughter. At nine o'clock, when supper was over, the servants came in; everybody knelt down, and

Mlle de Boisteilleul said the evening prayers aloud. At ten o'clock the whole house was asleep, except for my grand-mother, who was read to by her maid until one o'clock in the morning.

The Comte de Bedée's château was situated two or three miles from Plancoët, in a lofty and pleasant position. Everything about it breathed joy: my uncle's joviality was inexhaustible. He had three daughters, Caroline, Marie, and Flore, and a son, the Comte de la Bouëtardais, a counsellor in the High Court, who all shared his high spirits. Monchoix was full of cousins from all around; there was music, dancing, hunting, and general merry-making from morning to night. My aunt, Mme de Bedée, seeing my uncle gaily squandering his capital and his income, would not unnaturally get angry with him; but nobody listened to her, and her bad temper only added to her family's good humour, especially as my aunt herself was addicted to a good many fads and fancies: she always had a big, fierce hunting dog lying in her lap, and a tame boar following her around which filled the château with its grunting. When I came from my father's house, so dark and silent, to this house of gaiety and noise, I found myself in a veritable paradise. This contrast became more strik-ing when my family had settled in the country: going from Combourg to Monchoix was like going from the desert into the world, from the keep of a medieval baron to the villa of a Roman prince.

On Ascension Day 1775 I left my grandmother's house for Notre-Dame de Nazareth with my mother, my aunt De Boisteil-leul, my uncle De Bedée and his children, my wet-nurse, and my foster-brother. I was wearing a white gown, a white hat, white shoes and gloves, and a blue silk sash. We reached the abbey at ten o'clock in the morning. The monastery, standing at the roadside, looked older than it was on account of a quin-cunx of elms planted in the time of Jean V of Brittany. The quincunx led into the cemetery: the Christian could not reach the church except by way of the burial ground: it is through death that one enters into the presence of God.

The monks were already in their stalls; the altar was lit by a multitude of tapers; lamps hung down from the various arches;

in Gothic buildings there is so to speak a succession of perspectives and horizons. The beadles came to meet me ceremoniously at the door and led me into the choir. There three chairs had been put out: I took my place on the middle one; my wet-nurse sat on my left, my foster-brother on my right.

The Mass began: at the Offertory the priest turned towards me and read out certain prayers, after which my white clothes were removed and hung like an ex-voto below a picture of the Virgin. I was then dressed in a purple habit. The Prior delivered a discourse on the efficacy of religious vows; he recalled the story of the Baron de Chateaubriand who travelled to the East with St Louis; he told me that perhaps I too would one day go to Palestine and visit that Virgin of Nazareth to whom I owed my life through the intercession of the prayers of the poor, which always carried weight with God. After listening to the Benedictine's exhortation, I always dreamt of the pilgrimage to Jerusalem, and in the end I made it.

I have been dedicated to religion, and the garments of my innocence have rested on its altars; but it is not my clothes which should be hung now in its churches, it is my sufferings.

I was brought back to Saint-Malo. It is there, on the seashore between the Château and Fort Royal, that the children gathered together; it is there that I was brought up, a companion of the waves and the winds. One of the first pleasures I ever tasted was battling with the storms, and playing with the waves which retreated before me or chased after me on the shore. Another pastime was making monuments which my playmates called *fours*, or cakes, out of the sand on the beach. Since that time, I have often seen castles built to last for ever which have collapsed more quickly than my palaces of sand.

My fate having been irrevocably decided, I was abandoned to an idle childhood. A smattering of English, drawing, hydrography, and mathematics seemed more than sufficient for the education of a little boy destined in advance for the rough life of a sailor.

I grew up at home free of all control; we no longer lived in the house where I was born: my mother occupied a large house in the Place Saint-Vincent, almost opposite the gate leading to

Le Sillon. The young urchins of the town had become my closest friends; I filled the courtyard and the staircases of the house with them; I resembled them in every respect; I spoke their language; I shared their manners and behaviour; I was dressed like them, unbuttoned and untidy like them; my shirts were in ribbons; I never had a pair of stockings that was not full of holes; I trailed around in old down-at-heel shoes, which came off with every step I took; I often lost my hat and sometimes my coat. My face was dirty, scratched, and bruised, my hands black. I looked so peculiar that my mother, in the midst of an angry outburst, could not help laughing and exclaiming: 'How ugly he is!'

Shut up at night in their city under the same lock and key, the people of Saint-Malo formed a single family. Their manners were so innocent that young women who sent to Paris for ribbons and veils were regarded as worldly creatures whose scandalized companions would have nothing more to do with them. A marital misdemeanour was an unheard-of occurrence; when a certain Comtesse d'Abbeville was suspected of infidelity, a plaintive ballad was written on the subject which people sang while crossing themselves. However the poet, faithful in spite of himself to the traditions of the troubadours, sided against the husband, whom he called a monster and a barbarian.

On certain days of the year, the people of the town and the countryside came together at fairs called assemblies, which were held on the islands and in the forts around Saint-Malo; they went to these fairs on foot at low tide and in boats at high tide. The crowds of sailors and peasants; the covered wagons; the caravans of horses, donkeys, and mules; the competition between the stallkeepers; the tents pitched on the shore; the processions of monks and confraternities winding their way through the crowd with their banners and crosses; the rowing-boats and sailing-boats coming and going; the ships coming into the port or anchoring in the roads; the artillery salvoes, the ringing of bells; all this combined to lend these gatherings noise, movement, and variety.

I was the only witness to these fairs who did not share in the general merriment. I went to them without any money to buy toys or cakes. Shunning the contempt which follows in the wake of ill-fortune, I sat a long way from the crowd, beside the pools of water which the sea maintains and renews in the hollows of the rocks. There I amused myself watching the auks and gulls flying past, gazing into the bluish distance, picking up seashells, and listening to the music of the waves among the reefs. In the evening, at home, I was not much happier; I had an intense dislike for certain dishes, but I was forced to eat them. I used to look imploringly at La France, who would nimbly remove my plate when my father was looking the other way. The same strictness applied in the matter of warmth: I was not allowed to approach the fireplace. We have come a long way from the severe parents of that time to the fond parents of today.

On feast-days I used to be taken with my sisters on a pilgrimage to the various shrines of the city, to the chapel of Saint-Aaron and to the convent of La Victoire; the sweet voices of a few women hidden from sight fell upon my ear: the music of their canticles mingled with the roaring of the waves. When, in winter, at the hour of evening service, the cathedral filled with people; when old sailors on their knees and young women and children holding little candles read from their prayer-books; when the multitude, at the moment of benediction, recited in unison the *Tantum ergo*; when, in between these songs, the Christmastide squalls battered at the stained-glass windows of the basilica, shaking the roof of the nave which had once echoed with the lusty voices of Jacques Cartier and Duguay-Trouin, I experienced an extraordinary feeling of religion. I did not need La Villeneuve to tell me to fold my hands to call upon God by all the names my mother had taught me; I could see the heavens opening, the angels offering up our incense and our prayers; I bent my head: it was not yet burdened with those cares which weigh so heavily upon us that one is tempted never to raise one's head again once one has bowed it before an altar.

One sailor, coming away from these services, would set sail fortified against the night, while another would come back into port using the illuminated dome of the church as a guide: thus religion and danger were always face to face, and their images presented themselves to my mind inextricably linked together. I had scarcely been born before I heard talk of death: in the evening, a man would go through the streets ringing a bell, to tell the Christians to pray for one of their deceased brethren. Almost every year, boats sank before my eyes, and while I was playing on the beach, the sea would deposit at my feet the corpses of foreign seamen who had died far from home. Mme de Chateaubriand used to say to me, as St Monica said to her son: *Nihil longe est a Deo*: 'Nothing is far from God.' My education had been entrusted to Providence: it did not spare me its lessons.

Dedicated to the Virgin, I came to know and love my protectress, whom I confused with my guardian angel: her picture, which had cost La Villeneuve a half-sou, was pinned to the wall above my bed. I should have lived in the days when people used to say to Mary: 'Sweet Lady of Heaven and earth, mother of pity, fountain of all good, who bore Jesus Christ in your precious womb, most sweet and beautiful Lady, I thank and implore you.'

The first thing I ever learnt by heart was a sailor's hymn to the Virgin which I have since heard being sung in a shipwreck. Even today I still repeat that paltry rhyme with as much pleasure as poetry by Homer; a Madonna wearing a Gothic crown and a blue silk dress with a silver fringe inspires greater devotion in me than a Raphael Virgin.

If only that peaceable *Star of the Seas* had been able to still the turmoil of my life! But I was to know no rest, not even in my childhood; like the Arab's date-tree, my trunk had scarcely sprung from the rock before it was battered by the wind.

I have told how my precocious rebellion against Lucile's mistresses laid the foundations of my evil reputation; a playmate completed it.

My uncle, M. de Chateaubriand du Plessis, who lived at Saint-Malo like his brother, had, again like him, four daughters and two sons. Of my two cousins, Pierre and Armand, who were my first companions, the former became one of the Queen's pages and the latter was sent to school as being destined for the priesthood. Pierre, when he had served his time as a page, entered the Navy and was drowned off the coast of Africa. Armand, after being shut up in school for many years, left France in 1790, served throughout the Emigration, made a score of intrepid journeys in a longboat to the Brittany coast, and finally came and died for the King on the Grenelle Plain on Good Friday 1809, as I have already mentioned, and as I shall say once more when I come to recount his unhappy fate.

Deprived of the company of my two cousins, I replaced it with a new friendship.

The second floor of the house where we lived was occupied by a gentleman called Gesril who had a son and two daughters. This son had been brought up differently from myself; he was thoroughly spoilt and everything he did was a subject for admiration: he liked nothing better than fighting, unless it was provoking a quarrel of which he would appoint himself arbitrator. He was always playing tricks on the maids he met taking children out for a walk, and his pranks, magnified into dreadful crimes, were the talk of the town. His father laughed at everything he did, and the naughtier *Joson* was, the more he was loved. Gesril became my great friend and gained an unbelievable ascendancy over me: I learnt from this master, although my character was the exact opposite of his. I loved playing by myself and never tried to pick a quarrel with anybody: Gesril loved games and noise and gloried in childish squabbles. When some street-urchin spoke to me, Gesril would ask me: 'Why do you put up with him?' At this I imagined that my honour was compromised and I would fly at the impudent youth, however big or however old he might be. My friend would watch the fight and applaud my courage, but never lifted a finger to help me. Sometimes he raised an army from all the boys he met, dividing his conscripts into two gangs, and we would skirmish on the beach with stones as weapons.

This tendency to push others into adventures of which he remained a spectator might lead one to imagine that Gesril did not show much courage in later life; yet it was he who, on a smaller stage, probably surpassed Regulus in heroism; only Rome and Livy were wanting to ensure his fame. He had become a naval officer and was taken prisoner in the Quiberon landing,* when the action was over and the English went on cannonading the Republican army, Gesril plunged into the sea, swam out to the ships lying offshore, and told the English to cease fire, explaining that the émigrés had surrendered. They wanted to save him, throwing him a rope and urging him to climb on board. 'I am a prisoner on parole,' he shouted from the water, and he swam back to land: he was shot with Sombreuil and his companions.

Gesril was my first friend; both of us misjudged in our childhood, we were drawn together by the instinct of what we might become one day.

Two adventures brought this first part of my story to an end and produced a notable change in the manner of my upbringing.

We were on the beach one Sunday, along Le Sillon beyond the Porte Saint-Thomas, where thick stakes had been driven into the sand to protect the walls against the sea. We were in the habit of climbing on to these stakes to watch the first waves of the incoming tide pass beneath us. The places were taken as usual; there were several little girls among the little boys. Of the latter, I was the farthest out to sea, having nobody in front of me but a pretty little thing called Hervine Magon, who was laughing with pleasure and crying with fright. Gesril was at the other end of the row of stakes, nearest the shore.

The tide was coming in, the wind rising; already the maids and valets were calling out: 'Come down, Mademoiselle! Come down, Monsieur!' Gesril waited for a big wave to arrive; when it swept in between the piles, he pushed the child sitting next to him; the boy fell on to another, and he on to the next: the whole line went over like a row of skittles, but each one was steadied by his neighbour; there was only the little girl at the end of the line on to whom I collapsed who, having nobody to support her, fell into the water. The ebb swept her off her feet; there was

---

* In 1795 an émigré army under the Vicomte de Sombreuil landed at Quiberon with English naval support; those émigrés who were not killed in the ensuing battle were taken prisoner and shot.

a chorus of shrieks, and all the maids hitched up their skirts
and waded into the sea, each one seizing her charge and boxing
its ears. Hervine was rescued, and declared that François had
pushed her over. The maids bore down upon me; I got away
from them and ran home to barricade myself in the cellar, with
the female army hot in pursuit. Fortunately my mother and
father were out. La Villeneuve defended the door valiantly and
cuffed the enemy vanguard. The real cause of the trouble, Gesril, came to my help: he went up to his room and with his two
sisters threw jugfuls of water and baked apples at the attacking
force. They raised the siege at nightfall, but the news spread
through the town, and the Chevalier de Chateaubriand, aged
nine, passed for an evil character, a descendant of those pirates
of whom St Aaron had purged his rock.

This is the other adventure:

I was going one day with Gesril to Saint-Servan, a suburb
separated from Saint-Malo by the trading port. To get there at
low tide, you cross the water-courses on narrow bridges of flat
stones which are covered when the tide comes in. The servants
accompanying us had been left a long way behind. At the end
of one of the bridges we saw two cabin-boys coming towards
us. Gesril said to me: 'Are we going to let those ragamuffins
pass?' and promptly shouted at them: 'Into the water with you,
ducks!' They, in their capacity as cabin-boys, refused to see the
joke and continued to come forward; Gesril retreated; we stationed ourselves at the end of the bridge and, picking up pebbles
from the beach, we hurled them at the cabin-boys. They bore
down on us, forcing us to give ground, armed themselves too
with pebbles, and drove us back to our servants. Unlike Horatius I was not wounded in the eye: a stone struck me so hard
that it practically cut off my left ear, which hung down over my
shoulder.

I did not give a thought to my injury but only to my return
home. When my friend came home with a black eye and a torn
coat, he was comforted, caressed, coddled, and given a change
of clothing: in similar circumstances I was scolded and punished. The injury I had received was a dangerous one, but
nothing La France could say would persuade me to go home,

I was so frightened at the idea. I went and hid on the second floor of the house with Gesril, who bound my head up in a towel. This towel put him in a merry mood: it reminded him of a mitre; he turned me into a bishop and made me celebrate High Mass with him and his sisters until supper-time. The pontiff was then obliged to go downstairs, his heart beating wildly. Surprised to see my face covered with bruises and blood, my father said nothing; my mother gave a shriek of horror; La France explained what had happened, making excuses for me; I was nonetheless given a good dressing-down. My ear was patched up, and M. and Mme de Chateaubriand resolved to separate me from Gesril as soon as possible.

I believe it was that year that the Comte d'Artois came to Saint-Malo: he was treated to the sight of a naval battle. Looking down from the bastion of the powder-magazine, I saw the young prince in the midst of the crowd on the shore: in his glory and my obscurity, how great was the unknown quantity of fate! Thus, unless my memory is at fault, Saint-Malo has seen only two Kings of France, Charles IX and Charles X.

Such was my childhood. I do not know whether the strict upbringing I was given is good in principle, but it was adopted by my family without any set purpose and as a natural consequence of their temperaments. What is certain is that it made my ideas less like those of other men; what is even more certain is that it marked my feelings with a melancholy character born of the habit of suffering at a time of life of weakness, improvidence, and joy.

It may occur to some of my readers that this system of education was likely to make me detest my parents. This was not at all the case; the memory of their strictness is almost dear to me; I honour and esteem their great qualities. When my father died, my comrades in the Navarre Regiment were witnesses to my grief. As for my mother, it is to her that I owe the consolation of my life, since it is to her that I owe my faith; I listened to the Christian truths that came from her lips with the same fervour as Pierre de Langres studying at night in a church, by the light of the lamp burning before the Blessed Sacrament. Would my mind have been better developed if I had been sent to school earlier? I doubt it: these waves, these winds, this solitude which were my first masters were probably better suited to my native dispositions; perhaps I have these wild teachers to thank for certain qualities I would otherwise lack. The fact is that no system of education is intrinsically preferable to another: do the children of today love their parents more because they address them familiarly and no longer fear them? Gesril was spoilt in the same house where I was scolded: we both of us grew up decent men and affectionate and respectful sons. Something you consider bad may bring out your child's talents; something you consider good may stifle those same talents. God's wisdom is infinite; it is Providence which guides our footsteps when it destines us to play a part on the stage of this world.

THREE
Youth

My mother had never relinquished her desire that I should be given a classical education. The sailor's life for which I was destined 'would not be to my taste', she used to say; in any event she thought it advisable to render me capable of following another career. Her piety led her to hope that I would decide upon the Church. She therefore proposed that I should be sent to a school where I would learn mathematics, drawing, fencing, and English; she did not mention Greek and Latin for fear of alarming my father, but she intended that I should be taught those languages, secretly to begin with, and then openly when I had made sufficient progress. My father accepted her proposal, and it was agreed that I should enter the College of Dol. This town was chosen because it lay on the road from Saint-Malo to Combourg.

In the course of the severe winter which preceded my scholastic internment, the house where we were living caught fire; I was rescued by my eldest sister, who carried me through the flames. M. de Chateaubriand, who had retired to his château, sent word to his wife to join him in the spring.

I was to accompany my sisters to Combourg: we set off in the first fortnight of May. We left Saint-Malo at sunrise, my mother, my four sisters, and I, in a huge old-fashioned berline with extravagantly gilded panels, exterior footboards, and purple tassels at the four corners of the roof. We were drawn by eight horses decked out like mules in Spain, with bells hanging from their necks and attached to the reins, and housings and woollen fringes in various colours. While my mother sighed and my

sisters talked without stopping, I looked and listened and mar-
velled at every turn of the wheels: this was the first journey of
a Wandering Jew whose travels would never end. If a man only
changed place, well and good ... but his life and his heart
change too.

Our horses were rested at a fishing village on the Cancale
beach. Afterwards we crossed the marshes and the busy town
of Dol: passing the door of the school to which I was soon to
return, we turned inland.

For ten mortal miles we saw nothing but heaths ringed with
woods, fallow land which had barely been cleared, fields of
poor, short, black corn and scanty oats. We passed charcoal-
burners leading strings of ponies with lank, tangled manes, and
long-haired peasants in goatskin tunics driving gaunt oxen
along with shrill cries or walking behind heavy ploughs, like
fauns tilling the soil. Finally we came to a valley in which, close
to a pond, there rose the spire of a village church; the towers of
a feudal castle could be seen above the trees of a wood lit by the
setting sun.

Coming to the foot of the hill, we forded a stream; another
half-hour, and we left the highway to drive alongside a quin-
cunx, down an avenue of trees whose tops mingled above our
heads: I can still remember the moment when I entered this
shade and the mixture of fear and joy which I experienced.

Leaving the darkness of the wood, we crossed a forecourt
planted with walnut-trees, adjoining the steward's house and
garden, and passed through a gateway into a grassy courtyard
known as the Green Court. On the right were long stables and
a clump of chestnut-trees; on the left another clump of chestnut-
trees. At the far end of the courtyard, which rose gradually, the
château stood between two groups of trees. Its bleak, grim
façade, topped by a machicolated covered gallery, linked two
towers of disparate age, material, height, and thickness, which
were surmounted by crenellations and a pointed roof, like a
bonnet on top of a Gothic crown.

There were a few barred windows here and there in the bare
expanse of wall. A wide, straight, rigid staircase of twenty-two
steps, without banisters or parapet, had been built across the

filled-in moat in place of the old drawbridge and led up to the door of the château in the centre of the façade. Over this door there could be seen the coat of arms of the Lords of Combourg and the slits through which the arms and chains of the draw-bridge used to pass.

The coach drew up at the foot of the staircase; my father came forward to greet us. The reunion of his family moment-arily softened his temper to such an extent that he was ex-tremely pleasant to us. We went up the stairs and through an echoing entrance-hall with a Gothic ceiling into a little inner courtyard.

From this courtyard we went into the building which faced south over the pond and linked the two little towers. The whole château was in the form of a four-wheeled carriage. We found ourselves straight away in a room formerly known as the guardroom. There was a window at each end of this room, and two more at the sides. To make these four windows bigger, it had been necessary to pierce walls eight to ten feet thick. Two corridors which sloped like the corridor in the Great Pyramid led from the outer corners of the room to the little towers. A spiral staircase inside one of these towers connected the guard-room with the upper storey: such was the south building.

The building between the two big towers, looking north over the Green Court, consisted of a sort of dark, square dormi-tory which was used as a kitchen, the entrance-hall, the staircase, and a chapel. Over these rooms there was the drawing-room known as the Salon des Archives, or the Salon des Armoiries, or the Salon des Oiseaux, or the Salon des Chevaliers, so called on account of a ceiling studded with coloured coats of arms and painted birds. The recesses of the narrow, trefoiled win-dows were so deep that they formed little rooms with granite benches along the walls. Add to all this, in the various parts of the building, secret passages and staircases, dungeons and keeps, a maze of open and covered galleries, walled-up vaults; everywhere silence, darkness, and a face of stone: such was the Château of Combourg.

A supper which was served in the guardroom and which I ate greedily brought to an end the first happy day of my life.

True happiness is not expensive; if it costs dear, then it is of an inferior nature.

I had scarcely awoken the next morning before I went to explore the grounds of the château and celebrate my new-found solitude. The staircase faced north-west. Sitting at the head of this staircase, you had before you the Green Court and, farther on, a kitchen garden lying between two groves of trees: one, on the right (the quincunx along which we had come the day before), was called the Little Mall, the other, on the left, the Great Mall; the latter was a wood of oaks, beeches, sycamores, elms, and chestnut-trees. Mme de Sévigné in her time spoke highly of the shade given by these old trees; since then, one hundred and forty years had been added to their beauty.

On the opposite side, to the south and east, the countryside presented a very different picture; from the windows of the great hall you could see the houses of Combourg, a pond, the causeway beside this pond which carried the highroad to Rennes, a water-mill, and a meadow covered with herds of cows and separated from the pond by the causeway. Alongside this meadow there stretched a hamlet appertaining to a priory founded in 1149 by Rivallon, Lord of Combourg, where you could see a mortuary statue of him recumbent in his knightly armour. From the pond, the land rose gradually, forming an amphitheatre of trees from which there projected the spires of village churches and the turrets of manor-houses. On the far horizon, between the west and the south, the heights of Bécherel were silhouetted against the sky. A terrace lined with great ornamental box-trees encircled the foot of the château on that side, passed behind the stables, and wound down to the garden adjoining the Great Mall.

My first stay at Combourg was of short duration. Scarcely a fortnight had passed before I witnessed the arrival of the Abbé Portier, the principal of Dol College; I was delivered into his hands, and I followed him in spite of my tears.

I was not entirely a stranger to Dol, where my father was a canon, as the descendant and representative of the house of Guillaume de Chateaubriand, Sire de Beaufort, the founder in 1529 of one of the first stalls in the cathedral choir. The Bishop of Dol was M. de Hercé, a friend of my family and a prelate of very moderate political views, who, on his knees and holding a crucifix, was shot with his brother the Abbé de Hercé at Quiberon, in the Field of Martyrdom. On my arrival at the school I was placed under the special care of M. l'Abbé Leprince, who taught rhetoric and had a thorough knowledge of geometry: he was a handsome man with a nice wit, who loved the arts and could paint portraits with reasonable competence. He undertook to teach me mathematics; the Abbé Égault, who was in charge of the fourth form, became my Latin master; I studied mathematics in my own room, Latin in the common schoolroom.

It took some time for an owl of my sort to accustom himself to the cage of a school and to regulate his flight by the sound of a bell. I could not win those ready friends procured by wealth, for there was nothing to be gained from a poor wretch who did not even have a weekly allowance; nor did I join a clique, for I hate protectors. In the school games I did not presume to lead others, but at the same time I refused to be led: I was not fitted to be either a tyrant or a slave, and so I have remained.

Even so it happened that quite soon I became the centre of a set; later on, in my regiment, I exerted the same power: ordinary ensign that I was, the senior officers used to spend their evenings with me and preferred my rooms to the café. I do not know why this was, unless it had something to do with my ability to enter into the spirit and join in the way of life of other people. I enjoyed hunting and running as much as reading and writing. It is still a matter of indifference to me whether I chat about the most trivial matters or discuss the most serious subjects. But I have no liking for wit, which is wellnigh repugnant to me, although I am not exactly a simpleton. No human failing shocks me with the exception of mockery and conceit, which I find it hard to suffer patiently; I find that other people are always superior to me in some respect, and if by some chance I feel that I have an advantage over them the idea embarrasses me.

Qualities which my early upbringing had left dormant awoke in me at school. My aptitude for work was remarkable, my memory extraordinary. I made rapid progress in mathematics, a subject to which I brought a clarity of conception which astonished the Abbé Leprince. At the same time I showed a decided taste for languages. The rudiments, which are the bane of most schoolboys, I found easy to acquire; I awaited the time for the Latin lesson with a sort of impatience, as a relaxation after my sums and geometrical figures. In less than a year I reached the level of a good second-former. By some singularity, my Latin phrases fell so naturally into pentameters that the Abbé Égault called me the Elegist, a name by which my schoolmates knew me for long enough.

I went to Combourg for the holidays. Château life in the vicinity of Paris can give no idea of château life in a provincial backwater.

In the way of property, the estate of Combourg possessed only some barren heaths, a few mills, and the two forests Bourgouët and Tanoërn in a part of the country where timber is practically worthless. But Combourg was rich in feudal rights; these rights were of various kinds: some determined certain rents for certain concessions, or regulated customs born of the old political order; the others seem to have been nothing but amusements to begin with.

My father had revived some of these latter rights, in order to avert their prescription. When the whole family was gathered together, we used to take part in these old-fashioned entertainments: the three principal ones were the Saut des Poissonniers, the Quintaine, and a fair called the Angevine.* Peasants in clogs and breeches, men of a France which is now no more, watched these games of a France which was then no more. There was a prize for the victor, a forfeit for the vanquished.

The Quintaine maintained the tradition of the tournaments of old: it probably had some connexion with the military ser-

---

* The Saut des Poissonniers was a Maundy Thursday custom by which all the men who had sold fish during Lent had to jump into the pond; the Quintaine was a sort of tournament in which commoners who had married during the year tilted on horseback at a dummy originally named after a Turk called Quintain; the Angevine was held on 7 September, not 4 September as stated by Chateaubriand.

vice of the fiefs. The forfeits had to be paid in old copper coinage, up to the value of two *moutons d'or à la couronne* of 25 Parisian sols each.

The fair known as the Angevine was held in the pond meadow every year on 4 September, my birthday. The vassals were obliged to parade under arms and came to the château to raise the banner of the lord of the manor; from there they went to the fair to keep order and to enforce the collection of a toll due to the Counts of Combourg for every head of cattle, a sort of royalty. During this time my father kept open house. There was dancing for three days on end: for the masters in the great hall, to the scraping of a violin; for the vassals in the Green Court, to the nasal whine of a bagpipe. People sang and cheered and fired arquebusades. These noises mingled with the lowing of the cattle at the fair; the crowds wandered through the woods and gardens, and at least once a year Combourg saw something akin to merriment.

Thus I enjoy the singular distinction of having been present at the races of the Quintaine and the proclamation of the Rights of Man; of having seen the local militia of a Breton village and the National Guard of France, the banner of the Lords of Combourg and the flag of the Revolution. I am as it were the last surviving witness of feudal life.

The visitors who were received at the château consisted of the leading inhabitants of the village and the local aristocracy: these good people were my first friends. The most important local inhabitant was a certain M. Potelet, a retired sea-captain of the India Company, who used to tell stirring tales of Pondicherry. As he recounted these stories with his elbows on the table, my father was always tempted to throw his plate in his face. After him came the tobacco bonder, M. Launay de la Bliardière, the father, like Jacob, of a family of twelve children, nine girls and three boys, the youngest of whom, David, was a playmate of mine. This good man took it into his head to become a nobleman in 1789; he had left it rather late! In this household there was a great deal of happiness and a great many debts. The seneschal Gesbert, the fiscal attorney Petit, the tax collector Le Corvaisier, and the chaplain the Abbé Chalmel made up the society of Combourg. I have not met people of greater distinction in Athens.

I returned to Dol, much to my regret. The following year, plans were made by the army for a landing on Jersey,* and a camp was established near Saint-Malo. Troops were billeted at Combourg, and M. de Chateaubriand, out of courtesy, put up in succession the colonels of the Touraine and Conti Regiments: one was the Duc de Saint-Simon and the other the Marquis de Causans. A score of officers were invited to my father's table every day. The pleasantries of these strangers offended me; their walks disturbed the peace of my woods. It was through seeing the lieutenant-colonel of the Conti Regiment, the Marquis de Wignacourt, galloping beneath the trees that the idea of travel first entered my head.

When I heard our guests talking about Paris and the Court I fell into a state of melancholy; I tried to guess what society was like; I gained a vague, confused impression, but soon lost my bearings. Looking at the world from the quiet realms of innocence, I felt giddy, as one does when looking down at the ground from one of those towers that soar into the sky.

One thing delighted me, however, and that was the parade. Every day the new guard would march past, led by drummer and band, at the foot of the staircase in the Green Court. M. de Causans suggested showing me the camp on the coast, and my father gave his consent.

I was taken to Saint-Malo by M. de la Morandais, a gentleman of good family, but whom poverty had reduced to being the steward of the Combourg estates. He wore a coat of grey camlet with a little silver band at the collar, and a grey felt cap with earflaps and a peak in front. He put me behind him, on the crupper of his mare Isabelle. I held on to the belt of his hunting-knife, which was fastened outside his coat: I was delighted.

We stopped for dinner at a Benedictine abbey which, for want of a sufficient number of monks, had just been incorpor-

* In support of the Americans in their War of Independence.

ated in a more important community of the order. We found
nobody there but the bursar, who had been given the task of
disposing of the furniture and selling the timber. He provided
us with an excellent meatless dinner in what had been the
Prior's library: we ate a considerable number of new-laid eggs
with some huge carp and pike. Through the arcade of a cloister
I could see some great sycamores bordering a pond. The axe
struck at the foot of each tree, its top trembled in the air, and it
fell to make a show for us. Carpenters from Saint-Malo were
busy sawing off green branches as one trims a young head of
hair, or squaring the fallen trunks. My heart bled at the sight of
those decimated woods and that deserted monastery. The general sack of religious houses has since reminded me of that
spoliation of an abbey which for me was a portent of things to
come.

My brother was at Saint-Malo when M. de la Morandais
left me there. He said to me one evening: 'Get your hat: I am
taking you to the theatre.' I lost my head and went straight to
the cellar to look for my hat which was in the attic. A company
of strolling players had just arrived. I had already seen
puppet-shows, and I imagined that in a theatre you saw mari-
onettes far superior to those in the street.

My heart beating wildly, I came to a wooden building in a
deserted street, and went along some dark corridors, not without a certain feeling of apprehension. A little door was opened,
and there I was with my brother in a box half-full of people.

The curtain had risen, the play begun: it was Diderot's *Le
Père de famille*. I saw two men walking up and down the stage
and talking to each other, with everybody looking at them. I
took them for the managers of the puppet-show who were
chatting outside the home of the Old Woman who lived in a
shoe, while they waited for the audience to arrive; the only
thing that surprised me was that they should discuss their business so loudly and that they should be listened to in silence. My
astonishment grew when other characters coming on to the
stage started waving their arms about and weeping, and everybody took to crying out of sympathy. The curtain fell without
my having understood a word of all this. My brother went

down to the foyer during the interval between the two plays. Left in the box among strangers whose company was a torment to me in my shyness, I would have liked nothing better than to be back at school. Such was the first impression I obtained of the art of Sophocles and Molière.

The third year of my life at Dol was marked by the wedding of my two eldest sisters: Marie-Anne married the Comte de Marigny and Bénigne the Comte de Québriac. They accompanied their husbands to Fougères, giving as it were the signal for the dispersal of a family whose members were soon to separate. My sisters received the nuptial blessing at Combourg on the same day, at the same time, at the same altar, in the château chapel. They wept and my mother wept; I was surprised at their sorrow: I understand it today. I never attend a christening or a wedding without smiling bitterly or experiencing a pang. After being born, I know no greater misfortune than that of giving birth to a human being.

That same year saw a revolution in my person as in my family. Chance put into my hands two very different books, an unexpurgated Horace and a history of *Bad Confessions*. The spiritual upheaval which these two books brought about in me is unbelievable: a new world came into being around me. On the one hand, I obtained insight into secrets incomprehensible to one of my age, an existence different from mine, and charms of an unknown nature in a sex in which I had seen only a mother and sisters; on the other hand, ghosts dragging chains behind them and vomiting fire spoke to me of eternal punishment for a single hidden sin. I began to lose sleep; at night I thought I could see black hands passing in turn across my curtains: I came to imagine that these hands were cursed by religion, and this idea added to my terror of the infernal shades. I searched in vain in heaven and in hell for the explanation of a double mystery. Affected both morally and physically, I continued in my innocence to fight against the storms of a premature passion and the terrors of superstition.

If, since that time, I have been able to depict with some degree of verisimilitude the movements of the heart mingled with Christian remorse, I am convinced that I owe this achieve-

ment to the chance which introduced me at the same time to
two inimical empires. The havoc which an evil book wrought
in my imagination was compensated for by the terror which
another book inspired in me, and this in turn was so to speak
modified by the pleasurable thoughts which certain unveiled
pictures had left with me.

The holidays in the course of which I entered upon my twelfth
year were sad ones; the Abbé Leprince accompanied me to
Combourg. I never went out except with my tutor; we went for
long walks together. He was dying of consumption; he was
silent and melancholy; I was scarcely any merrier. We walked
for hours without saying a word. One day we lost our way in
the woods; M. Leprince turned to me and asked:

'Which way shall we go?'

I replied without hesitation:

'The sun is setting; just now it is striking the window of the
great tower; let us go that way.'

That evening M. Leprince recounted this incident to my
father: the future traveller showed himself in my decision.
Many a time, seeing the sun go down in the forests of America,
I have remembered the woods of Combourg; my memories
echo one another.

The Abbé Leprince suggested that I should be given a horse;
but in my father's opinion, the only thing a naval officer need
know how to handle was a ship. I was accordingly reduced to
secretly riding two fat coach-horses or a big piebald. The latter
was not Turenne's *Pie*, one of those battle-steeds which the
Romans called *desultorios equos* and trained to help their masters; it was a moon-eyed Pegasus which stamped when it was
trotting and bit my legs when I set it at a ditch. I have never
cared much for horses, although I have led the life of a Tartar;
and contrary to the effect which my early training should have
produced, I ride with greater elegance than sureness.

A fever, the germs of which I had brought with me from the
marshes of Dol, rid me of M. Leprince. A quack happened to
be passing through the village; my father, who had no faith in
doctors, had great faith in charlatans: he sent for the empiric,

who guaranteed to cure me in twenty-four hours. He came back the next day in a green coat trimmed with gold braid, a wide powdered wig, huge ruffles of dirty muslin, imitation diamonds on his fingers, worn black satin breeches, bluey-white silk stockings, and shoes with enormous buckles.

He opened my bed-curtains, felt my pulse, made me put out my tongue, jabbered a few words in an Italian accent on the necessity of purging me, and gave me a little piece of caramel to eat. My father approved of this treatment, for he maintained that all illness was caused by indigestion, and that for every kind of disorder you should purge a patient till he bled.

Half an hour after swallowing the caramel, I was seized with a terrible vomiting; M. de Chateaubriand was told of this, and threatened to have the poor devil thrown out of the tower window. The latter, utterly terrified, took off his coat and rolled up his shirt-sleeves, making the most grotesque gestures imaginable. With each movement, his wig turned in every direction; he echoed my cries, adding after each: *'Che? Monsou Lavandier?'* This M. Lavandier was the village chemist, who had been called in to help. I did not know, in the midst of my pain, whether I should die from taking the man's medicaments or from roaring with laughter at his behaviour.

The effects of this overdose of emetic were countered and I was set on my feet again. The whole of our life is spent wandering round our grave; our various illnesses are so many puffs of wind which bring us a little or a great deal nearer port. The first dead person I ever saw was a canon of Saint-Malo; he lay lifeless on his bed, his face distorted by the final convulsions. Death is beautiful, and she is our friend; yet we do not recognize her, because she appears to us in a mask and her mask terrifies us.

I was sent back to school at the end of autumn.

Mathematics, Greek, and Latin occupied the whole of my winter at school. What time was not devoted to study was given up to those childhood games which are the same all over the world. The little English boy, the little German, the little Italian, the little Spaniard, the little Iroquois, and the little Bedouin all bowl the hoop and throw the ball. Brothers of one great family, children lose their common features only when they lose their innocence, which is the same everywhere. Then the passions, modified by climates, governments, and customs, create different nations; the human species ceases to speak and understand the same language; society is the real Tower of Babel.

One morning I was engrossed in a game of prisoner's base in the school playground when I was told that I was wanted. I followed the servant to the main gate. There I found a stout, red-faced man, with an abrupt, impatient manner and a fierce voice; he was carrying a stick in his hand and was wearing an untidy black wig, a torn cassock with the ends tucked into the pockets, dusty shoes, and stockings with holes in the heels.

'You little scamp,' he said, 'aren't you the Chevalier de Chateaubriand de Combourg?'

'Yes, Monsieur,' I replied, quite taken aback by his manner of speaking.

'And I,' he went on, almost foaming at the mouth, 'I am the last of the elder branch of your family; I am the Abbé de Chateaubriand de la Guerrande; take a good look at me.'

The proud ecclesiastic put his hand into the fob pocket of a pair of old plush breeches, took out a mouldy six-franc crown piece wrapped in a piece of dirty paper, flung it at me, and stamped off, muttering his matins with a furious air. I have since discovered that the Prince de Condé had offered this rustic rector the post of tutor to the Duc de Bourbon. The scandalized priest replied that the Prince, as the owner of the Barony of Chateaubriand, ought to know that the heirs to that barony could *have* tutors but could not possibly *be* tutors. This arrogance was the cardinal failing of my family; in my father it was hateful; my brother pushed it to ridiculous lengths; it has come down to a certain extent to his eldest son. I am not sure that I myself, despite my republican inclinations, have entirely shaken it off, although I have taken every care to conceal it.

The time drew near for making my first communion, when it was customary in my family to decide upon the child's future condition. This religious ceremony took the place among young

Christians of the assumption of the *toga virilis* among the Romans. Mme de Chateaubriand had come in order to be present at the first communion of a son who, after being united to his God, would be parted from his mother.

My piety appeared to be sincere; I edified the whole school; my eyes glowed with religious ardour; my fasts were so frequent as to make my masters uneasy. They feared the effects of excessive devoutness; their enlightened piety sought to temper my fervour.

My confessor was the superior of the Eudist seminary, a man of fifty with a stern appearance. Every time I presented myself at the confessional, he questioned me anxiously. Surprised at the unimportance of my sins, he did not know how to reconcile my distress with the trivial nature of the secrets I confided to him. The nearer Easter came, the more pressing did the priest's questions become. 'Aren't you keeping something back?' he would ask. I replied: 'No, father.' 'Haven't you committed such and such a sin?' 'No, father.' And it was always: 'No, father.' He dismissed me with obvious misgivings, sighing and gazing into the depths of my soul, while I left his presence looking as pale and shifty as a criminal.

I was to receive absolution on the Wednesday in Holy Week. I spent Tuesday night praying and reading with terror the book of *Bad Confessions*. At three o'clock on the Wednesday afternoon, we set out for the seminary, accompanied by our parents. All the vain renown which has since attached itself to my name would not have given Mme de Chateaubriand an iota of the pride which she felt as a Christian and a mother at seeing her son preparing to participate in the great mystery of our religion.

On arriving at the church, I prostrated myself before the altar and lay there as if I had been annihilated. When I stood up to go to the sacristy, where the superior was waiting for me, my knees trembled beneath me. I threw myself at the priest's feet; it was only in the most broken of voices that I was able to say the *Confiteor*. 'Well, have you forgotten nothing?' asked the man of God. I remained silent. He started questioning me

again, and the inevitable 'No, father' came from my lips. He
lapsed into meditation, asking counsel of Him who conferred
upon the Apostles the power of binding and loosing souls.
Then, making an effort, he prepared to give me absolution.

If Heaven had shot a thunderbolt at me, it would have
caused me less dread. I cried:

'I have not confessed everything!'

This awe-inspiring judge, this delegate of the Supreme Arbiter, whose face filled me with such fear, became the tenderest of
shepherds. He clasped me in his arms and burst into tears.

'Come now, dear child,' he said, 'courage!'

I shall never experience a like moment in the whole of my
life. If the weight of a mountain had been lifted from me, I
should not have felt more relieved: I sobbed with happiness. I
venture to say that it was on that day that I became a decent,
upright man; I felt that I could never survive a feeling of
remorse: how great the remorse for a crime must be, when I
could suffer so dreadfully for concealing the minor misdemean-
ours of a child! But also how divine this religion is which can
thus take hold of our best instincts! What moral precepts can
ever take the place of these Christian institutions?

The first admission made, the rest came easily: the childish
offences which I had concealed, and which would have made
the world smile, were weighed in the balance of religion. The
superior was in an embarrassing position; he would have liked
to postpone my communion, but I was about to leave Dol College to enter the Navy shortly afterwards. With great perspicacity
he discovered in the very character of my youthful sins, insignificant though they were, the nature of my propensities; he was
the first man to fathom the secret of what I might become. He
divined my future passions; he did not conceal from me the
good he thought he saw in me, but he also predicted the evils to
come.

'After all,' he said, 'even if you have little time for your penance, you have been cleansed of your sins by your courageous,
though tardy, confession.'

Raising his hand, he pronounced the words of absolution.

On this second occasion, the dreadful hand showered on my head nothing but the heavenly dew; I bent my brow to receive it; my feelings partook of the joy of the angels. Then I ran to embrace my mother, who was waiting for me at the foot of the altar. I no longer appeared the same person to my masters and schoolmates: I walked with a light step, my head high and a radiant expression on my face, in all the triumph of repentance.

The next day, Maundy Thursday, I was admitted to the sublime and moving ceremony which I have vainly endeavoured to describe in *Le Génie du christianisme*. I might have felt here as elsewhere my usual little humiliations: my nosegay and my clothes were less impressive than those of my companions; but that day everything was of God and for God. I know exactly what Faith is: the Real Presence of the Victim in the Blessed Sacrament on the altar was as manifest to me as my mother's presence by my side. When the Host was laid on my tongue, I felt as though a light had been kindled within me. I trembled with veneration, and the only material thing that occupied my mind was the fear of profaning the sacramental bread.

Three weeks after my first communion, I left Dol College. I retain pleasant memories of that house: our childhood leaves something of itself in the places it has embellished, just as a flower communicates a perfume to the objects it has touched. To this day I feel moved when I think of the dispersal of my first companions and my first masters. The Abbé Leprince, appointed to a living near Rouen, did not survive much longer; the Abbé Égault obtained a rectorship in the diocese of Rennes; and I saw the good principal, the Abbé Portier, die at the beginning of the Revolution; he was a learned, gentle, simple-hearted man. The memory of that obscure teacher will always be dear and venerable to me.

At Combourg I found food for my piety in a mission whose exercises I followed. I received the sacrament of Confirmation on the manor steps, with the peasant boys and girls, from the hand of the Bishop of Saint-Malo. Afterwards a cross was erected; I helped to hold it steady while it was being fixed on its

YOUTH   47

base. It is still there: it stands in front of the tower in which my father died.* For thirty years it has seen no one appear at the windows of that tower; it is no longer saluted by the children of the château; every springtime it waits for them in vain; it sees none return but the swallows, more faithful to their nest than man to his house. How happy I should be if my life had been spent at the foot of that mission cross, if my hair had been whitened only by the years which have covered the arms of that cross with lichen!

I did not wait long before leaving for Rennes, where I was to continue my studies and complete my mathematics course, in preparation for my examination as a Naval Guard at Brest.

Rennes seemed to me a Babylon, the school a world. The number of masters and boys, and the size of the buildings, the garden, and the playgrounds struck me as immense; I grew accustomed to it all, however. For the price of a few punches, I acquired over my new schoolmates the same ascendancy I had exercised over my old companions at Dol. Young Bretons are quarrelsome scamps; on half-holidays we challenged each other to fights in the shrubberies of the Benedictines' garden, which was known as the Thabor; we used compasses fastened to the end of a walking-stick, or else we engaged in hand-to-hand fights which were more or less treacherous or courteous according to the gravity of the challenge. There were umpires who decided whether a forfeit was due, and what weapons the champions should employ. The fight did not end until one of the two parties admitted that he was beaten. I found my old friend Gesril here, presiding over these engagements as he had done at Saint-Malo. He offered to act as my second in a fight I had with Saint-Riveul, a young nobleman who became the first victim of the Revolution. I fell under my adversary, refused to surrender, and paid dearly for my pride. Like Jean Desmarets on his way to the scaffold, I said: 'I cry mercy to God alone.'

I met at this school two men who have since become famous in different ways: Moreau, the general, and Limoëlan, the

* The cross, made of wood, has since disappeared.

author of the infernal machine,* who is now a priest in America. There is only one portrait of Lucile in existence, and this
poor miniature is by Limoëlan, who turned portrait-painter
during the revolutionary troubles. Moreau was a day-boy,
Limoëlan a boarder. Rarely have such strange destinies been
found together at the same time, in the same province, in the
same small town, and at the same school.

The prefect was in the habit of going round the corridors
after lights out to see if all was well: to do this he looked
through a hole which had been made in all the doors. Limoëlan, Gesril, Saint-Riveul, and I all slept in the same room.
Several times we had stopped up the hole with paper, but all in
vain; the prefect poked the paper out and caught us jumping
over our beds and breaking our chairs.

One evening Limoëlan, without telling us what he intended
to do, persuaded us to go to bed and put out the lights. Soon
we heard him get up, go to the door, and then return to bed. A
quarter of an hour later, the prefect came along on tiptoe. As he
not unreasonably regarded us with suspicion, he stopped at our
door, listened, looked, and failed to see any light . . .†

'Who did that?' he shouted, rushing into the room. Limoëlan started choking with laughter and Gesril asked in a nasal
voice in his half-innocent, half-ironical way: 'What is it, sir?'
Where upon Saint-Riveul and I began laughing like Limoëlan
and hid our faces under the bedclothes.

They could get nothing out of us: we were heroic. We were
all four imprisoned in the vaults: Saint-Riveul dug his way
under a door leading into the farmyard; he put his head into
this mole-hill, and a pig ran up and made as if to eat his brains
out; Gesril slipped into the school cellars and opened up a cask
of wine; Limoëlan knocked down a wall, and I, climbing up to
a ventilator, stirred up the mob in the street with my speeches.
The dreadful author of the infernal machine playing this prank
on a school prefect reminds one of the young Cromwell inking

* Limoëlan was involved in the attempt to kill Bonaparte in December 1799 in
the Rue Saint-Nicaise.
† Here a scatological detail was suppressed by Chateaubriand in 1846.

the face of another regicide who signed Charles I's death warrant after him.

Although the schooling at Rennes College was very religious, my fervour abated: the number of my masters and schoolmates multiplied the occasions for distraction. I made progress in the study of languages; I became strong in mathematics, for which I have always had a pronounced leaning: I would have made a good naval officer or sapper. I was good at chess, billiards, shooting, and fencing; I drew tolerably well; I would have sung well too, if my voice had been trained. All this, combined with the way in which I was brought up and the life I have led as a soldier and traveller, explains why I have never played the pedant or displayed the stupid conceit, the awkwardness, and the slovenly habits of the men of letters of former days, still less the arrogance and self-assurance, the envy and blustering vanity of the new authors.

I spent two years at Rennes College; Gesril left eighteen months before I did. He entered the Navy. Julie, my third sister, was married in the course of these two years to the Comte de Farcy, a captain in the Condé Regiment, and settled with her husband at Fougères, where my two eldest sisters, Mmes de Marigny and de Québriac, were already living. Julie's wedding took place at Combourg, and I was present. There I met the Comtesse de Trojolif, who distinguished herself by her courage on the scaffold; a cousin and close friend of the Marquis de la Rouërie, she was involved in his conspiracy. I had not until then seen beauty except in my own family; I was disturbed by the sight of it in the face of a strange woman. Every step in life opened up new horizons before me; I heard the distant and seductive voice of the passions which were coming to me; I hurried to meet these sirens, drawn by an unfamiliar music. It so happened that, like the High Priest of Eleusis, I had a different incense for each divinity. But could the hymns which I sang while burning this incense be called 'perfumes', like the poems of the hierophant?*

*

* The mystical hymns of Orpheus were called *The Perfumes*.

After Julie's marriage, I set out for Brest. On leaving the great College of Rennes I did not feel the same regret that I had felt on leaving the little College of Dol; perhaps I had lost that innocence which makes everything attractive to us; time was beginning to develop it. My guide and mentor in my new position was one of my maternal uncles, the Comte Ravenel du Boisteilleul, a vice-admiral, one of whose sons, a distinguished artillery officer in Bonaparte's armies, married the only daughter of my sister the Comtesse de Farcy.

On my arrival at Brest I did not find my cadet's commission waiting for me; some accident had delayed it. I remained what was called an *aspirant*, and as such was exempt from the usual studies. My uncle put me to board in the Rue de Siam at a cadets' hostel, and introduced me to the naval commander, the Comte d'Hector.

Left for the first time to my own resources, instead of making friends with my future messmates, I withdrew into my usual solitude. My habitual society was confined to my masters in fencing, drawing, and mathematics.

The sea which I was to meet with on so many coasts washed, at Brest, the tip of the Armorican Peninsula: beyond that prominent cape there lay nothing but a boundless ocean and unknown worlds; my imagination revelled in this infinity. Often, sitting on some mast that had been laid along the Quai de Recouvrance, I watched the movements of the crowd: ship-wrights, sailors, soldiers, custom-house officers, and convicts passed to and fro before me. Passengers embarked and disem-barked, pilots conned their ships, carpenters squared blocks of wood, rope-makers lit fires under coppers which gave out clouds of smoke and the healthy smell of tar. Bales of merchan-dise and sacks of victuals were carried backwards and forwards; artillery trains were rolled from the sea to the magazines, from the magazines to the sea. Here, carts backed into the water to take on cargoes; there, garnets lifted loads, while cranes lowered stones and dredging-machines dug up alluvium. Forts repeated signals, launches came and went, vessels got under sail in the docks.

One day I had set off in the direction of the far end of the

port, towards the sea: it was warm; I lay down on the beach
and fell asleep. Suddenly I was awakened by an awe-inspiring
din; I opened my eyes like Augustus to see the triremes in the
anchorage of Sicily after the victory over Sextus Pompey: the
reports of guns followed one after another; the roads were
crowded with ships; the great French squadron was returning after the signing of peace.* The ships manoeuvred under
sail, hoisted their lights, showed their colours, turned their
poops, bows, or broadsides to the shore, stopped short by
suddenly dropping anchor, or continued to skim the waves.
Nothing has ever given me a higher idea of the human mind;
man seemed at that moment to have borrowed something from
Him who said to the sea: 'You shall go no further. *Non pro-
cedes amplius.*'

All Brest hurried to the port. Launches left the fleet and came
alongside the mole. The officers with which they were crowded,
their faces bronzed by the sun, had that foreign look which one
brings back from another hemisphere, and an ineffable air of
gaiety, pride, and daring, as befitted men who had just restored
the honour of the national ensign. These naval officers, so
deserving and illustrious, these companions of Suffren, La
Motte-Picquet, Couëdic, and D'Estaing, who had come through
the enemy's fire unscathed, were to fall one day under the fire
of their fellow countrymen.

I was watching the gallant troop go by when one of the officers broke away from the others and fell upon my neck: it
was Gesril. He seemed taller, but weak and ailing from a sword-
thrust he had received in the chest. He left Brest the same
evening to join his family. I saw him only once after that,
shortly before his heroic death; I will explain in what circumstances later. Gesril's sudden appearance and departure led me
to make a resolution which changed the course of my life: it
was written that that young man should exert an absolute
influence over my destiny.

It can be seen how my character was shaping, the turn my
ideas were taking, and what were the first symptoms of my

* The Peace of Versailles, 1783.

genius; for I can speak of that genius as an illness, whatever it may have been, rare or common, worthy or unworthy of the name I give it for want of another word to express my meaning. If I had been more like other men, I should have been happier: anybody who, without depriving me of my intelligence, could have killed what is called my talent would have done me a friendly service.

When the Comte de Boisteilleul took me to see M. d'Hector, I heard young and old sailors recounting their campaigns and talking of the countries they had visited: one had arrived from India, another from America; this one was about to set off on a journey round the world, while another was due to join the Mediterranean station, to visit the shores of Greece. My uncle pointed out La Pérouse to me in the crowd, a new Cook, whose fate has remained the secret of the tempests.*
I listened to everything and I looked at everything, without uttering a word; but there was no sleep for me that night; I spent it, in imagination, fighting battles or discovering unknown lands.

Be that as it may, seeing Gesril return to his parents, I decided that there was nothing to prevent me from going home to my own. I should have greatly liked serving in the Navy, if my spirit of independence had not unfitted me for service of any kind: I am inherently incapable of obedience. Voyages tempted me, but I felt that I should enjoy them only in solitude, left to follow my fancy. At last, giving the first proof of my fickleness, without telling my uncle Ravenel, without writing to my parents, without asking anybody's permission, and without waiting for my cadet's commission, I left one morning for Combourg, where I arrived as if I had dropped from the skies.

To this day I am still astonished to think how, in view of the terror with which my father inspired me, I could have dared to take such a step; and what is just as astonishing is the man-

---

* All trace of the explorer La Pérouse was lost in 1788. In 1828 the wrecks of his ships were found on the coast of Vanikoro, an island in the Santa Cruz group.

ner in which I was received. I expected an explosion of violent wrath, and I was given a quiet and gentle welcome. My father merely shook his head, as if to say: 'Here's a pretty kettle of fish!' My mother embraced me with all her heart, grumbling at the same time, and my Lucile kissed me in an ecstasy of joy.

FOUR
Manhood

Between the last date attached to these *Memoirs*, January 1814 at the Vallée-aux-Loups, and today's date, July 1817 at Montboissier, three years and six months have elapsed. Did you hear the Empire fall? No: nothing has disturbed the tranquillity of this spot. Yet the Empire has collapsed; the immense ruin has fallen in the course of my life, like Roman remains that have tumbled into the bed of some unknown stream. But events matter little to one who holds them of no account; a few years escaping from the hands of the Eternal will do justice to all these noises by means of an endless silence.

I have recounted my return to Combourg and my reception by my father, my mother, and my sister Lucile.

The reader will perhaps remember that my three other sisters had married and were living on the estates of their new families, in the vicinity of Fougères. My brother, whose ambition was beginning to develop, was more often in Paris than at Rennes. He first bought a post as *maître des requêtes* which he sold in order to take up a military career. He entered the Royal Cavalry Regiment; he then joined the diplomatic corps and accompanied the Comte de la Luzerne to London, where he met André Chénier; he was on the point of obtaining the Vienna Embassy when our troubles broke out. He applied for the Constantinople Embassy, but found that he had a formidable rival in the person of Mirabeau, who had been promised this embassy as a reward for joining the Court party. My brother had therefore more or less taken leave of Combourg by the time I came to live there.

Entrenched in his manor, my father now never left it, not even to attend the sittings of the States of Brittany. My mother went to Saint-Malo for six weeks every year, at Easter; she looked forward to this time as a time of release, for she detested Combourg. A month before the journey, it was discussed as if it were a dangerous enterprise; preparations were made; the horses were rested. On the eve of departure, everyone went to bed at seven in the evening, in order to get up at two in the morning. My mother, to her great satisfaction, set off at three, and spent the whole day covering thirty miles.

Lucile, who had been received as a canoness in the Chapter of L'Argentière, was about to be transferred to that of Remiremont: pending this move, she remained buried in the country.

As for myself, after my escape from Brest, I declared my wish to embrace the ecclesiastical state: the truth is that I was only trying to gain time, for I did not know what I wanted. I was sent to Dinan College to complete my humanities. I knew Latin better than my masters, but I began learning Hebrew. The Abbé de Rouillac was the principal of the college, and the Abbé Duhamel my tutor.

M. de Chateaubriand, who found it saved him money to keep me at home, and my mother, who hoped that I would persist in my religious vocation but who would have had scruples about bringing pressure to bear on me, no longer insisted on my residing in college, so that I found myself imperceptibly settling down under the paternal roof.

I should take pleasure in recalling my parents' way of life even if it were no more to me than a touching memory; but I shall describe it all the more readily in that the picture I shall draw will appear to have been traced from the vignettes in medieval manuscripts: whole centuries separate the present day from the days I am about to depict.

On my return from Brest, the masters of the Château of Combourg were four: my father, my mother, my sister, and myself. A cook, a chambermaid, two footmen, and a coachman composed the entire domestic staff: a hunting dog and two old mares were hidden away in a corner of the stable. These twelve living creatures were lost to sight in a manor-house where a hundred knights with their ladies, squires and varlets and King Dagobert's chargers and hounds might almost have gone unnoticed.

In the whole of the year, not a single stranger presented himself at the château, except for a few gentlemen, such as the Marquis de Montlouet and the Comte de Goyon-Beaufort, who asked to be put up on their way to plead a cause before the High Court. They used to arrive in winter, on horseback, with pistols at their saddle-bows and hunting-knives at their sides, and followed by a manservant, also on horseback, with a big livery trunk behind him.

My father, who was always very punctilious, used to receive them bareheaded on the steps, out in the wind and rain. Once inside the château, these country gentlemen would talk about their Hanovenan campaigns, their family affairs, and their lawsuits. At night they were shown to the north tower, to Queen Christina's bedchamber, a guest-room containing a bed seven foot square, hung with two sets of curtains in green muslin and crimson silk, and supported by four gilt Cupids. The next morning, when I came down to the great hall and looked out of the windows at the countryside covered with floods or frost, all that I saw was two or three travellers on the causeway beside the pond: they were our guests riding towards Rennes.

These strangers did not know a great deal about life; nonetheless, through them our view was extended a few miles beyond the horizon of our woods. As soon as they had gone we were reduced on weekdays to conversation among ourselves and on Sundays to the company of the village commoners and the local gentry.

On Sundays, if the weather was fine, my mother, Lucile, and I went to the parish church across the Little Mall and along a country lane; when it rained, we went by way of the abominable Rue de Combourg. We were not carried, like the Abbé de Marolles, in a light chariot drawn by four white horses captured from the Turks in Hungary. My father went to the parish church only once a year, to perform his Easter duties; during the rest of the year he heard Mass in the château chapel. Sitting in the pew of the lord of the manor, we received the incense and the prayers in front of the black marble tomb of Renée de Rohan, next to the altar; a symbol of mortal honours: a few grains of incense before a sepulchre!

The bleak tranquillity of the Château of Combourg was increased by my father's taciturn, unsociable temperament. Instead of gathering his family and his servants close to him, he had scattered them to the four corners of the building. His bedroom was in the small east tower, and his study in the small west tower. The furniture of this study consisted of three chairs upholstered in black leather and a table covered with title-deeds and parchments. A genealogical tree of the Chateaubriand family hung over the chimney-piece, and in one window-recess there were all sorts of firearms, from the pistol to the blunderbuss. My mother's room was situated above the great hall, between the two small towers: it had a parquet floor and was adorned with faceted Venetian mirrors. My sister occupied a closet adjoining my mother's room. The chambermaid slept a long way away, in the main building between the two great towers. As for myself, I was tucked away in a kind of isolated cell at the top of the turret containing the staircase which connected the inner courtyard with the various parts of the château. At the foot of this staircase, my father's valet and the other manservant slept in vaulted cellars, while the cook was garrisoned in the great west tower.

My father got up at four o'clock in the morning, winter and summer alike: he went into the inner courtyard to call and wake his valet at the entrance to the turret staircase. A cup of coffee was brought to him at five; he then worked in his study until midday. My mother and sister breakfasted in their separate rooms at eight o'clock. I had no fixed time either for rising or for breakfasting; I was supposed to study until midday: most of the time I did nothing.

At half past eleven, the bell rang for dinner, which was served at midday. The great hall did duty as both dining-room and drawing-room: we dined and supped at one end, on the east side: after the meal we went and sat at the other end, the west side, in front of a huge fireplace. The great hall was wainscoted, painted pale grey, and adorned with old portraits ranging from the reign of François I to that of Louis XIV; among these portraits one could recognize studies of Condé and Turenne: a picture representing Achilles killing Hector beneath the walls of Troy hung over the chimney-piece.

After dinner we stayed together until two o'clock. Then, if it was summer, my father went fishing, inspected his kitchen gardens, or took a walk round the park; if it was autumn or winter he went shooting. My mother retired to the chapel, where she spent a few hours in prayer. This chapel was a gloomy oratory, decorated with fine pictures by the greatest masters such as one scarcely expected to find in a feudal castle in the depths of Brittany. I still have in my possession a *Holy Family* by Albani, painted on copper, which comes from this chapel: it is all that remains to me of Combourg.

Once my father was out and my mother at her prayers, Lucile shut herself up in her room and I either returned to my cell or went out to roam the fields.

At eight o'clock the bell rang for supper. After supper, when the weather was fine, we sat out on the steps. My father shot at the screech-owls which flew out from the battlements at nightfall. My mother, Lucile, and I gazed at the sky, the woods, the last rays of the sun, the first stars. At ten o'clock we went in and retired to bed.

The autumn and winter evenings were different. When supper was over and the four of us had moved from the table to the fireplace, my mother sank with a sigh on to an old day-bed covered in Siam; a little table with a candle on it was put in front of her. I sat beside the fire with Lucile; the servants cleared the table and withdrew. My father then set off on a walk which lasted until he went to bed. He was dressed in a white petersham robe, or rather a kind of cloak which I have never seen on anyone else. His half-bald head was covered with a big white bonnet which stood upright. When, in the course of his walk, he went some distance from the fireplace, the huge hall was so badly lighted by the one solitary candle that he disappeared from sight; he could only be heard walking in the darkness: then he slowly returned towards the light, gradually emerging from the shadows like a ghost, with his white robe, his white bonnet, his long pale face. Lucile and I exchanged a few words in a low voice when he was at the other end of the hall; we fell silent when he drew near to us. He asked as he passed by: 'What were you talking about?' Terror-stricken, we made no answer; he continued his walk. For the rest of the evening nothing could be heard but the measured sound of his steps, my mother's sighs, and the murmur of the wind.

The château clock struck ten; my father stopped; the same spring which had lifted the hammer of the clock seemed to have arrested his steps. He pulled out his watch, wound it up, took a great silver candlestick holding a tall candle, went for a moment into the small west tower, then returned, candle in hand, and made for his bedroom, which led off from the small east tower. Lucile and I stood on his way; we kissed him and wished him good night. He offered us his dry hollow cheek without replying, walked on, and withdrew into the depths of the tower, whose doors could be heard closing behind him.

The spell was broken: my mother, my sister, and I, turned into statues by my father's presence, recovered the functions of life. The first effect of our disenchantment took the form of a torrent of words: we made silence pay dearly for having oppressed us.

When this flow of words had ceased, I called the chambermaid and escorted my mother and my sister to their rooms. Before I left them, they made me look under the beds, up the chimneys, and behind the doors, and inspect the surrounding staircases, passages, and corridors. All the traditions of the château concerning robbers and ghosts returned to their memory. The servants were convinced that a certain Comte de Combourg with a wooden leg, who had been dead three centuries, appeared at certain times, and that he had been seen in the great staircase in the turret; sometimes, too, his wooden leg walked on its own, accompanied by a black cat.

These stories took up all the time my mother and sister spent preparing for the night; they got into bed dying with fright; I retired to the top of my turret; the cook returned to the main tower, and the servants went down to their vaults.

The window of my keep opened on to the inner courtyard;

in the daytime I had a view of the battlements opposite, where hart's-tongue flourished and a wild plum-tree grew. A few martins, which in summer dived with shrill cries into the holes in the walls, were my sole companions. At night I could see only a few stars. When the moon was shining and sinking in the west, I knew it by the beams which came through the diamond-shaped window-panes and fell on my bed. Screech-owls, flitting from one tower to the next, passed time and again between the moon and me, outlining on my curtains the mobile shadow of their wings. Banished to the loneliest part of the château, at the entrance to the galleries, I did not miss a single murmur of the darkness. Sometimes the wind seemed to be running along light-footed; sometimes it uttered mournful plaints; all of a sudden my door was shaken violently, groans came from the vaults, and then these sounds would die away, only to begin once more. At four o'clock in the morning, the voice of the master of the house, calling his valet at the entrance to the ancient cellars, echoed round the château like the voice of the last phantom of the night. For me this voice took the place of the sweet music with which Montaigne's father used to awaken his son.

The Comte de Chateaubriand's unusual idea of making a child sleep by itself at the top of a tower may have had its inconvenient side, but it turned out to my advantage. This rough treatment left me with the courage of a man, without robbing me of that lively imagination of which people nowadays try to deprive the young. Instead of attempting to persuade me that ghosts did not exist, my mother and father forced me to stand up to them. When my father asked me, with a sarcastic smile: 'Is the Chevalier afraid?' he could have made me sleep with a corpse. When my mother said to me: 'My child, nothing happens without God's permission; you have nothing to fear from evil spirits as long as you remain a good Christian', I was more reassured than by all the arguments of philosophy. My success was so complete that the night winds, in my lonely tower, served merely as playthings for my fancies and wings for my dreams. My imagination, kindled into flame and spreading in all directions, failed to find adequate nourish-

ment anywhere and could have devoured heaven and earth. It
is this moral condition which I must now endeavour to describe.
Immersed once more in my youth, I am going to try to capture
myself in the past, to depict myself such as I was, such as perhaps I wish I were today, despite the torments I endured at the
time.

I had scarcely returned from Brest to Combourg than a revolution took place in my existence; the child vanished and the
grown man appeared, with all his passing joys and his enduring
sorrows.

To begin with, everything became a passion with me, pending the arrival of the passions themselves. When, after a silent
dinner, at which I had not dared either to speak or to eat,
I succeeded in making my escape, my delight was indescribable. I could not go down the steps straight away: I should have
flung myself down the whole flight. I was obliged to sit on one
of the steps to allow my excitement to subside; but as soon as
I had reached the Green Court and the woods, I began running,
jumping, leaping, skipping, and frolicking about until I fell
down exhausted, panting for breath, drunk with merriment
and freedom.

My father took me shooting. I acquired a taste for the sport
and carried it to excess; I can still see the field where I killed my
first hare. In autumn I would often stay for four or five hours
waist-deep in water, waiting for wild duck at the edge of a
pond; to this day my heart gives a leap when I see a dog point.
However, in my initial enthusiasm for the sport there was an
element of independence; crossing ditches, tramping across
fields, marshes, and moors, finding myself with a gun in a deserted spot, strong and lonely, all this was in my nature. On my
shooting expeditions, I would go so far that I had not the
strength to walk back, and the gamekeepers were obliged to
carry me on a litter of branches.

Yet the pleasures of the chase no longer satisfied me; I was
afflicted with a longing for happiness which I could neither control nor understand; my mind and my heart ended up by forming
as it were two empty temples, without altars or sacrifices; it was

not yet known what god was to be worshipped in them. I grew up beside my sister Lucile: our friendship was the whole of our life.

Lucile was tall and endowed with remarkable, but solemn beauty. Her pale features were framed in long black tresses; she often fixed her gaze upon the sky or cast looks around her which were full of sadness or fire. Her bearing, her voice, her smile, her face, all had something pensive and melancholy about them.

Lucile and I were of no use to one another. When we spoke of the world, it was of that which we carried within ourselves, a world which bore little resemblance to the real world. She saw me as her protector, while I saw her as my friend. She was afflicted by gloomy thoughts which I had difficulty in dispelling: at seventeen she mourned the passing of her youth and wanted to bury herself in a convent. Everything to her was care, sorrow, or anguish: an expression she was looking for or an illusion she was entertaining would torment her for months on end. I have often seen her with one arm thrown over her head, dreaming immobile and inanimate; the life in her, drawn towards her heart, ceased to be visible; her breasts even no longer rose and fell. Her attitude, her melancholy, her grace lent her the appearance of a funeral Genius. I would try at such times to comfort her, and the next moment I myself would be plunged into unaccountable despair.

Lucile liked reading some pious book, alone in the evening: her favourite oratory was the junction of two country roads, marked by a stone cross and a poplar whose long stylus rose into the sky like a pencil. My devout mother, captivated by the sight, said that her daughter reminded her of a Christian girl of the Early Church, praying at one of those stations called *laures*.

My sister's concentration of mind gave rise to some extraordinary mental phenomena: in her sleep, she dreamt prophetic dreams; in her waking hours, she seemed to read the future. On one of the landings of the staircase in the great tower there was a clock which struck the hours in the silence. Lucile, when she could not sleep, would go and sit on the stairs opposite the

clock and watch its face by the light of her lamp placed on the
floor. When the two hands met at midnight and in their dreadful conjunction engendered the hour of crimes and disturbances,
Lucile heard sounds which revealed distant deaths to her. She
happened to be in Paris a few days before the Tenth of August,*
staying with my other sisters near the Carmelite convent, and
looking at a mirror, she gave a cry and said: 'I have just seen
Death come in.' On the moors of Scotland, Lucile would have
been one of Walter Scott's mystic women, gifted with second
sight; on the moors of Brittany, she was nothing more than a
lonely creature endowed with beauty, genius, and misfortune.

The life which my sister and I led at Combourg increased the
exaltation natural to our age and character. Our principal distraction consisted of walking side by side in the Great Mall, in
spring on a carpet of primroses, in autumn on a bed of withered leaves, in winter on a sheet of snow embroidered with the
footprints of birds, squirrels, and stoats. Young as the primroses, sad as the withered leaves, we were in harmony with our
recreations.

It was in the course of one of these walks that Lucile, hearing
me speak rapturously of solitude, said to me: 'You ought to
write that down.' This remark revealed the Muse to me; a divine
inspiration passed over me. I began stammering out poetry, as if
it had been my natural language; night and day I sang of my
pleasures, in other words of my woods and valleys; I composed
a multitude of little idylls or pictures of Nature. I wrote in verse
long before writing in prose: M. de Fontanes used to maintain
that I had been equipped with both instruments.

Did this talent which friendship prophesied for me ever
come to me? How many things have I awaited in vain! In the
Agamemnon of Æschylus, a slave is posted as sentry on the roof
of the palace of Argos; his eyes strain to make out the agreed
signal for the return of the ships; he sings to relieve the tedium

---

* 10 August 1792, when a riot brought about the downfall of the constitutional monarchy, followed by the September massacres in the Paris prisons,
including the Carmelite convent.

of his vigils, but the hours pass and the stars set, and the torch never shines. When, after many years, its tardy light appears above the waves, the slave is bent beneath the weight of time; nothing remains for him but to reap misfortune, and the chorus tells him that 'an old man is a shadow wandering in the light of day'. ὄναρ ἡμερόφαντον ἀλαίνει.

In the first flush of inspiration I invited Lucile to imitate me. We spent days in mutual consultation, telling each other what we had done and what we meant to do. We undertook works in common; guided by our instincts, we translated the finest and saddest passages in Job and Lucretius on life: the *Taedet animam meam vitae meae*, the *Homo natus de muliere*, the *Tum porro puer, ut saevis projectus ab undis navita*, and so forth. Lucile's thoughts were nothing but feelings; they had difficulty in coming forth from her soul; but when she succeeded in expressing them, they were beyond compare. She has left behind some thirty pages in manuscript; it is impossible to read them without being profoundly moved. The elegance, the sweetness, the dreaminess, and the passionate feeling of these pages present a combination of the Greek genius and the Germanic genius.

My brother sometimes accorded a few brief moments to the hermits of Combourg. He usually brought with him a young counsellor at the High Court of Brittany, M. de Malfilâtre, a cousin of the unfortunate poet of the same name. I believe that Lucile, unknown to herself, had conceived a secret passion for this friend of my brother's, and that this stifled passion lay at the root of my sister's melancholy. She was moreover afflicted with Rousseau's folly though without his pride: she thought that everybody was in a conspiracy against her. She came to Paris in 1789, accompanied by that sister Julie whose death she has deplored with a tenderness tinged with the sublime. All who met her admired her, from M. de Malesherbes to Chamfort. Thrown into the revolutionary crypts at Rennes, she came close to being incarcerated in the Château of Combourg, which had been turned into a gaol during the Terror. After her release

from prison, she married M. de Caud,* who left her a widow a
year later. On my return from my emigration, I was reunited
with the friend of my childhood: I will tell you how she disappeared when it pleased God to afflict me.

I have returned from Montboissier, and these are the last lines
that I shall write in my hermitage;† I have to leave it, filled with
the fine striplings which in their serried ranks already hide and
crown their father. I shall never again see the magnolia which
promised its blossom to the tomb of my Floridan, the Jerusalem
pine and the cedar of Lebanon consecrated to the memory of
Jerome, the Granada laurel, the Greek plane-tree, the Armorican oak, at whose feet I depicted Blanca, sang of Cymodocée,
invented Velléda. These trees were born and grew with my
dreams, of which they were the hamadryads. They are about to
pass under another's sway: will their new master love them as I
have loved them? Perhaps he will let them die or cut them down:
it is my fate to keep nothing on this earth. Bidding farewell to
the woods of Aulnay, I shall recall the farewell which I bade
long ago to the woods of Combourg: all my days are farewells.
    The taste for poetry with which Lucile had inspired me was
like fuel added to the flames. My feelings acquired new strength;
vain ideas of glory passed through my mind; for a moment I
believed in my *talent*, but soon enough, recovering a proper
mistrust of myself, I began to entertain doubts about that talent, as I have continued to do ever since. I looked on my work
as an evil temptation; I felt angry with Lucile for having aroused
a regrettable propensity within me; I stopped writing and took
to mourning my future glory as one might mourn a glory that
was past.
    Returning to my former state of idleness, I became more
aware of what was lacking in my youth: I was a mystery to

---

* Lieutenant-Colonel Jacques de Caud was sixty-nine when he married Lucile,
then thirty-one, in August 1796; he died in March 1797.
† The Vallée-aux-Loups, to which Chateaubriand returned in November
1817 and which he found himself obliged to sell.

myself. I could not see a woman without feeling embarrassed; I blushed if she spoke to me. My shyness, already excessive in anybody's company, was so great with a woman that I would have preferred any torture to being left alone with her: yet no sooner had she gone than I longed for her to return. The descriptions of Virgil, Tibullus, and Massillon, it is true, presented themselves to my memory; but the image of my mother and my sister, covering everything with its purity, made thicker the veils which Nature sought to raise; filial and brotherly love deceived me with regard to any less disinterested affection. If the loveliest slaves of a seraglio had been handed over to me, I would not have known what to ask of them: chance enlightened me.

A neighbour of the Combourg domain came to spend a few days at the château with his wife, who was extremely pretty. Something, I forget exactly what, happened in the village; everyone ran to one of the windows of the great hall to look. I got there first, our fair guest followed hard on my heels, and I turned round to give her my place. Involuntarily she blocked my way, and I found myself pressed between her and the window. I ceased to be conscious of what was happening around me.

At that moment I became aware that to love and be loved in a manner which was unknown to me must be the supreme happiness. If I had done what other men do, I should soon have come to know the pains and pleasures of the passion whose seeds I carried within me; but everything in me assumed an extraordinary character. The fervour of my imagination, my shyness, and my solitude were such that, instead of going out into society, I fell back upon myself; for want of a real object of my love, I evoked, by the strength of my vague longings, a phantom which never left my side. I do not know whether the history of the human heart offers another example of this nature.

I accordingly created a woman in my imagination out of all the women whom I had seen: she had the figure, the hair, and the smile of the guest who had pressed me to her bosom; I gave her the eyes of one of the girls of the village, the complexion of another. The portraits of the great ladies of the time of François

I, Henri IV, and Louis XIV which adorned the drawing-room
provided me with other features, and I even borrowed certain
charms from the pictures of the Virgin that hung on church
walls.

This invisible charmer accompanied me wherever I went; I
talked to her as to a real person. She varied according to my
mood: now Aphrodite unveiled, now Diana dressed in dew and
air, now Thalia with her laughing mask, now Hebe bearing the
cup of youth, she often became a fairy who subjected Nature to
my authority. I was for ever retouching my canvas, taking one
attractive feature from my beauty to replace it with another. I
also changed her finery, borrowing elements from every country, every age, every art, every religion. Then, when I had created
a masterpiece, I scattered my lines and colours once more; my
unique woman turned into a crowd of women, in whom I idol-
ized separately the charms I had adored in unison.

Pygmalion was less enamoured of his statue: my trouble was
how to please mine. Recognizing in myself none of the qualities
required to arouse affection, I lavished upon myself all that
I lacked. I rode like Castor and Pollux; I played the lyre like
Apollo; Mars wielded his arms with less strength and skill; a
hero of history or romance, I heaped fictitious adventures on
fiction itself! The shades of Morven's daughters, the sultanas of
Baghdad and Granada, the ladies of medieval castles, baths,
perfumes, dances, Asiatic delights were all evoked for me by a
magic wand.

A young queen would come to me, decked in diamonds and
flowers (it was my sylph). She sought me out at midnight, through
gardens of orange-trees, in the galleries of a palace washed by
the waves of the sea, on the balmy shore of Naples or Messina,
beneath a sky of love bathed in the light of Endymion's star;
she moved forward, a living statue by Praxiteles, in the midst of
motionless statues, pale pictures, and silent frescoes whitened
by the moonlight: the soft sound of her progress across the
marble mosaic mingled with the imperceptible murmur of the
waves. The royal jealousy surrounded us. I fell upon my knees
before the sovereign of Enna's plains; the silken tresses from
her loosened diadem fell caressingly on my brow as she bent

her sixteen-year-old head over my face, and her hands rested on my breast, throbbing with respect and desire.

When I emerged from these dreams and found myself once more a poor, obscure little Breton without fame, beauty, or talents, who would attract no one's attention, who would go unnoticed, whom no woman would ever love, I was seized with despair: I no longer dared look up at the dazzling image I had created to accompany me.

This delirium lasted two whole years, during which my spiritual faculties reached the highest pitch of exaltation. I used to speak very little, but now I did not speak at all; I still used to study, but now I tossed my books aside; my taste for solitude became more pronounced than ever. I displayed all the symptoms of a violent passion; my eyes grew hollow, I lost weight, I could not sleep, I was absent-minded, melancholy, ardent, and unsociable. My days passed in a manner that was wild, weird, insensate, and yet full of delight.

In summer, on stormy days, I used to climb to the top of the great west tower. The thunder rumbling in the garrets, the rain pounding on the cone-shaped roofs of the towers, and the lightning furrowing the clouds and marking the brass weathercocks with an electric flame aroused my enthusiasm: like Ismen on the ramparts of Jerusalem, I invoked the thunder, hoping that it would bring me Armida.

If the sky was clear, I crossed the Great Mall, around which lay meadows divided by hedges of willow-trees. In one of these willows I had established a seat, like a nest; there, isolated between heaven and earth, I spent hours with the warblers; my nymph was by my side. I also associated her image with the beauty of those spring nights that are filled with the freshness of the dew, the sighs of the nightingale, and the murmur of the breeze.

Heaven and earth no longer meant anything to me; I forgot the former especially; but though I no longer prayed aloud, it listened to the voice of my secret misery: for I suffered, and suffering is a prayer.

*

Bound more closely than ever to my phantom and unable to enjoy what did not exist, I was like those mutilated men who dream of joys to which they can never attain and conjure up fantasies whose pleasures rival the tortures of hell. Moreover I had a presentiment of the misery of my future destinies: skilled in the art of self-inflicted suffering, I had placed myself between two sources of despair: sometimes I considered myself a mere cipher, incapable of rising above the common herd; sometimes I thought that I could feel within myself qualities which would never be appreciated. A secret instinct warned me that as I made my way in the world I should find nothing of what I sought.

Everything contributed to my bitterness and disgust: Lucile was unhappy; my mother did not console me; my father made me conscious of the horror of life. His gloominess increased with the years; old age stiffened his soul as it did his body; he spied on me constantly in order to scold me. When I returned from my wild excursions and saw him sitting on the steps, I would rather have died than enter the château. Yet this was only postponing my torture: obliged to appear at supper, I sat down guiltily on the edge of my chair, my cheeks wet with rain and my hair tangled. Under my father's gaze I sat motionless, with sweat covering my forehead: the last glimmer of reason left me.

I now come to a moment when I need strength to confess my weakness. The man who tries to take his life shows not so much the vigour of his soul as the feebleness of his nature.

I owned a fowling-piece whose worn trigger often went off when it was uncocked. I loaded this gun with three bullets and went to a remote part of the Great Mall. I cocked the gun, placed the muzzle in my mouth, and struck the butt against the ground; I did this several times, but the gun did not go off; the appearance of a gamekeeper interrupted me. An involuntary and unconscious fatalist, I concluded that my hour had not come, and I postponed the execution of my plan to another day. If I had killed myself, all that I have been would have been buried with me; nothing would have been known of the story which had led to my catastrophe; I should have swelled the crowd of nameless sufferers, and I should not have induced others to follow me by leaving a trail of sorrows as a wounded man leaves a trail of blood.

Those who might be disturbed by these descriptions and tempted to imitate these follies, those who might attach themselves to my memory by means of my illusions, must remember that they are listening only to a dead man's voice. Reader, whom I shall never know, nothing remains: nothing is left of me but what lies in the hands of the living God who has judged me.

An illness, the fruit of this unruly life, put an end to the torments which brought me the first inspirations of the Muse and the first attacks of the passions. These passions, ill-defined as yet, which taxed my soul so sorely resembled the storms at sea which rush in from every point of the compass: an inexperienced pilot, I did not know in which direction I should spread my sail to the uncertain winds. My breast swelled, and a fever took hold of me; an excellent doctor called Cheftel, whose son was involved in the Marquis de la Rouërie affair, was called in from Bazouches, a little town some fifteen miles from Combourg. He examined me carefully, prescribed certain medicaments, and declared that above all else it was essential to remove me from my present way of life.

I was in danger for six weeks. One morning my mother came and sat down on my bed and said:

'It is time for you to come to a decision; your brother is in a position to obtain a benefice for you; but before going into the seminary, you must think well, for although I would like you to embrace the ecclesiastical state, I would rather see you a man of the world than a scandalous priest.'

Those who have read the preceding pages will be able to judge whether my pious mother's proposal came at a timely moment. In the major events of my life, I have always known at once what to avoid: I am prompted by my sense of honour. If I became a priest, I should find myself ridiculous. If I became a bishop, the majesty of my office would overawe me and I should recoil respectfully from the altar. Should I, as a bishop, strive to acquire virtues or should I content myself with concealing my vices? I felt too weak to adopt the first course, too honest to adopt the second. Those who call me hypocritical and ambitious do not know me: I shall never achieve success in this life, precisely because I lack one passion and one vice: ambition and hypocrisy. In me the first would be at most a form of injured pride; I might sometimes wish to be a minister or a king in order to laugh at my enemies, but after twenty-four hours I should throw my portfolio or my crown out of the window.

I accordingly told my mother that I did not feel a strong enough vocation for the Church. For the second time I was changing my plans: I had not wanted to become a sailor, and now I no longer wanted to be a priest. There remained the Army, which tempted me; but how would I stand the loss of my independence and the constraint of European discipline? I hit on an absurd idea: I declared that I would go to Canada to clear forests or to India to join the army of one of the princes of that country.

By one of those contrasts which are to be found in all men, my father, normally so reasonable, was never greatly shocked by an adventurous project. He grumbled to my mother about my changes of mind, but decided to despatch me to India. I was sent off to Saint-Malo, where a ship was being fitted out for Pondicherry.

Two months went by: I found myself back on my native island, this time alone; Villeneuve had just died there. When I went to weep for her beside the poor, empty bed on which she had breathed her last, I noticed the little wicker go-cart in which I had learnt to stand upright in this melancholy world. I pictured my old nurse lying in bed and fixing her feeble gaze on that basket on wheels: this first memorial of my life facing the last memorial of the life of my second mother, the thought of the prayers for her charge which dear Villeneuve addressed to Heaven on leaving this world, this proof of an attachment so constant, disinterested, and pure, broke my heart with tenderness, gratitude, and sorrow.

There was nothing else at Saint-Malo to remind me of my

past: in the harbour I looked in vain for the ships in whose rigging I had played; they had gone or been broken up; in the town, the house where I was born had been turned into an inn. I was scarcely out of my cradle, and already a whole world had disappeared. I was a stranger in my childhood haunts, and people who met me asked me who I was, for the sole reason that my head had risen a few inches higher above the ground towards which it will sink again in a few years. How rapidly and how often we change our illusions and our way of life! Friends leave us, others take their place; our relationships alter: there is always a time when we possessed nothing of what we now possess, and a time when we have nothing of what we once had. Man does not have a single, consistent life: he has several laid end to end, and that is his misfortune.

A letter summoned me back to Combourg: I arrived, I supped with my family, my father did not utter a word, my mother sighed, Lucile looked dismayed; at ten o'clock we retired to bed. I questioned my sister; she knew nothing. At eight o'clock the next morning I was sent for. I went downstairs: my father was waiting for me in his study.

'Chevalier,' he said, 'you must renounce your follies. Your brother has procured you a second-lieutenant's commission in the Navarre Regiment. You are to go first to Rennes and then to Cambrai. Here are a hundred louis: spend them wisely. I am old and ill; I have not long to live. Conduct yourself as a man of honour and never bring disgrace on your name.'

He kissed me. I felt that stern, wrinkled face press tenderly against mine: it was the last paternal embrace I was to receive.

At that moment the Comte de Chateaubriand, a man usually so formidable in my eyes, appeared to me simply as a father infinitely worthy of my affection. I seized his emaciated hand and wept. He was beginning to suffer from the paralysis which killed him; his left arm kept giving a convulsive jerk which he was obliged to check with his right. It was holding his arm in this way, after handing me his old sword, that, without giving me time to recover my composure, he led me to the cabriolet which was waiting for me in the Green Court. He made me get in before him. The postilion drove off while I bade farewell to my mother and sister, dissolved into tears on the steps.

I drove along the causeway beside the pond; I saw the reeds inhabited by the swallows, the mill-stream and the meadow; I cast a look at the château. Then, like Adam after his sin, I went forth into unknown country, and 'the world was all before me'.*

Since then I have seen Combourg only three times. After my father's death we all met there, in mourning, to divide our inheritance and take leave of each other. On another occasion I accompanied my mother to Combourg: she was engaged in furnishing the castle in readiness for the arrival of my brother, who was bringing my sister-in-law to Brittany. My brother never came; with his young wife, he was soon to receive from the hand of the executioner a very different pillow from that prepared by my mother's hand. Finally I passed through Combourg a third time on my way to Saint-Malo to set sail for America. The château was empty, and I had to put up at the steward's lodge. When, walking along the Great Mall, I came to the end of a dark path and caught sight of the deserted steps, the closed door, and the shuttered windows, I fainted. I made my way back to the village as best I could, sent for my horses, and left in the middle of the night.

After an absence of fifteen years, and before leaving France once more to go to the Holy Land, I went to Fougères to embrace what remained of my family. I had not the heart to go on a pilgrimage to the fields with which the most vital part of my existence is connected. It was in the woods of Combourg that I became what I am, that I began to feel the first attacks of that boredom which I have dragged with me through life, of that sadness which has been my joy and my despair. There I sought for a heart which could beat with mine; there I saw my family gather together only to disperse. There my father dreamt of seeing his name established, the fortunes of his house revived: another illusion which time and revolution have dispelled. Of

* Milton: *Paradise Lost.*

six children that we were, only three remain: my brother, Julie, and Lucile are no more; my mother has died of grief, and my father's ashes have been snatched from his grave.

If my works survive me, if I am destined to leave behind a name, perhaps one day, guided by these *Memoirs*, some traveller will come and visit the places I have described. He will be able to recognize the château, but he will look in vain for the great wood: the cradle of my dreams has vanished like the dreams themselves. Left standing by itself on its rock, the ancient keep mourns for the oaks, its old companions which surrounded it and protected it against the tempest. Isolated like that keep, I too have seen falling around me the family which graced my days and lent me its shelter: fortunately my life is not built on this earth as firmly as the towers in which I spent my youth, and man offers less resistance to the storms than the monuments raised by his hands.

FIVE

Soldier and Courtier

It is a long way from Combourg to Berlin, from a young dreamer to an old minister. In the foregoing pages I find these words: 'In how many places have I begun writing these *Memoirs*, and in what place shall I complete them?'

Nearly four years have passed between the date on which I wrote down the facts which I have just recounted and that on which I am resuming these *Memoirs*. A thousand things have happened; a new man has appeared in me, the politician: I do not care greatly for him. I have defended the liberties of France, which alone can secure the continuation of the legitimate monarchy. With the help of the *Conservateur*, I have put M. Villèle into power; I have seen the Duc de Berry die and paid homage to his memory. In order to reconcile all parties, I have left France and accepted the Berlin Embassy.*

Yesterday I was at Potsdam, an ornate barrack, now empty of soldiers: I studied the mock Julian† in his mock Athens. At Sans-Souci I was shown the table at which a great German monarch turned the maxims of the Encyclopaedists into little French verses; Voltaire's room, decorated with wooden monkeys and parrots; the mill which he who laid waste whole provinces made a point of respecting; the tombs of the horse César and the greyhounds Diane, Amourette, Biche, Superbe, and Pax. The royal infidel took pleasure in profaning even the religion of

---

* Chateaubriand was appointed French Ambassador to the Court of Prussia in November 1820 and wrote this chapter in Berlin in the spring of 1821.
† Frederick II, who considered himself a 'philosopher-king', after the manner of the Emperor Julian.

the tomb by raising mausoleums to his dogs; he had marked out a burial-place for himself beside them, not so much to show his contempt for mankind as to parade his belief in nothingness.

I was taken to see the new palace, which is already falling into decay. In the old palace of Potsdam, they preserve the tobacco stains, the worn and soiled armchairs, indeed every relic of the renegade prince's uncleanliness. This place immortalizes at once the dirtiness of the cynic, the impudence of the atheist, the tyranny of the despot, and the glory of the soldier.

Only one thing attracted my attention: the hands of a clock fixed at the moment of Frederick's death. I was deceived by the immobility of the picture: hours do not suspend their flight; it is not man that stops time, it is time that stops man. What is more, it does not matter what part we have played in life; the brilliance or obscurity of our doctrines, our wealth or poverty, our joys or sorrows make no difference to the number of our days. Whether the hands of the clock move over a golden or a wooden face, whether the face is large or small, and whether it fills the bezel of a ring or the rose-window of a cathedral, the hour has one and the same duration.

Evenings in Berlin are long. I occupy a house belonging to the Duchess of Dino. My secretaries leave me as soon as night falls. When there is no entertainment at Court to celebrate the wedding of the Grand Duke and Grand Duchess Nicholas, I stay at home. Sitting all by myself in front of a cheerless stove, I can hear nothing but the shout of the sentry at the Brandenburg Gate and the steps in the snow of the man who whistles the hours. How shall I spend my time? Reading? I have scarcely any books. What if I were to continue my *Memoirs*?

You left me on the road from Combourg to Rennes: I alighted in this latter town at the house of a relative of mine. He informed me with great delight that a lady of his acquaintance, who was going to Paris, had a seat to spare in her carriage, and that he undertook to persuade this lady to take me with her. I accepted, cursing my relative's courtesy. He settled the matter and soon afterwards presented me to my travelling-companion, a sprightly, unselfconscious milliner, who burst out laughing when she saw me. The horses arrived at midnight and we set off.

There I was, in a post-chaise alone with a woman in the middle of the night. How was I, who had never looked at a woman in my life without blushing, to make the descent from the height of my dreams to this terrifying reality? I did not know where I was; I huddled in my corner of the carriage for fear of touching Mme Rose's gown. When she spoke to me, I stammered without being able to reply. She was obliged to pay the postilion and to see to everything, for I was incapable of raising a finger. At daybreak she looked with fresh amazement at this great booby with whom she regretted having saddled herself.

As soon as the scenery began to change and I ceased to recognize the dress and accent of the Breton peasants, I fell into a profound depression, which increased the contempt in which Mme Rose held me. I became aware of the feeling I had inspired, and I received from this first contact with the world an impression which time has not completely effaced. I was born shy but not shamefaced; I felt modesty on account of my age but not embarrassment. When it dawned on me that I was ridiculous because of the good side of my nature, my shyness turned into an insurmountable timidity. I could not speak another word: I felt that I had something to hide, and that this something was a virtue; I made up my mind to hide myself in order to wear my innocence in peace.

We drew nearer Paris. Coming down from Saint-Cyr, I was struck by the width of the road and the neatness of the fields. Soon we reached Versailles: the orangery and its marble stairs amazed me. The success of the American War had resulted in trophies for Louis XIV's palace; the Queen reigned there in all the splendour of her youth and beauty; the throne, so close to its fall, seemed to have never been more firmly established. And I, an obscure passer-by, was destined to outlive this pomp, to survive to see the woods of Trianon as deserted as those which I had just left behind.

At last we entered Paris. I saw an amused expression on every face, and thought that people looked at me to make fun

of me. Mme Rose told the postilion to drive to the Hôtel de
l'Europe in the Rue du Mail and lost no time in getting rid of
her simpleton. I had scarcely got out of the carriage than she
said to the porter:

'Give this gentleman a room. Your servant,' she added, nodding her head at me.

I never saw Mme Rose again.

A woman preceded me up a dark, steep staircase, holding a
labelled key in her hand; a Savoyard followed me with my little
trunk. When she reached the third floor, the chambermaid
opened the door of a bedroom; the Savoyard put the trunk
across the arms of a chair.

'Does Monsieur require anything?' asked the chambermaid.

'No,' I replied.

Somebody whistled three times; the chambermaid shouted:
'Coming!' rushed out, shut the door, and ran downstairs with
the Savoyard. When I found myself alone in my room, I felt
such a strange pang that I came close to taking the road back
to Brittany. I remembered everything I had heard about Paris; a
score of things embarrassed me. I should have liked to go to
bed, but the bed was not made; I was hungry, but I did not
know how to set about dining. I was afraid of making a fool of
myself. Ought I to call the hotel people? Ought I to go downstairs? To whom should I apply? I ventured to put my head out
of the window: all I could see was a small inner yard, as deep
as a well, across which people came and went who would never
give a thought to the prisoner on the third floor. I went and sat
down again by the dirty recess in which I was to sleep, reduced
to studying the figures on the paper with which its walls were
hung. The sound of voices arose in the distance, grew louder,
drew nearer; my door opened, and in came my brother and
one of my cousins, the son of a sister of my mother's who had
made a rather poor marriage. Mme Rose had taken pity on the
simpleton after all, and had sent word to my brother, whose
address she had been given at Rennes, that I had arrived in
Paris. My brother embraced me. My cousin Moreau was a big
fat man, smeared all over with snuff, who ate like an ogre,

talked a great deal, was always dashing about, puffing and choking, with his mouth half-open and his tongue half-out, knew everybody, and spent his time in gambling-dens, ante-rooms, and drawing-rooms.

'Well, Chevalier,' he said, 'here you are in Paris! I am going to take you to Madame de Chastenay's.'

Who was this woman whose name I had never heard before? This proposal turned me against my cousin Moreau.

'The Chevalier probably needs a rest,' said my brother. 'We will go and see Madame de Farcy, and then he shall come back to have dinner and go to bed.'

A feeling of joy entered my heart: the thought of my family in the midst of an indifferent world was like balm to me. We went out. Cousin Moreau made a fuss about the poor room I had been given, and urged my host to install me at least one floor further down. We got into my brother's carriage and drove to the convent where Mme de Farcy was living.

Julie had been in Paris for some time, in order to consult the doctors. Her charming face, her elegance, and her wit had soon made her much sought after. I have already said that she was born with a genuine talent for poetry. She became a saint, after having been one of the most attractive women of her times: the Abbé Carron has written her life.

When I saw her in Paris, she was in all the pomp of worldly luxury; she appeared covered with those flowers, adorned with those necklaces, and veiled in those scented fabrics which St Clement forbids the early Christian women. St Basil wishes the middle of the night to be for the solitary what the morning is for others, so that he may profit from the silence of Nature. The middle of the night was the hour when Julie went to gatherings at which her verses, recited by herself with marvellous euphony, formed the principal attraction.

Julie was infinitely lovelier than Lucile: she had tender blue eyes and dark hair which she wore in plaits or in long waves. Her hands and arms, which were models of whiteness and delicacy, added by their graceful movements something even more charming to her already charming appearance. She was radiant and lively, laughed often and unaffectedly, and showed teeth like pearls when she laughed. Countless portraits of women of Louis XIV's time resembled Julie, among others those of the three Mortemarts, but she was more elegant than Mme de Montespan.

She received me with that affection which only a sister can show. I felt safe and protected when I was enfolded in her arms, her ribbons, her lace, and her bouquet of roses. Nothing can take the place of a woman's loyalty, delicacy, and devotion; a man is forgotten by his brothers and friends and misjudged by his companions, but never by his mother, his sister, or his wife. When Harold was killed in the Battle of Hastings, his men could not recognize him among all the dead; they had to seek the help of a girl he loved. She came, and the unfortunate prince was found by Edith the swan-necked: *Editha Swaneshales, quod sonat collum cycni.*

My brother brought me back to my hotel; he ordered my dinner and left me. I dined alone, and went sadly to bed. I spent my first night in Paris pining for my moors and trembling at the uncertainty of my future.

At eight o'clock the next morning my fat cousin arrived; he had already done four or five errands.

'Well, Chevalier, we are going to have breakfast now; we shall dine with Pommereul, and this evening I shall take you to Madame de Chastenay's.'

This seemed to be my fate, and I resigned myself to it. Everything happened as my cousin had wished. After breakfast he said that he was going to show me Paris, and dragged me through the dirtiest streets around the Palais-Royal, telling me about the dangers to which a young man was exposed. We were punctual for our dinner appointment, which was at an eating-house. Everything which was served to us seemed bad to me. The conversation and the guests revealed a new world to me. The talk was about the Court, the financial proposals, the Academy's sitting, the women and intrigues of the day, the latest play, and the successes of actors, actresses, and authors.

There were several Bretons among the guests, including the Chevalier de Guer and Pommereul. The latter was a good talker, who has since written the history of some of Bonaparte's

campaigns, and whom I was destined to meet again when he
was at the head of the censorship.

After dinner my brother wanted to take me to the theatre,
but my cousin claimed me for Mme de Chastenay, and I went
with him to meet my fate.

I saw a beautiful woman, no longer in her first youth, but
still capable of inspiring love. She received me kindly, tried to
put me at my ease, and asked me about my province and my
regiment. I was awkward and embarrassed, and signalled to
my cousin to cut short the visit. But he, without so much as
glancing at me, talked endlessly about my merits, declaring
that I had written poetry at my mother's breast, and calling on
me to sing Mme de Chastenay's charms in verse. She released
me from this embarrassing situation, apologized for being
obliged to go out, and invited me to come back and see her the
next morning in so sweet a voice that I involuntarily promised
to obey.

I returned the next day alone: I found her in bed in an elegantly furnished room. She told me that she was a little out of
sorts, and that she had the bad habit of rising late. For the first
time in my life I found myself at the bedside of a woman who
was neither my mother nor my sister. She had noticed my shyness the day before, and conquered it so completely that I
managed to express myself with a certain volubility. I forget
what I said to her, but I can still see her look of astonishment.
She held out to me a half-bare arm and the most beautiful hand
in the world, and said with a smile:

'We shall tame you.'

I did not even kiss that beautiful hand; I withdrew in considerable confusion. The next day I left for Cambrai. Who was
this Mme de Chastenay? I have no idea: she passed through my
life like a charming shadow.

The mail-coach brought me to my garrison town. One of my
brothers-in-law, the Vicomte de Chateaubourg (he had married
my sister Bénigne, the Comte de Québriac's widow), had given
me letters of recommendation to some of the officers in my regiment. The Chevalier de Guénan, a man of very good breeding,

introduced me to a mess in which there dined a number of officers distinguished for their talents, MM. Achard, Des Maillis,
and La Martinière. The Marquis de Mortemart was colonel of
the regiment, the Comte d'Andrezel major: I was placed under
the particular protection of the latter. I have met both of them
in later years: one of them became my colleague in the Chamber of Peers; the other applied to me for certain services which
I was happy to render him. There is a melancholy pleasure in
meeting people we have known at different periods of our life
and in considering the changes which have occurred in their
existence and ours. Like markers left behind us, they trace the
way we have come through the desert of the past.

Joining my regiment in mufti, I had donned military dress
within twenty-four hours, and I felt as if I had always worn it.
My uniform was blue and white, like the clothes I had worn
under my vow years before: as a young man and as a child I
marched under the same colours. I was submitted to none of
the trials which the second-lieutenants were in the habit of
inflicting on newcomers: I do not know why they did not venture to indulge in this military horseplay with me. Before I had
been with the regiment a fortnight, I was treated as an old
hand. I learnt the practice and theory of firearms with ease; I
went through the ranks of corporal and sergeant to the applause
of my instructors. My room became the meeting-place of the
old captains as well as of the young second-lieutenants: the former went over their campaigns with me, while the latter
confided their love-affairs to me.

La Martinière used to fetch me to accompany him past the
door of one of the belles of Cambrai whom he worshipped; this
happened five or six times a day. He was extremely ugly, and
his face was pitted with pockmarks. He would tell me of his
passion while draining big glasses of red-currant syrup, which
I sometimes paid for.

Everything would have been perfect but for my passion for
clothes. At that time the army affected the stiffness of the Prussian uniform: a small hat, little curls worn close to the head, a
pig-tail tied very tightly, and a carefully buttoned coat. I disliked
this intensely; I submitted to these shackles in the morning, but

in the evening, when I hoped that none of my superior officers would see me, I put on a bigger hat, the barber brushed out my curls and loosened my pig-tail, and I unbuttoned and turned back the facings of my coat. In this amorous undress I would go courting on La Martinière's behalf under the cruel Fleming's windows. But one day I came face to face with M. d'Andrezel.

'What is the meaning of this, Monsieur?' said the terrible major. 'Consider yourself under arrest for three days.'

I felt somewhat humiliated, but I recognized the truth of the proverb that it is an ill wind that blows nobody good: I was delivered from my friend's love-affairs.

I read *Télémaque* again beside Fénelon's tomb: I was not really in the mood for the philanthropic story of the cow and the bishop.

It amuses me to recall the beginning of my career. Passing through Cambrai with the King, after the Hundred Days, I looked for the house where I had lived and the coffee-house I used to frequent: I could not find them: everything had disappeared, men and monuments.

In the same year* that I was serving my military apprenticeship at Cambrai, Frederick II died: I am now ambassador to that great king's nephew, and I am writing this part of my *Memoirs* in Berlin. That important news for the world at large was followed by sad news for me: Lucile wrote to tell me that my father had been carried off by a stroke two days after the Angevine Fair, one of the joys of my childhood.

Among the authentic documents which I am using as a guide I find my parents' death-certificates.

In the first certificate, the old society remains: M. de Chateaubriand is a *great and powerful lord*, etc, the witnesses are *noblemen* and *worthy burgesses*; among the signatories I find the Marquis de Montlouet, who used to stop at the Château of Combourg in the winter, and the Abbé Sévin, who found it so hard to believe that I was the author of *Le Génie du Christianisme*, faithful guests of my father's, even in his last abode. But

* 1786.

my father did not lie for long in his shroud: he was thrown out
of it when the France of old was thrown on to the garbage-heap.

In my mother's death-certificate, the globe turns on a different axis: a new world, a new era: the computation of the years
and even the names of the months have changed. Mme de Chateaubriand is now just a poor woman who breathes her last in
the house of *Citizeness* Gouyon; a gardener and a day-labourer
who cannot sign his name are the only witnesses to my mother's death; no relatives or friends; no funeral ceremony; the
only bystander, the Revolution.

I mourned the death of M. de Chateaubriand: it showed him
to me better than he was; I remembered neither his strictness
nor his weaknesses. I seemed to see him still walking in the
evenings up and down the great hall at Combourg; I was moved
at the thought of those family scenes. If my father's affection
for me was affected by the severity of his character, it was nonetheless deep for all that. He would, I feel sure, have mourned
me sincerely if Providence had called me before him. But would
he, if we had remained on earth together, have appreciated the
fame that has come to me? A literary reputation would have
wounded his aristocratic pride; he would have seen nothing but
degeneration in his son's gifts; even the Berlin Embassy, won by
the pen, not the sword, would have given him little satisfaction.
His Breton blood, moreover, made him a political malcontent,
a great opponent of taxation, and a violent enemy of the Court.
He read the *Gazette de Leyde*, the *Journal de Francfort*, the
Mercure de France, and the *Histoire philosophique des deux
Indes*, whose declamatory style delighted him; he called the
author, the Abbé Raynal, a 'master-mind'. In matters diplomatic, he was an anti-Mussulman: he declared that forty
thousand *Russian rascals* would march over the Janissaries'
bellies and take Constantinople. Yet Turkophobe though he
was, my father nonetheless bore a grudge against the *Russian
rascals* because of his encounters with them at Danzig.

I share M. de Chateaubriand's opinions regarding literary
and other reputations, but for different reasons. I do not know
of a fame in history that tempts me: if I had to stoop to pick up
at my feet and to my profit the greatest glory in the world,

I would not take the trouble. If I had moulded my own clay, perhaps I would have created myself a woman, out of sheer love for them; or if I had created myself a man, I would have endowed myself with beauty first of all; next, as a safeguard against boredom, that bitter enemy of mine, it would have suited me quite well to be an artist of genius, but unknown and using my talent only for the benefit of my solitude. In life weighed by its light weight, measured by its short measure, and stripped of all deception, there are only two things of real value: religion married with intelligence and love married with youth, that is to say the future and the present: the rest is not worth while.

With my father's death, the first act of my life came to an end: the paternal home became empty; I pitied it, as if it were capable of feeling solitude and desertion. Henceforth I was independent and master of my fortune: this freedom frightened me. What should I do with it? I mistrusted my powers and shrank away from myself.

I was given a furlough. M. d'Andrezel, appointed Lieutenant-Colonel of the Picardy Regiment, was leaving Cambrai: I acted as his courier. I passed through Paris, where I did not stop for so much as a quarter of an hour: I saw the moors of my native Brittany again with more joy than that with which the Neapolitan banished to our climes would look once more at the shores of Portici, the fields of Sorrento. My family gathered together at Combourg; we divided the inheritance; once that was done, we scattered like birds leaving the paternal nest. My brother, who had come from Paris, went back there; my mother settled at Saint-Malo; Lucile went away with Julie; I spent some time with Mmes de Marigny, de Chateaubourg, and de Farcy. Marigny, my eldest sister's château, is pleasantly situated, seven miles from Fougères, between two lakes, in the midst of woods, rocks, and meadows. I stayed there quietly for a few months; then a letter arrived from Paris to disturb my tranquillity.

Though he was on the point of entering the service and marrying Mlle de Rosanbo, my brother had not yet abandoned the long robe; for this reason he was not entitled to ride in the royal coaches. His eager ambition gave him the idea of obtaining the honours of the Court for me in order to prepare the way for his own elevation. Our proofs of nobility had been made out for Lucile when she was admitted to the Chapter of L'Argentière, so that everything was ready. My brother wrote to tell me that I was on the highroad to fortune; that I had already been granted the rank of cavalry captain, an honorary and courtesy rank; that it would be an easy matter to go on to secure my admission to the Order of Malta, by means of which I should enjoy rich benefices.

This letter struck me like a thunderbolt: the idea of returning to Paris and being presented at Court, when I all but fainted if I met three or four strangers in a drawing-room! The idea of imbuing me with ambition, when my only dream was to live in obscurity!

My first impulse was to reply to my brother that it was his duty, as the eldest, to uphold his name; that, as for myself, the obscure younger son of a Breton family, I should not resign from the service, because there was a chance of war, but that, though the King might need a soldier in his army, he had no need of a poor gentleman at his Court.

I lost no time in reading this romantic reply to Mme de Marigny, who shrieked with horror; she sent for Mme de Farcy, who laughed at me; Lucile would have supported me, but she did not dare to disagree with her sisters. They tore my letter out of my hands, and, weak as I always am in matters where I am concerned, I wrote to my brother that I was ready to go.

Go I did: I went to be presented at the first Court of Europe, to make the most splendid of starts in life; and I looked like a man being dragged to the galleys or on the point of being sentenced to death.

I entered Paris by the same road I had taken the first time; I went to the same hotel, in the Rue du Mail; it was the only one I knew. I was given a room opposite my old one, but a little larger and overlooking the street.

My brother, either because he was embarrassed by my manners or because he took pity on my shyness, did not take me into society and introduced me to nobody. He lived in the Rue des Fossés-Montmartre; I went there to have dinner with him every day at three o'clock; we then separated till the next day. My fat cousin Moreau was no longer in Paris. I walked past Mme de Chastenay's house two or three times, without daring to ask the porter what had become of her.

Autumn set in. I got up at six, went to the riding-school, and breakfasted. Fortunately at that time I had a passion for Greek; I translated the *Odyssey* and the *Cyropaedia* until two o'clock, interspersing my labours with historical studies. At two o'clock I dressed and went to my brother's rooms; he asked me what I had been doing and what I had seen; I replied: 'Nothing.' He shrugged his shoulders and turned his back on me.

One day there was some noise outside; my brother ran to the window and called to me: I refused to leave the armchair in which I lay stretched out at the back of the room. My poor brother warned me that I should die unknown, of no use to myself or my family. At four o'clock I went back to my hotel and sat down at my window. Two girls of fifteen or sixteen used to come at that hour and start sketching at the window of a house opposite. They had noticed my punctuality, as I had theirs. Now and then they raised their heads to look at their neighbour; I was infinitely grateful to them for this mark of attention: they were my only company in Paris.

When night fell, I went to see a play; I took pleasure in the desert of the crowd, although it always cost me a little effort to buy my ticket at the door and mix with other men. I revised the ideas about the theatre which I had formed at Saint-Malo. I saw Mme de Saint-Huberti as Armida, and decided that there had been something lacking in the sorceress of my creating. When I did not imprison myself in the Opéra or at the Français, I wandered from street to street or along the embankments until ten or eleven at night. To this day I cannot see the row of street-lamps from the Place Louis XV to the Barrière des Bons-Hommes without remembering the agonies I went through when I took that road to go to Versailles for my presentation.

*

The dread day arrived: I had to set out for Versailles more dead than alive. My brother took me there the day before my presentation and introduced me to Marshal de Duras, a worthy man with a mind so commonplace that it cast a certain vulgarity on his fine manners; nonetheless, the good marshal scared me terribly.

The next morning I went by myself to the palace. One has seen nothing if one has never seen the pomp of Versailles, even after the disbanding of the old royal household: Louis XIV was still present.

Everything went well so long as I had only to go through the guardrooms: military pomp has always pleased me and never awed me. But when I entered the ante-chamber of the Great Hall and found myself among the courtiers, my agony began. The gentlemen in waiting looked at me; I heard them asking who I was. One has to remember the former prestige of royalty to realize the importance of a presentation in those days. A mysterious aura of destiny clung to the debutant; he was spared the patronizing look of contempt which, coupled with extreme politeness, composed the inimitable manners of the grandee. Who could tell whether this particular debutant might not become the master's favourite? Everyone respected in him the future familiarity with which he might be honoured. Nowadays we rush to the palace with even greater eagerness than before and, curiously enough, without any illusions: a courtier reduced to living on truths is in serious danger of dying of hunger.

When the King's levee was announced, those persons who had not been presented withdrew; I experienced a feeling of vanity: I was not proud of remaining, but I should have felt humiliated at leaving. The door of the King's bedchamber opened: I saw the King, in accordance with tradition, complete his toilet, in other words take his hat from the hand of the first gentleman in waiting. The King came towards me on his way to Mass; I bowed; Marshal de Duras presented me:

'Sire, the Chevalier de Chateaubriand.'

The King looked at me, returned my bow, hesitated, and appeared to be on the point of stopping to speak to me. I should have replied with complete self-assurance: my shyness had van-

ished. To speak to the commander of the Army, to the head of
the State, seemed a simple matter to me, though I could not
understand why. The King, whose embarrassment was greater
than mine, could not think of anything to say to me, and passed
on. The vanity of human destinies: this sovereign whom I was
seeing for the first time, this powerful monarch was Louis XVI
six years removed from the scaffold! And this new courtier at
whom he scarcely glanced, charged with separating bones from
bones,* after having been presented, upon proof of nobility, to
the majesty of St Louis's heir, would one day be presented,
upon proof of fidelity, to his dust! A twofold mark of respect to
the twofold royalty of the sceptre and the pen! Louis XVI
could have answered his judges as Christ answered the Jews:
'Many good works I have shown you; for which of those works
do you stone me?'

We hurried to the gallery to see the Queen on her way back
from the chapel. She soon appeared with a glittering and
numerous retinue; she made a stately curtsey to us; she seemed
delighted with life. And those beautiful hands, which bore with
such grace the sceptre of so many kings, were destined, before
being bound by the executioner, to mend the rags of the widow,
a prisoner in the Conciergerie!

My brother had obtained a sacrifice from me, but it was not
in his power to make me go any further with it. It was in vain
that he begged me to stay at Versailles in order to attend the
Queen's cards in the evening.

'You will be presented to the Queen,' he said, 'and the King
will speak to you.'

He could not have given me a better reason for running
away. I lost no time in going to hide my glory in my humble
hotel, happy to have escaped from Court, but seeing still before
me the dreadful day of the carriages, 19 February 1787.†

---

* In 1815 Chateaubriand was a member of the commission appointed to iden-
tify Louis XVI's remains in the Madeleine graveyard.
† The *Gazette de France* of 27 February 1787 states that Chateaubriand and
three other debutants, 'who had earlier had the honour of being presented to
the King, had, on the 19th, that of riding in His Majesty's carriages and following him in the hunt'.

The Duc de Coigny informed me that I was to hunt with the King in the forest of Saint-Germain. I set out early in the morning to meet my fate, dressed in the uniform of a debutant, a grey coat, red jacket and breeches, lace-topped riding-boots, a hunting-knife at my side, and a little gold-laced French hat. There were four of us debutants at the Palace of Versailles: myself, the two Messieurs de Saint-Marsault, and the Comte d'Hautefeuille. The Duc de Coigny gave us our instructions: he warned us not to cut across the hunt, as the King flew into a passion if anyone came between him and the quarry. The Duc de Coigny bore a name fatal to the Queen.* The meet was at Le Val, in the forest of Saint-Germain, a domain leased by the Crown from Marshal de Beauvau. The custom was for the horses of the first hunt in which debutants took part to be provided by the royal stables.

The drums beat the general salute: a voice gave an order, and the guard presented arms. There was a shout of 'The King!' The King came out and entered his carriage: we rode in the carriages behind. It was a far cry from this hunting expedition with the King of France to my hunting expeditions on the moors of Brittany, and an even farther cry to my hunting expeditions with the savages of America: my life was to be full of these contrasts.

We reached the rallying-point, where a considerable number of saddle-horses, held in hand under the trees, were showing signs of impatience. The carriages drawn up in the forest with the guards standing by; the groups of men and women; the packs held in with difficulty by the huntsmen; the barking of the hounds, the neighing of the horses, and the sound of the horns made up an extremely lively scene. The hunts of our kings recalled both the old and new customs of the monarchy, the rude pastimes of Clodion, Chilpéric, and Dagobert, and the elegant amusements of François I, Henri IV, and Louis XIV.

I was too full of my reading not to see everywhere Comtesses de Chateaubriand, Duchesses d'Étampes, Gabrielles d'Estrées,

---

* He was highly unpopular, and the fact that he was a favourite of the Queen was held against Marie Antoinette.

La Vallières, and Montespans. My imagination seized on the historic side of this hunt, and I felt completely at ease: besides, I was in a forest, and therefore at home.

Alighting from the carriage, I handed my ticket to the huntsmen. A mare called L'Heureuse had been picked for me, a fast animal but hard-mouthed, skittish, and capricious; a fair likeness of my fate, which has always tended to set its ears back. The King mounted and rode off; the hunt followed him, taking different roads. I was left behind, struggling with L'Heureuse, who refused to let her new master straddle her; in the end, however, I managed to leap on to her back: the hunt was already far away.

At first I mastered L'Heureuse fairly well; compelled to shorten her pace, she bent her neck, shook her bit, which was white with foam, and bounded along sideways; but once she got near the scene of action, there was no holding her. She pushed out her head, forcing my hand down on the saddlebow, and galloped straight into a group of hunters, sweeping aside everything in her way, and stopping only when she collided with the horse of a woman whom she nearly knocked over, to the accompaniment of roars of laughter from some and screams of terror from others. I have tried in vain today to remember the name of this woman, who listened politely to my apologies. Nothing else was talked of but the debutant's 'adventure'.

I had not come to the end of my trials. About half an hour after my mishap, I was riding across a long clearing in a deserted part of the wood: there was a summerhouse at the end, and I began thinking about these palaces scattered around the Crown forests, in memory of the long-haired kings and their mysterious pleasures. A shot rang out; L'Heureuse turned sharply, plunged into the thicket, and carried me to the very spot where the roebuck had just been killed: the King appeared.

I then remembered, but too late, the Duc de Coigny's warning words: the wretched Heureuse had done for me. I leapt to the ground, pushing my mare back with one hand and sweeping my hat off with the other. The King looked and saw a debutant who had beaten him to the kill; he felt the need to say something; instead of flying into a passion, he said in a good-natured voice and with a loud laugh:

'He did not hold out long.'

This was the only remark Louis XVI ever addressed to me. People came up from every side; they were astonished to find me 'talking' with the King. The debutant Chateaubriand created a sensation with his two 'adventures'; but, as has always happened since, he did not know how to turn either his good or his bad fortune to account.

The King brought three other bucks to bay. As debutants were allowed to hunt only the first animal, I went back to Le Val with my companions to wait for the hunt to return.

The King arrived at Le Val; he was in high spirits and talking about the incidents of the chase. We drove back to Versailles. A fresh disappointment lay in store for my brother; instead of going to dress in order to be present at the unbooting, the moment of triumph and favour, I jumped into my carriage and returned to Paris, delighted to be free of my honours and tribulations. I told my brother that I was determined to go back to Brittany.

Satisfied at having made his name known, and hoping one day to bring to maturity, by means of his own presentation, what had proved abortive in mine, he put no obstacle in the way of the departure of so eccentric a brother.

Such was my first experience of town and Court. Society struck me as even more odious than I had imagined it; but although it frightened me, it did not dishearten me; I felt in some confused way that I was superior to what I had seen. I took an invincible dislike to the Court; this dislike, or rather this contempt, which I have been unable to conceal, will either prevent me from succeeding or will topple me from the summit of my career.

It should be added that if I judged the world without knowing it, the world, for its part, knew nothing of me. Nobody guessed, when I made my debut, what I might be capable of achieving, and when I returned to Paris nobody guessed it any better. Since attaining my melancholy fame, I have been told by a good many people: 'How promptly we should have picked you out, if we had met you in your youth!' This obliging assurance is nothing but an illusion produced by an established reputation. Outwardly men look very much alike: it is no use Rousseau's telling us that he had a pair of small, attractive eyes: it is nonetheless certain, witness his portraits, that he had the appearance of a schoolmaster or a cantankerous cobbler.

To have done with the Court, I must add that after revisiting Brittany and coming back to Paris to live with my younger sisters, Lucile and Julie, I plunged more deeply than ever into my solitary habits. You may ask what came of the story of my presentation. It went no further.

'Then you never hunted with the King again?'

'No more than I did with the Emperor of China.'

'And you never went back to Versailles?'

'I twice went as far as Sèvres; my courage failed me, and I returned to Paris.'

'So you derived no benefit from your position?'

'None at all.'

'Then what did you do?'

'I got bored.'

'So you felt no ambition?'

'Oh, yes: by dint of worry and intrigue, I achieved the glory of publishing an idyll in the *Almanach des Muses** whose appearance nearly killed me with hope and fear. I would have given all the King's carriages to have written the ballad *O ma tendre Musette!* or *De mon Berger volage.*

'Good for anything with other people, good for nothing where I am concerned: there you have me.'

---

* This idyll, entitled *L'Amour de la campagne* and signed 'The Chevalier de C . . .', appeared in the *Almanach des Muses* for 1790.

SIX

The French Revolution

Everything in the previous chapter was written in Berlin. I have returned to Paris for the christening of the Duc de Bondeaux,* and I have resigned my embassy out of political loyalty to M. de Villèle who has left the Cabinet. Restored to a life of leisure, let me pick up my pen again. The more these *Memoirs* fill up with the years I have lived, the more they remind me of the lower bulb of an hour-glass showing how much of my life has fallen: when all the sand has passed through, I would not turn over my glass timepiece, if God gave me the power to do so.

The new solitude into which I entered in Brittany, after my presentation, was no longer that of Combourg; it was not so complete, nor so serious, nor, to tell the truth, so obligatory: I was free to leave it, and so it lost its value. An escutcheoned old lady and an emblazoned old baron, watching over the last of their daughters and the last of their sons in a feudal manor, appeared in the guise of what the English call 'characters': there was nothing provincial or narrow about that life, because it was not ordinary life.

At my sisters' homes, the province met together in the midst of the field: neighbours danced at one another's houses or put on plays in which I performed occasionally and incompetently. In winter one had to suffer, at Fougères, the society of a little town, with its balls, assemblies, and dinners, and I could not live forgotten as I had in Paris.

On the other hand, I had not seen the Army and the Court without undergoing a change in my ideas: in spite of my natural

* Chateaubriand returned on 26 April 1821 for the christening on 1 May.

inclinations, an indefinable force within me rebelled against obscurity and urged me to emerge from the shadows. Julie loathed provincial life, while the instinct of genius and beauty impelled Lucile towards a wider stage.

I consequently experienced a feeling of dissatisfaction with my existence which told me that this existence was not my destiny.

Nonetheless, I still loved the country, and around Marigny it was delightful. My regiment had changed its quarters: the first battalion was stationed at Le Havre, the second at Dieppe; I joined the latter: my presentation at Court lent me a certain distinction. I acquired a taste for my profession; I worked hard at my drill, and was put in charge of new recruits whom I marched up and down the pebbly beach: the sea has formed the background to most of the scenes in my life.

I went back to Fougères for six months' leave of absence. The presiding genius there was a noble spinster called Mlle de la Belinaye, the aunt of that Comtesse de Trojolif of whom I have already spoken. A pleasant but ugly sister of an officer in the Condé Regiment attracted my admiration: I did not have the courage to raise my eyes to beauty; it was only in the presence of a woman's imperfections that I dared to venture a respectful tribute.

Mme de Farcy, who was always ailing, finally decided to leave Brittany. She persuaded Lucile to accompany her; Lucile in turn overcame my repugnance; we set off together for Paris: a sweet partnership of the three youngest birds of the brood.

My brother was married; he lived with his father-in-law, the Président de Rosanbo, in the Rue de Bondy. We arranged to settle near by: through the good offices of M. Delisle de Sales, who lived in the Saint-Lazare villas, at the top of the Faubourg Saint-Denis, we secured an apartment in these same villas.

M. de Malesherbes had three daughters, Mmes de Rosanbo, d'Aulnay, and de Montboissier: he loved Mme de Rosanbo best, because of the similarity between her opinions and his. The Président de Rosanbo also had three daughters, Mmes de Chateaubriand, d'Aulnay, and de Tocqueville, and a son whose brilliant intelligence is combined with perfect Christian piety.

M. de Malesherbes delighted in the company of his children, grandchildren, and great-grandchildren. Many a time, in the early days of the Revolution, I saw him arrive at Mme de Rosanbo's house, hot from some political controversy, toss his wig to one side, lie down on the carpet of my sister-in-law's room, and let the mob of children crawl all over him with a tremendous din. He would have been a man of rather vulgar manners but for a certain brusqueness which saved him from being commonplace: at the first words which came from his lips one recognized the scion of an old family and the great magistrate. His natural virtues had been tainted with a little affectation by the philosophy which he mingled with them. He was full of knowledge, courage, and integrity, but so violent and hot-blooded that one day, talking to me about Condorcet, he said: 'That man was a friend of mine; today, I would have no scruples about killing him like a dog.' The tide of the Revolution swept over him, and his death brought him glory. This great man would have remained hidden within his merits if misfortune had not revealed him to the world. A noble Venetian lost his life just as he discovered his title-deeds in the collapse of an old palace.

M. de Malesherbes's frank demeanour freed me from all constraint. He considered me reasonably well educated; this was our first point of contact: we discussed botany and geography, his favourite subjects of conversation. It was through talking with him that I conceived the idea of undertaking a journey in North America to discover the sea which first Hearne and later Mackenzie saw. We also agreed about politics: the idealistic feelings which lay at the bottom of our first troubles appealed to the independence of my character; the natural antipathy which I felt for the Court gave added force to this inclination. I was on the side of M. de Malesherbes and Mme de Rosanbo against M. de Rosanbo and my brother, whom we nicknamed 'the rabid Chateaubriand'. The Revolution would have carried me with it if only it had not begun with a series of crimes: I saw the first head carried on the end of a pike, and I recoiled. In my eyes murder will never be an object of admiration or an argument for freedom; I know of nothing more servile, contemptible, cowardly, and stupid than a terrorist. Have I not met in France the whole of this race of Brutus in the service of Caesar and his police? The levellers, regenerators, and cut-throats had turned into valets, spies, and sycophants, and even less naturally into dukes, counts, and barons: how thoroughly medieval!

Lastly, what attached me even more to the illustrious old man was his predilection for my sister: in spite of the Comtesse Lucile's shyness, we succeeded, with the aid of a little champagne, in persuading her to take part in a little play on the occasion of M. de Malesherbes's birthday; she gave such a touching performance that she turned that good and great man's head. He was even more insistent than my brother that she should be translated from the Chapter of L'Argentière to that of Remiremont, which insisted on the strict and difficult proofs of the 'sixteen quarterings'. Philosopher though he was, M. de Malesherbes possessed the principles of birth to a high degree.

This picture of men and society at the time of my debut must be spread over a period of about two years, from 25 May 1787, the date of the closing of the first Assembly of Notables, to 5 May 1789, that of the opening of the States General. During these two years, my sisters and I did not live all the time in Paris, nor in the same part of Paris. I will now regress and take my readers back to Brittany.

I should add that I was still obsessed by my illusions; although I missed my woods, I had found a new solitude in remote times instead of places. In old Paris, in the precincts of Saint-Germain-des-Prés, in monastery cloisters, in the vaults of Saint-Denis, in the Sainte-Chapelle, in Notre-Dame, in the narrow streets of the Cité, and at the humble door of Héloïse, I saw my enchantress again; but beneath the Gothic arches and among the tombs she had assumed a deathly appearance: she was pale and looked at me with melancholy eyes; she was just the shadow or the spirit of the dream which I had loved.

It was at this time that my brother, pursuing his plans, decided to obtain my admission to the Order of Malta. In order to do this it was necessary for me to receive the tonsure: this could be given me by M. Cortois de Pressigny, the Bishop of Saint-Malo. I therefore went to my native city, where my good mother had settled; she no longer had her children around her and spent her days in church, her evenings knitting. Her absent-mindedness was unbelievable: I met her one morning in the street, carrying one of her slippers under her arm by way of a missal. From time to time a few old friends would find their way to her retreat and they would talk about the good old days. When she and I were alone, she would improvise beautiful stories for me in verse.

As Mme de Chateaubriand was a real saint, she prevailed upon the Bishop of Saint-Malo to give me the tonsure, although he had scruples on the subject: to give the mark of the ecclesiastic to a soldier and a layman seemed to him to be a profanation not far removed from simony. M. Cortois de Pressigny, now Archbishop of Besançon and a peer of France, is a worthy and deserving man. He was young at that time, a protégé of the Queen's, and on the highroad to success, which he reached later by a better road: persecution.

Dressed in uniform, with my sword at my side, I went down on my knees at the prelate's feet; he cut two or three hairs from the crown of my head; this was called the tonsure, of which I received a formal certificate. With this certificate, it was possible for me to obtain an income of two hundred thousand livres, once my proofs of nobility had been accepted in Malta: an abuse, no doubt, in the ecclesiastical order, but a useful thing in the political order of the old constitution. Was it not better for a kind of military benefice to be attached to the sword of a soldier than to the cloak of an abbé who would have spent the revenue of his fat living in the streets of Paris?

The fact that I received the tonsure, which I was given for the foregoing reasons, has led ill-informed biographers to state that I began by entering the Church.

This happened in 1788. I had horses and rode in the country or galloped beside the waves, the moaning friends of my youth; I would dismount and play with them; the whole barking family of Scylla sprang up to my knees to fondle me: *Nunc vada* *latrantis Scyllae.** I have travelled far and wide to admire the scenes of nature: I could have contented myself with those which my native land offered me.

There is nothing more delightful than the countryside for some fifteen miles round Saint-Malo. The banks of the Rance, from the mouth of the river to Dinan, are enough in themselves to deserve the traveller's attention, forming as they do a constant medley of rocks and greenery, sandbanks and forests, creeks and hamlets, ancient manors of feudal Brittany and modern dwelling-houses of trading Brittany.

Every peasant, sailor, and ploughman owns a little white cottage with a garden: among the vegetables, the currant-bushes, the rose-trees, the irises, and the marigolds in this garden, you will find a set of Cayenne tea, a head of Virginia tobacco, a Chinese flower, or some such souvenir of another shore and another sun: this is the owner's chart and itinerary. The tenant-farmers on the coast come from fine Norman stock; the women are tall, slender, and agile, and wear grey woollen bodices, short petticoats of calamanco and striped silk, and white stockings with coloured clocks. Their foreheads are shaded by a broad head-dress in dimity or cambric, with flaps which stand up in the form of a cap or float like a veil. A silver chain hangs in loops at their left side. Every morning in the spring, these daughters of the North, stepping out of their boats as if they were coming once again to invade the country, carry to market baskets of fruit and shells filled with curds: when, with one hand, they balance on their heads black jars full of milk or flowers, when the pinners of their caps set off their blue eyes, their pink faces and their fair hair beaded with dew, the Valkyries of the *Edda*, of whom the youngest is the Future, or the Canephores of Athens, were not as graceful. Is this picture still a faithful likeness? Those women are doubtless no longer alive; nothing remains of them but my memories.

The year 1789, of such importance in our history and in the history of the human race, found me on the moors of my native

* Now the waves of barking Scylla . . . (Anon.).

Brittany; indeed I was unable to leave the province until rather late, and did not reach Paris until after the sack of the Maison Réveillon, the opening of the States General, the constitution of the Third Estate as a National Assembly, the Tennis Court oath, the Royal Speech of 23 June, and the joining of the clergy and the nobles to the commons.

There was considerable activity along the road I took: in the villages the peasants were stopping coaches, asking to see passports, and interrogating passengers. The nearer we came to the capital, the more the excitement grew. Passing through Versailles, I saw troops quartered in the orangery, artillery trains parked in the courtyards, the temporary hall of the National Assembly erected in the Place du Palais, and deputies coming and going among groups of sightseers, palace servants, and soldiers.

In Paris the streets were blocked by crowds waiting outside the bakers' shops: passers-by stood talking at street-corners; tradesmen came out of their shops to hear and give the latest news on their doorsteps; at the Palais-Royal, agitators gathered together: Camille Desmoulins began to stand out from the rest.

I had scarcely arrived, together with Mme de Farcy and Mme Lucile, at a hotel in the Rue de Richelieu, when a riot started: the mob rushed to the Abbaye to release some French Guards who had been arrested on their officers' orders. The non-commissioned officers of an artillery regiment quartered at the Invalides joined the people. The defection of the army was beginning.

The Court, alternately giving way and offering resistance, a mixture of obstinacy and weakness, of bravado and fear, allowed itself to be dictated to by Mirabeau, who demanded that the troops should be removed, and yet did not agree to remove them: it accepted the affront but did not remove the cause of it. In Paris a rumour spread that an army was arriving by way of the Montmartre sewer, and that dragoons were going to force the gates. Somebody suggested taking up the street pavements and carrying the paving-stones up to the fifth floors of the houses, in order to drop them on the tyrant's satellites: everyone set to work. In the midst of this confusion, M. Necker was ordered to resign. The new ministry was made up of MM.

de Breteuil, de la Galaisière, de la Vauguyon, de la Porte, Foullon, and Marshal de Broglie. They took the places of MM. de
Montmorin, de la Luzerne, de Saint-Priest, and de Nivernais.

A Breton poet, newly arrived, had asked me to take him to
Versailles. There are people who will go to see gardens and
fountains while empires are being overthrown: scribblers in
particular possess this faculty of isolating themselves in their
mania in the course of the greatest events; their phrase or stanza
is everything to them.

I took my Pindar at Mass-time into the gallery of Versailles.
The Court was radiant: M. Necker's dismissal had raised everyone's spirits; all felt sure of victory; possibly Sanson and Simon*
were among the crowd, and witnessed the delight of the Royal
Family.

The Queen passed by with her two children; their fair
hair seemed to be waiting for crowns. Mme la Duchesse d'
Angoulême, aged eleven, drew all eyes by her virginal dignity.
The little Dauphin walked under his sister's protection, and M.
Du Touchet followed his pupil; he noticed me and obligingly
pointed me out to the Queen. Casting a smiling glance in my
direction, she made the same gracious bow to me which she had
given me on the day of my presentation. I shall never forget that
look of hers which was so soon to be extinguished. Marie
Antoinette, when she smiled, shaped her lips so clearly that,
horrible to relate, the recollection of that smile enabled me to
recognize the jaw-bone of the daughter of kings when the head
of the unfortunate woman was discovered in the exhumations
of 1815.

The counter-stroke to the blow struck in Versailles resounded
in Paris. On my return I passed a crowd carrying busts
of M. Necker and M. le Duc d'Orléans, covered with crape.
They were shouting: 'Long live Necker! Long live the Duc
d'Orléans!' and among these shouts there could be heard
another that was bolder and more unexpected: 'Long live Louis
XVII!' Long live the child whose very name would have been

* Sanson was the public executioner appointed by Louis XVI, whom he guillotined in 1793; Simon was a cobbler who became tutor to Louis XVII.

forgotten in the funeral inscription of his family, if I had not recalled it to the memory of the Chamber of Peers! If Louis XVI had abdicated, Louis XVII been placed on the throne, and M. le Duc d'Orléans declared Regent, what would have happened?

In the Place Louis XV, the Prince de Lambesc, at the head of the Royal-Allemand Regiment, drove the crowd back into the Tuileries gardens and wounded an old man: suddenly the tocsin sounded. The sword-cutlers' shops were broken into, and thirty thousand muskets taken from the Invalides. The mob armed itself with pikes, staves, pitchforks, sabres, and pistols; Saint-Lazare was sacked, the city gates burnt down. The electors of Paris took over the government of the capital, and in a single night sixty thousand citizens were organized, armed, and equipped as National Guards.

On 14 July came the fall of the Bastille. I was present, as a spectator, at this attack on a few pensioners and a timid governor: if the gates had been kept closed, the mob could never have entered the fortress. I saw two or three cannon-shots fired, not by the pensioners, but by French Guards who had already climbed up to the towers. The Governor, De Launay, was torn from his hiding-place, and after undergoing a thousand outrages, was killed on the steps of the Hôtel de Ville; Flesselles, the provost of the merchants of Paris, had his brains blown out: this was the sight which heartless optimists thought so fine. In the midst of these murders, the mob indulged in wild orgies, as in the troubles in Rome under Otho and Vitellius. The 'victors of the Bastille', happy drunkards declared conquerors by their boon companions, were driven through the streets in hackney carriages; prostitutes and *sans-culottes*, who were at the beginning of their reign, acted as their escort. The passers-by took off their hats, with a respect born of fear, before these heroes, some of whom died of fatigue in the midst of their triumph. The keys of the Bastille multiplied; they were sent to all the important fools in the four quarters of the world. How many times have I missed the chance of making my fortune! If I, a spectator, had inscribed my name on the list of the victors, I should be in receipt of a pension today.

The experts hurried along to conduct a post-mortem examination of the Bastille. Temporary cafés were installed under canvas; people crowded into them as at Longchamp or the Saint-Germain fair; carriages drove slowly past or stopped at the foot of the towers, the stones of which were being thrown down among clouds of dust. Elegantly dressed women and fashionable young men, standing on different levels of the Gothic ruins, mingled with the half-naked workmen who were demolishing the walls to the acclamations of the crowd. At this meeting-place could be seen the most famous orators, the best-known men of letters, the most celebrated painters, the most renowned actors and actresses, the most popular dancers, the most illustrious foreigners, the grandees of the Court and the ambassadors of Europe: old France had come here to finish, new France to begin.

Louis XVI went to the Hôtel de Ville on the 17th; a hundred thousand men, armed like the monks of the League, received him. He was harangued by MM. Bailly, Moreau de Saint-Méry, and Lally-Tolendal, who all wept: the last has remained prone to tears. The King gave way to emotion in his turn; he stuck an enormous tricolour cockade in his hat, and was declared there and then to be *a good man, Father of the French, and King of a free people*, a people which, by virtue of its freedom, was preparing to cut off the head of that good man, its father and king.

A few days after this reconciliation, I was standing at the window of my hotel with my sisters and some Breton acquaintances when we heard shouts of 'Bolt the doors, bolt the doors!' A troop of ragamuffins appeared at one end of the street; from the midst of this troop there rose a couple of standards which we could not see clearly at that distance. As they came nearer, we made out two dishevelled and disfigured heads, which Marat's forerunners were carrying, each at the end of a pike: they were the heads of MM. Foullon and Bertier. The others with me all drew back from the windows; I remained. The murderers stopped in front of me and stretched the pikes up towards me, singing, dancing, and jumping up in order to bring the pale effigies closer to my face. One eye in one of these heads had started out of its socket and was hanging down on the dead man's face; the pike was projecting through the open mouth, the teeth of which were biting on the iron.

'Brigands!' I cried, filled with an indignation which I was unable to contain. 'Is that how you understand liberty?'

If I had had a gun, I should have fired at those wretches as at a pack of wolves. They howled with fury, and beat at the main door in the hope of breaking it in and adding my head to those of their victims. My sisters fainted; the cowards in the hotel heaped reproaches on me. The murderers, who were being pursued, did not have time to break into the house and made off. Those heads, and others which I saw soon afterwards, changed my political tendencies; I was horrified by these cannibal feasts, and the idea of leaving France for some distant land began to take root in my mind.

The 5th of October arrived. I did not witness the events of that day. Accounts of what had happened reached the capital early on the 6th. We were told at the same time to expect a visit from the King. I was as bold in public places as I was timid in drawing-rooms: I felt that I was born for solitude or the forum. I hurried to the Champs-Élysées. First there appeared some guns, ridden by harpies, thieves, and prostitutes making obscene remarks and filthy gestures. Next, in the midst of a horde of people of every age and sex, the Lifeguards came marching by; they had exchanged hats, swords, and bandoliers with the National Guards, and each of their horses carried two or three fishwives, dirty, drunk, and dishevelled bacchantes. After them came the deputation from the National Assembly, followed by the royal carriages, rolling along in a dusty forest of pikes and bayonets. Tattered rag-pickers and butchers with blood-stained aprons wrapped around their thighs, bare knives at their belts and their shirtsleeves rolled up, clung to the carriage doors; other sinister guards had climbed on to the roof; yet others hung on to the footboard or perched on the box. They fired off muskets and pistols, shouting:

'Here come the baker, the baker's wife, and the baker's boy!'

By way of an oriflamme, held high in the air by Swiss halberds, there were carried before the descendant of St Louis the heads of two Lifeguards, powdered and curled by a Sèvres wigmaker.

The astronomer Bailly told Louis XVI at the Hôtel de Ville that the *humane, respectful, and loyal* people had just *conquered* its King, and the King for his part, *greatly touched and highly pleased*, declared that he had come to Paris *of his own free will*; unworthy falsehoods born of violence and fear which at that time dishonoured all men and all parties. Louis XVI was not insincere: he was weak; weakness is not insincerity, but it takes its place and fulfils its functions; the respect which the virtues and misfortunes of the saintly, martyred King must inspire in us render any expression of human judgement wellnigh sacrilegious.

The sittings of the National Assembly presented a sight of an interest which the sittings of our 'Chambers' are far from approaching. One had to get up early to obtain a seat in the crowded galleries. The deputies arrived eating, talking, and gesticulating; they formed groups in various parts of the house according to their opinions. The order of the day was read out after that, the subject agreed upon was discussed, or else an extraordinary motion. It was not a matter of insipid points of law; there was nearly always some scheme of destruction on the agenda. The deputies spoke for or against; everybody improvised as best he could. The debate grew stormy; the galleries joined in the discussion, applauding and cheering, hissing and booing the speakers. The president rang his bell, while the deputies shouted at one another from bench to bench. Mirabeau the Younger took his opponent by the collar; Mirabeau the Elder cried:

'Silence to the "thirty votes"!'

One day I was sitting behind the Royalist opposition; in front of me was a noble from the Dauphiné, a swarthy little man, who jumped on to his seat in a fury and said to his friends:

'Let us fall upon those ragamuffins, sword in hand!'

He pointed to where the majority were sitting. The ladies of the Market, knitting in the galleries, heard him, rose from their seats, and all shouted at once, holding their stockings in their hands and foaming at the mouth:

'To the lantern with them!'

The Vicomte de Mirabeau, Lautrec, and a few young nobles suggested taking the galleries by assault.

Soon this din was drowned by another: some petitioners, armed with pikes, appeared at the bar.

'The people are starving,' they said. 'It is time to take strong measures against the aristocrats and to *rise to the level of the situation.*'

The president assured these citizens of his respect for their opinions. 'We have our eyes on the traitors,' he replied, 'and the Assembly will see that justice is done.'

At this a fresh tumult broke out: the deputies of the Right shouted that they were heading for anarchy; the deputies of the Left retorted that the people was free to express its will, that it had the right to complain of the abetters of despotism, sitting in the very midst of the nation's representatives: they spoke in these terms of their colleagues to that sovereign people which was waiting for them under the street lamps.

The evening sittings surpassed the morning sittings in violence and scandal: people speak better and more boldly by candlelight. In the evening the Riding-hall became a veritable playhouse, in which was enacted one of the greatest dramas in the world. The leading characters still belonged to the old order of things: their terrifying substitutes, hidden behind them, spoke little or not at all. At the end of a stormy discussion, I saw a common-looking deputy mount the tribune, a man with a grey, impassive face and neatly dressed hair, decently clad like the steward of a good house or a village notary who was careful of his appearance. He read out a long and boring report, and nobody listened to him; I asked his name: it was Robespierre. The men who wore shoes were ready to leave the drawing-rooms, and already the clogs were kicking at the door.

When, before the Revolution, I read the history of public disturbances among various nations, I could not understand how it was possible to live in those times; I was surprised that Montaigne could write with such spirit in a château which he could not walk round without running the risk of being taken prisoner by bands of Leaguers or Protestants.

The Revolution made me understand the possibility of living in such conditions. Moments of crisis produce a reduplication of life in men. In a society which is dissolving and reforming, the struggle of two geniuses, the clash between past and future, and the mixture of old customs and new form a transitory amalgam which does not leave a moment for boredom. Passions and characters, set at liberty, display themselves with an energy which they do not possess in the well-regulated state. The breaches of the laws, the emancipation from duties, customs, and proprieties, and even the dangers of everyday life all add to the interest of this disorder. The human race perambulates the streets in holiday mood, having got rid of its schoolmasters and returned for a moment to a state of nature, and does not begin to feel the need for social restraint again until it bears the yoke of the new tyrants engendered by licence.

I cannot depict the society of 1789 and 1790 better than by comparing it with the architecture of the time of Louis XII and François I, when the Greek orders began to be combined with Gothic style, or rather by likening it to the collection of ruins and tombstones of all ages which were heaped pell-mell, after the Terror, in the cloisters of the Petits-Augustins: except that the ruins of which I speak were alive and constantly changing. In every corner of Paris there were literary gatherings, political meetings and theatrical entertainments; future celebrities wandered about unrecognized in the crowd, like souls on the shores of Lethe before enjoying the light. I saw Marshal Gouvion-Saint-Cyr acting in Beaumarchais's *La Mère coupable* at the Théâtre du Marais. One went from the Club des Feuillants to the Club des Jacobins, from the ballroom and gaming-house to the meetings in the Palais-Royal, from the gallery of the National Assembly to the gallery in the open air. The streets were full of popular deputations, cavalry pickets, and infantry patrols passing to and fro. Walking beside a man in a French coat, with powdered hair, a sword at his side, a hat under his arm, pumps, and silk stockings, one could see a man wearing his hair short and without powder, an English dress-coat, and an American cravat. At the theatres, the actors gave out the latest news, and the pit sang patriotic ditties. Topical plays drew packed houses: if an abbé appeared on the stage the audience would shout: 'Jack Priest! Jack Priest!' and the abbé would reply: 'Messieurs, long live the nation!' People flocked to hear Mandini and his wife, Viganoni, and Rovedino sing at the Opera-Buffa after hearing the *Ça ira* howled in the streets; they went to admire Mme Dugazon, Mme Saint-Aubin, Carline, little Olivier, Mlle Contat, Molé, Fleury, and the young Talma after seeing Favras hanged.

The walks on the Boulevard du Temple and the Boulevard des Italiens, also known as Coblentz, and the paths in the Tuileries Gardens were thronged with smartly dressed women: three young daughters of the composer Grétry shone there, pink and white like their dresses: all three died soon after. 'She fell asleep for ever,' said Grétry, speaking of his eldest daughter, 'sitting on my lap, as beautiful as she was in life.' A multitude of carriages ploughed across the muddy crossroads where the *sans-culottes* splashed about, and the beautiful Mme de Buffon could be seen sitting by herself in a phaeton belonging to the Duc d'Orléans, waiting at the door of some club.

All that was elegant and tasteful in aristocratic society met at the Hôtel de La Rochefoucauld, at the soirées of Mmes de Poix, d'Hénin, de Simiane, and de Vaudreuil, or in the few salons of the upper magisterial circle that remained open. At M. Necker's, at M. le Comte de Montmorin's, at the houses of the different ministers, there gathered together (with Mme de Staël, the Duchesse d'Aiguillon, Mmes de Beaumont and de Sérilly) all the new celebrities of France with all the freedom of the new manners. The shoemaker knelt to measure your foot in the uniform of an officer of the National Guard; the monk who on Friday trailed his black or white frock along the ground appeared on Sunday in a round hat and a lay coat; the clean-shaven Capuchin read the paper in a tavern, and a nun sat quietly in the midst of a group of frivolous women: a sister or an aunt who had been turned out of her convent. The mob visited these monasteries which had been thrown open to the world, like the travellers who, at Granada, wander through the deserted halls of the Alhambra, or, at Tivoli, linger beneath the columns of the Sibyl's temple.

For the rest, many duels and love-affairs, prison liaisons, and political friendships, mysterious meetings among ruins, under a calm sky, in the midst of Nature's peace and poetry; remote, silent, solitary walks, mingled with undying oaths and indefinable affections, accompanied by the dull roar of a vanishing world, the distant noise of a crumbling society, which threatened to crush in its fall these joys placed at the foot of events. Those who had lost sight of one another for twenty-four hours could not be sure of ever meeting again. Some took the road of revolution; others made plans for civil war; others set off for Ohio, sending on ahead plans of country houses to be built among the savages; yet others went to join the Princes: all this cheerfully and often without a sou in their pockets, the Royalists declaring that the whole thing would be stopped one of these mornings by a decree of Parliament, and the patriots, just as light-hearted in their hopes, announcing the reign of peace, happiness, and liberty.

My regiment, which was garrisoned at Rouen, preserved its discipline until quite a late date. It had a brush with the mob over the execution of the actor Bordier,* who suffered the last sentence pronounced by the old High Court; hanged one day, he would have been a hero the next, if he had lived another twenty-four hours. Finally, however, an insurrection started among the soldiers of the Navarre Regiment. The Marquis de Mortemart emigrated: his officers followed him. I had neither adopted nor rejected the new ideas; as little disposed to attack them as I was to serve them, I felt no desire either to emigrate or to continue my military career: I therefore resigned my commission.

Freed from all bonds, I had, on the one hand, somewhat heated arguments with my brother and the Président de Rosanbo, and on the other, equally bitter discussions with Ginguené, La

---

* Bordier and a Lisieux solicitor called Jourdain started a riot in Rouen on the night of 3 August 1789 for which they were hanged.

Harpe, and Chamfort. Ever since my early youth, my political impartiality had pleased nobody. What is more, I attached importance to the questions raised at that time only in so far as they concerned such general concepts as human liberty and dignity; personal politics bored me; my real life lay in higher regions.

One idea obsessed me, the idea of going to the United States: I needed a useful purpose for my journey; I proposed, as I have said in these *Memoirs* and in several of my works, to discover the North-West Passage. This project was not out of keeping with my poetic nature. Nobody took any notice of me; like Bonaparte, I was then a mere second-lieutenant unknown to the outside world; both of us emerged from obscurity at the same time, I to seek fame in solitude, he to seek glory among other men. I had not attached myself to any woman, and my sylph still dominated my imagination. I looked forward to the blissful happiness of making my fantastic journeys through the forests of the New World in her company. Through the influence of another variety of nature, my flower of love, my nameless phantom of the Armorican woods, grew into *Atala* in the shady groves of Florida.

M. de Malesherbes made me positively excited about this voyage. I used to go and see him in the morning: sitting with our noses glued to maps, we compared the different charts of the Arctic Circle; we calculated the distances between the Behring Straits and the other end of Hudson Bay; we read the various narratives of English, Dutch, French, Russian, Swedish, and Danish sailors and travellers; we inquired into the routes to be adopted on land to reach the shores of the Polar Sea; we discussed the difficulties to be overcome, the precautions to be taken against the rigours of the climate, the attacks of wild animals, and the scarcity of provisions. The great man said to me:

'If I were young, I should go with you and spare myself the sight of all the crime, treachery, and folly which I see around me. But at my age a man must die where he is. Do not forget to write to me by every ship, to keep me informed of your progress and your discoveries: I will bring them to the notice of the ministers. It is a pity that you know no botany.'

After these conversations, I would read Tournefort, Duhamel, Bernard de Jussieu, Grew, Jacquin, Rousseau's Dictionary, the elementary floras; I ran to the Jardin du Roi, and soon I considered myself a second Linnaeus.

At last, in January 1791, I made up my mind in all seriousness. The chaos was increasing: it was enough to bear an *aristocratic* name to be exposed to persecution: the more conscientious and moderate your opinions, the more they rendered you liable to suspicion and attack. I therefore decided to strike my tents: I left my brother and my sisters in Paris, and made for Brittany.

At Fougères I met the Marquis de la Rouërie: I asked him to give me a letter of recommendation for General Washington. 'Colonel Armand' (the name by which the marquis was known in America) had distinguished himself in the American War of Independence. He became famous in France through the royalist conspiracy which made such touching victims in the Désilles family. Having died while organizing this conspiracy, he was exhumed and recognized, thus bringing about the ruin of his hosts and his friends. The rival of La Fayette and Lauzun and the predecessor of La Rochejaquelein, the Marquis de la Rouërie was a livelier character than they: he had fought more than the first; he had carried off opera-singers like the second; he would have become the comrade-in-arms of the third. He used to scour the woods in Brittany in the company of an American major, and with a monkey perched on his horse's crupper. The law students at Rennes loved him for his boldness of action and his freedom of ideas: he had been one of the twelve Breton nobles sent to the Bastille. His figure and his manners were elegant, his appearance smart, his features charming, and he resembled the portraits of the young lords of the League.

I chose Saint-Malo as my port of embarkation, so as to be able to embrace my mother. I have told in the third chapter of these *Memoirs* how I passed through Combourg and what feelings oppressed me there. I spent two months at Saint-Malo, busying myself with preparations for my voyage, as I had done before when I was intending to leave for India.

I struck a bargain with a captain called Dujardin, who was to carry to Baltimore the Abbé Nagot, Superior of the Saint-Sulpice Seminary, together with several seminarists in their principal's care. These travelling companions would have been more to my liking four years earlier: from being a zealous Christian I had become a free-thinker. This change in my religious opinions had been brought about by reading philosophical works. I believed in all good faith that a religious mind was partly paralysed, that there existed truths which it was unable to comprehend, however superior it might be in other respects. This smug pride led me astray: I inferred in the religious mind that absence of a faculty which is to be found in fact in the philosophic mind: the limited intelligence thinks that it sees everything because it keeps its eyes open; the superior intelligence consents to shut its eyes because it sees everything within. Finally, one thing completed my misery: the groundless despair which I carried in the depths of my heart.

A letter from my brother has fixed the date of my departure in my memory: he wrote to my mother from Paris, informing her of Mirabeau's death.* Three days after the arrival of this letter, I joined my ship, which was lying in the roads; my luggage had already been put on board. We weighed anchor, a solemn moment for sailors. The sun was setting when the coasting pilot left us, after putting us through the channels. The sky was overcast, the breeze slack, and the swell beat heavily against the reefs a few cables' length from our ship.

My gaze remained fixed on Saint-Malo, where I had just left my mother in tears. I could see the steeples and domes of the churches where I had prayed with Lucile, the walls, the ramparts, the forts, the towers, the beaches where I had spent my childhood with Gesril and my other playmates; I was abandoning my storm-tossed country just when she had lost a man who could never be replaced. I was going away equally uncertain about my country's destinies and my own: which of us was to

* 2 April 1791.

perish, France or I? Should I ever see France and my family again?

A calm set in at nightfall and halted us at the mouth of the roads; the lights of the town and the beacons were kindled: these lights which twinkled beneath my paternal roof seemed at once to smile at me and bid me farewell, while lighting my way through the rocks, the darkness of the night, and the blackness of the waves.

I was setting out with nothing but my youth and my illusions; I was leaving a world whose dust I had trod and whose stars I had counted for a world whose soil and sky was unknown to me. What was to become of me if I attained the object of my voyage? If I had roamed the polar shores the years of discord which have crushed so many generations with so much din would have fallen silently over my head; society would have changed its appearance in my absence. It is probable that I should never have had the misfortune to become a writer; my name would have remained unknown, or would have won only that discreet fame which is less than glory, which is scorned by envy and left to happiness. Who can tell whether I should have recrossed the Atlantic, or whether I should have settled down in the solitary wastes explored and discovered at my risk and peril, like a conqueror in the midst of his conquests?

But no, I was to return to my native land, there to change the nature of my misfortunes, there to be something very different from what I had been before. The sea in whose lap I was born was about to become the cradle of my second life; she carried me on my first voyage as if at my nurse's breast, in the arms of the confidant of my first tears and my first joys.

In the absence of any wind, the ebb-tide carried us out to sea, the lights on the shore grew gradually smaller and finally disappeared. Worn out by reflections, vague regrets, and even vaguer hopes, I went below to my cabin: I turned in, rocked in my hammock to the sound of the waves caressing the side of the ship. The wind rose; the unfurled sails hanging about the masts filled out; and when I went up on deck the next morning, the land of France was out of sight.

Here my destinies changed. 'Again to sea!' as Byron sang.

SEVEN

To America

Thirty-one years after embarking, as an ordinary second-lieutenant, for America, I embarked for London with a passport worded as follows:

'Give passage to His Lordship the Vicomte de Chateaubriand, Peer of France, Ambassador of the King to His Britannic Majesty, etc.'

No description: my greatness was such as to make my face known wherever I went. A steamship chartered for my special use brought me from Calais to Dover. On setting foot on English soil, on 5 April 1822, I was saluted by the guns of the fort.* An officer came on behalf of the commandant to offer me a guard of honour. When I arrived at the Shipwright Inn, the landlord and waiters received me with bare heads and hanging arms. The Mayoress invited me to an evening party in the name of the fairest ladies of the town. M. Billing, attaché to my Embassy, was waiting for me. A dinner of enormous fishes and monstrous quarters of beef restored the vigour of M. l'Ambassadeur, who had no appetite and was not in the least tired. The local populace, gathered beneath my windows, filled the air with loud hurrahs. The officer returned and, contrary to my wishes, posted sentries at my door. The next day, after making a lavish distribution of the money of the King my master, I set off for London, to the roar of guns, in a light carriage drawn by four fine horses driven at a lively trot by two smart postilions. My staff followed in other coaches; couriers dressed

* Chateaubriand landed in the evening of 4 April and arrived in London on the 5th. He wrote this chapter in London between April and September 1822.

in my livery accompanied the cavalcade. We drove through Canterbury, attracting the attention of John Bull and the occupants of the other carriages we passed. At Blackheath, a common once frequented by highwaymen, I found a newly built village. Soon I saw before me the immense skull-cap of smoke which covers the city of London.

Plunging into the gulf of black mist, as if into one of the mouths of Tartarus, and crossing the whole town, whose streets I recognized, I arrived at the Embassy in Portland Place. The chargé d'affaires, M. le Comte Georges de Caraman, the embassy secretaries, M. le Vicomte de Marcellus, M. le Baron E. Decazes, M. de Bourqueney, and the attachés welcomed me with dignified politeness. All the ushers, porters, valets, and footmen of the house were assembled on the pavement. I was handed the cards of the English ministers and the foreign ambassadors, who had already been informed of my imminent arrival.

On 17 May in the year of grace 1793, I disembarked at Southampton for the same city of London, an obscure and humble traveller from Jersey. No mayoress noticed my arrival; the mayor of the town, William Smith, gave me on the 18th a travel permit for London, to which was attached an extract from the Alien Bill. My description read as follows:

'François de Chateaubriand, French officer in the emigrant army, five feet four inches high, thin shape, brown hair, and pitted with the small Pox.'

I humbly shared the cheapest of carriages with some sailors on leave; I changed horses at the meanest of inns; poor, sick, and unknown, I entered a rich and famous city over which Mr Pitt held sway; I took a lodging at six shillings a month under the lathing of a garret which a cousin from Brittany had found for me at the end of a little street off the Tottenham Court Road.

Now obscurity of a different kind envelops me in London. My political position throws my literary fame into the shade: there is not a fool in the three kingdoms but prefers Louis XVIII's Ambassador to the author of *Le Génie du christianisme*. I shall see how matters turn out after my death, or when

I have ceased to fill M. le Duc Decaze's place at the Court of George IV, a succession as incongruous as the rest of my life.

Since my arrival in London as French Ambassador, one of my greatest pleasures has been to leave my carriage at the corner of some square and to wander on foot through the back streets which I frequented in former days, the popular suburbs where misfortune takes refuge under the protection of a kindred suffering, the obscure shelters which I haunted with my companions in distress, not knowing whether I should have any bread to eat the next day, I whose table today is covered with three or four courses. At all those narrow, humble doors which were once open to me, I see only unfamiliar faces. I no longer meet my fellow countrymen roaming the streets, recognizable by their gestures, their gait, and the style and age of their clothes. I no longer come across those martyred priests wearing the clerical collar, the big three-cornered hat, and the long, black, threadbare frock-coat, whom the English used to greet as they passed. Wide streets lined with palaces have been cut, bridges built, walks planted with trees: Regent's Park, near Portland Place, occupies the space of the old meadows filled with herds of cows. A cemetery which formed the view from the dormer window of one of my attic rooms has disappeared within the precincts of a factory. When I go to see Lord Liverpool, I find it difficult to discover the spot where Charles I's scaffold stood; new buildings, closing in on Charles II's statue, have encroached, like forgetfulness itself, upon memorable events.

How much I regret, in the midst of my insipid grandeur, that world of tribulations and tears, those times in which I mingled my sorrows with those of a colony of fellow sufferers. It is true, then, that everything changes, that misfortune itself comes to an end, like prosperity! What has become of my brothers in emigration? Some are dead, while the others have suffered various fates: like myself, they have seen their families and friends disappear: they are less happy in their native land than they were on foreign soil. Had we not on that soil our meetings, our amusements, our celebrations, and above all our youth? Mothers of families and girls starting life in adversity brought home the weekly fruit of their toil and went to join in some dance of

into the country, into the little garden of some unfrequented
tavern, and drink a cup of bad tea on a wooden bench, while
we talk of our insane hopes and our ungrateful country, discuss
our troubles, and look for ways and means of helping one
another or some relative in even worse plight than ourselves.

That is what I have been feeling and saying to myself in these
first days of my embassy in London. I can escape from the melancholy which assails me beneath my roof only by saturating
myself in a less oppressive melancholy in Kensington Gardens.
These gardens at least have not changed; the trees alone have
grown taller; here, in this still solitary place, the birds build
their nests in peace. It is no longer even the fashion to meet
here, as in the days when the loveliest of Frenchwomen, Mme
Récamier, used to walk here followed by the crowd. From the
edge of the deserted lawns of Kensington I love to watch the
horses riding across Hyde Park, and the carriages of the fashionable young men, among which figures my empty tilbury,
while I, a poor little emigrant noble once more, walk along the
path where the exiled confessor used to say his breviary.

It was in Kensington Gardens that I planned the *Essai historique*; that, reading over the diary of my travels beyond the
sea, I drew from it the loves of *Atala*; it was here too, after
wandering far and wide across the fields beneath a lowering
sky, which turned yellow as if pervaded with a polar light, that
I jotted down in pencil the first sketch of the passions of *René*.
At night I deposited in the *Essai historique* and *Les Natchez* the
harvest of my daydreams. The two manuscripts marched
abreast, although I often lacked the money to buy paper for
them, and was obliged, for want of thread, to fasten the pages
together with nails pulled out of the battens in my attic.

These places where I received my earliest inspirations impress
me with a sense of their power; they reflect upon the present
the gentle light of my memories; I feel in the mood to take up
my pen again. So many hours are wasted in embassies! I have
just as much time here as in Berlin to continue my *Memoirs*, an
edifice which I am building out of dead bones and ruins. My
secretaries here in London want to go to picnics in the morning
and to balls at night: nothing could please me better! The footmen

their country. Attachments were formed in the course of con-versations in the evening, after work, on the grass at Hampstead or Primrose Hill. In chapels decorated by our own hands, in old tumbledown buildings, we prayed together on 21 January and on the anniversary of the Queen's death,* and were moved by a funeral oration pronounced by the emigrant curé of our village. We strolled beside the Thames, to watch ships laden with the world's riches entering port or to admire the country houses at Richmond, we who were so poor and who had lost the shelter of the paternal roof: all these things gave us true happiness.

When I come home in 1822, instead of being received by a shivering friend who opens the door of our attic to me, addresses me with easy familiarity, and beds down on a pallet next to mine, covering himself with his thin coat and using the moonlight as a lamp, I pass by the light of torches between two rows of lackeys, ending in five or six respectful secretaries. Rid-dled on the way with the words *Monseigneur*, *Milord*, *Your Excellency*, *Monsieur l'Ambassadeur*, I come at last to a drawing-room hung with gold and silk.

'I beg you, gentlemen, to leave me! A truce to these Milords! What do you want me to do with you? Go and laugh in the Chancery, as if I were not here. Do you think you can persuade me to take this masquerade seriously? Do you think me fool enough to imagine that I have changed my nature because I have changed my coat? The Marquess of Londonderry is com-ing, you say; the Duke of Wellington has asked for me; Mr Canning is looking for me; Lady Jersey expects me to din-ner with Mr Brougham; Lady Gwydir hopes to see me at ten o'clock in her box at the Opera, Lady Mansfield at midnight at Almack's.'

Mercy! Where can I hide? Who will deliver me? Who will save me from this persecution? Come back, happy days of pov-erty and loneliness! Return to life, companions of my exile! Come, old comrades of the camp-bed and the pallet, let us go

---

* Louis XVI was guillotined on 21 January 1793, Marie Antoinette on 16 October 1793.

in their turn, Peters, Valentine, Lewis, go to the ale-house, and
the maids, Rose, Maria for a walk through the streets: I am
delighted. They leave me the key of the outside door: *Monsieur
l'Ambassadeur* is left in charge of his house; if anybody knocks,
he will open the door. Everybody has gone out; here I am, on
my own: let me set to work.

Twenty-two years ago, as I have just remarked, I sketched
out *Les Natchez* and *Atala* in London; now, in my *Memoirs*, I
have come to the period of my travels in America: it all fits
together perfectly. Let us wipe out those twenty-two years, as
they have in fact been wiped out of my life, and set off for the
forests of the New World: the story of my embassy will come at
its proper time, when God pleases; but provided I stay here for
a few months, I shall have time and leisure enough to go from
the Niagara Falls to the Army of the Princes in Germany, and
from the Army of the Princes to my withdrawal to England.
The Ambassador of the King of France will be able to tell the
story of the French emigrant in the very place where the latter
spent his exile.

The last chapter ended with my embarkation at Saint-Malo.
Soon we left the Channel, and the huge waves coming from the
west told us that we had reached the Atlantic.

The boatswain of my ship was an old supercargo called Pierre
Villeneuve, whose very name appealed to me because of the
kindly Villeneuve of my childhood. He had served in India,
under the Bailli de Suffren, and in America under the Comte
d'Estaing; he had been involved in countless engagements.
Leaning against the bows of the ship, beside the bowsprit, like
an army veteran sitting under the pergola of his little garden in
the moat of the Invalides, Pierre, chewing a plug of tobacco
which filled out his cheek like a gumboil, described to me the
clearing of the decks, the effect of the gunfire below decks, and
the havoc caused by cannon-balls ricocheting against the gun-
carriages, the guns, and the timber-work. I made him tell me
about the Indians, the Negroes, and the planters. I asked him
how the trees were shaped, what was the colour of earth and

sky, the taste of the fruit; whether pineapples were better than peaches, palm-trees more impressive than oaks. He explained all this to me with the aid of comparisons taken from things I knew: the palm-tree was a big cabbage; an Indian's dress was like my grandmother's; camels looked like hunchbacked donkeys; all the peoples of the East, and especially the Chinese, were cowards and thieves. Villeneuve came from Brittany, and we never failed to end up by singing the praises of the incomparable beauty of our native land.

The bell interrupted our conversations; it struck the watches and the time for dressing, for the roll-call, and for meals. In the morning, at a given signal, the crew lined up on deck, stripped off their blue shirts, and put on others which were drying in the shrouds. The discarded shirts were promptly washed in tubs in which this school of seals also soaped their brown faces and their tarred paws.

At the midday and evening meals, the sailors, sitting in a circle round the mess-can, one after the other, in an orderly fashion and without any attempt at cheating, dipped their tin spoons into the soup which splashed about with the rolling of the ship. Those who were not hungry sold their ration of biscuit or salt meat to their messmates for a plug of tobacco or a glass of brandy. The passengers took their meals in the captain's cabin. In fine weather a sail was spread over the stern of the ship, and we dined with a view of a blue sea, flecked here and there with white marks where it was touched by the breeze.

Wrapped in my cloak, I stretched myself out at night on the deck. My eyes contemplated the stars above me. The swollen sail sent back to me the coolness of the breeze which rocked me beneath the dome of heaven: half-asleep and driven onwards by the wind, I was borne along to new skies and new dreams.

Among my fellow passengers there was a young Englishman. Francis Tulloch had served in the artillery: he was a painter, a musician, and a mathematician, and he spoke several languages. The Abbé Nagot, the Superior of the Sulpicians, had met the Anglican officer and made a Catholic of him: he was taking his neophyte to Baltimore.

I struck up a friendship with Tulloch: as I was an ardent free-thinker at the time, I urged him to return to his parents. The sight which lay before our eyes filled him with admiration. We used to rise at night, when the deck was given up to the officer of the watch and a few sailors who smoked their pipes in silence: *Tuta aequora silent.**

The ship rolled at the mercy of the slow and silent waves, while sparks of fire ran with the white foam along her sides. Thousands of stars shining in the dark blue of the heavenly dome, a boundless sea, infinity in the sky and on the waves! Never has God impressed me with His greatness more than during those nights when I had immensity over my head and immensity beneath my feet.

Westerly winds, interspersed with periods of calm, delayed our progress. By 4 May we had got no farther than the Azores. On the 6th, at about eight in the morning, we came in sight of the Isle of the Peak; for long centuries this volcano commanded unnavigated seas; a useless beacon by night, an unseen land-mark by day.

We anchored in a poor roadstead, with a rocky bottom, in forty-five fathoms of water. The island of Graciosa, before which we were moored, displayed to us hills that were a little swollen in outline like the ellipses of an Etruscan amphora: they were draped in the green of their cornfields and gave off a pleasant smell of wheat peculiar to the harvests of the Azores. In the midsts of these carpets, we could see the dividing lines of the fields, formed by volcanic stones, half black and half white, piled one on top of the other. On the summit of a mound there stood an abbey, a monument of an old world on new soil; at the foot of this mound, the red roofs of the town of Santa Cruz were mirrored in a pebbly creek. The whole island, with its indentations of bays, capes, coves, and promontories, dupli-cated its inverted landscape in the sea. As an outer protection it had a girdle of rocks jutting vertically from the waves. In the background of the picture, the volcanic cone of the Peak, planted

* The sea is calm and silent (Virgil).

on a cupola of clouds, pierced the aerial perspective beyond Graciosa.

It was decided that I should go ashore with Tulloch and the mate; the longboat was lowered and rowed towards the island, which was about two miles away. We noticed some movement on the beach; a praam put out in our direction. As soon as she had come within earshot, we made out a number of monks in her. They hailed us in Portuguese, Italian, English, and French, and we replied in all four languages. The island was in a state of alarm, for our vessel was the first big ship that had ventured to anchor in the dangerous roadstead where we were riding the tide. What is more, it was the first time the islanders had ever seen the tricolour flag; they did not know whether we hailed from Tunis or Algiers: Neptune had not recognized the standard carried so proudly by Cybele. When they saw that we had human forms and that we understood what was said to us, they were overjoyed. The monks helped us into their boat and we rowed merrily towards Santa Cruz, where we had some difficulty in landing because of the rather rough surf.

The whole island came running to meet us. Four or five alguazils, armed with rusty pikes, took charge of us. His Majesty's uniform attracted the honours in my direction, and I was taken for the leading member of the deputation. We were escorted to the Governor's hovel, where His Excellency, dressed in a shabby green uniform which had once been gold-laced, granted us a solemn audience: he gave us permission to take in fresh supplies.

Our monks took us to their monastery, a roomy and well-lighted building provided with balconies. Tulloch had found a fellow countryman: the principal brother, who bustled about seeing to our needs, was a sailor from Jersey, whose ship had gone down with all hands off Graciosa. The sole survivor of the wreck, and not lacking in intelligence, he had become an apt pupils of the catechists; he had learnt Portuguese and a few words of Latin; the fact of his being an Englishman had told in his favour, and they had converted him and made a monk of him. The Jersey sailor found it much more to his liking to be lodged, boarded, and clothed at the altar than to climb the rigging to take in the mizzen topsail. He had not forgotten his old trade: it was a long time since he had heard his language spoken, and he was delighted to meet someone who knew it; he laughed and swore like a true apprentice. He showed us over the island.

The houses in the villages, built of wood and stone, were adorned with outer galleries which gave a clean look to these huts, because they let in a great deal of light. The peasants, nearly all of them vine-growers, were half-naked and bronzed by the sun; the women, short and yellow-skinned like mulattoes, but sprightly and gay, took a naïve pride in their appearance, with their posies of syringa and their rosaries worn as crowns or necklaces.

The hillsides were covered with vine-stocks, the wine from which resembled that of Fayal. Water was scarce, but wherever a spring welled, there grew a fig-tree and stood an oratory with a portico painted in fresco. The arches of the portico framed views of the island and the sea. It was on one of these fig-trees that I saw a flock of blue teal settle that were not of the web-footed variety. The tree had no leaves, but it bore red fruit set like crystals. When it was adorned with the cerulean birds, which drooped their wings, its fruit appeared to be a bright purple, while the tree seemed suddenly to have grown a blue foliage.

We were served with a good supper by the monks after our excursion, and we spent the night drinking with our hosts. The next day about noon, our supplies having been taken on board, we returned to the ship. The monks promised to attend to our letters for Europe. The ship had been in danger on account of a stiff south-easterly wind which had risen. We weighed anchor; but it was caught in the rocks, and we lost it as expected. We set sail: the wind continued to freshen, and soon we had left the Azores behind.

The wind forced us to bear north, and we arrived at the Banks of Newfoundland. Some floating icebergs were drifting around in the midst of a pale, cold mist.

The men of the trident have games which have been handed down to them by their predecessors: when you cross the Line, you must resign yourself to receiving *baptism*; it is the same ceremony in the tropics as on the Banks of Newfoundland, and wherever it is held, the leader of the masquerade is always called the Old Man of the Tropics. Tropical and dropsical are synonymous terms for the sailor, so that the Old Man of the Tropics has an enormous paunch. He is dressed, even when he is in his native tropics, in all the sheepskins and fur jackets the crew can muster between them; and he squats in the main-top, giving a roar every now and then. Everybody looks up at him: he starts clambering down the shrouds with all the clumsiness of a bear and stumbling like Silenus. As he sets foot on deck he utters fresh roars, gives a bound, seizes a pail, fills it with sea-water, and empties it over the heads of those who have never crossed the Equator or never reached the ice-line. You may flee below decks, jump on to the hatches, or climb up the masts: the Old Man of the Tropics comes after you. A generous tip marks the end of these games of Amphitrite, which Homer would have extolled, just as he sang of Proteus, if Old Oceanus had been known in his entirety in the days of Ulysses; but at that time, only his head could be seen at the Pillars of Hercules; his body lay hidden and covered the world.

We steered for the islands of Saint-Pierre and Miquelon, looking for a new port of call. When we came in sight of the former, one morning between ten o'clock and noon, we were almost on top of it; its coast showed like a black hump through the mist.

We anchored in front of the capital of the island: we could not see it, but we could hear the sounds on land. The passengers lost no time in disembarking; the Superior of Saint-Sulpice, who had been continuously plagued by sea-sickness, was so weak that he had to be carried ashore. I took a room apart from the rest and waited for a squall to blow away the mist and show me the place where I was living and, so to speak, the faces of my hosts in this land of shadows.

The port and roadstead of Saint-Pierre are situated between the east coast of the island and a long-shaped islet called the Ile aux Chiens, or Isle of Dogs. The port, known as the Barachois, stretches inland and ends in a brackish pool. Some barren hills are crowded together in the centre of the island: one or two stand apart and overhang the sea; others have at their foot a skirt of turfy moorland which has been levelled out. The look-out hill can be seen from the town.

The Governor's house faces the wharf. The church, the rectory, and the provision warehouse are to be found in the same area; next come the houses of the naval commissioner and the harbour-master. From there, the one street of the town runs over the pebbles along the beach.

I dined two or three times with the Governor, an extremely polite and obliging officer. He grew a few European vegetables on a slope outside. After dinner he showed me what he called his garden. A sweet, delicate smell of heliotrope came from a small patch of flowering beans; it was not wafted to us by a gentle breeze from home, but by a wild Newfoundland wind which had no connexion with the exiled plant, no attractive element of reminiscence or delight. In this perfume which was no longer breathed in by beauty, purified in its breast, or diffused in its wake, in this perfume of a changed dawn, a different culture, another world, there lingered all the melancholy of nostalgia, absence, and youth.

From the garden we went up towards the hills, and stopped at the foot of the flagstaff in front of the look-out. The new French flag waved over our heads; like Virgil's women, we looked at the sea, *flentes*:* it separated us from our native land! The Governor was uneasy: he belonged to the defeated order; what is more, he was bored in this lonely spot, which was suited to a dreamer like myself, but which was a thankless abode for a man interested in public affairs and not endowed with that all-absorbing passion which banishes the rest of the world from sight. My host inquired after the Revolution; I asked him for news of the North-West Passage. He was in the van of the wilderness, but he knew nothing of the Eskimos and received nothing from Canada but partridges.

One morning I went by myself to the Cap-à-l'Aigle to see the sun rise in the direction of France. There, a wintry stream formed

* Weeping.

a cascade which with its last leap reached the sea. I sat on a rocky ledge with my feet hanging over the water foaming at the bottom of the cliff. A young fisher-girl appeared on the upper slopes of the hill; she was bare-legged, in spite of the cold, and was walking in the dew. Tufts of dark hair showed from under the kerchief bound round her head; over this kerchief she wore a hat made of the reeds that grew in the country and shaped like a boat or a cradle. A bunch of purple heather peeped out of her bosom, which was outlined beneath the white fabric of her shift. Now and then she bent down to gather the leaves of an aromatic plant known in the island as *natural tea*. With one hand she dropped these leaves into a basket which she carried in the other. She saw me: without showing any alarm, she came and sat next to me, putting her basket down beside her, and began looking at the sun like myself, with her legs dangling over the sea.

We stayed for a few minutes without speaking; finally I proved myself the bolder of the two and asked:

'What are you gathering there? The season for bilberries and atocas is over.'

She raised two big dark eyes, looked at me shyly but proudly, and answered:

'I was picking tea.'

She showed me her basket.

'Are you taking this tea home to your father and mother?'

'My father is away fishing with Guillaumy.'

'What do you do on the island in winter?'

'We make nets; we fish the lakes by breaking the ice; on Sundays we go to Mass and Vespers and sing hymns; and then we play with the snow and watch the boys hunting the polar bears.'

'Will your father be back soon?'

'Oh, no: the captain is taking the ship to Genoa with Guillaumy.'

'But Guillaumy will be coming back?'

'Oh, yes, next season, when the fishermen return. He is going to bring me a striped silk bodice, a muslin petticoat, and a black necklace.'

'And you will be all decked out for the wind, the mountains, and the sea. Would you like me to send you a bodice, a petti- coat, and a necklace?'

'Oh, no!'

She got to her feet, picked up her basket, and ran down a steep path beside a fir-grove, singing a Mission hymn in a loud, clear voice. She scattered as she ran some lovely birds, called egrets because of the tuft on their heads; she looked as though she were one of their number. When she got to the sea, she leapt into a boat, unfurled the sail, and sat down at the rudder; one might have taken her for Fortune: she sailed away from me.

After taking on stores and replacing the anchor lost at Gra- ciosa, we left Saint-Pierre. Sailing south, we reached the latitude of 38°, and were becalmed a short distance from the coasts of Maryland and Virginia. The misty sky of the northern regions had been succeeded by a clear, cloudless sky; we could not see the land, but the scent of the pine forests was wafted to us. Daybreak and dawn, sunrise and sunset, dusk and nightfall were all admirable. I was never tired of gazing at Venus, whose rays seemed to envelop me like my sylph's tresses in the past.

One day an incident occurred which very nearly put an end to my plans and my dreams. The heat was overpowering; the ship, lying in a dead calm and weighed down by its masts, was rolling heavily: roasting on deck and wearied by the motion of the vessel, I decided to have a bathe, and although we had no boat out, I dived into the sea from the bowsprit. All went well to begin with, and several passengers followed my example. I swam about without looking at the ship; but when I happened to turn my head, I saw that the current had already carried her some distance away from me. The sailors, alarmed by the situ- ation, had thrown a rope to the other swimmers. Sharks appeared in the wake of the ship, and shots were fired at them to drive them away. The swell was so heavy that it slowed me down and exhausted my strength. There was a whirlpool below me, and at any moment the sharks might make off with one of my arms or legs. On board, the boatswain was trying to lower a boat, but the tackle had to be fixed first, and all this took time.

By the greatest good fortune, an almost imperceptible breeze sprang up; the ship, answering to the helm a little, came nearer to me; I was just able to catch hold of the rope, but my companions in foolhardiness were already clinging to it; when we were pulled to the ship's side, I was at the end of the line, and they bore on me with their whole weight. In this way they fished us out one after another, an operation which lasted a long time. The rolling continued; at every roll, we either plunged six or seven feet into the water or else we were lifted as many feet up in the air, like fish at the end of a line; at the last immersion, I felt as if I were about to faint; one more roll, and it would have been all up with me. I was hoisted on deck half-dead; if I had been drowned, what a good riddance that would have been for me and the rest!

Two days after this incident, we came in sight of land. My heart beat wildly when the captain pointed it out to me: America! It was barely indicated by the tops of a few maple-trees above the horizon. The palm-trees at the mouth of the Nile have since indicated the coast of Egypt to me in the same way. A pilot came on board; we entered Chesapeake Bay. That same evening a boat was sent ashore to obtain fresh provisions. I joined the party, and soon I trod American soil.

Gazing around me, I remained motionless for a few moments. This continent, which had been unknown for possibly the whole of antiquity and many centuries in modern times; the first wild destiny of that continent and its second destiny after the arrival of Christopher Columbus; the supremacy of the European monarchies shaken in this new world; the old society ending in young America; a republic of an unfamiliar type foreshadowing a change in the human mind; the part which my country had played in these events; these seas and shores owing their independence in part to the French flag and French blood; a great man issuing from the midst of the discord and the wilderness; Washington living in a flourishing city on the same spot where William Penn had bought a patch of forest-land; the United States passing on to France the revolution which France had supported with her arms; lastly, my own fate, the virgin muse which I had come to abandon to the passion of a new variety of nature; the discoveries which I hoped to make in the deserts which still extended their broad kingdom behind the narrow domain of a foreign civilization: such were the thoughts that revolved in my mind.

We walked towards the nearest house. Woods of balsam-trees and Virginian cedars, mocking-birds, and cardinal tanagers proclaimed by their appearance and shade, their song and colour, that we were in a new clime. The house, which we reached after half an hour, was a cross between an English farmhouse and a West Indian hut. Herds of European cows were grazing in pastures surrounded by fences, on which striped squirrels were playing. Blacks were sawing up logs of wood, whites tending tobacco-plants. A Negress of thirteen or fourteen, practically naked and singularly beautiful, opened the gate to us like a young Night. We bought some cakes of Indian corn, chickens, eggs, and milk, and returned to the ship with our demijohns and baskets. I gave my silk handkerchief to the little African girl: it was a slave who welcomed me to the soil of liberty.

We weighed anchor to make our way to the roads and port of Baltimore: as we approached, the waters narrowed; they were smooth and still; we appeared to be sailing up a lazy river lined with avenues. Baltimore looked as if it lay at the far end of a lake. Opposite the town there rose a wooded hill, at the foot of which they had begun building. We moored alongside the quay. I slept on board and did not go ashore till the next day. I went to stay at the inn with all my luggage; the seminarists retired to the establishment prepared for them, whence they have since scattered all over America.

What became of Francis Tulloch? The following letter was delivered to me in London on 12 April 1822:

Thirty years have elapsed, my dear viscount, since our journey to Baltimore, and it is extremely doubtful whether you will remember even so much as my name; but if I am to judge by the feelings of my heart, which has always been loyal and true to you, this is not the case, and I flatter myself that you would not be displeased to see me again. Although we live almost opposite each other (as you will see from the address on this letter), I am only too well aware how many things separate us. But show the slightest desire to see me and I shall be happy to prove to you, to the best of my ability, that I am still, as I have always been, your faithful and devoted

Francis Tulloch

Friday, 12 April.
30 Portland Place.

So Tulloch was in London; he did not become a priest; he is married; his adventures have come to an end like mine. This letter testifies to the truthfulness of my *Memoirs* and the accuracy of my recollections. Who could have given evidence of an *alliance* and a *friendship* formed thirty years ago at sea, if the other contracting party had not come upon the scene? But what a sad and retrogressive perspective this letter opens up to me! In 1822 Tulloch had reappeared in the same city as myself, in the same street as myself; the door of his house was opposite mine, just as when we had met on the same ship, on the same deck, with his cabin facing mine. How many other friends of mine shall I never see again! Every night, as he lies down to rest, a man can count his losses: only his years never leave him, although they pass one by one; when he reviews them and calls their numbers, they reply: 'Present!' Not a single one is absent from the roll-call.

Baltimore, like all the other capital cities of the United States, did not have the same dimensions then as it has today: it was a pretty little Catholic town, neat and lively, whose customs and society bore a close resemblance to the customs and society of Europe. I paid the captain my passage-money and gave him a farewell dinner. I booked my seat in a stage-coach which went three times a week to Pennsylvania. I got into it at four o'clock in the morning and found myself rolling along the highways of the New World.

The road we took, which had been marked out rather than made, crossed a somewhat flat stretch of country: there were scarcely any trees, a few farms, some thinly scattered villages.

The climate was French, and swallows flew over the rivers as they did over the pond at Combourg.

As we drew near to Philadelphia, we met peasants going to market, public carriages, and private carriages. Philadelphia struck me as a fine town, with wide streets, some of which were planted with trees, which intersected each other at right angles at regular intervals from north to south and east to west. The Delaware runs parallel to the street which follows its west bank. This river would be considered a large one in Europe: nobody in America thinks it worth mentioning; its banks are low and not particularly picturesque.

At the time of my journey (1791), Philadelphia did not yet extend as far as the Shuylkill; the ground running in the direction of that tributary had been divided into lots, and houses were being built on them here and there.

Philadelphia offers a monotonous appearance. In general, what is missing from the Protestant cities of the United States is great works of architecture: the Reformation, young in years, and sacrificing nothing to the imagination, has rarely erected those domes, those airy naves, those twin towers with which the old Catholic religion has crowned Europe. Not a single monument in Philadelphia, New York, or Boston soars above the mass of walls and roofs: the eye is saddened by this uniform level.

Putting up at first at a hotel, I later took a room in a boarding-house patronized by planters from San Domingo and Frenchmen who had emigrated with other ideas than mine. A land of freedom offering asylum to people fleeing from freedom: there could be no better proof of the supreme value of generous institutions than this voluntary exile of the supporters of absolute power in a pure democracy.

A man arriving like myself in the United States, full of enthusiasm for the peoples of classical antiquity, a colonist looking everywhere for the rigidity of early Roman life, was bound to be shocked at the luxuriousness of the carriages, the frivolity of the conversations, the inequality of fortunes, the immorality of the banks and gaming-houses, the noisiness of the ball-rooms and theatres. In Philadelphia I might easily have thought myself in Liverpool or Bristol. The common people were an attractive sight; the Quaker girls with their grey dresses, their little uniform bonnets, and their pale faces, looked positively beautiful.

At that period of my life I had a great admiration for republics, although I did not consider them a practical possibility at the stage of world history which we had reached: I knew liberty as the Ancients understood it, and liberty the daughter of the manners of a new-born society; but I knew nothing of that liberty which is the daughter of enlightenment and of an old civilization, that which the representative republic has shown to be a reality: God grant that it may last! In order to be free, a man is no longer obliged to plough his own small field, to curse the arts and sciences, or to have hooked nails and a dirty beard.

When I arrived in Philadelphia, General Washington was not there: I was obliged to wait for him for about a week. I saw him go past in a carriage drawn by four prancing horses driven four-in-hand. Washington, according to the ideas I held at that time, was necessarily Cincinnatus; Cincinnatus in a chariot conflicted somewhat with my republic of the Roman year 296. Could Washington the Dictator be anything but a peasant driving his oxen along with a goad and holding the handle of his plough? But when I went to see him with my letter of recommendation, I found once again the simplicity of the ancient Roman.

A little house, which looked like the other houses near by, was the palace of the President of the United States: there were no sentries, not even any footmen. I knocked, and a young maidservant opened the door. I asked her if the General was at home; she replied that he was. I said that I had a letter for him. The maid asked me my name, which is difficult to pronounce in English and which she could not remember. She then said quietly: 'Walk in, sir', and led the way along one of those narrow corridors which serve as entrance-halls in English houses: she showed me into a parlour where she asked me to wait for the General.

I felt no emotion: neither greatness of soul nor greatness of fortune impresses me; I admire the former without being overawed by it; the second fills me with pity rather than respect: no man's face will ever disturb me.

A few minutes later the General came in: tall in stature, and calm and cold rather than noble in bearing, he resembled his portraits. I handed him my letter in silence; he opened it, and his eyes went straight to the signature, which he read aloud, exclaiming:

'Colonel Armand!'

This was the name by which he knew the Marquis de la Rouërie and by which the latter had signed himself.

We sat down. I explained to him as best as I could the purpose of my journey. He answered in monosyllables in English and French, and listened to me with a sort of astonishment; I noticed this, and said to him with some spirit:

'But it is not as difficult to discover the North-West Passage as it is to create a nation, as you have done.'

'Well, well, young man!' he exclaimed, giving me his hand.

He invited me to dinner the next day, and we parted.

I took good care to keep the appointment. There were only five or six guests. The conversation turned upon the French Revolution. The General showed us a key from the Bastille. These keys, as I have already remarked, were silly toys which were distributed to all and sundry. Three years later, the exporters of locksmiths' wares could have sent the President of the United States the bolt of the prison of the monarch who gave freedom to both France and America. If Washington had seen the *victors of the Bastille* in the gutters of Paris, he would have had less respect for his relic. The seriousness and strength of the Revolution did not spring from those bloody orgies. At the time of the revocation of the Edict of Nantes, in 1685, the same mob from the Faubourg Saint-Antoine demolished the Protestant church at Charenton with just as much zeal as when it laid waste the church of Saint-Denis in 1793.

I left my host at ten o'clock in the evening, and never saw him again; he went away the next day, and I continued my journey.

Such was my meeting with the soldier-citizen, the liberator of a world. Washington went to his grave before a little fame attached itself to my footsteps; I passed before him as the most insignificant of human beings; he was in all his glory, I in all my obscurity; my name may not have lingered so much as one whole day in his memory: yet I am fortunate indeed that his gaze should have fallen upon me! I have felt warmed by it for the rest of my life: there is virtue in the gaze of a great man.

EIGHT
With the Savages

I was impatient to continue my journey. It was not the Americans that I had come to see, but something entirely different from the men I knew, something more in keeping with the normal order of my ideas; I longed to throw myself into an enterprise for which I was equipped with nothing but my imagination and my courage.

At the time when I decided to try to discover the North-West Passage, it was not known whether North America extended towards the Pole and joined Greenland, or whether it terminated in some sea adjoining Hudson Bay and the Behring Straits. In 1772 Hearne had discovered the sea at the mouth of Copper Mine River, in latitude 71° 15′ N. and longitude 119° 15′ W. of Greenwich.

On the Pacific coast, the efforts of Captain Cook and other sailors after him had left certain doubts. In 1787 a ship was said to have entered an inland sea of North America; according to the story told by the captain of this ship, what had been taken for an uninterrupted coastline to the north of California was really just a closely knit chain of islands. The British Admiralty sent Vancouver to verify these reports, which proved to be false. Vancouver had not yet made his second voyage.

In the United States, in 1791, people were beginning to talk about the route taken by Mackenzie: starting from Fort Chippeway on Mountains Lake, on 3 June 1789, he made his way down to the Arctic Ocean by the river to which he gave his name.

This discovery might have made me change direction and head due north; but I would have had scruples about altering

the plan which M. de Malesherbes and I had agreed upon. I
decided, therefore, to travel west so as to strike the north-west
coast above the Gulf of California; from there, following the
outline of the continent, and keeping the sea in sight all the
time, I hoped to explore the Behring Straits, double the north-
ernmost cape of America, come down east along the shores of
the Arctic Ocean, and return to the United States by way of
Hudson Bay, Labrador, and Canada.

What means did I possess to carry out this prodigious pere-
grination? None whatever. Most of the French explorers have
been solitary men, left to their own resources; only very rarely
has the Government or some company employed or assisted
them. Englishmen, Americans, Germans, Spaniards, and Portuguese have accomplished, with the support of the national will,
what in our case impoverished individuals have begun in vain.
Mackenzie and others after him have made conquests in the
vast expanse of America, for the benefit of the United States
and Great Britain, which I had dreamt of making for the
aggrandizement of my native land. If I had succeeded, I should
have had the honour of bestowing French names on hitherto
unknown regions, of endowing my country with a colony on
the Pacific coast, of taking the rich fur trade away from a rival
Power, and of preventing that Power from opening up a shorter
route to the Indies by putting France herself in possession of
that route. I have put these plans on record in my *Essai historique*, published in London in 1796, and the plans in question
were taken from the manuscript account of my travels written
in 1791. These dates prove that in both my ideas and my writings I was ahead of the latest explorers of the Arctic ice-fields.

I obtained no encouragement in Philadelphia. I realized then
that the purpose of this first voyage would not be achieved, and
that my present expedition was destined to be only the prelude
to a second and longer voyage. I wrote to this effect to M. de
Malesherbes, and while awaiting the future, I promised to
poetry whatever should be lost to science. And indeed, if I failed
to find in America what I was looking for, the Arctic world, it so
happened that I did find there a new muse.

A stage-coach, similar to the one which had brought me

from Baltimore, took me from Philadelphia to New York, a
gay, crowded, commercial city, which was nevertheless far
from being what it is today, and even farther from what it will
be in a few years' time, for the United States grow faster than
this manuscript. I went on a pilgrimage to Boston to salute the
first battlefield of American liberty. I saw the plains of Lexing-
ton; I sought there, as I have since sought at Sparta, the grave
of those warriors who died *in obedience to the sacred laws of
their country*.* A notable example of the concatenation of
human affairs: a finance Bill passed by the English Parliament
in 1765 creates a new empire on this earth in 1782, and causes
one of the oldest kingdoms of Europe to disappear from the
world in 1789!

I embarked at New York on the packet sailing for Albany,
which is situated in the upper reaches of the Hudson River.
There were a considerable number of passengers. Towards
evening on the first day, we were served with a collation of fruit
and milk; the women sat on the benches on deck, and the men
at their feet. Conversation was not maintained for long: at the
sight of a beautiful natural picture, one involuntarily falls
silent.

   Arriving at Albany, I went in search of a Mr Swift, for whom
I had been given a letter. This Mr Swift traded in furs with the
Indian tribes enclosed in the territory ceded by England to the
United States; for the civilized Powers, whether republican or
monarchical, unceremoniously divide among themselves land
in America which does not belong to them. After listening to
what I had to say, Mr Swift raised some eminently reasonable
objections. He told me that I could not undertake a voyage of
this importance on the spur of the moment, alone, without
help, without support, and without letters of recommendation
for the English, American, and Spanish posts through which I
should have to pass; that if I had the good fortune to cross so
many desolate wastes, I should come to frozen regions where I

* Chateaubriand later admitted his mistake in looking for the grave of Leoni-
das and his three hundred Spartans at Sparta instead of Thermopylae.

should die of cold and hunger: he advised me to begin by accli-
matizing myself, and urged me to learn the Sioux, Iroquois,
and Eskimo languages and to spend some time living with the
trappers and the agents of the Hudson's Bay Company. Once I
had completed this preliminary training, I could then, in four
or five years' time, and with the assistance of the French Government, proceed on my hazardous mission.

This advice, whose justice, in my heart of hearts, I was
forced to admit, annoyed me. If I had relied on my own judgement, I should have set off there and then for the Pole, as one
would set out from Paris to Pontoise. I concealed my annoyance from Mr Swift, and asked him to find me a guide and
some horses to take me to Niagara and Pittsburgh: from Pittsburgh I would go down the Ohio and collect ideas which would
be useful to me in my future plans. I was still thinking of following my original route.

Mr Swift engaged a Dutchman for me who spoke several
Indian dialects. I bought a couple of horses and left Albany.

The whole stretch of country between that town and Niagara is now inhabited and cleared; the New York Canal crosses
it; but at that time a considerable part of this territory was
unoccupied.

When, after crossing the Mohawk, I entered some woods
where no trees had been felled, I was seized with a sort of
intoxication of independence: I went from tree to tree, left and
right, saying to myself:

'Here there are no roads, no cities, no monarchies, no republics, no presidents, no kings, no men.'

And in order to see whether I was really reinstated in my
original rights, I indulged in wild antics which infuriated my
guide, who secretly believed me to be mad.

Alas, I imagined that I was alone in that forest in which I
held my head so high! But suddenly I almost ran into the side
of a shelter. Under the roof of that shelter, my astonished eyes
beheld the first savages I had ever seen. There were a score of
them, men and women, all daubed with paint like sorcerers,
with half-naked bodies, slit ears, crows' feathers on their heads,
and rings in their noses. A little Frenchman, his hair all curled

and powdered, wearing an apple-green coat, a drugget jacket, and a muslin jabot and ruffles, was scraping a pocket fiddle and making those Iroquois dance *Madelon Friquet*. M. Violet (for that was his name) was the savages' dancing-master. They paid him for his lessons in beaver skins and bears' hams. He had been a scullion in General Rochambeau's service during the American War. After the departure of our army, he had stayed in New York with the intention of instructing the Americans in the fine arts. Success had widened the scope of his ambitions, and the new Orpheus was now carrying civilization to the savage hordes of the New World. Speaking to me of the Indians, he always said: 'These savage ladies and gentlemen.' He took great pride in the nimbleness of his pupils, and indeed I have never seen such capering. Holding his little violin between his chest and his chin, M. Violet would tune the magic instrument and then call out to the Iroquois:

'Take your places!'

And the whole troop would start leaping about like a band of demons.

It was a terrible experience for a disciple of Rousseau, this introduction to savage life through a dancing-lesson given to some Iroquois by General Rochambeau's sometime scullion. I was tempted to laugh, but I felt cruelly humiliated.

I bought a complete outfit from the Indians: two bearskins, one to serve as a demi-toga, the other as a bed. I added to my new apparel the red cap in ribbed cloth, the cloak, the belt, the horn for calling in the dogs, and the bandoleer of the typical trapper. My hair hung over my bare neck, and I wore a long beard: I looked like an amalgam of savage, hunter, and missionary. I was invited to a hunt which was to take place the next day to track down an American badger, an animal which is now practically extinct in Canada, like the beaver.

We set off in boats before dawn to go up a river coming out of the forest in which the badger had been seen. There were about thirty of us, including Indians as well as American and Canadian trappers: part of the troop walked alongside the flotilla with the dogs, and the women carried our provisions.

We did not find the badger, but we killed some lynxes and musk-rats. The Indians used to go into deep mourning when they had accidentally killed any of the latter animals, for the female of the musk-rat is, as everybody knows, the mother of the human race. The Chinese, who are more observant, maintain that the rat changes into a quail, the mole into an oriole.

Our table was abundantly furnished with river birds and fish. The dogs are trained to dive, so that when they are not hunting they go fishing: they plunge into the rivers and seize the fish even when they are at the bottom of the water. The women cooked our meals over a big fire around which we took our places. We had to lie flat, with our faces close to the ground, to protect our eyes against the smoke, which hung in a great cloud above our heads and preserved us after a fashion from the stings of the mosquitoes.

M. Violet gave me letters of credence for the Onondagas, the remnant of one of the six Iroquois nations. I came first of all to the Lake of the Onondagas. The Dutchman picked a suitable spot in which to pitch our camp: in the curve of a river flowing from the lake. We drove two forked stakes into the ground, six feet apart, and hung a long pole horizontally in the forks of these stakes. Strips of birch bark, one end resting on the ground and the other on the transversal pole, formed the sloping roof of our palace. Our saddles had to serve as pillows and our cloaks as blankets. We fastened bells to our horses' necks and turned them loose in the woods near our camp: they did not wander far.

The next day I went to pay a call on the sachem of the Onondagas; I reached his village at ten o'clock in the morning. I was promptly surrounded by a crowd of young savages who spoke to me in their language, mixed with English phrases and a few French words; they were noisy and light-hearted, like the first Turks I saw, later on, when I landed on the soil of Greece. These Indians, enclosed in clearings made by the whites, have houses and cattle of their own; their huts are full of utensils bought at Quebec, Montreal, Niagara, and Detroit on the one hand, and in the markets of the United States on the other.

The explorers of the interior of North America found in a
state of nature, among the various savage tribes, the different
forms of government known to the civilized peoples. The Iroquois belonged to a race which seemed destined to conquer all
the other Indian races, if strangers had not come to empty his
veins and arrest his genius. That fearless creature was not overawed by firearms when they were first used against him; he
stood fast in the midst of the whistling of bullets and the roar
of gun-fire, as if he had heard these sounds all his life; he seemed
to pay no more attention to them than to a storm. As soon as
he was able to lay his hands on a musket, he made better use of
it than a 'European. He did not substitute it for the tomahawk,
the scalping-knife, the bow and arrow; he kept these weapons,
adding to them the carbine, the dagger, and the axe; it seemed
as if he could never have enough arms to satisfy his valour.
Doubly equipped with the murderous instruments of Europe
and America, his head decked with plumes, his ears slit, his
face daubed with various colours, his arms tattooed and
smeared with blood, this champion of the New World became
as redoubtable in appearance as he was in battle, on the shores
which he defended foot by foot against the invaders.

The Onondaga sachem or chief was an old Iroquois in the
fullest sense of the word: he kept up in his person the ancient
traditions of the wilderness.

English writers never fail to call the Indian sachem *the old
gentleman*. Well, the old gentleman is completely naked; he
wears a feather or a fishbone stuck through his nostrils, and
sometimes covers his head, which is as smooth and round as a
cheese, with a laced three-cornered hat, as a European sign of
honour. Does not the Abbé Velly depict history with the same
realism? The Frankish chieftain Chilpéric rubbed his hair with
sour butter, *infundens acido comam butyro*, daubed his cheeks
with woad, and wore a striped jacket or a tunic made of the
skin of some animal; he is represented by Velly as a prince magnificent to the point of ostentation in his furniture and retinue,
voluptuous to the point of debauchery, and scarcely believing
in God, whose ministers were the butt of his mockery.

The sachem of the Onondagas received me well and invited

me to sit down on a mat. He spoke English and understood French; my guide knew Iroquois: conversation was easy. Among other things, the old man told me that although his nation had always been at war with mine, he had always respected it. He complained about the Americans; he considered them greedy and unfair, and regretted that in the division of the Indian territories his tribe had not gone to increase the lot of the English.

The women served us with a meal. Hospitality is the last virtue which the savages have retained in the midst of European civilization; it is well known what that hospitality was like in the past; the hearth was as sacred as the altar.

When a tribe was driven out of its woods, or when a man came and asked for hospitality, the stranger began what was called the dance of the supplicant. The child touched the threshold and said: 'Here is the stranger.' And the chief replied: 'Child, bring the man into the hut.' The stranger, coming in under the child's protection, sat down among the ashes of the hearth. And the woman sang the song of consolation: 'The stranger has found a mother and a wife; the sun will rise and set for him as of old.'

These customs give the impression of having been borrowed from the Greeks: Themistocles, calling on Admetus, kisses the *penates* and his host's young son (at Megara I may have trodden on the poor woman's hearthstone, under which Phocion's cinerary urn was hidden); while Ulysses, visiting Alcinous, says to Arete: 'Noble Arete, daughter of Rhexenor, after suffering cruel misfortunes, I throw myself at your feet.' And having said this, the hero goes and sits among the ashes of the hearth . . .

I took leave of the old sachem. He had been present at the capture of Quebec. In the shameful years of Louis XV's reign, the episode of the Canadian War consoles us as if it were a page of our ancient history discovered in the Tower of London.

Montcalm, given the task of defending Canada unaided, against forces which are regularly replenished and four times his own in number, fights successfully for two years, defeating Lord Loudon and General Abercromby. At last his luck deserts him; he falls wounded beneath the walls of Quebec, and two days later breathes his last: his grenadiers bury him in a hole made by a bombshell, a grave worthy of the honour of our arms! His noble enemy Wolfe dies facing him; he pays with his own life for Montcalm's life and for the glory of expiring on a few French flags.

My guide and I mounted our horses again. Our route became more difficult, with nothing but a line of felled trees to indicate it. The trunks of these trees served as bridges over the streams or as fascines in the quagmires. The American settlers were at this time moving towards the Genesee concessions. These concessions were sold at prices which varied according to the richness of the soil, the quality of the trees, the course and force of the water.

It has been observed that the settlers are often preceded in the woods by bees: these are the vanguard of the farmers, the symbols of the industry and civilization whose coming they herald. Strangers to America, where they arrived in the wake of Columbus, these peaceful conquerors have robbed a new world of flowers only of those treasures of whose use the natives were ignorant; and they have employed those treasures to no other effect than to enrich the soil from which they took them.

The clearings along both sides of the road I was travelling presented a curious mixture of natural and civilized conditions. In a corner of a wood which had never known any sound but the yells of the savage and the belling of the stag, one came across a ploughed field; and from the same vantage-point one could see an Indian's wigwam and a planter's cabin. Some of these cabins, which had already been completed, reminded one of the neatness and cleanliness of Dutch farm-houses; others were only half-finished and had no roof but the sky.

I was received in these dwellings which were the result of a morning's work, and inside I often found a family equipped with the amenities of European civilization: mahogany furniture, a piano, carpets, and mirrors, a few steps from an Iroquois's hut. In the evening, when the farm-workers had returned from the woods with their axes and hoes, the windows were thrown open. My host's daughters, with their lovely

fair hair dressed in ringlets, would stand round the piano singing the duet from Paisiello's *Pandolfetto*, or some *cantabile* by
Cimarosa, all this in full view of the wilderness, and sometimes
to the murmuring sound of a waterfall.

In the better districts small towns were established. The
spire of a new church shot up from the heart of an old forest.
Since the English take their customs with them wherever they
go, after crossing tracts of country containing no trace of
human habitation, I would suddenly see an inn-sign swinging
from the branch of a tree. Trappers, planters, and Indians mingled together at these caravanserais: the first time I put up at
one, I swore that it would be the last.

Entering one of these hostelries, I stood amazed at the sight
of an enormous bed built in a circle round a post: each traveller
took his place in this bed with his feet against the post in the
middle and his head at the circumference of the circle, so that
the sleepers were arranged symmetrically like the spokes of a
wheel or the sticks of a fan. After some hesitation, I got into
this contraption, because I could see no one else in it. I was
beginning to doze off when I felt something sliding against me:
it was the leg of my big Dutchman: I have never experienced a
more horrible sensation in the whole of my life. I jumped out of
the hospitable bed, cordially cursing the customs of our good
forefathers. I went and slept in my cloak in the moonlight: this
bedfellow at least was all sweetness, freshness, and purity.

On the bank of the Genesee we found a ferry-boat. A troop
of settlers and Indians crossed the river with us. We pitched
camp in meadows bright with butterflies and flowers. Dressed
in our varied costumes, and sitting in different groups round
our fires, with our horses tethered or grazing, we looked like a
caravan. It was there that I first made the acquaintance of the
rattlesnake, which allows itself to be bewitched by the sound of
a flute. The Greeks would have turned my Canadian into
Orpheus, the flute into a lyre, and the snake into Cerberus or
perhaps Eurydice.

We rode on towards Niagara. When we had come to within
twenty miles of our destination, we saw, in an oak-grove, the
camp-fire of some savages who had stopped for the night on

the bank of a stream where we ourselves were thinking of bivouacking. We took advantage of their preparations: after
grooming our horses and getting ready for the night, we
accosted the little band. Crossing our legs tailor-fashion, we sat
down among the Indians around the fire and started roasting
our maize cakes.

The family consisted of two women, two children who had
not yet been weaned, and three braves. The conversation
became general, that is to say interspersed with a few words
from me and a great many gestures; then each one fell asleep
where he was sitting. I alone stayed awake, and went to sit by
myself on a tree-root which ran along the bank of the stream.

The moon showed above the tree-tops; a balmy breeze,
which that Queen of the Night brought with her from the East,
seemed to precede her through the forests, as if it were her cool
breath. The solitary luminary climbed higher and higher in the
sky, now pursuing her course, now crossing clusters of clouds
which resembled the peaks of a chain of snow-capped mountains. All would have been peace and silence but for the falling
of a few leaves, the passing of a sudden gust of wind, the hoot-
ing of a brown owl; in the distance I could hear the dull roar of
the Niagara Falls, which in the still of the night echoed from
wilderness to wilderness before dying away in the lonely forests. It was during nights such as that that an unknown muse
appeared to me; I listened to the accents of her voice and
marked them down in my book, by the light of the stars, as an
ordinary musician might write down the notes dictated to him
by some great master of harmony.

The next day, the Indians armed themselves while the women
collected their baggage. I distributed a little gunpowder and
vermilion among my hosts. We parted, touching our foreheads
and breasts. The braves gave the marching-cry and set off in
front; the women followed after, carrying the children, who,
slung in furs on their mothers' backs, turned their heads to
look at us. I followed this procession with my eyes until the
whole troop had disappeared among the trees of the forest.

The Niagara Falls savages in the English dependency were
entrusted with the task of policing that side of the frontier. This

weird constabulary, armed with bows and arrows, prevented us from passing. I had to send the Dutchman to the fort at Niagara for a permit in order to enter the territory of the British government. This saddened me a little, for I remembered that France had once ruled over both Upper and Lower Canada. My guide returned with the permit: I still have it; it is signed: *Captain Gordon*. Is it not strange that I should have found the same English name on the door of my cell in Jerusalem? As I wrote in my *Itinéraire*: 'Thirteen pilgrims had inscribed their names on the door and walls of the room: the first was called Charles Lombard, and he visited Jerusalem in 1669; the last was John Gordon, and the date of his stay is 1804.'

I spent two days in the Indian village, where I wrote another letter to M. de Malesherbes. The Indian women busied themselves with various tasks; their babies were slung in nets from the branches of a tall purple beech. The grass was covered with dew, the wind smelt sweet as it came out of the forest, and the cotton-plants, turning their capsules upside down, looked like white rose-trees. The breeze rocked the aerial cradles with an almost imperceptible movement; the mothers got up now and then to see if their children were asleep and had not been awakened by the birds.

The Indian village was some eight or ten miles from the Falls: it took my guide and me nearly four hours to cover this distance. Already, six miles away, a column of mist indicated the position of the waterfall to me. My heart beat with joy mingled with terror as I entered the wood which concealed from my view one of the most awe-inspiring sights that Nature has offered to mankind.

We dismounted, and leading our horses by the bridle, we made our way across heaths and copses until we reached the bank of the Niagara River, seven or eight hundred paces above the Falls. As I was moving forward, the guide caught me by the arm; he stopped me at the very edge of the water, which was going past with the swiftness of an arrow. It did not froth or foam, but glided in a solid mass over the sloping rock; its silence before its fall contrasted with the roar of the fall itself. The Scriptures

often compare a nation to mighty waters: this was a dying
nation which, robbed of its voice by the agony of death, was
hurling itself into the abyss of eternity.

The guide continued to hold me back, for I felt so to speak
drawn towards the river, and I had an involuntary longing to
throw myself in. First I would look upstream at the river-banks,
then downstream at the island which divided the waters, and
the spot where those waters stopped all of a sudden, as if they
had been cut off in mid-air.

After a quarter of an hour of perplexity and admiration I
went on to the Falls. The reader can find in the *Essai sur les
Révolutions* and *Atala* the two descriptions I have made of the
scene. Today, great highroads lead to the cataract; there are
inns on both the American and English banks, and mills and
factories beneath the chasm.

I have seen the cascades of the Alps with their chamois and
those of the Pyrenees with their lizards; I have not been far
enough up the Nile to see its cataracts, which are mere rapids;
I make no mention of the waters of Terni and Tivoli, graceful
adornments for ruins or subjects for the poet's song: *Et prae-
ceps Anio ac Tiburni lucus.**

Niagara eclipses everything. I gazed for a long time at this
cataract whose existence was revealed to the old world, not by
puny travellers like myself, but by missionaries who, seeking
solitude for the love of God, would throw themselves on their
knees at the sight of some marvel of Nature and receive martyrdom as they came to the end of their hymn of admiration.
Our priests saluted the natural splendours of America and consecrated them with their blood; our soldiers clapped their
hands at the sight of the ruins of Thebes and presented arms to
Andalusia: the whole genius of France lies in the twin army of
our camps and our altars.

I was holding my horse's bridle twisted round my arm when
a rattlesnake started rustling in the bushes. The startled horse
reared up and backed towards the Falls. I was unable to release
my arm from the reins; the horse, growing more terrified every

* And the swift Anio and the sacred wood of Tibur (Horace).

moment, dragged me after it. Already its fore-feet were off the ground; crouching on the edge of the abyss, it maintained its position only by the strength of its loins. It was all up with me, when the animal, itself astonished at the new danger confronting it, swung round away from the Falls. If I had died in the Canadian forest, would my soul have carried to the supreme tribunal the sacrifices, the good works and virtues of Père Jogues and Père Lallemand,* or empty days and futile fantasies?

This was not the only danger I encountered at Niagara. A ladder of creepers was used by the savages to get down to the lower basin; it was broken at this time. Wishing to see the Falls from below, I ignored my guide's protests and started clambering down the side of an almost perpendicular rock. In spite of the roar of the water foaming below me, I kept my head and got to within forty feet of the bottom. At that point, however, the bare, vertical rock offered me no further foothold; I was left hanging by one hand to the last root, feeling my fingers opening under the weight of my body: few men have spent two minutes such as those I counted then. My tired hand let go; I fell. By an incredible stroke of good fortune, I found myself on the edge of a rock upon which I should have been smashed into a thousand pieces, and I was not conscious of any serious injury. I was a few inches from the abyss and I had not rolled into it; but when the cold and damp began to penetrate my body, I saw that I had not got off so lightly: my left arm was broken above the elbow. The guide, who was looking down at me and to whom I made signs of distress, ran off to fetch some savages. They hoisted me with ropes up an otters' path, and carried me to their village. I had only a simple fracture: a couple of splints, a bandage, and a sling were enough to cure me.

We eventually set out for the lands known at that time by the general name of the Floridas, and now divided into the states of Alabama, Georgia, South Carolina, and Tennessee.

---

* Two French Jesuit missionaries. The former was killed by the Mohawks in 1646; the latter died at Quebec in 1673.

The savages of Florida tell of an island in the middle of a lake which is inhabited by the most beautiful women in the world. The Muskhogulges have repeatedly tried to conquer it, but this Eden flees before their canoes, a natural symbol of those dreams which retreat before our desires. The country also boasted a fountain of youth: who would wish to live his life over again?

These fables came close to assuming a sort of reality in my eyes. Just when we least expected it, we saw a flotilla of canoes, some with oars and the others with sails, come out of a bay. They landed at the island on which we had pitched camp. Manning them were two families of Creeks, the one consisting of Seminoles, the other of Muskhogulges, including some Cherokees and Burnt-woods. I was struck by the grace of these savages, who in no way resembled those of Canada.

The Seminoles and Muskhogulges are fairly tall, and, by an extraordinary contrast, their mothers, wives, and daughters are the smallest women known in America.

The Indian women who landed near us, born of mixed Cherokee and Castilian stock, were tall in stature. Two of them looked like Creoles from San Domingo or Mauritius but were yellow-skinned and delicate like women of the Ganges. These two Floridan women, who were cousins on the father's side, served as my models, the one for Atala, the other for Céluta: they surpassed the portraits I painted of them only by that variable and fugitive truth of nature, that physiognomy of race and climate which I was unable to render. There was something indefinable in that oval face, in that dusky complexion which one seemed to see through a light, orange-tinted film of smoke, in that soft black hair, in those narrow eyes, half-hidden beneath the veil of two satiny eyelids which opened lazily; in short, in the dual charm of the Indian and the Spanish woman.

The meeting with our hosts resulted in a certain change in our movements: our trading agents began asking questions about horses, and it was decided that we should go and settle down near the studs.

The plain on which our camp was established was covered with bulls, cows, horses, bisons, buffaloes, cranes, turkeys, and pelicans: these birds mottled the green background of the savannah with white, black, and pink streaks.

Our traders and trappers were stirred by many passions: not passions of race, education, or prejudice, but natural passions, full-blooded and absolute, making straight for their object, with no witnesses but a tree fallen in the depths of an unknown forest, an uncharted valley, a nameless river. The relations between the Spaniards and the Creek women formed the basis of most adventures: the Burnt-woods played the principal part in these romances. One story was famous: that of a dealer in brandy who had been seduced and ruined by a 'painted woman' or courtesan. This story, put into Seminole verse under the title of *Tabamica*, used to be sung on the way through the woods. Carried off in their turn by the settlers, the Indian women soon died neglected and forsaken in the Spanish town of Pensacola: their misfortunes went to swell the *Romanceros* and to be classed with the laments of Ximena.

The earth is a charming mother; we come forth from her womb; in childhood, she holds us to her breasts, which are swollen with milk and honey; in youth and manhood, she lavishes upon us her cool waters, her harvests, and her fruits; she offers us, wherever we may go, shade, a bath, a table, and a bed; when we die, she opens her bosom to us again and throws a coverlet of grass and flowers over our remains while she secretly transforms us into her own substance to be reproduced in some new and graceful shape. That is what I said to myself when I awoke and my first glance fell upon the sky, the canopy of my bed.

The hunters had set out for their day's work, and I remained behind with the women and children. I never left the side of my two sylvan goddesses: one was proud, the other sad. I could not understand a single word of what they said to me; but I went to fetch water for their cup, twigs for their fire, mosses for their bed. They wore the short skirt and the wide, slashed sleeves of Spanish women, the bodice and cloak of Indian women. Their bare legs were cross-gartered with birch laces. They plaited their hair with posies of flowers or filaments of rushes: they covered their breasts with chains and glass necklaces. Purple berries hung from their ears, and they had a pretty talking parrot, the bird of Armida, which they fastened on their shoulder like an emerald or carried in a hood on their hand, as the great ladies of the tenth century carried their hawks. To harden their breasts and arms, they rubbed themselves with the apoya or rattan-cane. In Bengal the nautch-girls chew the betel-nut, and in the Levant the almes suck the mastic of Chio; the Floridan women crushed between their bluey-white teeth tears of liquid-ambar and roots of libanis, which combined the fragrance of angelica, cedrat, and vanilla. They lived in an atmosphere of perfumes emanating from themselves, like orange-trees and flowers living in the pure exhalations from their leaves and chalices. I amused myself by putting some little ornament on their heads: they submitted, showing mild alarm; magicians themselves, they thought that I was casting a spell over them. One of them, the 'proud' one, kept offering up prayers; she seemed to me half-Christian. The other one sang in a velvety voice, finishing every phrase on a note of stirring beauty. Sometimes they spoke sharply to each other: I thought I could recognize the accents of jealousy, but the 'sad' one wept, and silence was restored.

A fishing party was arranged. The sun had nearly set. In the foreground there were sassafras, tulip-trees, catalpas, and oaks from whose boughs there hung skeins of white moss. Behind there rose the most charming of trees, the papaw, which might have been taken for a stylus of chased silver, surmounted by a Corinthian urn. In the background there was a profusion of balsam-trees, magnolias, and liquidambars.

Abandoned by my companions, I rested by the edge of a clump of trees: its darkness, glazed with light, formed the penumbra in which I sat. Fireflies shone among the crape-coloured shrubs, disappearing from sight when they passed through the moonbeams. I could hear the sound of the rise and fall of the lake, the leaping of the goldfish, and the occasional cry of the diving-bird. My eyes were fixed on the water; I gradually fell into that state of drowsiness which is familiar to men who travel the world's highways; I no longer had any clear recollections;

I felt as if I were living and vegetating with Nature in a kind of pantheism. I leant back against the trunk of a magnolia-tree and fell asleep; my slumbers floated on a vague surface of hope.

When I emerged from this Lethe, I found myself between two women; the odalisks had returned; not wanting to awaken me, they had sat down silently by my side; then, either in a pretence of sleep or because they had really dozed off, their heads had fallen on my shoulders.

A breeze blew through the grove and deluged us with a shower of magnolia petals. Then the younger of the Seminoles began to sing: no man who is not sure of himself should ever expose himself to such temptation: one cannot tell what passions may enter with melody into a man's breast. A harsh, jealous voice replied to the woman's song: a Burnt-wood was calling the two cousins, they started and rose: dawn was beginning to break.

I have since repeated this scene, though without Aspasia, on the shores of Greece: going up to the columns of the Parthenon with the dawn, I saw Mount Cithaeron, Mount Hymettus, the Acropolis of Corinth, the tombs and the ruins, bathed in a dew of golden, transparent, shimmering light, which was reflected by the seas and wafted like a perfume by the breezes from Salamis and Delos.

We finished on the bank our voyage without words. At noon we struck camp to go and inspect the horses which the Creeks wished to sell and the traders to buy. Women and children, all were summoned to act as witnesses, as was the custom in solemn transactions. Stallions of every age and colour, foals and mares, with bulls, cows, and heifers, started racing and galloping around us. In the confusion I was separated from the Creeks. A group of men and horses collected at the edge of a wood. Suddenly I recognized my two Floridans among them; strong hands were seating them on the cruppers of two Barbary horses ridden bareback by a Burnt-wood and a Seminole. The mares galloped off, and the huge squadron followed them. The horses rushed, leaped, bounded, and neighed in the midst of the horns of the bulls and buffaloes, their hoofs colliding in mid-air, their tails and manes flying blood-stained behind them.

A whirlwind of ravenous insects swarmed around this wild cavalry. My Floridans disappeared from sight like Ceres' daughter, snatched away by the god of the underworld.

That is how everything proves abortive in my life, and why nothing is left me but pictures of what has passed me by: I shall go down to the Elysian Fields with more shades than any man has ever taken with him. The fault lies with my character: I am incapable of taking advantage of any piece of good fortune; I cannot take an interest in anything whatever that interests others. Except in religion, I have no beliefs. Shepherd or king, what would I have done with my sceptre or my crook? I would have grown equally weary of glory or genius, work or leisure, prosperity or misfortune. Everything tires me: I laboriously tow my boredom behind me, yawning away my life wherever I go.

The devil having spirited away the Muskhogulge maidens, I was told by the guide that a Burnt-wood who was in love with one of the two women had been jealous of me and had arranged with a Seminole, the brother of the other cousin, to take Atala and Céluta away from me. The guide referred to them bluntly as 'painted women', which wounded my vanity. I felt all the more humiliated in that the Burnt-wood, my favoured rival, was a lean, ugly, dark-skinned mosquito of a man, with all the characteristics of the insects which, according to the Grand Lama's entomologists, are animals whose flesh is inside their bones. Solitude appeared empty to me after my misadventure. I was short-tempered with my sylph, who nobly came running to console her faithless lover, like Julie when she forgave Saint-Preux his Parisian Floridans.* I lost no time in leaving the wilderness, in which I have since resuscitated the drowsy companions of my night. I cannot tell whether I gave back to them the life they gave me: at least I made a virgin of one and a virtuous wife of the other, by way of expiation.

We crossed the Blue Mountains again and approached the European clearings in the vicinity of Chillicothe. On the bank

---

* In Rousseau's novel *La Nouvelle Héloïse*.

of a stream I saw an American house: a farm-house at one end and a water-mill at the other. I went in, asked for food and shelter, and was well received.

My hostess showed me up a ladder to a room over the shaft of the hydraulic machine. My little casement-window, festooned with ivy and cobaeas with iris bells, overlooked the stream which flowed past, narrow and solitary, between two thick borders of willows, elms, sassafras, tamarinds, and Caroline poplars. The moss-covered millwheel turned in their shade, letting fall long ribbons of water. Perch and trout leaped about in the foam; wagtails flew from one bank to the other; and some birds of the kingfisher family fluttered their wings above the current.

How happy I should have been there with the 'sad' one, if only she had remained faithful to me, sitting dreaming at her feet with my head against her knees, listening to the noise of the weir, the turning of the wheel, the rolling of the millstone, the sifting of the bolter, the even beating of the clack, and breathing in the freshness of the water and the smell from the husks of the pearl barley.

Night fell. I went down to the farm parlour. It was lighted only by maize-straw and bean husks blazing in the hearth. The firearms of the master of the house, lying horizontally in the gun-rack, gleamed in the light from the fire-place. I sat down on a stool in the chimney-nook, near a squirrel which kept jumping from the back of a big dog to the shelf of a spinning-wheel and back again. A kitten installed itself on my knee to watch this game. The miller's wife put a large stewpot on the fire, whose flames played round the black base of the pot like a radiated crown of gold. While I watched the potatoes boiling for my supper, I read by the light of the fire, holding my head low down, an English newspaper which I had found lying on the floor between my legs. Printed in large letters I read the words: FLIGHT OF THE KING. It was the story of Louis XVI's attempted escape and the arrest of the unfortunate monarch at Varennes.*

---

* On 22 June 1791.

A sudden conversion took place in my mind. Rinaldo saw his weakness in the mirror of honour in Armida's gardens; I was not Tasso's hero, but the same looking-glass showed me my image in an American orchard. The clash of arms and the tumult of the world resounded in my ears beneath the thatch of a mill hidden in unfrequented woods. I said to myself: 'Go back to France', and abruptly brought my travels to a close.

Thus it was that my sense of duty upset my original plans and caused the first of those upheavals that have marked my career. The Bourbons no more needed a younger son from Brittany to return from abroad to offer them his obscure devotion than they have needed his services since he has emerged from his obscurity. If I had lit my pipe with the newspaper which changed the course of my life, and continued my journey, no one would have noticed my absence; my life at that time was unknown and weighed as little as the smoke from my calumet. A mild dispute between myself and my conscience flung me on the stage of the world. I could have done as I pleased, since I was the sole witness of the struggle; but of all witnesses, that is the one before whom I should most fear to blush.

Why is it that the wastes of Erie and Ontario present themselves to my mind with a charm which the splendid spectacle of the Bosphorus does not possess in my memory? It is because, at the time of my travels in the United States, I was full of illusions; the troubles in France began at the same time as my adult life; nothing was settled or complete either in myself or in my native land. Those days are dear to me because they remind me of the innocence of feelings inspired by my family and the pleasures of youth.

Fifteen years later, after my travels in the Levant, the Republic, swollen with ruins and tears, had poured like a torrent from the deluge into despotism. I no longer deluded myself with idle dreams; my recollections, henceforth finding their source in society and human passion, were no longer innocent and ingenuous. Disappointed in both my pilgrimages to the West and to the East, I had failed to discover the passage to the Pole, I had failed to win glory on the banks of the Niagara, where I had gone in search of it, and I had left it undisturbed in the ruins of Athens.

Setting out to be an explorer in America and returning to be a soldier in Europe, I did not go the whole length of either of these careers: an evil genie snatched the staff and the sword away from me, and put the pen in my hand. Another fifteen years have elapsed since, looking at the night sky over Sparta, I recalled the countries which had already seen my peaceful or troubled sleep: in the woods of Germany, on the commons of England, on the plains of Italy, on the high seas, and in the Canadian forests I had already greeted the same stars which I saw shining over the land of Helen and Menelaus. But what did it avail me to complain to the stars, the immobile witnesses of my vagrant destinies? One day their gaze will cease to tire itself by following me: in the meantime, indifferent to my fate, I will not ask those stars to exercise a gentler influence over it, or to restore to me that part of life which the traveller leaves behind him in the places he visits.

Returning to Philadelphia from the wilderness, as I have already said, having hurriedly written on the way *what I have just related*, like the old man in La Fontaine, I did not find the bills of exchange I expected; this was the beginning of the financial difficulties in which I have been plunged ever since. Fortune and I took a dislike to each other at first sight. According to Herodotus, certain Indian ants used to amass piles of gold; according to Athenaeus, the sun gave Hercules a golden ship in which to land on the island of Erythia, the home of the Hesperides: ant though I am, I do not have the honour of belonging to the great Indian family, and sailor though I am, I have never crossed the sea in anything but a wooden boat. It was a vessel of this kind which brought me back to Europe from America. The captain allowed me to make the crossing on credit. On 10 December 1791 I embarked with several of my fellow countrymen who, for a variety of reasons, were returning like myself to France. The ship's destination was Le Havre.

A westerly gale caught us at the mouth of the Delaware and drove us across the Atlantic in seventeen days. Often under bare poles, we were scarcely able to heave to. The sun did not appear once. The ship, steered by dead reckoning, flew before the waves. I crossed the ocean in shadow; never before had it looked so sad. I myself, sadder still, was returning from my first venture in life disappointed and deceived. 'Palaces are not built on the sea,' says the Persian poet Feryd-Eddyn. I felt a vague heaviness of heart, as at the approach of a great misfortune. Looking out over the waves, I asked them to tell me my destiny, or else I did some writing, more inconvenienced by their movement than disturbed by their threats.

Far from calming down, the tempest increased in force the nearer we came to Europe; but it blew steadily, and the uniformity of its rage produced a sort of furious lull in the livid sky and the leaden sea. The captain, having been unable to take the altitude, was uneasy; he went up into the shrouds and scanned the horizon through a telescope. A look-out was placed on the bowsprit, another in the fore-topsail of the mainmast. The sea turned choppy and the water changed colour, signs that we were approaching land: but what land?

I spent two nights walking the deck, to the accompaniment of the slapping of the waves in the darkness, the moaning of the wind in the rigging, and the leaping of the sea as it swept across the decks; all around us there was a mad riot of waves. Tired out by the jerks and jolts given by the ship, I went below early on the third night. The weather was terrible; my hammock creaked and rocked with every blow from the sea, which, breaking over the vessel, shook it from stem to stern. Soon I heard men running from one end of the deck to the other and coils of rope being thrown about: I experienced the movement one feels when a ship starts tacking. The hatch of the between-decks ladder was opened, and a frightened voice called for the captain: that voice, in the middle of the night and the storm, sounded ominous. I strained my ears, and thought I could hear some of the sailors talking about the lie of the coast. I jumped out of my hammock; a wave burst in and flooded the captain's cabin, knocking over tables, mattresses, chests, and firearms, and rolling them about pell-mell; I got up on deck half-drowned.

When I put my head out of the hatchway, a marvellous sight met my eyes. The ship had tried to put about; but, failing in the attempt, she had been embayed by the wind. By the light of the moon, which kept emerging from the clouds only to plunge into them again, we could see on both sides of the ship, through a yellow fog, a coast bristling with rocks. The sea was throwing up mountainous waves in the channel in which we lay trapped; now they scattered into foam and spray, now they presented an oily, vitreous surface, mottled with black, coppery, or greenish stains, according to the colour of the shoals over which they roared. For two or three minutes the moaning of the deep and that of the wind would be confused; the next moment, we could distinguish the swirling of the currents, the hissing of the reefs, the voice of the distant surge. From the hold of the ship there came sounds which made the hearts of the bravest sailors beat faster. The bows of the vessel cut through the thick mass of the waves with a hideous roar, and at the helm, torrents of water flowed away, seething and bubbling as at the opening of a sluice. In the midst of all this uproar, nothing was so alarming as a certain dull murmur, like that of a vase filling with water.

Lighted by a lantern and held down by weights, portulans, charts, and log-books lay spread out on a hen-coop. A squall of wind had put out the binnacle-lamp. Everyone was at logger-heads about the land. We had entered the Channel without noticing it; the ship, shuddering under every wave, was drifting between the islands of Guernsey and Alderney. It seemed as if we were bound to be wrecked, and the passengers packed their valuables to save them.

The crew included some French sailors; one of them, in the absence of a chaplain, started singing the hymn to Our Lady of Succour which was the first thing I had learnt as a child; I sang it again in sight of the coast of Brittany, almost under my mother's eyes. The American Protestant sailors joined in the singing of their French Catholic mates; danger teaches men how weak they are and unites them in prayer. All of us, passengers and sailors, were on deck, clinging to the rigging, the sheathing, the capstan, or the anchor bills to avoid being swept away by the sea or hurled overboard by the rolling of the ship. The captain shouted for an axe to cut away the masts; and the rudder, whose tiller had been abandoned, went swinging from side to side with a harsh creaking sound.

One experiment remained to be tried: the lead now registered only four fathoms on a sandbank which crossed the channel; it was just possible that the swell might carry us over the bank and into deep water, but who had the courage to seize the helm and take the responsibility for our common safety? One false turn of the tiller, and we were done for.

One of those men who spring from events and who are the spontaneous children of danger came to our rescue: a sailor from New York took the post deserted by the steersman. I can still see him in his shirt and canvas trousers, bare-footed and his hair tangled and wet, holding the tiller in his strong hands while he looked back over the stern at the sea which was to save or sink us. The great wave came towards us, stretching the whole width of the channel, rolling high without breaking, like one sea invading another; big white birds, flying a straight and steady course, preceded it like birds of death. The ship touched and stuck; there was complete silence; every face turned pale. The swell arrived: just as it touched us, the sailor put down the helm; the ship, on the point of falling on her side, presented her stern, and the swell, which seemed about to engulf us, lifted her up and over. The lead was heaved; it registered twenty-seven fathoms. A cheer rose to the heavens above, and we added a shout of 'Long live the King!' God did not hear it for Louis XVI; it benefited none but ourselves.

Although we were clear of the two islands, we were not out of danger; we could not get beyond the coast of Granville. At last the ebbing tide carried us out, and we doubled the cape of La Hougue. I experienced no fear during this semi-shipwreck and felt no delight at being saved. It is better to leave life while one is young than to be evicted from it by time. The next day we entered Le Havre. The whole population had come out to see us. Our top-masts were broken, our longboats had been swept away, our quarter-deck had been cut down, and we shipped water with every pitch of the vessel. I landed on the jetty. On 2 January 1792 I once more trod my native soil, which was soon to slip away again from under my feet. I brought with me no Eskimos from the polar regions, but two savages of an unknown species: Chactas and Atala.

NINE
With the Emigrant Army

I wrote to my brother in Paris giving him details of my crossing, telling him the reasons for my return, and asking him for the money I needed to pay my passage. My brother replied that he had forwarded my letter to my mother. Mme de Chateaubriand did not keep me waiting: she sent me the wherewithal to settle my debt and leave Le Havre. She told me that Lucile was with her, as well as my uncle Bedée and his family. This news persuaded me to go to Saint-Malo, so that I could consult my uncle on the subject of my proposed emigration.

On my way from Le Havre to Saint-Malo I had occasion to observe the divisions and misfortunes of France; the country mansions had been burnt or abandoned; the owners, to whom distaffs had been sent, had left; their womenfolk were living in hiding in the towns. The hamlets and small market towns were groaning under the tyranny of the clubs affiliated to the central Club des Cordeliers, which was later amalgamated with the Jacobins. The rival club, the Société Monarchique, or Société des Feuillants, had ceased to exist; the ignoble nickname of *sans-culotte* had become popular; the King was never referred to except as 'Monsieur Veto' or 'Monsieur Capet'.

I was given an affectionate welcome by my mother and my family, although they deplored the inopportune moment I had chosen for my return. My uncle, the Comte de Bedée, was preparing to go to Jersey with his wife, his son, and his daughters. The problem was how to raise enough money to enable me to join the Princes. My American journey had made a hole in my fortune; the property which belonged to me as the younger son of the family had been reduced to almost nothing by the suppression of feudal rights; the benefices which were to have accrued to me by virtue of my affiliation to the Order of Malta had fallen, like the rest of the clergy's riches, into the hands of the nation. This concourse of circumstances led to the most serious step in my life: my family married me off in order to obtain for me the means of going to get killed in support of a cause which I did not love.

There lived in retirement at Saint-Malo M. de Lavigne, a Knight of Saint-Louis and sometime Commander of Lorient. The Comte d'Artois had stayed with him in that town when he visited Brittany: the Prince was delighted with his host and promised to grant him any favour he might ask for in the future.

M. de Lavigne had two sons: one of them married Mlle de la Placelière. The two daughters born of this marriage lost both father and mother at an early age. The elder married the Comte du Plessix-Parscau, a captain in the Navy, the son and grandson of admirals, and now a Knight of the Order of St Louis and commander of the naval cadet corps at Brest; the younger was living with her grandfather and was seventeen years old when I arrived at Saint-Malo on my return from America. She was white-skinned, delicate, slim, and extremely pretty: she wore her lovely fair hair, which curled naturally, hanging down like a child's. Her fortune was estimated at five or six hundred thousand francs.

My sisters took it into their heads to make me marry Mlle de Lavigne, who had become greatly attached to Lucile. The whole affair was arranged without my knowledge. I had not seen Mlle de Lavigne more than three or four times; I recognized her at a distance on Le Sillon by her pink pelisse, her white dress, and her fair, wind-blown hair, when I was on the beach abandoning myself to the caresses of my old mistress, the sea. I felt that I possessed none of the requisite qualities of a husband. All my illusions were alive; nothing was exhausted in me; the very energy of my existence had doubled as a result of my travels. I was tormented by my muse. Lucile liked Mlle de Lavigne and saw this marriage as a means of obtaining a private fortune for me. 'Go ahead, then!' I said. In me the public man is inflexible; but the private man is at the mercy of whosoever wishes to dominate him, and to avoid an hour's wrangling I would become a slave for a century.

The consent of Mlle de Lavigne's grandfather, her uncle on her father's side, and her principal relatives was easily obtained; there remained an uncle on her mother's side, M. de Vauvert, to be won over; he was a great democrat and objected to his niece's marrying an aristocrat like myself, who was not one at all. We thought we could ignore him, but my pious mother insisted that the religious ceremony should be performed by a non-juring priest, and this could only be done in secret. M. de Vauvert knew this, and let the law loose upon us, on the grounds of rape and breach of the law, asserting that the grandfather, M. de Lavigne, had entered his second childhood. Mlle de Lavigne, who had become Mme de Chateaubriand without my having had any communication with her, was taken away in the name of the law and interned in the convent of La Victoire at Saint-Malo pending the decision of the courts.

There was no rape in all this, no breach of the law, no adventure, and no love; this marriage had only the worst part of a novel about it: truth. The case was tried and the court pronounced the marriage civilly valid. Since the members of both families were in agreement, M. de Vauvert abandoned his proceedings. The constitutional priest, heavily bribed, withdrew his protest against the first nuptial blessing, and Mme de Chateaubriand was released from the convent, where Lucile had imprisoned herself with her.

I now had a new acquaintance to make, and it brought me all I could wish for. I doubt whether a more acute intelligence than my wife's has ever existed: she guesses the thought and the word about to spring to the brow or the lips of the person with whom she is talking; it is impossible to deceive her. Mme de Chateaubriand has an original and cultured mind, writes in the most piquant style, tells a story to perfection, and admires me without ever having read two lines of my works: she would be afraid of finding ideas in them that differ from her own, or of discovering that people are not sufficiently enthusiastic about my merits. Although a passionate critic, she is well-informed and a good judge.

Mme de Chateaubriand's defects, if she has any, spring from the superabundance of her virtues; my own defects, which cannot be denied, result from the sterility of mine. It is easy to possess resignation, patience, a general obligingness, and an even temper when one takes to nothing, when one is bored by everything, and when one replies to good and ill-fortune alike with a wearied and wearying 'What does it matter?'

Mme de Chateaubriand is a better person than I am, though less easy to get on with. Have I been blameless in my behaviour to her? Have I accorded my companion all the attention which she deserved and which was hers by right? Has she ever complained? What happiness has she tasted in return for her unwavering affection? She has shared my misfortunes; she has been plunged into the prisons of the Terror, the persecutions of the Empire, the difficulties of the Restoration; she has not known the joys of motherhood to counterbalance her sorrows. Deprived of children, which she might perhaps have had in another marriage, and which she would have loved devotedly; blessed with none of the honour and affection which surround the mother of a family and console a woman for the loss of her best years, she has travelled, sterile and solitary, towards old age. Often separated from me, and prejudiced against literature, she finds no compensation in the pride of bearing my name. Timorous and trembling for me alone, she is robbed by her constantly renewed anxieties of both sleep and the time to cure her ills: I am her chronic infirmity and the cause of her relapses. Can I compare the few signs of impatience which she has shown me with the cares which I have caused her? Can I set my good qualities, such as they are, with her virtues which feed the poor and which have founded the Marie-Thérèse Infirmary* in the face of all manner of obstacles? What are my labours beside the good works of that Christian woman? When the two of us appear before God, it is I who will be condemned.

---

* In 1819 Mme de Chateaubriand founded a home in Paris for aged priests and old ladies of the nobility who had lost their fortunes in the Revolution. She handed it over to the Archbishopric of Paris in 1836 and was buried in the Infirmary chapel in 1847.

I was married at the end of March 1792, and on 20 April the Legislative Assembly declared war on Francis I, who had just succeeded his father Leopold; on the 10th of the same month, Benedict Labre had been beatified in Rome: there you have two different worlds. The war precipitated the rest of the aristocracy out of France. On the one hand, persecution became more severe; on the other, no Royalist could stay at home without being considered a coward: it was time for me to make my way to the camp which I had come so far to seek. My uncle Bedée and his family sailed for Jersey, and I set out for Paris with my wife and my sisters Lucile and Julie.

Paris in 1792 no longer looked the same as in 1789 and 1790; this was no longer the Revolution in its infancy, but a people marching drunkenly to its destiny, across abysses and by uncertain roads. The appearance of the people was no longer excited, curious, eager: it was threatening. In the streets one met only frightened or ferocious faces, people hugging the walls so as not to be seen or roaming around in search of their prey: timid eyes were turned away from you, or else grim eyes gazed into yours in order to fathom your secrets.

Variety in dress was a thing of the past; the old world was slipping into the background; men had donned the uniform cloak of the new world, a cloak which as yet was merely the last garment of the victims to come. Already the social licence displayed at the time of France's rejuvenation, the liberties of 1789, those wild and whimsical liberties of a social order which is breaking up and which has not yet turned to anarchy, were levelling themselves out beneath the sceptre of the people; one could sense the approach of a plebeian tyranny, fruitful, it is true, and full of hope, but also much more formidable than the decaying despotism of the old monarchy: for, since the sovereign people is ubiquitous, when it turns tyrant the tyrant is ubiquitous; it is the universal presence of a universal Tiberius.

With the Parisian population there was mingled an alien population of cut-throats from the south; the vanguard of the Marseillais whom Danton was bringing up for the Tenth of August and the September Massacres could be recognized by their rags, their bronzed complexions, and their look of cowardice and crime, but crime under a different sun: *in vultu vitium*, vice in the face.

The preparations for my departure dragged on interminably. My family had thought that they were arranging a rich marriage for me: it turned out that my wife's fortune was invested in Church securities; the nation undertook to pay them after its own fashion. What is more, Mme de Chateaubriand had lent the scrip of a large part of these securities to her sister, the Comtesse du Plessix-Parscau, who had emigrated. Money, therefore, was still wanting; we had no option but to borrow.

A notary obtained ten thousand francs for us: I was taking them home to the Cul-de-sac Férou, in the form of *assignats*, when I met one of my old messmates in the Navarre Regiment, the Comte Achard, in the Rue de Richelieu. He was a great gambler; he suggested going to the rooms of a certain M.— where we could talk: the devil urged me on: I went upstairs, I gambled, and I lost everything except fifteen hundred francs with which, full of remorse and confusion, I got into the first carriage that came along. I had never gambled before: gaming produced a sort of painful intoxication in me; if the passion had taken hold of me, it would have turned my brain. Half-distracted, I got out of the cab at Saint-Sulpice, leaving behind my pocket-book, which contained the remainder of my fortune. I ran home and said that I had left the ten thousand francs in a hackney-carriage.

I went out again, turned down the Rue Dauphine, crossed the Pont-Neuf, feeling tempted to throw myself into the water, and made my way to the Place du Palais-Royal, where I had taken the fateful vehicle. I questioned the Savoyards who watered the nags and described my particular cab; they gave me a number at random. The police superintendent of the district informed me that this number belonged to a job-master living at the top of the Faubourg Saint-Denis. I went to this man's house and stayed all night in the stable, waiting for the cabs to return: a considerable number arrived one after the other, but none of them was mine; finally, at two o'clock in the morning, I saw my chariot drive in. I had scarcely had time to recognize my two white steeds when the poor beasts, utterly worn out, dropped all of a piece on to the straw, their bellies distended and their legs stretched out as if they were dead.

The coachman remembered driving me. After me he had picked up a citizen who had asked to be taken to the Jacobins; after the citizen, a lady whom he had driven to No. 13 Rue de Cléry; after that lady, a gentleman whom he had set down at the Recollects in the Rue Saint-Martin. I promised the driver a tip and, as soon as the new day had dawned, I set out to look for my fifteen hundred francs, as I had gone in search of the North-West Passage. It seemed clear to me that the citizen of the Jacobins had confiscated them by the right of his sovereignty. The lady of the Rue de Cléry maintained that she had not seen anything in the coach. I reached my third stop without any hope; the coachman gave as good a description as he could of the gentleman he had driven. The porter exclaimed:

'Why, that's Père So-and-so!'

He led me through the corridors and the deserted apartments to the room of a Recollect who had been left behind to make an inventory of the furniture in the monastery. Sitting on a pile of rubbish in a dusty frock-coat, the monk listened to my story.

'Are you,' he asked, 'the Chevalier de Chateaubriand?'

'Yes,' I replied.

'Here is your pocket-book,' he said. 'I was going to bring it to you when I had finished: I found your address inside.'

It was this hunted and plundered monk, engaged in conscientiously counting up the relics of his cloister for his proscribers, who restored to me the fifteen hundred francs with which I was going to make my way into exile. Failing this little sum, I would not have emigrated: what would have become of me? My whole life would have been changed. I will be hanged if I would move a single step today to recover a million.

My brother and I obtained false passports for Lille: we were a couple of wine-merchants and members of the National Guard of Paris, whose uniform we wore, on our way to tender for the army supplies. My brother's valet, Louis Poullain, known as Saint-Louis, travelled under his own name; although he hailed from Lamballe, in Lower Brittany, he was going to see his family in Flanders. The day of our emigration was fixed for 15 July 1792, the day after the second Federation. We spent the 14th in the Tivoli Gardens, with the Rosanbo family, my sisters, and my wife. Tivoli belonged to M. Boutin, whose daughter had married M. de Malesherbes. Towards the end of the day, we saw a goodly number of federates wandering aimlessly around; written on their hats in chalk were the words: 'Pétion or death!' Tivoli, the starting-point of my exile, was to become a place of amusement and entertainment. The fifteen hundred francs I had recovered seemed to be a large enough fortune to bring me back in triumph to Paris.

On 15 July, at six o'clock in the morning, we got into the diligence: we had booked our seats in the cabriolet, by the driver; the valet, whom we were not supposed to know, squeezed himself into the inside with the other passengers. Saint-Louis walked in his sleep; in Paris he used to go looking for his master at night, with his eyes open but fast asleep. He used to undress my brother and put him to bed, sleeping all the time, replying 'I know, I know' to all that was said to him during his attacks, and waking up only when cold water was thrown in his face. He was a man of about forty, nearly six foot high, and as ugly as he was tall. This poor fellow, who was extremely respectful, had never served any other master than my brother; he was quite embarrassed when he had to sit down at table with us at supper-time. The other passengers, who were all great patriots, kept talking of hanging the aristocrats from the lanterns, which increased his dismay. The idea that at the end of all this he would have to pass through the Austrian Army, in order to fight in the Army of the Princes, completely turned his brain. He drank heavily and climbed into the diligence again; we went back to the coupé.

In the middle of the night we heard the passengers shouting, with their heads out of the windows:

'Stop, postilion, stop!'

The diligence stopped, the door was opened, and immediately male and female voices could be heard crying:

'Get out, citizen, get out! We can't stand this! Get out, you swine! He's a brigand! Get out, get out!'

We got out too, and saw Saint-Louis seized and flung out of the coach, get to his feet, look all round him with his wide-open but sleeping eyes, and start running off in the direction of Paris, without his hat and as fast as his legs could carry him. We were unable to acknowledge him, as that would have given us away; we had to leave him to his fate. Caught and put under arrest at the first village he came to, he stated that he was the servant of M. le Comte de Chateaubriand, and that he lived in the Rue de Bondy in Paris. The constabulary passed him on from one brigade to the next, until he eventually arrived at the Président Rosanbo's; the unfortunate man's depositions served to prove that we had emigrated, and to send my brother and sister-in-law to the scaffold.

The next morning, when the diligence stopped for breakfast, we had to listen to the whole story a score of times:

'The man was out of his mind; he was dreaming out loud; he kept saying strange things; he was probably a conspirator, a murderer fleeing from justice.'

The well-bred citizenesses blushed and waved large 'Constitutional' fans made of green paper. It was easy for us to recognize in these stories the effects of somnambulism, fear, and wine.

On arrival at Lille, we went in search of the person who was to take us across the frontier. The Emigration had its agents of deliverance who eventually became agents of perdition. The monarchical party was still powerful, the question undecided; the weak and cowardly worked for it while waiting to see how things turned out.

We left Lille before the gates were closed; we waited in a remote house and did not set off again until ten at night, when it was dark; we carried nothing except a stick in our hands; it was no more than a year since I had followed my Dutchman in the same way through the American forests.

We crossed cornfields through which there wound barely perceptible paths. French and Austrian patrols were scouring the countryside: we were liable to run into either, or to find ourselves facing a sentry's pistol. We saw solitary horsemen in the distance, sitting motionless, gun in hand; we heard horses' hoofs in country lanes; putting our ears to the ground, we made out the regular tramp of infantry on the march. After three hours spent alternately running and tiptoeing along, we reached a crossroads in a wood where a few belated nightingales were singing. A company of Uhlans concealed behind a hedge fell upon us with raised sabres. We shouted:

'Officers going to join the Princes!'

We asked to be taken to Tournay, saying that we were in a position to prove our identity. The officer in command placed us between his troopers and led us away.

When day broke, the Uhlans noticed our National Guard uniforms under our overcoats, and insulted the colours in which France was soon to dress a subjugated Europe . . .

My brother remained in Brussels with the Baron de Montboissier, who appointed him his aide-de-camp. I set out alone for Coblenz.

The Army of the Princes was no longer there. I crossed those empty kingdoms, *inania regna*; I saw the beautiful valley of the Rhine, the Temple of the barbarian muses, where ghostly knights would appear among the ruins of their castles and one can hear the clash of arms at night when war is near.

Between Coblenz and Treves, I fell in with the Prussian Army: I was going past the column when, coming up with the guards, I noticed that they were marching in battle order, with cannon in line; the King and the Duke of Brunswick were in the centre of the square, which was composed of Frederick's old grenadiers. My white uniform caught the King's eye: he sent for me; he and the Duke of Brunswick took off their hats and saluted the old French Army in my person. They asked me my name and regiment, and where I was going to join the Princes. This military welcome touched me: I replied with some emotion that, on learning in America of the King's misfortunes, I had returned to shed my blood in his service. The officers and generals with Frederick William gave a murmur of approval, and the Prussian sovereign said:

'Monsieur, one can always recognize the sentiments of the French aristocracy.'

He took off his hat again and stood uncovered and motionless until I had disappeared behind the grenadiers. Nowadays
people revile and abuse the emigrants; they are 'tigers who tore
at their mother's bosom'; at the time of which I speak, men followed the old examples, and honour ranked as high as country.
In 1792, fidelity to one's oath was still held to be a duty; today,
it has become so rare that it is regarded as a virtue.

The Army of the Princes was composed of gentlemen, classed
by provinces and serving as private soldiers: the aristocracy
was harking back to its origins and the origins of the monarchy
at the very moment when both the aristocracy and the monarchy were coming to an end, just as an old man reverts to his
childhood. There were also brigades of emigrant officers of different regiments who had likewise become privates once more:
among these were my messmates of Navarre, led by their colonel, the Marquis de Mortemart. I was strongly tempted to
enlist with La Martinière, even if he was still in love, but
Armorican patriotism carried the day. I enrolled in the seventh
Breton company, commanded by M. de Gouyon-Miniac. The
nobles of my province had provided seven companies; to these
was added an eighth consisting of young men of the Third
Estate: the steel-grey uniform of this last company differed
from that of the seven others, which was royal blue with ermine
facings. Men attached to the same cause and exposed to the
same dangers perpetuated their political inequalities by these
odious distinctions: the real heroes were the plebeian soldiers,
since there was no element of personal interest in the sacrifices
they made.

Enumeration of our little army:

Infantry of gentlemen-soldiers and officers; four companies
of deserters, dressed in the different uniforms of the regiments
from which they came; one artillery company; a few officers
from the engineers, with some guns, howitzers, and mortars of
various calibres (the gunners and the engineers, who nearly all
embraced the cause of the Revolution, were responsible for its
success abroad). A very fine cavalry, consisting of German
carabineers, musketeers under the command of the old Comte

de Montmorin, and naval officers from Brest, Rochefort, and Toulon, supported our infantry. The wholesale emigration of these last officers plunged the French Navy back into the state of weakness from which Louis XVI had extricated it. Never since the days of Duquesne and Tourville had our squadrons won greater glory. My comrades were delighted, but I had tears in my eyes when I saw those ocean dragoons go by who no longer commanded the ships with which they had humbled the English and delivered America. Instead of going in search of new continents to bequeath to France, these companions of La Pérouse sank into the mud of Germany. They rode the horse dedicated to Neptune; but they had changed their element, and the land was not for them. It was all in vain that their commander carried at their head the tattered ensign of the *Belle-Poule*, the sacred relic of the white flag, from whose shreds honour still hung, but victory had fallen.

We had tents, but we had little else. Our muskets, made in Germany, rubbishy weapons and incredibly heavy, broke our shoulders and were often in no condition to be fired. I went through the whole campaign with one of these firearms, whose hammer stubbornly refused to fall.

We stayed two days at Treves. It was a great pleasure for me to see some Roman ruins after seeing the nameless ruins of Ohio, and to visit that town which was sacked so often that Salvianus said of it: 'Fugitives from Treves, you ask for theatres, you beg the princes once again to provide a circus: for what state, I ask you, for what people, for what city? *Theatra igitur quaeritis, circum a principibus postulatis? Cui, quaeso, statui, cui populo, cui civitati?*'

Fugitives from France, where was the people for which we wished to restore the monuments of St Louis?

I sat down with my musket among the ruins; I took out of my haversack the manuscript account of my travels in America; I arranged the separate sheets on the grass around me; I revised and corrected a description of a forest, a passage from *Atala*, in the remains of a Roman amphitheatre, getting ready in this way to conquer France. Then I put away my treasure, the weight of which, added to that of my shirts, my cloak, my tin mess-can, my demijohn, and my little Homer, made me spit blood. I tried stuffing *Atala* into my cartridge-pouch with my useless ammunition; my comrades laughed at me and pulled out the sheets which stuck out on either side of the leather cover. Providence came to my rescue: one night, after sleeping in a hay-loft, I found when I awoke that my shirts had disappeared from my haversack; the thieves had left my papers. I gave thanks to God: that accident assured my 'fame' and saved my life, for the sixty pounds that weighed upon my shoulders would have given me consumption.

We were given orders to march on Thionville. We covered some fifteen miles a day. The weather was terrible; we tramped along through the rain and the mud singing: *O Richard, ô mon roi!* or *Pauvre Jacques!* When we arrived at the camping-ground, having no wagons or provisions, we went with our donkeys, which followed the column like an Arab caravan, to look for food in the farms and villages. We paid for everything scrupulously: nevertheless I was put on a fatigue duty for absent-mindedly taking a couple of pears from a château garden. A great steeple, a great river, and a great lord are bad neighbours, says the proverb.

We pitched our tents at random, and had to keep on beating the canvas to flatten out the threads and prevent the water coming through. We were ten soldiers to a tent; each in turn was given the cooking to do; one went for meat, another for bread, another for wood, another for straw. I was good at making soup, and was highly complimented on it, especially when I mixed milk and cabbage with the stew, in the Breton fashion. I had learnt to put up with smoke when I was with the Iroquois, so that I bore myself bravely in front of my fire of damp, green branches. This soldier's life is very amusing; I imagined myself still among the Indians. As we sat eating our meal in our tent my comrades asked me to tell them about my travels; they told me some fine stories in return; we all lied like a corporal in a tavern with a conscript footing the bill.

An army is generally composed of soldiers of roughly the same age, the same height, and the same strength. Ours was a very different body, a motley collection of grown men, old men, and children fresh from their dovecotes, jabbering Norman, Breton, Picard, Auvergnat, Gascon, Provençal and Languedocian. A father served with his sons, a father-in-law with his son-in-law, an uncle with his nephews, a brother with a brother; a cousin with a cousin. This strange host, ridiculous though it appeared, had something honourable and touching about it, because it was animated by sincere convictions; it presented an image of the old monarchy and provided a last glimpse of a dying world. I have seen old noblemen, stern-faced and grey-haired, dressed in torn coats with knapsacks on their backs and muskets slung over their shoulders, dragging themselves along with the aid of a stick and supported under the arm by one of their sons; I have seen young men lying wounded under a tree while a chaplain in frock-coat and stole knelt by their side, sending them to St Louis, whose heirs they had striven to defend. The whole of this needy troop, which did not receive a single sou from the Princes, made war at its own expense, while the Assembly's decrees finished the task of despoiling it and consigned our wives and mothers to prison.

Near our poor and obscure camp there was another that was brilliant and rich. At its headquarters one saw nothing but wagons full of eatables, one met no one but cooks, valets, and aides-de-camp. Nothing could have symbolized better the Court and the provinces, the monarchy that died at Versailles and the monarchy that died on Du Guesclin's heaths. We had come to loathe the aides-de-camp; outside Thionville, we shouted: 'Forward, the aides-de-camp!' just as the patriots used to shout: 'Forward, the officers!'

I felt a pang when, arriving one gloomy day in sight of some woods that lined the horizon, we were told that those woods were in France. Crossing the frontier of my country in arms had an effect on me which I find it impossible to convey: I had as it were a sort of revelation of the future, particularly as I shared none of my comrades' illusions, either with regard to the cause they were supporting or the hope of victory with which they deluded themselves; I was like Falkland in Charles

I's army. There was not a Knight of La Mancha, sick, lame,
and wearing a nightcap under his three-cornered beaver, but
was utterly convinced of his ability, alone and unaided, to put
fifty tough young patriots to flight. This honourable and admirable pride, a source of prodigious feats at other times, had not
infected me: I did not feel so sure of the strength of my invincible arm.

We reached Thionville on 1 September without having suffered
any reverse, for we had met nobody on the way. The cavalry
encamped on the right and the infantry on the left of the highroad running from the town towards Germany. The fortress
was not visible from the camping-ground; but six hundred
paces farther on there was a hill-crest dominating the Moselle
Valley. The naval cavalry linked the right flank of our infantry
to the Austrian corps of the Prince of Waldeck, while the
infantry's left flank was covered by the eighteen hundred horses
of the Maison-Rouge and Royal-Allemand Regiments. We dug
a trench along our front, piling our arms the whole length of it.
The eight Breton companies occupied two intersecting streets
of the camp, and the company of the Navarre officers, my former messmates, took up their positions below us.

Eventually the rumour spread that at last we were going to
see some action; the Prince of Waldeck was to try a frontal
assault while we were to cross the river and create a diversion
by a feint attack on the place from the direction of France.

Five Breton companies, including mine, the company of the
Picardy and Navarre officers, and the regiment of volunteers,
made up of young Lorraine peasants and deserters from various regiments, were ordered up for duty. We were to be
supported by the Royal-Allemand, the squadrons of musketeers, and the different corps of dragoons which were covering
our left flank: my brother was in this cavalry with the Baron de
Montboissier, who had married a daughter of M. de Malesherbes, Mme de Rosanbo's sister and therefore my sister-in-law's
aunt. We escorted three companies of Austrian artillery with
heavy guns and a battery of three mortars.

We started at six o'clock in the evening; at ten we crossed

the Moselle above Thionville on a copper pontoon-bridge. Dawn found us drawn up in order of battle on the left bank, with the heavy cavalry disposed in echelon on both flanks, and the light cavalry in front. At our second movement, we formed up in column and set off.

About nine o'clock we heard a volley fired on our left. A carabineer officer rode up at full speed to tell us that a detachment of Kellermann's army was about to join issue with us, and that fighting had already begun between the sharpshooters. The officer's horse had been hit by a bullet on the forehead; it kept rearing up, with foam streaming from its mouth and blood from its nostrils; the carabineer, sitting sword in hand on this wounded horse, was a splendid sight. The corps which had come from Metz was manoeuvring to take us in the flank; they had some field-guns whose fire fell among our regiment of volunteers. I heard the exclamations of a few recruits struck by cannon-balls; these last cries of youths snatched from life filled me with a feeling of profound pity: I thought of the poor mothers.

The drums beat the charge, and we rushed headlong at the enemy. We came so close that the smoke did not prevent us from seeing that terrible expression assumed by a man who is prepared to shed your blood. The patriots had not yet acquired the assurance that comes from lengthy experience of fighting and victory; their movements were feeble and fumbling; fifty grenadiers of the Old Guard would have sliced straight through a heterogeneous mass of undisciplined nobles of all ages; ten to twelve hundred infantrymen were shaken by a few shots from the Austrian heavy artillery; they turned tail; our cavalry pursued them for five miles or so.

A deaf-and-dumb German girl, called Libbe or Libba, had become attached to my cousin Armand and had followed him. I found her sitting on the grass, which was staining her dress with blood: her elbows were propped on her upturned knees; one hand, passed through her tangled yellow hair, supported her head. She was weeping as she looked at three or four dead men, new deaf-mutes, lying around her. She had not heard the claps of the thunderbolts of which she saw the effects; she could not hear the sighs which escaped her lips when she looked at Armand; she had never heard the voice of the man she loved, and she would not hear the first cry of the child which she bore in her womb; if the grave contained only silence, she would not know that she had been laid to rest in it.

After a fairly long halt, we resumed our march and arrived at nightfall under the walls of Thionville.

The drums were silent; orders were given in a whisper. In order to repulse any attempted sortie, the cavalry stole along the roads and hedges to the gate which we were to cannonade. The Austrian artillery, protected by our infantry, took up a position fifty yards from the outworks, behind a hurriedly constructed epaulement of gabions. At one o'clock in the morning of 6 September, a rocket sent up from the Prince of Waldeck's camp on the other side of the town gave the signal for action. The Prince opened up a brisk fire, to which the town made a vigorous reply. We started firing at the same time.

The besieged garrison, not thinking that we might have troops on this side and failing to foresee this assault, had left the southern ramparts unprotected; they soon made good the omission: a couple of batteries were mounted which penetrated our epaulements and put two of our guns out of action. The sky was on fire; we were enveloped in clouds of smoke. I behaved like a little Alexander: worn out with fatigue, I fell sound asleep, practically under the wheels of the gun-carriage where I was mounting guard. A shell, bursting six inches from the ground, sent a splinter into my right thigh. The shock awoke me, but I felt no pain and saw only from my blood that I was wounded. I bound up my thigh with my handkerchief. In the engagement on the plain, two bullets had struck my haversack during a wheeling movement. Atala, like a devoted daughter, placed herself between her father and the enemy's lead; she still had to withstand the fire of the Abbé Morellet.*

At four o'clock in the morning, the Prince of Waldeck ceased fire: we thought the town had surrendered, but the gates did

---

* The Abbé Morellet, of the Académie Française, was one of the fiercest critics of *Atala*.

not open, and we had to think about falling back. We retired to our positions after an exhausting march lasting three days.

The Prince of Waldeck had gone right up to the edge of the ditches, which he had tried to cross, hoping to bring about a surrender by means of the simultaneous attack on two fronts: divisions were still supposed to exist in the town, and we flattered ourselves with the hope that the Royalist party would bring the keys to the Princes. The Austrians, having fired in barbette, lost a considerable number of men; the Prince of Waldeck had an arm shot off. While a few drops of blood were being shed under the walls of Thionville, blood was flowing in torrents in the prisons of Paris: my wife and sisters were in greater danger than I.

We raised the siege of Thionville and set out for Verdun, which had surrendered to the Allies on 2 September. Longwy, the birthplace of François de Mercy, had fallen on 23 August. Everywhere, wreaths and festoons of flowers bore witness to the passage of Frederick William.

On 16 October, at the camp near Longwy, the captain of my company, M. de Gouyon-Miniac, handed me a perfectly honourable certificate of leave. At Arlon, we saw a file of horses and wagons on the highroad; the horses, some standing, others kneeling, others with their noses resting on the ground, were all dead, and their carcasses had gone stiff between the shafts: they might have been shades from a battlefield bivouacking on the banks of the Styx. My old classmate Ferron de la Sigonière asked me what I was planning to do, and I answered:

'If I can get as far as Ostend, I shall take a ship for Jersey where I shall find my uncle Bedée; from there I shall be able to join the Royalists in Brittany.'

The fever was sapping my strength; it was only with difficulty that I could support myself on my swollen thigh. I felt a new ailment taking hold of me. After twenty-four hours of vomiting, my face and body were covered with an eruption: confluent smallpox declared itself; it appeared and disappeared according as the temperature of the air varied. In this condition I set out on foot to make a journey of five hundred miles, rich to the extent of eighteen livres Tournois; all this for the greater glory of the monarchy.

I made my way by easy stages along the canals to Ostend; there I found some Bretons, my comrades-in-arms. We chartered a decked boat and set off down the Channel. We slept in the hold, on the shingle that served as ballast. My physical resources were finally exhausted. I could no longer speak; the swell of a rough sea brought me to the point of collapse. I could only just swallow a few drops of lemon and water, and when the weather forced us to put into Guernsey, everyone thought I was going to breathe my last; an emigrant priest read me the prayers for the dying. The captain, not wanting me to die on board his ship, ordered me to be put on the quay; they sat me down in the sun, with my back against a wall and my head turned towards the open sea, looking at that island of Alderney where, eight months before, I had faced death in a different form.

It would appear that I was fated to arouse pity. The wife of an English pilot happened to pass by; she was moved and called her husband, who, with the help of two or three sailors, carried me, the friend of the waves, into a fisherman's house; there they laid me on a comfortable bed, between wonderfully white sheets. The young woman took every possible care of the stranger: I owe her my life. The next day I was taken on board again. My hostess almost wept as she took leave of her patient: women have a heavenly instinct for misfortune. My lovely, fair-haired guardian, who looked like a figure in an old English print, pressed my swollen, burning hands between her cool, long hands; I was ashamed to touch something so beautiful with something so ugly.

We set sail and eventually reached the westernmost point of Jersey. One of my companions, M. du Tilleul, went to St Helier to see my uncle. M. de Bedée sent a carriage to fetch me the next morning. We drove right across the island: though I felt as if I were dying, I was charmed with its groves; but I talked nothing but nonsense about them, having fallen into delirium.

I lay four months between life and death. My uncle, his wife, his son, and his three daughters took it in turns to watch by my

bedside. I occupied an apartment in one of the houses which
they were beginning to build along the port: the windows of
my bedroom came down as far as the floor, and I was able to
see the sea from my bed. The doctor, M. Delattre, had forbidden the family to talk to me of serious matters, and especially
of politics. Towards the end of January 1793, seeing my uncle
come into my room in deep mourning, I trembled, for I thought
we had lost a member of our own family: he informed me of
the death of Louis XVI. I was not surprised: I had foreseen it.
I asked for news of my relatives: my sisters and my wife had
returned to Brittany after the September Massacres; they had
had considerable difficulty in leaving Paris. My brother, who
had gone back to France, was living at Malesherbes.

I began to get up and about; the smallpox had gone, but my
chest hurt and I was left with a weakness which remained for a
long time.

M. de Bouillon was the protector of the French refugees in Jersey: he dissuaded me from my plan to cross over to Brittany,
unfit as I was to endure a life of caves and forests; he advised
me to go to England, and there to look for an opportunity to
enter the regular service. My uncle, who was very ill provided
with money, began to feel the pinch with his large family; he
had found himself obliged to send his son to London to feed
himself on poverty and hope. Not wishing to be a burden to M.
de Bedée, I decided to relieve him of my presence.

Thirty louis which a Saint-Malo smuggler brought me made
it possible for me to put my plan into execution, and I booked
a berth on the packet for Southampton. I was deeply moved
when the time came to leave my uncle: he had looked after me
with a father's affection; with him were associated the few
happy moments of my childhood; he knew everything I loved;
I found in his features a certain resemblance to my mother. I
had left that excellent mother, and I was never to see her again;
I had left my sister Julie and my brother, and I was doomed to
meet them no more; I was leaving my uncle, and his jovial
countenance was never again to gladden my eyes. A few months
had been sufficient to bring about all these losses, for the death

of our friends is not to be reckoned from the moment when they die, but from that when we cease to live with them.

The packet on which I embarked was crowded with emigrant families. On board I made the acquaintance of M. Hingant, a former colleague of my brother's in the High Court of Brittany, a man of taste and intelligence of whom I shall have a great deal to say. A naval officer was playing chess in the captain's cabin; he did not remember my face, I had changed so much; but I recognized Gesril. We had not met since Brest; we were destined to part at Southampton. I told him of my travels, he told me of his. This young man, born near me among the waves, embraced his first friend for the last time in the midst of the waves which were soon to witness his glorious death.

I have already given the certificate of my landing from Jersey at Southampton at the beginning of the seventh chapter of these *Memoirs*. Here I am, then, after my travels in the forests of America and the camps of Germany, arriving as a poor emigrant, in 1793, in that land where I am writing all this in 1822, and where I am now a splendid ambassador.

TEN

Exile in England

Hingant, whom I had met on the Jersey packet, had become a close friend of mine. He was interested in literary matters, he was well informed, and he wrote novels in secret from which he read extracts to me. He was in lodgings not far from Baylie, at the end of a street leading into Holborn. Every morning at ten o'clock I had breakfast with him; we talked about politics and above all about my work. I told him how much I had built of my nocturnal edifice, the *Essai*; then I returned to my day-time occupation, translating. We met for dinner, at a shilling a head, in a public-house; afterwards we made for the fields. Often too we would go for walks alone, for both of us were fond of musing.

I would then wend my way towards Kensington or Westminster. Kensington appealed to me; I used to wander about the unfrequented part, while a splendid multitude filled the part adjacent to Hyde Park. The contrast between my poverty and their wealth, between my isolation and that crowd of people, amused me. I watched the young Englishmen passing by in the distance with that sense of embarrassed desire with which my sylph used to inspire me when, after decking her with all my extravagances, I scarcely dared raise my eyes to look at my handiwork. Death, which I thought I was approaching, added a certain mystery to this vision of a world from which I had almost departed. Did anyone's eyes rest on the foreigner seated at the foot of a fir-tree? Did some beautiful woman divine the unseen presence of René?

At Westminster I had a different pastime: in that maze of tombs I thought of mine ready to open to receive me. The bust of an insignificant person such as myself would never find a place among these illustrious effigies. Then I came to the tombs of the monarchs: Cromwell was no longer there and Charles I was not there at all. The ashes of a traitor, Robert d'Artois, lay beneath the flagstones which I trod with my loyal steps. The fate of Charles I had just been extended to Louis XVI; every day the steel reaped its harvest in France, and the graves of my relatives were already dug.

The singing of the choir and the conversation of the visitors interrupted my reflections. I could not come here often, for I was obliged to give the guardians of those who lived no more the shilling which was necessary for me to go on living. But then I would circle round the Abbey with the rooks, or stop to gaze at the towers, twins of unequal height, which the setting sun lit up with a blood-red glow against the black backdrop of the City's smoke.

One day, however, it so happened that, wishing to contemplate the interior of the basilica in the twilight, I became lost in admiration of its bold, capricious architecture. Dominated by the sentiment of the *sombre vastity of Christian churches* (Montaigne), I wandered slowly about and was overtaken by the night: the doors were closed. I tried to find a way out; I called for the usher and beat on the doors; all this noise, spread out in the silence, was lost; I had to resign myself to sleeping among the dead.

I amused Hingant with the story of my adventure, and we decided to have ourselves locked in at Westminster; but our poverty summoned us to the dead in a less poetic manner.

My funds were running out: Baylie and Deboffe had been bold enough, in return for a written promise of reimbursement in the event of no sale, to start printing the *Essai*; there their generosity ended, as was only natural; indeed I was surprised at their courage. The translations stopped coming in; Peltier, a man of pleasure, grew tired of for ever helping me. He would willingly have given me what he had, if he had not preferred to squander it; but hunting here and there for work and being helpful and patient were beyond him. Hingant too saw his treasure diminishing; the two of us were left with only sixty francs. We cut down our rations, as on a ship when the journey is prolonged. Instead of a shilling a head, we spent only six-pence on our dinner. With our morning tea, we reduced our bread by half and suppressed the butter altogether. This abstin-ence preyed on my friend's nerves. He became absentminded; he would prick up his ears and look as if he were listening to someone; in reply, he would either burst out laughing or start crying. Hingant believed in magnetism, and had clouded his brain with Swedenborg's rubbish. He told me every morning that he had been disturbed by noises during the night; if I sug-gested that he was imagining things he lost his temper. The anxiety which he caused me prevented me from feeling my own sufferings.

These were considerable for all that: our strict diet, com-bined with the work I was doing, inflamed my diseased chest; I began to have difficulty in walking and yet I spent my days and part of my nights out of doors, so as not to reveal my poverty. When we came to our last shilling, my friend and I agreed to keep it in order to make a pretence of breakfasting. We decided that we should buy a penny roll; that we should have some hot water and the teapot brought up as usual; that we should not put in any tea or eat the bread; but that we should drink the hot water with a few grains of sugar left at the bottom of the bowl.

Five days went by in this fashion. I was consumed with hun-ger; I burnt with fever; sleep had deserted me; I sucked pieces of linen which I had soaked in water; I chewed grass and paper. When I passed a baker's shop, the torment I endured was unspeakable. One bitter winter's night, I stood for two hours outside a shop which sold dried fruit and smoked meat, devour-ing everything I could see with my eyes: I could have eaten not only the foodstuffs but the boxes and baskets in which they were packed.

On the morning of the fifth day, fainting from inanition, I dragged myself to Hingant's room; I knocked at the door: it was locked. I called out; Hingant did not answer for some time; at last he got up and opened the door. He was laughing in an odd manner; his frock-coat was buttoned up; he sat down at the tea-table.

'Our breakfast is coming,' he said in a strange voice.

I thought I could see some blood on his shirt; I ripped open his coat; he had stabbed himself with a penknife in the left breast, leaving a wound two inches deep. I shouted for help. The maidservant went to fetch a surgeon. The wound was dangerous.

This new misfortune forced me to take action. Hingant, who was a counsellor at the High Court of Brittany, had refused to accept the salary which the British Government granted to French magistrates, just as I had declined the shilling a day doled out to all emigrants: I wrote to M. de Barentin and explained my friend's position to him. Hingant's relatives hurried to his aid and took him into the country. At that very moment my uncle Bedée sent me forty crowns, a touching gift from my persecuted family. I seemed to see all the gold of Peru before me: the mite of the prisoners of France supported the Frenchman in exile.

My destitution had impeded my work. As I had stopped delivering copy, printing had been suspended. Deprived of Hingant's company, I decided not to keep on my room at Baylie's at a guinea a month; I paid the quarter that was due and left. On a lower level than the needy emigrants who had been my first protectors in London were others even more poverty-stricken. There are degrees among the poor as among the rich; one can go from the man who keeps himself warm in winter by sleeping with his dog down to the man who shivers in his tattered rags. My friends found me a room better suited to my diminishing fortune (one is not always at the height of prosperity); they installed me in the vicinity of Marylebone Street, in a garret whose dormer-window overlooked a cemetery: every night the watchman's rattle told me that body-snatchers had been at work.

Those who are reading this part of my *Memoirs* have not noticed that I have interrupted them twice: once to offer a banquet to the Duke of York, the King of England's brother, and the second time to hold a reception on the anniversary of the King of France's return to Paris, on 8 July. This reception cost me forty thousand francs. Peers and peeresses of the British Empire, ambassadors, and distinguished foreigners crowded my splendidly decorated rooms. My tables shone with the glitter of London crystal and the gold of Sèvres porcelain. There was an abundance of the most delicate dishes, the finest wines, the loveliest flowers. Portland Place was filled with splendid carriages. Collinet and Almack's orchestra charmed the fashionable melancholy of the dandies and the dreamy beauty of the pensively dancing ladies. The Opposition and the Ministerial majority had called a truce, Lady Canning chatting with Lord Londonderry, Lady Jersey with the Duke of Wellington. Monsieur, who complimented me this year on my lavish hospitality of 1822, did not know, in 1793, that there existed not far from him a future Minister who, pending the arrival of fame and honours, fasted in a garret beside a cemetery as penance for his loyalty. I congratulate myself today on having been nearly shipwrecked, caught a glimpse of war, and shared the sufferings of the humblest classes of society, just as I am thankful for having met injustice and calumny in times of prosperity. I have profited from these lessons: life, without the misfortunes which give it gravity, is a child's bauble.

I was the man with forty crowns; but since equality of fortune had not yet been established and food had not grown any cheaper, there was nothing to offset the emptying of my purse. I could not count on any further help from my family, which was exposed in Brittany to the double scourge of the Chouan insurrection and the Terror. I saw nothing before me but the workhouse or the Thames.

But then the resourceful Peltier hunted me out, or rather brought me down from my eyrie. He had read in a Yarmouth newspaper that a society of antiquarians was preparing a history of the county of Suffolk, and that they were looking for a Frenchman capable of deciphering some twelfth-century French manuscripts in the Camden collection. The parson of Beccles was in charge of the whole enterprise, and it was a question of approaching him.

'This is just what you need,' Peltier told me. 'Go and decipher their old papers for them; you can go on sending the manuscript of the *Essai* to Baylie; I'll make the old rogue start printing again; and you'll come back to London with two hundred guineas, your book finished, and ready for anything!'

Upon reflection, the advice of my fellow countryman, a real character out of the books by my other fellow countryman Le Sage, did not seem so bad to me. After three days spent making inquiries and fitting myself out at Peltier's tailor, I set out for Beccles with some money lent me by Deboffe on the understanding that I was going to resume work on the *Essai*. I changed my name, which no Englishman was able to pronounce, to that of Combourg, which had been borne by my brother, and which reminded me of the sorrows and pleasures of my early youth. I took a room at the inn, and handed the local minister a letter from Deboffe, who was highly thought of in the English book world. The letter recommended me as a scholar of the first order. I was very well received, saw all the gentlemen of the district, and met two officers of our Royal Navy who gave French lessons in the neighbourhood.

I regained my strength; the excursions I made on horseback restored my health to some extent. England, viewed thus in detail, was sad but charming; wherever I went, I saw the same things under the same aspect. M. de Combourg was invited to every party. I had my studies to thank for the first alleviation of my lot. Cicero was right to recommend reading as an antidote to the sorrows of existence. The women were delighted to meet a Frenchman to talk French with.

The misfortunes of my family, which I learnt about from the newspapers, and which made me known by my real name (for I was unable to conceal my grief), increased the interest which people took in me. The newspapers announced the death of M. de Malesherbes; of his daughter, Mme la Présidente de Rosanbo; of his granddaughter, Mme la Comtesse de Chateaubriand; and of his grandson-in-law, the Comte de Chateaubriand, my brother, all executed together, on the same day, at the same hour, on the same scaffold.* M. de Malesherbes

---

* On 22 April 1794, at 5 p.m., in the Place de la Révolution.

was an object of admiration and veneration among the English; my family connexion with the defender of Louis XVI added to the kindness of my hosts.

My uncle Bedée informed me of the persecution suffered by the rest of my relatives. My aged and incomparable mother had been flung into a cart with other victims and taken from the depths of Brittany to the gaols of Paris, in order to share the fate of the son she had loved so dearly. My wife and my sister Lucile were awaiting sentence in the dungeons at Rennes; there had been talk of imprisoning them in the Château of Combourg, which had become a state fortress: their innocence was accused of the crime of my emigration. What were our sorrows on foreign soil compared with those of the French who had remained at home? And yet how unhappy we were, in the midst of the sufferings of exile, to know that our very exile was being made the pretext for the persecution of our loved ones!

Two years ago my sister-in-law's wedding ring was picked up in the gutter of the Rue Cassette, and brought to me. It was broken; the two hoops of the ring had come apart and hung together like the links of a chain; the names engraved inside were clearly legible. How had the ring come to be found there? Where and when had it been lost? Had the victim, imprisoned in the Luxembourg, passed along the Rue Cassette on her way to execution? Had she dropped the ring from the tumbril? Had the ring been torn from her finger after the execution? I was deeply moved at the sight of this symbol, which, by its broken condition and its inscription, reminded me of cruel events. Some mysterious fate was attached to this ring, which my sister-in-law seemed to have sent me from among the dead, in memory of herself and my brother. I have given it to her son:* may it not bring him bad luck!

The 9th of Thermidor saved my mother's life, but she was forgotten in the Conciergerie. The Conventional commissary found her.

'What are you doing here, citizeness?' he asked her. 'Who are you, and why do you stay here?'

---

* The Comte Louis de Chateaubriand (1790–1873).

My mother replied that, having lost her son, she took no interest in what was happening in the outside world, and it was a matter of indifference to her whether she died in prison or elsewhere.

'But perhaps you have some other children?' said the commissary.

My mother mentioned my wife and sisters who were incarcerated at Rennes. An order was sent to set them free, and my mother was compelled to leave the prison.

Ten miles from Beccles, in a little town called Bungay, there lived an English clergyman, the Rev. Mr Ives, a great Hellenist and mathematician. He had a wife who was still young, of charming appearance, mind, and manners, and an only daughter of fifteen. Introduced to this household, I was better received there than anywhere else. We drank in the old English fashion, and stayed at table for two hours after the ladies had withdrawn. Mr Ives, who had been to America, liked telling of his travels, hearing the story of my own, and talking about Newton and Homer. His daughter, who had studied intensively in order to please her father, was an excellent musician and sang as Mme Pasta sings today. She reappeared at tea-time and charmed away the old parson's infectious drowsiness. Leaning on the piano, I listened to Miss Ives in silence.

When the music was over, the young lady questioned me about France and about literature, asking me to draw up a plan of study for her; she particularly wanted to know the Italian authors, and begged me to give her some notes on the *Divina Commedia* and the *Gerusalemme*. Little by little I began to experience the timid charm of an affection born in the soul: I had decked out the Floridans, but I would not have dared to pick up Miss Ives's glove; I felt embarrassed when I tried to translate a passage from Tasso. I was more at ease with that chaster and more masculine genius, Dante.

Charlotte Ives's age and mine tallied. Into relationships formed in the midst of one's career there enters a certain melancholy; when two people do not meet at the very outset, the memories of the beloved are not mingled with that part of one's life when one breathed without knowing her: those days, which belong to other company, are painful to the memory and as it were distinct from one's existence. When there is a disproportion of age, the drawbacks increase; the older of the two began life before the younger was born; the younger is destined to remain alone in his turn: one has walked in a solitude this side of a cradle, while the other will cross a solitude that side of a tomb; the past was a desert for the first, and the future will be a desert for the second. It is difficult to be in love in all the circumstances that produce happiness: youth, beauty, opportunity, taste, character, grace, and age.

Having had a fall from my horse, I stayed for some time at Mr Ives's house. It was winter; the dreams of my life began to flee before reality. Miss Ives became more reserved; she stopped bringing me flowers; she would not sing for me any more.

If I had been told that I should pass the rest of my life in obscurity with this retiring family, I should have died of joy: love needs only permanence to be at once an Eden before the Fall and a Hosanna without end. See to it that beauty lasts, that youth endures, that the heart never wearies, and you reproduce Heaven. Love is so surely the supreme happiness that it is haunted by the illusion of perpetuity; it pronounces only irrevocable vows; in the absence of joy, it tries to make sorrow eternal; a fallen angel, it still speaks the language it spoke in the incorruptible abode; its hope is that it may never die; in its twofold nature and its twofold illusion on this earth it endeavours to perpetuate itself by immortal thought and inexhaustible generation.

I looked forward with dismay to the time when I should be obliged to go. On the eve of the day fixed for my departure, dinner was a gloomy meal. To my great surprise, Mr Ives withdrew at dessert, taking his daughter with him, and I remained alone with Mrs Ives: she was in a state of considerable embarrassment. I thought she was going to reproach me with an inclination which she might have discovered but which I had never mentioned. She looked at me, lowered her eyes, and blushed; bewitching as she was in her confusion, there was no sort of devotion that she might not have claimed for herself. At last, overcoming with an effort the reserve which had prevented her from speaking:

'Sir,' she said in English, 'you have noticed my confusion: I do not know if Charlotte pleases you, but it is impossible to deceive a mother's eyes: my daughter has undoubtedly conceived an attachment for you. Mr Ives and I have discussed the matter together: you suit us in every respect; we believe that you will make our daughter happy. You no longer have a country of your own; you have lost your relatives; your property has been sold; who then could call you back to France? Until you inherit our possesions, you will live with us.'

Of all the sorrows I had endured, this was the greatest and most painful. I threw myself at Mrs Ives's feet; I covered her hands with my kisses and my tears. She thought I was weeping with happiness, and she began to sob for joy. She stretched out her arm to pull the bell-rope; she called her husband and daughter.

'Stop!' I cried. 'I am a married man!'

She fell back in a faint.

I went out and, without going back to my room, left the house on foot. On arriving at Beccles I took the mail-coach for London, after writing a letter to Mrs Ives of which I regret that I did not keep a copy.

I have retained the sweetest, tenderest, and most grateful recollection of that event. Mr Ives's family was the only one which took a kindly interest in me and welcomed me with real affection. Poor, unknown, outlawed, and neither handsome nor attractive, I was offered an assured future, a country, a charming wife to draw me out of my shell, a mother of almost equal beauty to take the place of my aged mother, and a father of considerable learning who loved and cultivated literature to replace the father of whom Heaven had bereaved me; what did I possess to set against all that? No illusion could possibly enter into the choice they had made of me; I could have no doubt that I was loved. Since that time, I have met with only one attachment sufficiently lofty to inspire me with the same confidence. As for the interest of which I may subsequently have been the object, I have never been able to make out whether external causes, the noise of fame, the prestige of officialdom, and the glamour of high literary or political positions were not the covering which attracted the eager attention paid to me.

I returned to London, but found no peace: I had fled from my fate like a miscreant from his crime. How painful it must have been to a family so worthy of my homage, respect, and gratitude to suffer a sort of rejection by the stranger whom they had made welcome, and to whom they had offered a new home with a simplicity, an absence of suspicion, a lack of precaution almost patriarchal in character! I imagined Charlotte's grief and the just reproaches which they were entitled and bound to heap upon me: for, after all, I had taken pleasure in yielding to an inclination of which I knew the insuperable illegitimacy. Had I, then, made a vain attempt at seduction, without fully realizing the heinousness of my behaviour? But whether I stopped, as I did, in order to retain my self-respect, or ignored all obstacles in order to satisfy an inclination already stigmatized by my conduct, I could only have plunged the object of that seduction into sorrow or regret.

From these bitter reflections, I allowed my mind to turn to other thoughts not less filled with bitterness: I cursed my marriage, which, contracted in accordance with the false perceptions of a mind that had been very sick at the time, had thrown me off my course and was now robbing me of happiness. It did not occur to me that, on account of the sickly temperament to which I was subject and the romantic notions of freedom which I cherished, marriage with Miss Ives would have been just as painful to me as a more independent union.

One thing within me remained pure and charming, though profoundly sad: the image of Charlotte; and that image finally prevailed over my feelings of rebellion against my fate. I was tempted a hundred times to return to Bungay, not to appear before the troubled family, but to hide by the roadside to see Charlotte pass by, to follow her to the church where we had the same God, if not the same altar, in common, to offer that woman, through the medium of Heaven, the inexpressible ardour of my vows, and to pronounce, at least in thought, the prayer from the nuptial blessing which I might have heard from a clergyman's lips in that church.

The places where I had wandered, the times in question, and the words which I had exchanged with Charlotte, were engraved in my memory: I saw the smile of the wife who had been destined for me; I respectfully touched her black tresses; I pressed her lovely arms against my breast, like a chain of lilies which I might have worn round my neck. No sooner was I in some secluded spot than Charlotte, with her white hands, came to sit beside me. I divined her presence, as at night one breathes the perfume of flowers one cannot see.

Deprived as I was of Hingant's company, my walks, more solitary than ever, left me free to take with me the image of Charlotte. There is not a common, a road, or a church within thirty miles of London that I have not visited. The most deserted places, a field of nettles, a ditch planted with thistles, anything that was neglected by men, became favourite spots for me, and in those spots Byron already breathed. Resting my head on my hand, I gazed at the despised places; when their painful impression affected me too deeply, the memory of Charlotte came to delight me: at such moments I was like the pilgrim who, reaching a solitude within view of the rocks of Mount Sinai, heard a nightingale singing.

In London, people were surprised at my behaviour. I never looked at anyone, I never replied to anyone, I did not know what was said to me: my old companions began to think that I had gone mad.

What happened at Bungay after my departure? What became of that family to which I had brought joy and grief?

You will not have forgotten that I am at present Ambassador to the Court of George IV, and that I am writing in London, in 1822, of what happened to me in London in 1795.

Some official business obliged me, a week ago, to interrupt the narrative which I am resuming today. During this interval, my valet came and told me one morning, between twelve and one o'clock, that a carriage had stopped at my door and that an English lady was asking to see me. As I have made it a rule, in my public position, never to turn anyone away, I ordered the lady to be shown up.

I was in my study when Lady Sutton* was announced. I saw
a lady in mourning enter the room, accompanied by two handsome boys, also in mourning: one might have been sixteen, the
other fourteen years old. I went towards the stranger; she was
so moved that she could scarcely walk. She said to me in a fal-
tering voice:

'My lord, do you remember me?'

Yes, I remembered Miss Ives! The years which had passed
over her head had left only their springtime behind. I took her
by the hand, made her sit down, and sat by her side. I could not
speak; my eyes were full of tears; I gazed at her in silence through
those tears; I could tell that I had loved her deeply from what I
was experiencing. Finally I was able to say in my turn:

'And you, madam, do you remember me?'

She raised her eyes, which she had kept lowered till then,
and for sole reply gave me a smiling and melancholy glance like
a long remembrance. Her hand was still between mine. Charlotte said to me:

'I am in mourning for my mother; my father died some years
ago. These are my children.'

With these words, she drew away her hand and sank back
into her armchair, covering her eyes with her handkerchief.
Soon she went on:

'My lord, I am now speaking to you in the language which I
used to practise with you at Bungay. I feel ashamed: excuse me.
My children are the sons of Admiral Sutton, whom I married
three years after your departure from England. But I am not
sufficiently self-possessed today to enter into details. Permit me
to come again.'

I asked her for her address, and gave her my arm to escort
her to her carriage. She trembled, and I pressed her hand against
my heart.

I called on Lady Sutton the following day; I found her alone.
Then there began between us a series of those *Do you remember?* questions which bring back a whole lifetime. At each *Do
you remember?* we looked at one another, trying to discover in

* Misspelt 'Sulton' by Chateaubriand.

each other's faces those traces of time which measure so cruelly the distance from the starting-point and the length of the road that has been travelled. I said to Charlotte:

'How did your mother tell you . . . ?'

Charlotte blushed, and hastily interrupted me:

'I have come to London to ask if you would do something to help Admiral Sutton's children. The elder would like to go to Bombay. Mr Canning, who has been appointed Governor-General of India, is your friend; he might be willing to take my son with him. I should be most grateful to you, and I should like to owe to you the happiness of my first child.'

She laid a stress on these last words.

'Ah, madam,' I replied, 'what memories you bring back to me! What a change of destinies! You who received a poor exile at your father's hospitable board: you who did not scorn his sufferings; you who perhaps thought of raising him to a glorious and unhoped-for rank: it is you who now ask for his support in your own country! I will see Mr Canning; your son, however much it hurts me to give him that name, your son shall go to India, if it only depends on me. But tell me, madam, how does my new position affect you? In what way do you regard me at present? That title of *my lord* which you use seems very harsh to me.'

Charlotte replied:

'I don't think you have changed, or even aged. When I spoke about you to my parents in your absence, I always gave you the title of *my lord*; it seemed to me that it was yours by right; were you not the same to me as a husband, *my lord and master*?'

That lovely woman had something of Milton's Eve about her as she uttered these words: she was not born of another woman's womb; her beauty bore the imprint of the divine hand that had moulded it.

I hurried to see Mr Canning and Lord Londonderry; they made as many difficulties about a minor position as would have been made in France, but they promised to do what they could, as people promise at Court. I gave Lady Sutton an account of the steps I had taken. I saw her on three further occasions: at my fourth visit, she told me she was returning to

Bungay. This last meeting was a sad one. Charlotte talked to me once more of the past, of our secret life, of our readings, of our walks, of music, the flowers of the past, the hopes of bygone days.

'When I knew you,' she said, 'no one mentioned your name; now, who has not heard it? Do you know that I have a work and several letters in your handwriting? Here they are.' And she handed me a packet. 'Do not be offended if I choose to keep nothing of yours.' She began to cry. 'Farewell, farewell,' she said. 'Think of my son. I shall never see you again, for you will not come to see me at Bungay.'

'I will,' I cried. 'I shall come to bring you your son's commission.'

She shook her head unbelievingly, and withdrew.

On returning to the Embassy, I locked myself in my room and opened the packet. It contained nothing but a few unimportant notes I had written and a plan of study, with remarks on the English and Italian poets. I had hoped to find a letter from Charlotte; there was none there; but in the margins of the manuscript I saw some notes in English, French, and Latin: the faded ink and the youthful handwriting showed that it was a long time since they had been entered into those margins.

That is the story of my acquaintanceship with Miss Ives. As I finish telling it, it seems to me as if I were losing Charlotte a second time in the same island where I had lost her the first.

A letter from Julie, which I received soon after one from Fontanes, confirmed my feeling of growing isolation: Fontanes urged me to *work and become famous*; my sister begged me to *give up writing*; one proposed glory to me, the other oblivion. You have seen from my account of Mme de Farcy's life that she was given to such ideas: she had grown to hate literature because she regarded it as one of the temptations of her life.

Saint-Servan, 1 July 1798

My dear, we have just lost the best of mothers: it grieves me to inform you of this sad blow. When you cease to be the object of our solicitude, we shall have ceased to live. If you knew how many tears your errors had caused our venerable mother to shed;

how deplorable they appear to all who think and who profess not
only piety but reason; if you knew this, perhaps it would help to
open your eyes, to induce you to give up writing; and if Heaven,
moved by our prayers, permitted us to meet again, you would
find among us all the happiness one may enjoy on earth; you
would give us that happiness, for there is none for us as long
as you are not with us and we have reason to be anxious about
your fate.

Ah, why did I not follow my sister's advice? Why did I go on
writing? If my age had gone without my writings, would anything have been changed in the events and spirit of that age?

So I had lost my mother; so I had brought her distress in the
last hours of her life! While she was breathing her last far from
the last of her sons, and praying for him as she died, what was
I doing in London? Perhaps I was strolling in the cool of the
morning while the sweat of death was covering my mother's
forehead without having my hand there to wipe it away!

The filial affection which I retained for Mme de Chateaubri-
and went very deep. My childhood and youth were intimately
linked with the memory of my mother; everything that I knew
came from her. The idea that I had poisoned the last days of the
woman who bore me in her womb filled me with despair: I
flung copies of the *Essai* into the fire with horror, as the instrument of my crime; if it had been possible for me to destroy the
entire work, I should have done so without hesitation. I did not
recover from my distress until the thought occurred to me of
expiating my first work by means of a religious work: this was
the origin of *Le Génie du christianisme*.

'My mother,' I wrote in the first preface to that work, 'after
being flung, at the age of seventy-two, into dungeons where she
saw some of her children die, finally expired on a pallet to
which her misfortunes had reduced her. The recollection of my
errors cast a great bitterness over her last days; as she lay dying,
she instructed one of my sisters to recall me to the religion in
which I was brought up. My sister acquainted me with my
mother's last wish. When the letter reached me across the sea,
my sister herself was no more; she too had died from the effects

of her imprisonment. Those two voices from the tomb, that death which acted as Death's interpreter, made a powerful impression on me. I became a Christian. I did not yield, I must admit, to great supernatural enlightenment; my conviction came from the heart; I wept and I believed.'

I exaggerated my guilt: the *Essai* was not an impious book, but a book of doubt and sorrow. Through the darkness of that book there glides a ray of the Christian light that shone upon my cradle. No great effort was needed to return from the scepticism of the *Essai* to the certainty of *Le Génie du christianisme*.

When, after receiving the sad news of Mme de Chateaubriand's death, I decided suddenly to change the course of my life, the title of *Le Génie du christianisme*, which I found straight away, filled me with inspiration; I set to work, toiling away with the fervour of a son building a mausoleum to his mother. My materials had long since been collected and rough-hewn by my previous studies. I knew the works of the Fathers of the Church better than they are known in our times; I had studied them in order to dispute them, and having entered upon that road with evil intentions, instead of leaving it as a victor, I left it vanquished.

As to history proper, I had given it special attention when composing the *Essai sur les Révolutions*. The Camden manuscripts which I had recently examined had made me familiar with the manners and institutions of the Middle Ages. Finally, my monstrous manuscript of *Les Natchez*, totalling 2,393 folio pages, contained everything *Le Génie du christianisme* could possibly need in the way of nature descriptions; I could draw heavily on that source, as I had done for the *Essai*.

I wrote the first part of *Le Génie du christianisme*. MM. Dulau, who had become the accredited booksellers of the French emigrant clergy, undertook to publish it. The first sheets of the first volume were printed.

The work thus begun in London in 1799 was completed only in Paris in 1802: see the different prefaces to *Le Génie du christianisme*. A sort of fever consumed me during the whole time of writing; no one will ever know what it is like to carry at the same time in one's brain, in one's blood, and in one's soul, *Atala* and *René*, and to combine with the painful child-birth of those passionate twins the difficulties attending the conception of the other parts of *Le Génie du christianisme*. The memory of Charlotte penetrated and warmed me in my work, and if that were not enough, the first longing for fame inflamed my exalted imagination. This longing came to me from filial affection; I wanted to create a great stir, so that the noise of it might rise till it reached my mother's dwelling-place, and so that the angels might carry her my solemn expiation.

Separated from the Continent by a long war, the English at the end of the last century preserved their national manners and character. There was still only one people, in whose name the sovereign power was wielded by an aristocratic government; only two great classes existed, bound by ties of friendship and common interest: patrons and dependants. That jealous class called the *bourgeoisie* in France, which was beginning to arise in England, was as yet unknown: there was nothing between the rich landowners and the men who plied a trade. Everything had not yet become machinery in the manufacturing professions, folly in the privileged classes. Along the same pavements where one now sees dirty faces and men in overcoats there passed little girls in white cloaks, with straw hats fastened under the chin with a ribbon, and a basket containing fruit or a book on their arm; all kept their eyes lowered, and all blushed when one looked at them. 'Britain', says Shakespeare,* is 'in a great pool, a swan's nest'. Frock-coats without a jacket underneath were so unusual in London in 1793 that a woman who was weeping bitterly over the death of Louis XVI said to me:

'But, my dear sir, is it true that the poor King was dressed in a frock-coat when they cut off his head?'

The 'gentleman farmers' had not yet sold their patrimony in order to come and live in London; in the House of Commons they still formed that independent fraction which, alternating between the Opposition and the Ministry, upheld the ideas of liberty, order, and property. They hunted the fox or shot pheas-

* *Cymbeline*, Act III, Scene 4.

ants in the autumn, ate fat geese at Christmas, shouted 'Hurrah!' for roast beef, grumbled about the present, praised the past, cursed Pitt and the war, which sent up the price of port, and went to bed drunk only to begin the same life all over again the next day. They were convinced that the glory of Great Britain would never fade as long as they sang *God save the King*, maintained the rotten boroughs, kept the game laws in force, and secretly sent hares and partridges to market under the name of 'lions' and 'ostriches'.

The Anglican clergy was learned, hospitable, and generous; it had received the French clergy with true Christian charity. The University of Oxford printed at its own expense and distributed gratis among the curés a New Testament according to the Latin Vulgate, with the imprint: *In usum cleri Gallicani in Anglia exulantis*. As for English high society, I, a poor exile, saw nothing of it but the outside. When there was a reception at Court or at the Princess of Wales's, ladies went by sitting side-ways in sedan-chairs; their great hoop-petticoats protruded through the door of the chair like altar-hangings. They themselves, on those waist-high altars, looked like madonnas or pagodas. Those fine ladies were the daughters whose mothers the Duc de Guiche and the Duc de Lauzun had adored; those daughters are, in 1822, the mothers and grandmothers of the little girls who come to my house to dance in short frocks to the music of Collinet's flute, swift-growing generations of flowers.

I began to turn my eyes towards my native land. A great revolution had taken place. Bonaparte had become First Consul and was restoring order by means of despotism; many exiles were returning; the upper Emigration in particular was losing no time in collecting what was left of its fortune: loyalty was dying at the head, while its heart still beat in the breasts of a few half-naked country gentlemen. Mrs Lindsay had gone; she wrote to MM. de Lamoignon to return; she also invited Mme d'Aguesseau, the sister of MM. de Lamoignon, to cross the Channel. Fontanes wrote to suggest that I should finish the printing of *Le Génie du christianisme* in Paris. Though I had not forgotten my country, I felt no desire to see it again; gods more powerful than the paternal *Lares* held me back; I no longer had any home or possessions in France; my motherland had become for me a bosom of stone, a breast without milk; I should not find my mother there, or my brother, or my sister Julie. Lucile was still alive, but she had married M. de Caud and no longer bore my name; my young 'widow' knew me only through a union of a few months, through misfortune, and through an absence of eight years.

If I had been left to myself, I do not know that I should have had the strength to leave, but I saw my little circle breaking up; Mme d'Aguesseau offered to take me to Paris, and I gave in. The Prussian Minister obtained a passport for me in the name of Lassagne, an inhabitant of Neuchâtel. MM. Dulau stopped the printing of *Le Génie du christianisme*, and gave me the sheets that had been set up. I detached the sketches of *Atala* and *René* from *Les Natchez*; I locked the rest of the manuscript in a trunk which I entrusted to my hosts in London, and I set out for Dover with Mme d'Aguesseau: Mrs Lindsay was waiting for us at Calais.

That was how I left England in 1800; my heart was occupied with other things than it is at the time of writing, in 1822. I brought nothing back from the land of exile but dreams and regrets; today my head is full of scenes of ambition, of politics, of splendours, and of Courts, all so ill-suited to my nature. How many events are heaped up in my present existence! Pass, men, pass; my turn will come. I have unfolded only a third of my days before your eyes; if the sufferings which I have undergone have weighed upon my vernal serenity, now, as I enter upon a more fruitful period of life, the germ of *René* will develop, and bitterness of another kind will be blended with my narrative. What shall I not have to say as I speak of my country; of her revolutions, whose initial stages I have already recounted; of the Empire and the colossus whose fall I witnessed; of the Restoration in which I played so considerable a part, that Restoration which is glorious today in 1822, but which nonetheless I can see only through a kind of fateful mist?

Here I end this book, which brings me to the spring of 1800.

Arriving at the close of my first career, I see opening before me the writer's career; from being a private individual I am about to become a public figure; I am leaving the virginal and silent shelter of solitude to enter the dusty and noisy crossroads of the world; broad day is going to light up my dreaming life, light to penetrate my kingdom of shadows. I cast a melancholy glance at these books which contain my unremembered hours; I seem to be bidding a last farewell to my old home; I am taking leave of the thoughts and dreams of my youth as of sisters and sweethearts whom I am leaving by the family hearth and whom I shall never see again.

We took four hours to cross from Dover to Calais; I slipped into my country under the cover of a foreign name: doubly hidden beneath the obscurity of the Swiss Lassagne and my own, I entered France with the century.

PART TWO

CONSULATE AND EMPIRE
1800–1814

ONE
Madame de Beaumont

The person who occupied the greatest place in my existence on my return from the Emigration was Mme la Comtesse de Beaumont. She lived for part of the year at the Château de Passy, near Villeneuve-sur-Yonne, which M. Joubert inhabited during the summer. Mme de Beaumont returned to Paris and expressed the desire to meet me.

To make a long chain of regrets of my life, Providence decreed that the first person to treat me kindly at the outset of my public career should also be the first to disappear. Mme de Beaumont opens the funeral procession of those women who have passed before me. My most distant memories rest on ashes, and they have gone on falling from coffin to coffin; like the Indian Pandit, I recite the prayers for the dead until the flowers of my rosary have faded.

Mme de Beaumont was the daughter of Armand-Marc de Saint-Hérem, Comte de Montmorin, French Ambassador in Madrid, Commandant in Brittany, member of the Assembly of Notables in 1787, and Minister of Foreign Affairs under Louis XVI, who was very fond of him; he died on the scaffold, where he was followed by several members of his family.

Mme de Beaumont was plain rather than attractive in appearance, and very like the portrait of her by Mme Lebrun. Her face was thin and pale; her eyes were almond-shaped and would perhaps have been too bright if an extraordinary sweetness had not half-extinguished her glances and caused them to shine languidly, as a ray of light is softened by passing through crystal water. Her character had a sort of rigidity and impatience which came from the strength of her feelings and the inward suffering which she experienced. Endowed with a lofty soul and great courage, she was born for the world, from which her spirit had withdrawn out of choice and unhappiness; but when a friendly voice summoned that solitary intelligence, it came forth and spoke to you in words from Heaven. Mme de Beaumont's extreme fragility made her slow of expression, and this slowness was touching; I knew this sorely afflicted woman only at the time of her flight; she was already mortally sick, and I devoted myself to her sufferings. I had taken lodgings in the Rue Saint-Honoré, at the Hôtel d'Étampes, near the Rue Neuve-du-Luxembourg. In this latter street Mme de Beaumont occupied an apartment looking out over the gardens of the Ministry of Justice. I went to see her every evening, with her friends and mine, M. Joubert, M. de Fontanes, M. de Bonald, M. Molé, M. Pasquier, and M. de Chênedollé, men who have made their mark in literature and public life.

The success of *Atala* having induced me to make a fresh start on *Le Génie du christianisme*, two volumes of which were already in print, Mme de Beaumont offered to give me a room in the country, in a house which she had rented at Savigny. I spent six months in this retreat of hers, with M. Joubert and our other friends.

The house stood at the entrance to the village, on the Paris side, near an old highroad known in those parts as the Chemin de Henri IV: there was a vine-covered slope behind, and in front Savigny Park, ending in a wooded screen and crossed by the little River Orge. On the left, the plain of Viry stretched away as far as the springs of Juvisy. There were valleys all around, where we used to go in the evening in search of new walks.

In the morning we breakfasted together; after breakfast I withdrew to start work; Mme de Beaumont had the goodness to copy out the quotations which I marked for her. This noble woman offered me shelter when I had none; without the peace which she gave me, I might never have finished a work which I had been unable to complete during my misfortunes.

I shall always remember certain evenings spent in this refuge of friendship: on returning from our walks, we gathered together beside an ornamental fresh-water pool which had been installed in the middle of a plot of grass in the kitchen-garden. Mme Joubert, Mme de Beaumont, and I sat on a bench; Mme Joubert's son rolled about on the grass at our feet; that child has already disappeared. M. Joubert walked by himself along a gravel path; a couple of watchdogs and a cat played around us, while pigeons cooed on the edge of the roof. What happiness this was for a man newly returned from exile, after spending eight years in utter isolation, except for a few days which had passed all too quickly! It was generally during these evenings that my friends made me talk about my travels: I have never described the wilderness of the New World as well as on these occasions. At night, when the windows of our rustic drawing-room were opened, Mme de Beaumont would point out certain constellations, telling me that I should remember one day that she had taught me to know them: since I have lost her, I have several times stood not far from her grave in Rome, in the middle of the Campagna, and searched the sky for the stars whose names she told me: I have seen them shining above the Sabine Hills; the protracted rays of those stars came down and struck the surface of the Tiber. The spot where I saw them above the woods of Savigny, and the places where I have seen them since, the mobility of my destinies, and the sign that a woman had left for me in the sky to remind me of her: all this broke my heart. By what miracle does man agree to do what he must do on earth, he who is doomed to die?

Soon afterwards there appeared one of those souls in pain which are of a different species from other souls and which, on their way through life, mingle their exceptional unhappiness with the vulgar sufferings of mankind: it was my sister Lucile.

After my arrival in France I had written to my family to inform them of my return. Mme la Comtesse de Marigny, my eldest sister, was the first to come to see me, went to the wrong street, and met five MM. Lassagne,* the last of whom came up through a cobbler's trap-door to answer to his name. Mme de Chateaubriand came in her turn: she was charming, and full of all the qualities calculated to give me the happiness which

* The name Chateaubriand had adopted in order to return to France.

I have found with her since we have been reunited. Mme la
Comtesse de Caud, Lucile, came next. M. Joubert and Mme de
Beaumont were smitten with a passionate fondness and a tender
pity for her. There then began between them a correspondence
which ended only with the death of the two women who had
bent towards one another like two flowers of the same kind on
the point of fading away. Mme Lucile having stopped at Versailles on 30 September 1802, I received this note from her:

> I write to ask you to thank Madame de Beaumont on my behalf
> for the invitation she has sent me to go to Savigny. I hope to have
> that pleasure in about a fortnight's time, unless there is some obs-
> tacle on Madame de Beaumont's side.

Mme de Caud came to Savigny as she had said she would.

I have told you how, in my youth, my sister, a canoness of
the Chapter of L'Argentière, and destined for that of Remiremont, had conceived an attachment for M. de Malfilâtre, a
counsellor at the High Court of Brittany, which, remaining
locked in her breast, had increased her natural melancholy.
During the Revolution, she married M. le Comte de Caud, and
lost him after fifteen months of marriage. The death of Mme la
Comtesse de Farcy, a sister for whom she had a tender affection, added to Mme de Caud's sadness. She then attached
herself to Mme de Chateaubriand, my wife, and gained an
ascendancy over her which had unfortunate effects, for Lucile
was violent, masterful, and unreasonable, and Mme de Chateaubriand, pursued by her caprices, hid from her in order to
render her the services which a richer friend does to a suscep-
tible and less fortunate friend.

Lucile's genius and character had almost reached the degree
of madness of Jean-Jacques Rousseau; she imagined that she
was being persecuted by secret enemies: she gave Mme de
Beaumont, M. Joubert, and myself false addresses at which to
write to her; she examined the seals of her letters to see whether
they had been broken; she wandered from one home to another,
unable to stay with either my sisters or my wife; she had taken

a dislike to them, and Mme de Chateaubriand, after showing her a devotion surpassing all that one could imagine, had finally broken down under the burden of such a cruel affection.

Another blow had struck Lucile: M. de Chênedollé, who was living near Vire, had gone to see her at Fougères; soon there was talk of a marriage, but this fell through. Everything failed my sister all at once, and, thrown back upon herself, she no longer had the strength to bear her misfortunes. This plaintive spectre rested for a moment on a stone in the smiling solitude of Savigny: so many hearts there had welcomed her joyfully. They would so gladly have restored her to a life of sweet reality. But Lucile's heart could beat only in an atmosphere made expressly for her and which no one else had ever breathed. She swiftly consumed the days of the separate world in which Heaven had placed her. Why had God created a being only to suffer? What mysterious connexion can there be between a suffering temperament and an eternal principle?

After the adoption of the Concordat by the Legislative Body in 1802, Lucien Bonaparte, then Minister of the Interior, gave a reception for his brother; I was invited, as having rallied the Christian forces and led them back to the charge. I was in the gallery when Napoleon entered; he made a pleasant impression on me; I had never seen him before except at a distance. His smile was gentle and beautiful; his eyes were admirable, particularly on account of the way in which they were set beneath his forehead and framed in his eyebrows. There was as yet no charlatanism in his glance, nothing theatrical or affected. Le Génie du christianisme, which was then making a considerable stir, had struck a chord in Napoleon. A prodigious imagination animated that cold-blooded politician; he would not have been what he was if the Muse had not been there; reason carried out the ideas of the poet. All those men who lead great lives are a compound of two natures, for they must be capable of both inspiration and action: one conceives the plan, the other puts it into execution.

Bonaparte saw me and recognized me, I do not know how. When he came towards me no one knew whom he was making for; rank after rank opened up; each person hoped that the Consul would stop at him; he looked as if he felt a certain impatience with those illusions. I hid behind my neighbours; Bonaparte suddenly raised his voice and said:

'Monsieur de Chateaubriand!'

I was then left standing by myself, for the crowd drew back and soon gathered together again to form a circle around the two of us. Bonaparte addressed me with simplicity; without paying me any compliments, without any idle questions, without any preamble, he spoke to me straight away about Egypt and the Arabs, as if I had always been a close friend of his and we were simply continuing a conversation we had already begun.

'I was always greatly impressed,' he said, 'when I saw the sheikhs fall on their knees in the middle of the desert, turn towards the East, and touch the sand with their foreheads. What was the unknown thing which they were worshipping in the East?'

Bonaparte interrupted himself and broached another idea without any transition:

'Christianity! Haven't the ideologists tried to make an astronomical system of it? And if that should be so, do they think they can persuade me that Christianity is a little thing? If Christianity is the allegory of the movement of the spheres, the geometry of the stars, the free-thinkers may say what they please: in spite of themselves, they have still left a considerable measure of greatness to *the infamous thing*.'*

Suddenly Bonaparte moved away. As with Job, in my darkness, 'a spirit passed before me, the hair of my flesh stood up. There stood one whose countenance I knew not, and I heard the voice, as it were, of a gentle wind.'

My days have been but a series of visions; Hell and Heaven have continually opened up beneath my feet or above my head, without giving me time to explore their darkness or their light. Once on the shore of each of the two worlds, I met the man of the last century and the man of the new century: Washington and Napoleon. I conversed for a moment with each; both sent

* Voltaire always referred to the Church, and by extension to Christianity, as *l'infâme*.

me back to solitude, the first through a kindly wish, the second through a crime.*

As a result of this meeting, Bonaparte thought of me for Rome: he had decided at a glance where and how I could be of use to him. It mattered little to him that I had no experience of public affairs, that I was entirely unfamiliar with practical diplomacy; he believed that some minds are capable of understanding and have no need of apprenticeship. He was a great discoverer of men: but he wanted them to possess talent only for him, and even then on condition that that talent was not greatly renowned; jealous of every reputation, he regarded it as an usurpation of his own: there was to be no one but Napoleon in the universe.

When I left France, we were all greatly deluded about Mme de Beaumont's condition; she wept frequently, and her will has shown that she believed her case to be hopeless. However, her friends, without communicating their fears to one another, tried to reassure each other; they believed in miracles performed by the waters and consolidated by the sunshine of Italy; they separated and took different roads: their rendezvous was Rome.

A letter from M. Ballanche dated 30 Fructidor† informed me of the arrival of Mme de Beaumont, who had reached Lyons from Le Mont-d'Or on her way to Italy. He told me that I need not fear the misfortune which I dreaded, and that the sick woman's health seemed to be improving.

On reaching Milan, Mme de Beaumont met M. Bertin, who had been called there on business; he had the kindness to take charge of the poor traveller, and he accompanied her to Florence, where I had gone to meet her. I was shocked by her appearance. She had only just enough strength left to smile. After a few days' rest, we left for Rome, travelling at walking pace to avoid jolting. Mme de Beaumont was the object of assiduous attention everywhere: this lovable woman, so ill and forlorn, had an irresistible charm. The very maids at the inns gave way to this sweet commiseration.

* The execution of the Duc d'Enghien, as will be seen in the next chapter.
† 17 September 1803.

In Rome I had rented a lonely house for her near the Piazza d'Espagna, at the foot of the Monte Pincio; it had a little garden with orange-trees growing against the wall and a courtyard with a fig-tree in it. There I installed my dying friend. I had had considerable difficulty in obtaining this retreat, for there is a prejudice in Rome against diseases of the chest, which are held to be infectious.

At that period of the revival of social distinctions, everything that had belonged to the old monarchy was sought after. The Pope inquired after the daughter of M. de Montmorin; Cardinal Consalvi and the members of the Sacred College followed His Holiness's example; Cardinal Fesch himself showed Mme de Beaumont until the day of her death marks of deference and respect which I would not have expected of him.

To begin with, Mme de Beaumont experienced a certain relief. The patient herself began again to believe in her life. I had the satisfaction of thinking that at least Mme de Beaumont would never leave me again: I intended to take her to Naples in the spring, and from there to send in my resignation to the Minister for Foreign Affairs. M. d'Agincourt, that true philosopher, came to see the bird of passage, which had stopped at Rome before going on to unknown lands; M. Boguet, already the oldest of our painters, also called. These reinforcements of hope encouraged the sick woman, and lulled her with an illusion which in her heart of hearts she no longer retained.

The improvement which the air of Rome had produced in Mme de Beaumont did not last: true, the signs of an immediate collapse disappeared; but it seems that the last moment always lingers as if to deceive us. Two or three times I had tried taking the patient for a drive; I attempted to divert her thoughts by showing her the beauties of the country and the sky: nothing interested her any more. One day I took her to the Colosseum: it was one of those October days that are to be seen only in Rome. She managed to get out of the carriage, and went and sat on a stone facing one of the altars placed in the precincts of the building. She raised her eyes and looked slowly round those porticoes which had themselves been dead so many years, and which had seen so many die; the ruins were adorned with briars and columbines yellowed by autumn and bathed in light. The dying woman then lowered her eyes step by step, from the sun down to the arena, fixed them on the altar cross, and said to me:

'Let us go: I am cold.'

I took her home; she went to bed and never rose again.

The doctors, whom I had called together again after the experiment of the drive, told me that nothing but a miracle could save Mme de Beaumont. She was obsessed by the idea that she would not survive All Souls' Day, 2 November; then she remembered that one of her relatives, I do not know which, had died on 4 November. I told her that she was letting her imagination run away with her, and that she would soon see that her fears were groundless. She replied, to console me:

'Oh, yes, I shall live longer than that!'

She noticed a few tears which I was trying to hide from her; she held out her hand to me and said:

'You are a child; weren't you expecting this?'

On the eve of her death, Thursday, 3 November, she seemed more composed. She spoke to me about the disposal of her fortune and said, speaking of her will, that 'everything was settled, but that everything still remained to be done, and that she would have been glad of only two hours in which to see to it all'. In the evening, the doctor told me that he felt obliged to warn the patient that the time had come for her to think of putting her conscience in order: I broke down for a moment; the fear of shortening the little time which Mme de Beaumont still had to live by the formal preparations for death horrified me. I railed against the doctor, and then begged him to wait at least until the following day.

I spent a restless night, with this secret locked in my heart. The patient did not allow me to spend it in her room. I remained outside, trembling at every sound I heard: when the door was opened a little way, I saw the feeble glow of a dying night-light.

On Friday, 4 November, I went in, followed by the doctor. Mme de Beaumont noticed my agitation, and said:

'Why are you looking like that? I have had a good night.'

The doctor thereupon deliberately told me aloud that he

wanted to speak to me in the next room. I went out: when I returned, I no longer knew whether I was alive or dead. Mme de Beaumont asked me what the doctor had wanted to say to me. I flung myself on my knees beside her bed and burst into tears. She lay for a moment without speaking, looked at me, and said in a firm voice, as if she wanted to give me strength:

'I did not think it was going to be quite so quick: well, the time has come to say good-bye. Send for the Abbé de Bonnevie.'

The Abbé de Bonnevie, having obtained the necessary powers, came to see Mme de Beaumont. She told him that she had always had a profound religious feeling at heart, but that the terrible misfortunes which had befallen her during the Revolution had caused her for some time to doubt the justice of Providence; that she was prepared to admit her errors and to commend herself to the eternal mercy of God; but that she hoped that the ills she had suffered in this world would shorten the period of her expiation in the next. She made a sign to me to withdraw, and remained alone with her confessor.

I saw him come back an hour later, wiping his eyes and saying that he had never heard more beautiful language, nor seen such heroism. The parish priest was sent for to administer the sacraments. I returned to Mme de Beaumont's bedside. When she saw me she asked:

'Well, are you pleased with me?'

She spoke feelingly of what she deigned to call 'my kindness' to her: oh, if at that moment I had been able to buy back a single one of her days by the sacrifice of all my own, how gladly would I have done so! Mme de Beaumont's other friends, who were not present on this occasion, had at least only once to weep for her, whereas I stood at the head of that bed of pain in which man hears his last hour strike, with every smile of the patient's giving me life once more and taking it away again as it faded from her lips. A terrible idea occurred to me: I realized that Mme de Beaumont had not suspected until her last breath the very real attachment I had for her: she kept showing her surprise, and seemed to be dying at once disconsolate and delighted. She had imagined that she was a burden to me, and had wanted to go in order to set me free.

The priest arrived at eleven o'clock: the room filled up with that crowd of idle onlookers which cannot be prevented from following a priest around in Rome. Mme de Beaumont faced the formidable solemnity without the slightest sign of fear. We went down on our knees, and the patient received both Communion and Extreme Unction. When everyone had gone, she made me sit on the edge of her bed and spoke to me for half an hour about my affairs and my plans with the greatest nobility of mind and the most touching friendship; she urged me above all to live with Mme de Chateaubriand and M. Joubert; but was M. Joubert going to go on living?

She asked me to open the window because she felt stifled. A ray of sunshine lit up her bed and this seemed to raise her spirits. She then reminded me of plans for retiring to the country which we had sometimes discussed, and she began to cry.

Between two and three in the afternoon, Mme de Beaumont asked Mme Saint-Germain, an old Spanish lady's-maid who served her with an affection worthy of so kind a mistress, to transfer her to another bed; the doctor forbade this, fearing that Mme de Beaumont might die in the course of the move. She then told me that she could feel the death-agony approaching. Suddenly she flung back her blanket, held out her hand to me, and pressed mine convulsively, her eyes wandering from side to side. With her free hand she made signs to someone she could see standing at the foot of her bed; then, bringing the hand back to her breast, she said:

'It is there!'

Utterly dismayed, I asked her if she could recognize me: she smiled faintly in the midst of her delirium, and gave me a little nod of the head: her speech was already no longer of this world. The convulsions lasted only a few minutes. We supported her in our arms, the doctor, the nurse, and myself: one of my hands rested on her heart, which could be felt against her thin bones; it was beating fast like a watch unwinding its broken chain. Oh, moment of fear and horror, I felt it stop! We let down on to her pillow the woman who had found rest; her head drooped. A few locks of her hair fell over her forehead; her eyes were closed; eternal night had fallen. The doctor held a mirror and a light to her mouth: the mirror was not clouded by the breath of life, and the light remained immobile. It was all over.

Usually those who weep are able to indulge their tears in peace, while others take it upon themselves to see to the last rites of religion: as representing, on behalf of France, the Cardinal Minister, who was absent at the time, and as the only friend of M. de Montmorin's daughter and therefore responsible to her family, I was obliged to attend to everything; I had to choose the place of burial, see to the depth and width of the tomb, order the shroud, and give the carpenter the measurements of the coffin.

Two monks watched by this coffin, which was to be carried to San Luigi dei Francesi. One of these fathers was from Auvergne and a native of Montmorin itself. Mme de Beaumont had expressed a desire to be buried in a piece of cloth which her brother Auguste, the only one to escape the scaffold, had sent her from Mauritius. This cloth was not in Rome; all that we could find was a piece of it which she always carried about with her. Mme Saint-Germain fastened this strip around the body with a cornelian containing a lock of M. de Montmorin's hair. The French ecclesiastics were invited; the Princess Borghese lent her family hearse; Cardinal Fesch had left orders, in the event of an only too predictable accident, to send his livery and his carriages. On Saturday, 5 November, at seven o'clock in the evening, by the light of torches and in the midst of a great multitude, Mme de Beaumont passed along the road which all of us have to take.

TWO

The Execution of the
Duc d'Enghien

Two days before 21 March,* I dressed to go and take leave of
Bonaparte at the Tuileries; I had not seen him again since the
time when he had spoken to me at Lucien's. The gallery in
which he was receiving was full; he was accompanied by Murat
and a principal aide-de-camp; he walked along almost without
stopping. As he approached, I was struck by the alteration in
his face: his cheeks were hollow and livid, his eyes hard, his
complexion pale and blotchy, his expression gloomy and fierce.
The attraction which he had previously exerted upon me
ceased; instead of remaining in his path, I moved aside in order
to avoid him. He glanced at me as if he were trying to recognize
me, took a few steps towards me, then turned and walked
away. Had I appeared to him as a warning? His aide-de-camp
noticed me: when the crowd concealed me, this aide-de-camp
tried to catch sight of me between the people standing in front
of me, and once again drew the Consul in my direction. This
game went on for nearly a quarter of an hour, I always drawing
back, Napoleon always following me without knowing it. I
have never been able to account for the aide-de-camp's behaviour. Did he take me for a suspicious character whom he had
never seen before? Did he, if he knew who I was, want to force
Bonaparte to talk to me? Whatever the truth of the matter,

* The date of the execution of Louis-Antoine-Henri de Bourbon, Duc
d'Enghien (1762–1804). When Cadoudal's conspiracy was discovered, Bonaparte acted on reports that D'Enghien was involved, violated the neutral
territory of Baden, where the duke was living, and had him taken to Vincennes. In the early morning of 21 March 1804 he was tried by a military
court, sentenced to death, and shot in the castle moat.

Napoleon went on into another room. Satisfied at having done my duty in presenting myself at the Tuileries, I withdrew. From the joy which I have always felt at leaving palaces, it is clear that I was not born to enter them.

On returning to the Hôtel de France, I said to several of my friends:

'Something strange must be happening that we know nothing about, for Bonaparte cannot have changed to that extent, unless he is ill.'

M. Bourrienne heard about my strange forecast; he has merely confused the dates; here is what he writes:

'On his return from seeing the First Consul, M. de Chateaubriand told his friends that he had noticed a great change in the First Consul and something sinister in his expression.'

Yes, I noticed it: a superior intelligence does not bring forth evil without pain, because that is not its natural fruit, and it ought not to bear it.

Two days later, on 21 March, I got up early, for the sake of a memory that was sad and dear to me. M. de Montmorin had built himself a house at the corner of the Rue Plumet, on the new Boulevard des Invalides. In the garden of this house, which was sold during the Revolution, Mme de Beaumont, when little more than a child, had planted a cypress-tree, and she had occasionally taken pleasure in showing it to me as we passed: it was to this cypress-tree, of which I alone knew the origins and history, that I was going to say good-bye. It still exists, but it is pining away and scarcely rises as far as the window beneath which a hand which has vanished loved to tend it. I can distinguish that poor tree from among three or four others of the same species; it seems to know me and to rejoice when I approach; melancholy breezes bend its yellowed head a little towards me, and it murmurs at the window of the deserted room: there is a mysterious understanding between us, which will cease when one or the other of us falls.

After paying my pious tribute, I went down the Boulevard and the Esplanade des Invalides, and crossed the Pont Louis XV and the Tuileries Gardens, which I left near the Pavillon Marsan by the gate which now opens into the Rue de Rivoli.

There, between eleven o'clock and midday, I heard a man and a woman who were shouting out some official news; passers-by were stopping, suddenly petrified by these words:

'Verdict of the special military commission convened at Vincennes, sentencing to death *the man known as Louis-Antoine-Henri de Bourbon, born on the 2nd of August 1772 at Chantilly.*'

This cry fell upon me like a thunderbolt; it changed my life, just as it changed Napoleon's. I returned home, and said to Mme de Chateaubriand:

'The Duc d'Enghien has just been shot.'

I sat down at a table and began writing my resignation. Mme de Chateaubriand raised no objection and watched me writing with great courage. She had no illusions about the danger which I was incurring: General Moreau and Georges Cadoudal were being tried; the lion had tasted blood, and this was not the moment to irritate him.

M. Clausel de Coussergues arrived; he too had heard the sentence being made public. He found me pen in hand: my letter, from which, out of consideration for Mme de Chateaubriand, he made me omit certain angry phrases, was sent off; it was addressed to the Minister for Foreign Affairs. The wording mattered little: my opinion and my crime lay in the fact of my resignation: Bonaparte made no mistake about that.

Long afterwards, in conversation with M. de Fontanes, he remarked that my resignation was one of the things that had most impressed him. M. de Talleyrand had an official letter sent to me in which he graciously reproached me for depriving his department of my talents and services. I returned the expenses of my installation, and everything was apparently finished. But by daring to leave Bonaparte, I had placed myself on his level, and he was turned against me by all the force of his perfidy, as I was turned against him by all the force of my loyalty. Until the day he fell, he held the sword suspended over my head: sometimes he returned to me from a natural inclination and tried to engulf me in his fatal prosperity; sometimes I was drawn to him by the admiration with which he inspired me, and by the idea that I was witnessing a transformation of society and not a mere change of dynasty: but our respective natures, antipathetic in so many respects, always gained the upper hand, and if he would gladly have had me shot, I should have felt no great compunction about killing him.

Alas, we had suffered too many different tyrannies, and our characters, crushed by a succession of hardships and oppressions, no longer had enough energy to allow our grief to wear mourning for young Condé for very long: gradually the tears dried up; fear overflowed in congratulations on the First Consul's escape from danger; it wept with gratitude at having been saved by such a sacred sacrifice. Nero, at Seneca's dictation, wrote the Senate a letter of apology for the murder of Agrippina; the delighted Senators heaped blessings on the magnanimous son who had not hesitated to pluck out his heart by such a salutary act of matricide. Society soon returned to its pleasures: it was afraid of its mourning: after the Terror, the victims who had been spared danced, tried their best to look happy, and, fearing that they might be suspected of the crime of memory, displayed the same gaiety as when they went to the scaffold.

I at least can rejoice that I was neither troubled by fear, nor affected by contagion, nor carried away by evil example. The satisfaction which I feel today at what I did then is proof to me that conscience is no illusion. Happier than all those potentates, than all those nations which fell at the feet of the victorious soldier, I turn again with pardonable pride to this page which I have kept as my only possession and which I owe only to myself. In 1807, with my heart still moved by the murder which I have just related, I wrote the following lines; they caused the *Mercure* to be suppressed, and placed my liberty in jeopardy once more:

When, in the silence of abjection, no sound can be heard save that of the chains of the slave and the voice of the informer; when all tremble before the tyrant, and it is as dangerous to incur his favour as to merit his displeasure, the historian appears, entrusted with the vengeance of the nations. Nero prospers in vain, for Tacitus has already been born within the Empire; he grows up unknown beside the ashes of Germanicus, and already a just Providence has delivered into the hands of an obscure child the glory of the master of the world. If the historian's role is a fine one, it often has its dangers; but there are altars such as that of honour which, though deserted, demand further sacrifices: the god has not been annihilated because the temple is empty. Wherever there remains a chance for fortune, there is no heroism in trying it; magnanimous actions are those whose foreseeable result is adversity and death. After all, what do reverses matter if our name, pronounced by posterity, makes a single generous heart beat two thousand years after we have lived?

The death of the Duc d'Enghien, by introducing a new principle into Bonaparte's conduct, marred the perfection of his understanding: he was obliged to adopt as a shield maxims of which he did not have the total force at his disposal, for his glory and his genius constantly falsified them. He became an object of fear and suspicion; men lost confidence in him and his destiny; he was compelled to see, if not to seek out, men whom he would never have seen before and who, as a result of his action, considered that they had become his equals: the contagion of their impurity began to overtake him. He did not dare to reproach them for anything, for he no longer possessed the virtuous freedom to blame. His great qualities remained the same, but his good dispositions became impaired and no longer supported his great qualites; corrupted by that original stain, his nature deteriorated.

Will the ashes of Bonaparte be exhumed, as those of the Duc d'Enghien have been? If I could have had my way, this latter victim would still be sleeping unhonoured in the moat of Vincennes Castle. This excommunicate would have been left, like Raymond de Toulouse, in an open coffin; no man's hand would have dared to conceal beneath a plank the sight of this witness to the incomprehensible judgements and anger of God. The abandoned skeleton of the Duc d'Enghien and Napoleon's lonely grave on St Helena would have made a pair: there would have been nothing more commemorative than those remains, face to face, at opposite ends of the earth.

It is here where I am writing this, here at Chantilly, that the Duc d'Enghien was born: *Louis-Antoine-Henri de Bourbon, born on 2 August 1772 at Chantilly*, says the sentence of death. It is on this lawn that he played as a child: every trace of his footsteps has vanished. And the victor of Freiburg, Nördlingen, Lens, and Senef,* where has he gone with his *victorious but now lifeless hands*? And his descendants, the Condé of Johannisberg and Berstheim, and his son, and his grandson, where are they? That castle, those gardens, those fountains *that were silent neither by day nor by night*, what has become of them? Mutilated statues, lions with a claw or a jaw restored; trophies sculptured in a crumbling wall; coats of arms with faded fleurs-de-lis; foundations of razed turrets; some marble coursers above empty stables no longer enlivened by the neighing of the horse of Rocroi; beside a riding-school, a high unfinished gate: that is what is left of the memories of a heroic race; a will tied with a rope has changed the owners of the inheritance.†

On various occasions the whole forest has fallen under the axe. People of bygone ages have hunted in these preserves, once so noisy, now so silent. What was their age and what were their passions when they halted at the foot of these oaks? What dreams occupied their minds? Obscure men that we are, what are we beside those famous men? We shall disappear, never to return; you, sweet-william, who lie on my table beside this paper, and whose belated little flower I have gathered among the heather, you will be born again; but as for us, we shall not come to life again with the scented solitary which has diverted my thoughts.

---

* Louis II, Prince de Condé (1621–86), known as the Great Condé. The phrases in italics are taken from Bossuet's funeral oration.
† The Duc d'Enghien's father, the last of the Condés, was found hanged in his apartment at Saint-Leu-Taverny in 1830; he left Chantilly and the bulk of his fortune to the Duc d'Aumale, Louis-Philippe's fifth son.

The Death of Lucile

A new and grievous sorrow surprised me at Villeneuve. To tell you about it, I must go back a few months before my journey to Switzerland. I was still living in the house in the Rue Miromesnil when, in the autumn of 1804, Mme de Caud came to Paris. The death of Mme de Beaumont had completed the derangement of my sister's mind; she came close to refusing to believe in the reality of that death, to suspecting some mystery in that disappearance, or to including Heaven in the number of the enemies who made fun of her misfortunes. She had no money; I had found an apartment in the Rue Caumartin for her, deceiving her as to the rent and as to the arrangements which I persuaded her to make with the keeper of an eating-house. Like a flame about to go out, her genius shed its brightest light; she was bathed in its radiance. She would write a few lines which she would throw into the fire, or else copy out of books some thoughts in harmony with the disposition of her soul. She did not stay long in the Rue Caumartin; she went to live with the Dames Saint-Michel, in the Rue du Faubourg Saint-Jacques: Mme de Navarre was the superior of the convent. Lucile had a little cell overlooking the garden: I noticed that she followed with her eyes, with a sort of gloomy longing, the nuns walking in the enclosure around the vegetable plots. One could guess that she envied the saints and, going further, aspired to become an angel. I will sanctify these *Memoirs* by depositing in them, as a relic, the following letter from Mme de Caud, written before she took wing for her eternal home:

My dear brother, do not grow weary of my letters or of my company; remember that soon you will be released for ever from my importunities. My life is casting its last light, like a lamp which has burnt out in the darkness of a long night, and which sees the breaking of the dawn in which it is to die. Glance back, I beg you, my dear, at the early moments of our existence; remember that we were often seated on the same lap, and pressed together against the same bosom; that already you added your tears to mine, that from the earliest days of your life you protected and defended my frail existence, that our games united us and that I shared your first studies. I will not speak to you of our adolescence, of the innocence of our thoughts and our pleasures, nor of the need we both felt to see each other all the time. If I recall the past, I frankly confess, my dear, that it is to revive the image of myself in your heart. When you left France for the second time, you entrusted your wife to my care, and you made me promise never to part from her. True to this precious engagement, I voluntarily held out my hands to be chained, and entered those places destined only for victims condemned to death. In those dwellings I felt no anxiety except as to your fate; I consulted the forebodings of my heart incessantly about you. When I had recovered my freedom, in the midst of the misfortunes which overwhelmed me, it was only the thought of our reunion that kept me alive. Now that I have lost for ever the hope of spending my life at your side, bear with my sorrow. I shall become resigned to my destiny, and it is only because I am still fighting against it that I am suffering such cruel anguish; but when I have submitted to my fate ... And what a fate! Where are my friends, my protectors and my riches? Who cares about my life, that life abandoned by all and weighing down entirely upon itself? O Lord, are not my present woes enough for someone as weak as I am, without adding to them the fear of the future? Forgive me, my dear, I will resign myself; I will fall asleep, in a deathlike slumber, upon my destiny. But during the few days which I have to spend in this city, let me look for my last consolation in you; let me believe that my presence is dear to you. ...

This poignant and wholly admirable letter is the last I received; it alarmed me on account of the added sadness of which it

bears the stamp. I hurried to the Dames Saint-Michel; my sister
was walking in the garden with Mme de Navarre; she came in
when she heard that I had gone up to her room. She made a
visible effort to collect her thoughts, and now and then her lips
twitched convulsively. I begged her to be reasonable, to stop
writing such unjust and heartrending things to me, and to stop
thinking that I could ever grow weary of her. She seemed to
grow a little calmer at the words which I repeated to comfort
and console her. She told me that she believed that the convent
was doing her harm, and that she would feel better living by
herself, somewhere near the Jardin des Plantes, where she could
see doctors and go for walks. I urged her to do as she wished,
adding that in order to help her maid Virginie, I would let her
have old Saint-Germain. This proposal seemed to give her considerable pleasure, reminding her as it did of Mme de Beaumont,
and she assured me that she would start looking for her new
lodgings. She asked me how I was thinking of spending the
summer; I told her that I should be going to Vichy to join my
wife, and then to M. Joubert's at Villeneuve, returning to Paris
from there. I suggested that she might care to accompany us.
She replied that she wished to spend the summer alone, and
that she was going to send Virginie back to Fougères. I left her;
she seemed more composed.

Mme de Chateaubriand left for Vichy, and I got ready to follow her. Before leaving Paris I went again to see Lucile. She was
affectionate; she spoke to me about her writings. I encouraged
the great poet to work hard; she kissed me, wished me a good
journey, and made me promise to come back soon. She saw me
to the staircase landing, leant over the banisters, and quietly
watched me go down. When I reached the bottom I stopped
and, raising my eyes, called out to the unhappy woman who
was still looking at me:

'Good-bye, my dear sister! I shall see you soon! Take care of
yourself. Write to me at Villeneuve. I will write to you. I hope
that next winter you will agree to live with us.'

That evening I saw the worthy Saint-Germain; I gave him his
instructions and some money, so that he might secretly reduce
the price of anything she might require. I told him to keep me

informed of everything that happened and not to fail to call me back if he needed to see me. Three months went by. When I arrived at Villeneuve, I found two fairly reassuring letters about Mme de Caud's health; but Saint-Germain forgot to tell me about my sister's new lodgings. I had begun to write her a long letter when Mme de Chateaubriand suddenly fell dangerously ill: I was at her bedside when I was brought a fresh letter from Saint-Germain; I opened it: a single horrifying line told me of the sudden death of Lucile.

I have cared for many graves in my life: it fell to my lot and my sister's destiny that her ashes should be scattered to the four winds. I was not in Paris when she died; I had no relatives there; kept at Villeneuve by my wife's critical condition, I was unable to go and attend to those sacred remains; instructions sent from afar arrived too late to prevent a common burial. Lucile knew no one and had not a single friend; she was known only to Mme de Beaumont's old manservant, as if he had been charged with linking those two destinies together. He alone followed the forsaken coffin, and he himself had died before Mme de Chateaubriand's sufferings allowed me to bring her back to Paris.

My sister was buried among the poor. In which cemetery was she laid to rest? In what motionless wave of the ocean of the dead was she engulfed? In what house did she die, after leaving the community of the Dames de Saint-Michel? If, by making inquiries, if, by examining municipal archives and parish registers, I should come across my sister's name, what would that avail me?* Would I find the same cemetery keeper? Would I find the man who dug a grave that has remained nameless and unrecorded? Would the rough hands that were the last to touch that pure clay remember it? What nomenclator of the shades could show me the obliterated grave? Might he not make a mistake? Since Heaven has so willed it, may Lucile be lost for ever! I find in this absence of locality a difference from the burials of my other friends. My predecessor in this world

* The death certificate was later discovered, though not by Chateaubriand. Lucile died at No. 6 Rue d'Orléans, on 9 November 1804.

and the next is praying to the Redeemer for me; she is praying to Him from the midst of the pauper remains among which her own are mingled: thus does Lucile's mother and mine rest lost among the preferred of Jesus Christ. God will have been able to recognize my sister; and she, who cared so little for this world, was bound to leave no trace of her passage. She has left me, that saintly genius. Not a day has passed but I have wept for her. Lucile loved to hide; I have made a solitude for her in my heart: she shall leave it only when I have ceased to live.

Those are the true, the only events of my real life! What did I care, when I lost my sister, about the thousands of soldiers falling in battle, the crumbling of thrones, and the changes taking place in the face of the world?

Lucile's death struck at the roots of my soul: it was my childhood in the midst of my family, the first vestiges of my existence, that were disappearing. Our lives resemble those fragile buildings shored up in the sky by flying buttresses; the latter do not crumble all at once, but collapse one after another; they go on supporting some gallery when they have already abandoned the sacrarium and the cradle of the edifice. Mme de Chateaubriand, still bruised by Lucile's imperious caprices, saw only a deliverance for the Christian woman who had attained eternal peace. Let us be gentle if we would be regretted: great genius and superior qualities are mourned only by the angels.

FOUR

Bonaparte and the Chateaubriands

By a series of arrangements, I had become the sole proprietor of the *Mercure*. By the end of June 1807, M. Alexandre de Laborde published the account of his journey in Spain; in July I published in the *Mercure* the article from which I have quoted certain passages when dealing with the death of the Duc d'Enghien: '*When, in the silence of abjection*, etc.' Bonaparte's successes, far from subduing me, had roused me to revolt; I had gathered fresh energy from my feelings and the storms. It was not in vain that my face was bronzed by the sun,* nor had I exposed myself to the wrath of Heaven to tremble with darkened brow before the anger of a man. If Napoleon had done with the kings, he had not done with me. My article, falling in the midst of his successes and splendours, caused a sensation in France: countless manuscript copies were made and distributed; several subscribers to the *Mercure* cut out the article and had it bound separately: it was read in drawing-rooms and hawked from house to house. One has to have lived at that time to understand the effect produced by a voice thundering all alone in the silence of the world. The noble feelings which had been thrust down to the bottom of men's hearts revived. Napoleon flew into a passion: one is less irritated by reason of the offence received than by reason of the opinion one has formed of oneself. What was this? Someone daring to despise his very glory, to brave for the second time the man at whose feet the world lay prostrate!

---

* A reference to Chateaubriand's journey in the Middle East from July 1806 to June 1807 which he described in his *Itinéraire de Paris à Jérusalem*.

'Does Chateaubriand think that I am an idiot, that I don't understand him?' he roared. 'I'll have him cut down on the steps of the Tuileries!'

He gave orders to suppress the *Mercure* and to have me arrested. My property perished; my person escaped by a miracle: Bonaparte had to busy himself with the world; he forgot me, but I remained under a constant threat.

My position was a deplorable one: when I felt bound to act according to the dictates of my sense of honour, I found myself burdened with my personal responsibility and with the worry which I caused my wife. Her courage was great, but she suffered nonetheless for it, and these storms which fell upon me one after the other disturbed her life. She had suffered so much for me during the Revolution! It was only natural that she should long for a little peace. The more so in that Mme de Chateaubriand admired Bonaparte unreservedly; she had no illusions about the Legitimacy; she was for ever predicting what would happen to me on the return of the Bourbons.

The first chapter of these *Memoirs* is dated 4 October 1811 at the Vallée-aux-Loups: there I give a description of the little retreat which I bought to hide me at that time.* Leaving our apartment at Mme de Coislin's, we first of all went to live in the Rue des Saints-Pères, in the Hôtel de Lavalette, which took its name from the owners of the establishment.

M. de Lavalette was a thick-set man who wore a plum-coloured coat and carried a gold-headed cane. He became my business manager, if it can be said that I have ever had any business. He had been buttery officer to the King, and what I did not eat up he drank.

Towards the end of November, seeing that the repairs to my cottage were making no progress, I decided to go and supervise them. We arrived at the Vallée in the evening. We did not take the ordinary road, but went in through the gate at the bottom of the garden. The soil of the drive, soaked with rain, prevented the horses from going forward; the carriage fell over on its side.

* August 1807.

A plaster bust of Homer, which had been placed beside Mme de Chateaubriand, was thrown out of the window and broke its neck: a bad omen for *Les Martyrs*, on which I was working at the time.

The house, full of workmen laughing, singing, and hammering away, was warmed by burning wood-shavings and lighted by candle-ends; it looked like a hermitage illuminated at night by pilgrims, in the woods. Delighted to find two rooms more or less ready, in one of which the table had been laid, we sat down to supper. The next day, awakened by the sound of the hammers and the songs of the husbandmen, I saw the sun rise with less anxiety than the master of the Tuileries.

I made some extensions to my cottage; I improved the appearance of its brick wall with a portico supported by two black marble columns and two white marble caryatids: I remembered that I had been to Athens. I planned to add a tower to the end of the building; in the meantime I had imitation battlements built on to the wall separating me from the road, thus anticipating the fashion for things medieval which is all the rage at the moment. The Vallée-aux-Loups is the only thing that I regret of all that I have lost; it is written that nothing shall remain to me. After losing the Vallée, I planted the Marie-Thérèse Infirmary, and now I have left that too. I defy fate now to attach me to the smallest plot of earth; henceforth my only garden shall be those avenues, honoured with such splendid names, around the Invalides, along which I stroll with my lame or one-armed colleagues. Not far from these walks, Mme de Beaumont's cypress raises its head; in these deserted spaces, the great and gay Duchesse de Châtillon once leant upon my arm. Now I give my arm only to time: it is heavy enough. . . .

Armand de Chateaubriand, whom you have seen as the companion of my childhood, and whom you met again in the Army of the Princes with the deaf and dumb Libba, had remained in England. He married in Jersey and was entrusted with the correspondence of the Princes. Setting sail on 25 September 1808, he was landed at eleven o'clock the same evening on the coast of Brittany, near Saint-Cast. The boat's crew consisted of eleven men; only two were Frenchmen, Roussel and Quintal.

Armand went at once to the house of M. Delaunay-Boisé-Lucas the elder, who lived in the village of Saint-Cast, where the English had once been driven back to their ships: his host advised him to go back, but the boat had already set off on the homeward journey to Jersey. Armand, having come to an agreement with M. Boisé-Lucas's son, handed him the despatches with which he had been entrusted by M. Henry-Larivière, the Princes' agent.

> I went to the coast on 29 September [*he says in the course of one of his interrogations*], and waited there for two nights without seeing my boat. As the moon was very bright, I withdrew, and returned on 14 or 15 October. I stayed there until the 24th of the same month. I spent every night among the rocks, but to no purpose; my boat did not come. During the day I went to the Boisé-Lucas's. The same boat with the same crew, including Roussel and Quintal, was to have come to fetch me. As for the precautions taken in conjunction with Boisé-Lucas the elder, there were none apart from those which I have already described.

The dauntless Armand, landed a few steps from his home, as if on the inhospitable shore of the Crimea, looked in vain across the waves, by the light of the moon, in search of the boat which could have saved him. In bygone days, when I had already left Combourg and was preparing to go to India, I had cast my melancholy gaze across the same waves. From the rocks of Saint-Cast where Armand lay, from the Cap de la Varde where I had sat, a few miles of sea-water, over which our eyes have gazed in opposite directions, have witnessed the cares and divided the destinies of two men, joined by ties of name and blood. It was also in the midst of the same waves that I met Gesril for the last time. Often, in my dreams, I see Gesril and Armand washing the wounds in their foreheads in the deep, while the sea with which we used to play in our childhood comes lapping blood-red at my feet.

Armand succeeded in setting off in a boat bought at

Saint-Malo, but, driven back by the north-west wind, he was obliged to put in once more. At last, on 6 January, helped by a sailor called Jean Brien, he launched a little stranded dinghy and got hold of another which was afloat. He describes his voyage, which recalls my own adventures, in the following words taken from his examination on 18 March:

From nine o'clock in the evening, when we set sail, till two o'clock in the morning, the weather favoured us. Judging then that we were not far from the rocks called the Mainquiers, we lay to on our anchor, intending to wait for daylight; but the wind freshened and, fearing that it would grow even stronger, we set off once more. A few minutes later, the sea became very rough, and since our compass had been broken by a yardarm, we remained uncertain as to the course we were taking. The first land that came in sight on the 7th (it was probably about midday) was the coast of Normandy, which made us tack about, and we returned again and lay to near some rocks called Écreho, situated between the Normandy coast and Jersey. The strong contrary winds forced us to stay in that position all the rest of that day and the whole of the 8th. On the morning of the 9th, as soon as it was light, I said to Depagne that it seemed to me that the wind had decreased, seeing that our boat was not straining much, and I told him to look which way the wind was blowing. He said that he could no longer see the rocks near which we had dropped anchor. I then realized that we were adrift and that we had lost our anchor. The violence of the storm left us no alternative but to make for the coast. As we could see no land, I did not know how far we were from it. It was then that I threw my papers into the sea, after taking the precaution of fastening a stone to them. We then sailed before the wind and made the coast at about nine o'clock in the morning, at Bretteville-sur-Ay, in Normandy.

We were met on the coast by the custom-house officers, who took me out of my boat half-dead; my feet and legs were frostbitten. Both of us were put up at the house of the lieutenant of the Bretteville brigade. Two days later, Depagne was taken to the prison at Coutances, and I have not seen him since. A few days after that, I myself was transferred to the gaol in that town; the

next day I was taken by the sergeant to Saint-Lô, and stayed for
eight days with the said sergeant. I appeared once before the Prefect of the department, and on 26 January I left with the captain
and the sergeant of the constabulary for Paris, where I arrived on
the 28th. They took me to the office of M. Desmarets, at the Ministry of Police, and from there to the prison of La Grande-Force.

Armand had the winds, the waves, and the imperial police
against him; Bonaparte was in league with the storms. The
gods indulged in a great expenditure of wrath against a paltry
human life.

The packet which Armand had thrown into the sea was cast
up by it on the beach at Notre-Dame-d'Alloue, near Valognes.
The papers contained in this packet were produced in evidence
at the trial; there were thirty-two of them. Quintal, returning to
the beaches of Brittany with his boat to fetch Armand, had
also, by an obstinate fatality, been shipwrecked on the Normandy coast a few days before my cousin. The crew of Quintal's
boat had talked; the Prefect of Saint-Lô had learnt that M. de
Chateaubriand was the leader of the Princes' enterprises. When
he heard that a boat manned by only two men had run aground,
he had no doubt that Armand was one of the two, for all the
fishermen spoke of him as the most fearless sailor that had ever
been seen.

Taken to Paris and imprisoned in La Force, Armand under-
went a secret interrogation at the military gaol of the Abbaye.
General Hulin, who had become Military Commandant of Paris,
appointed Captain Bertrand of the first demi-brigade of veterans
judge-advocate of the military commission instructed, by a
decree of 25 February, to take cognizance of Armand's case.

The people implicated were M. de Goyon, whom Armand
had sent to Brest, and M. de Boisé-Lucas the younger, whom he
had instructed to deliver letters from Henry-Larivière to MM.
Laya and Sicard in Paris.

In a letter of 13 March addressed to Fouché, Armand wrote:

May the Emperor deign to restore to liberty men now languishing
in prison for having shown me too much kindness. In any event,

may liberty be restored to them all in like measure. I commend
my unfortunate family to the Emperor's generosity.

This incomprehension of a man with human feelings addressing himself to a hyena is painful to behold. Bonaparte was not
the lion of Florence: he did not give up the child at the sight of
the mother's tears. I had written to ask Fouché for an audience;
he granted me one and assured me with all the coolness of
revolutionary frivolity 'that he had seen Armand, that I could
set my mind at rest; that Armand had told him that he would
die well, and that he did in fact look extremely resolute'. If I
had suggested to Fouché that he too should die, would he have
retained that deliberate tone and that superb insouciance with
regard to himself?

I applied to Mme de Rémusat, asking her to deliver to the
Empress a letter for the Emperor containing a plea for justice
or mercy. Mme la Duchesse de Saint-Leu told me, at Arenenberg, of the fate of my letter: Josephine gave it to the Emperor;
he seemed to hesitate as he read it, then, coming across some
words which offended him, he flung it impatiently into the fire.
I had forgotten that one should show pride only on one's own
behalf.

M. de Goyon, condemned with Armand, suffered his sentence. Yet Mme la Baronne-Duchesse de Montmorency, Mme
de Matignon's daughter, with whom the Goyons were connected, was induced to intercede in his favour. A Montmorency
in service should have been able to obtain anything, if the pros-
titution of a name had been enough to win over an old
monarchy to a new power. Mme de Goyon, though unable to
save her husband, saved young Boisé-Lucas. Everything contributed to this misfortune, which struck down only unknown
persons; one would have thought that it was the end of the
world that was in question, what with storms on the waves,
ambushes on land, Bonaparte, the sea, Louis XVI's murderers,
and perhaps some *passion*, the mysterious spirit of earthly
catastrophes. No one else noticed these things; they struck me
alone and lived on only in my memory. What did Napoleon
care about the insects crushed by his hand on his crown?

On the day of the execution,* I wanted to accompany my comrade on his last battlefield; I could not find a carriage, and hurried on foot to the Grenelle Plain. I arrived, drenched in sweat, a second too late: Armand had just been shot against the outer wall of Paris. His skull was shattered; a butcher's dog was licking up his blood and his brains. I followed the cart which took the bodies of Armand and his two companions, plebeian and noble, Quintal and Goyon, to the Vaugirard Cemetery, where I had buried M. de la Harpe. I saw my cousin for the last time without being able to recognize him: the lead had disfigured him; he had no face left: I could not observe the ravages of time in it, nor even see death within its shapeless, bleeding orb; he remained young in my memory as at the time of the Siege of Thionville. He was shot on Good Friday: Christ crucified appears to me at the end of all my misfortunes. When I walk along the rampart of the Grenelle Plain, I stop to look at the marks left by the shooting, which can still be seen on the wall. If Bonaparte's bullets had left no other traces, he would no longer be talked about.

* 31 March 1809.

FIVE
Napoleon in Russia

When Bonaparte crossed the Niemen, eighty-five million, five hundred thousand souls recognized his sovereignty or that of his family; half the population of Christendom obeyed him; his orders were carried out over an area of nineteen degrees latitude and thirty degrees longitude. Never had such a gigantic expedition been seen before; never will its like be seen again.

On 22 June, at his headquarters at Wilkowiski, Napoleon declared war:

'Soldiers, the second Polish War has begun; the first ended at Tilsit; Russia is carried away by Fate: her destiny must be fulfilled.'

Moscow replied to this voice which was still young through the mouth of its Metropolitan, aged one hundred and ten:

'The City of Moscow welcomes Alexander, its Saviour, like a mother in the arms of her loving sons, and sings Hosanna! Blessed be he who comes!'

Bonaparte addressed himself to Destiny, Alexander to Providence.

On 23 June 1812, Bonaparte made out the Niemen in the darkness; he ordered three bridges to be thrown across it. The following evening, a few sappers crossed the river in a boat; they found nobody on the other bank. A Cossack officer in command of a patrol came up to them and asked them who they were.

'Frenchmen.'

'Why have you come to Russia?'

'To fight you.'

The Cossack disappeared into the forest; three sappers fired into the trees; there was no reply, only universal silence.

Bonaparte had spent a whole day lying on his bed, weak yet restless: he could feel something withdrawing from him. The columns of our armies advanced through the Forest of Pilwisky under cover of darkness, like the Huns who were led by a doe across the Palus-Meotides. The Niemen could not be seen; to recognize it, one had to touch its banks.

In broad daylight, instead of the Muscovite battalions or the Lithuanian populace advancing to meet their liberators, nothing could be seen but bare sands and deserted forests. 'Three hundred paces from the forest,' writes Ségur, 'the Emperor's tent stood on the loftiest eminence. Around it, all the hills and slopes and valleys were covered with men and horses.'

The combined forces under Napoleon's orders amounted to six hundred and eighty thousand, three hundred infantry and one hundred and seventy-six thousand, eight hundred and fifty cavalry. In the War of the Succession, Louis XIV had six hundred thousand men under arms, all of whom were French. The regular infantry, under Bonaparte's personal command, was divided into ten corps. These corps consisted of twenty thousand Italians, eighty thousand men from the Confederation of the Rhine, thirty thousand Poles, thirty thousand Austrians, twenty thousand Prussians, and two hundred and seventy thousand Frenchmen.

The army crossed the Niemen; Bonaparte himself passed over the fateful bridge and set foot on Russian soil. He stopped and watched his soldiers marching by, then disappeared from sight and galloped at random through the forest, as if summoned to a congress of spirits on the heath. He returned; he listened; the army listened: they imagined that they could hear the rumble of gunfire in the distance, and they rejoiced; it was only a storm; the prospect of battle faded. Bonaparte took shelter in a deserted monastery, a doubly peaceful refuge.

It has been said that Napoleon's horse stumbled and that someone was heard to murmur: 'A bad omen; a Roman would turn back.' This is the old story of Scipio, of William the

Conqueror, of Edward III, and of Malesherbes setting out for
the revolutionary tribunal.

The troops took three days to cross the river; then they fell
into line and started to advance. Napoleon pressed forward;
time called out to him: 'March! March!' as Bossuet used to say.

At Vilna, Bonaparte received Senator Vibicki of the Diet of
Warsaw: a Russian envoy, Balaschoff, presented himself next;
he declared that negotiations were still possible, that Alexander
was not the aggressor, and that the French had invaded Russia
without declaring war. Napoleon replied that Alexander was
nothing but a parade-ground general and that he had only
three generals: Kutusoff, whom he, Bonaparte, did not bother
his head about since he was a Russian; Bennigsen, who had
been too old for his job six years before and was now in his
second childhood; and Barclay, who was on the retired list. The
Duc de Vicence, considering himself insulted by something
Bonaparte had said during the conversation, broke in angrily:

'I am a good Frenchman; I have already proved it; I will
prove it again by repeating that this war is ill-advised and dangerous, and that it will be the ruin of the army, France, and the
Emperor.'

Bonaparte had asked the Russian envoy: 'Do you really
think that I care a rap about your Polish Jacobins?' Mme de
Staël records this last remark; her friends in high places kept
her well informed. She declares that there existed a letter
written to Romanzoff by one of Bonaparte's ministers, who
suggested erasing the words Poland and Polish from European
treaties: overwhelming proof of Napoleon's contempt for his
brave petitioners.

Bonaparte asked Balaschoff how many churches there were
in Moscow: on hearing the reply, he exclaimed:

'What, as many churches as that at a time when nobody is
Christian any more?'

'I beg your pardon, sire,' said the Muscovite, 'the Russians
and the Spaniards still are.'

Balaschoff having been sent off with some unacceptable
proposals, the last hope of peace vanished. The bulletins said:
'So this is the Russian Empire, which seemed so formidable

from a distance! It is nothing but a desert. It will take Alexander longer to gather his recruits together than Napoleon to reach Moscow.'

When he reached Vitebsk, Bonaparte was tempted for a moment to call a halt there. Returning to his headquarters, after seeing Barclay fall back yet again, he flung his sword on to some maps and exclaimed:

'I am stopping here! My 1812 campaign is over: my 1813 campaign will do the rest.'

He would have been well-advised to have kept to this resolution which all his generals were urging upon him. He had counted on receiving new peace proposals: seeing nothing of the sort coming his way, he became bored; he was only twenty days from Moscow. 'Moscow the holy city!' he kept saying. His eyes flashed, his brow darkened: the order to advance was given. Certain representations were made to him; he ignored them. Questioned as to his opinion, Daru replied that 'he could not see either the purpose of such a war or the need for it'. The Emperor retorted: 'Do people think I am mad? Do they think I fight for the fun of it?' Had they not heard him, the Emperor, say that 'the Spanish War and the Russian War were two cankers eating into France's vitals'? But it needed two to make peace, and not a single letter had come from Alexander.

And who was responsible for these *cankers?* These inconsequences tend to go unnoticed, and can even be used if need be as proof of Napoleon's naïve sincerity.

Bonaparte would have considered it degrading to admit that he had made a mistake. His soldiers complained that they no longer saw him except at the hour of battle, for ever sending them to their deaths, never keeping them alive; he remained deaf to these complaints. The news of the peace concluded between the Russians and the Turks surprised him but did not hold him back: he hurried towards Smolensk. The proclamations issued by the Russians declared: 'He is coming with treachery in his heart and loyalty on his lips, to put us in chains with his legions of slaves. Let us carry the cross in our hearts and steel in our hands; let us draw the teeth of this lion; let us overthrow the tyrant who has overthrown the world.'

On the heights of Smolensk, Napoleon caught up with the Russian army, which consisted of one hundred and twenty thousand men.

'I have them!' he cried.

At dawn on 17 August, Belliard pursued a band of Cossacks and hurled them into the Dnieper; when the curtain of troops had fallen back, the Russian army could be seen on the road to Moscow; it was withdrawing. Bonaparte's dream had eluded him once again. Murat, who had played a considerable part in the vain pursuit, felt such despair that he wanted to die. He refused to leave one of our batteries under fire from the citadel of Smolensk, which had not yet been evacuated. 'Get out, all of you! Leave me alone here!' he shouted. A terrible onslaught was launched against this citadel: lined up on the heights which form an amphitheatre above the town, our troops watched the battle raging below: when they saw the assault force plunging forward through fire and grapeshot, they clapped their hands as they had done at the sight of the ruins of Thebes.

During the night a fire attracted everyone's attention. One of Davoust's non-commissioned officers scaled the walls and entered the citadel through the smoke; the sound of voices reached him from a distance: pistol in hand, he went in that direction and, to his great surprise, he ran into a friendly patrol. The Russians had abandoned the town, and Poniatowski's Poles had occupied it.

From Smolensk, an army could be led equally well to St Petersburg and to Moscow. Smolensk should have warned the conqueror to stop; for a moment he thought of doing so. 'The Emperor,' says M. Fain, 'deeply discouraged, spoke of the possibility of stopping at Smolensk.' In the field-hospitals supplies were beginning to run out. General Gourgaud records that General Lariboisière was obliged to hand over the wadding of his guns to provide dressings for the wounded. But Bonaparte was carried away; he enjoyed watching at the two ends of Europe the two dawns that broke over his armies on scorching plains and frozen steppes.

Orlando,* in his narrow circle of chivalry, ran after Angelica; conquerors of the first order pursue a greater sovereign:
there can be no rest for them until they have clasped in their
arms the Earth-Goddess with her crown of towers, bride of
Time, daughter of Heaven, and mother of the gods. Obsessed
by his own existence, Bonaparte had reduced everything to the
limits of his person; Napoleon had taken possession of Napoleon; there was no longer anything in him but himself. So far he
had explored only famous places; now he was travelling a
nameless road along which Peter the Great had done little more
than sketch out the future cities of an empire that was not yet
a hundred years old. If examples were instructive, Bonaparte
might have felt anxious at the recollection of Charles XII passing through Smolensk on his way to Moscow. At Kolodrina
there was a murderous engagement; the corpses of the French
troops had been hurriedly buried, so that Napoleon could not
judge the extent of his losses. At Dorogobouj, he encountered
a Russian with a beard of dazzling whiteness covering his chest:
too old to follow his family and left alone in his house, he had
seen the marvels of the end of Peter the Great's reign, and now
watched, in silent indignation, the devastation of his country.

A succession of battles offered and refused brought the
French to the field of Borodino. At every bivouac, the Emperor
would discuss the situation with his generals, listening to their
arguments as he sat on some pine-branches or played with a
Russian cannon-ball which he poked about with his foot.

Barclay, the Livonian pastor who had become a general, was
the author of this system of retreats which gave autumn time to
overtake him: an intrigue at Court brought about his downfall.
Old Kutusoff, who had been beaten at Austerlitz because his
allies had refused to take his advice, which was to refuse battle
until the arrival of Prince Charles, took Barclay's place. In
Kutusoff the Russians saw a general of their own nation,
Suvuroff's pupil, the man who had defeated the Grand Vizier in
1811, and the author of the peace with the Sublime Porte,

* In the *Orlando Furioso* of Ariosto.

which was so necessary to Russia at this time. In the meantime a Muscovite officer presented himself at Davoust's outposts; he brought nothing but vague proposals; his real mission seemed to be to look and to examine: he was shown everything. The French, with their carefree, fearless curiosity, asked him what they would find between Viasma and Moscow.

'Pultava,'* he replied.

When he reached the heights of Borodino, Bonaparte saw that the Russian army had finally halted and was solidly entrenched. It consisted of one hundred and twenty thousand men and six hundred guns; the French had a similar force on their side. After examining the left wing of the Russian army, Marshal Davoust advised Napoleon to turn the enemy's flank.

'That would take me too long,' replied the Emperor.

Davoust pressed his point; he undertook to have completed his manoeuvre by six o'clock in the morning. Napoleon interrupted him sharply:

'Oh, you always want to turn the enemy's flank.'

A great stir had been noticed in the Muscovite camp; the troops were under arms; Kutusoff, surrounded by the popes and archimandrites, and preceded by the emblems of religion and a sacred icon rescued from the ruins of Smolensk, was speaking to his soldiers about Heaven and their native land, calling Napoleon the universal despot.

In the French camps too, in the midst of songs of battle and triumphant choruses mingled with cries of pain, a Christian voice was heard; it stood out from all the rest; it was the holy hymn rising by itself beneath the vaults of time. The soldier whose voice, calm yet full of emotion, lingered on after the others, was the aide-de-camp of the marshal in command of the Horseguards. This aide-de-camp had been in all the battles of the Russian campaign; he spoke of Napoleon like his greatest admirers, but he recognized his weaknesses; he corrected lying anecdotes and declared that the mistakes which had been

* Pultava was the town in the Ukraine where Charles XII of Sweden was defeated by the Russians in 1709.

committed were due to the leader's pride and the forgetfulness of God among his captains.

The day before the storm was extremely quiet. 'The sort of wisdom,' says M. de Baudus, 'which goes to the preparation of such cruel follies, is humiliating for human reason when one thinks about it in cold blood at the age which I have attained; for in my youth I found it most impressive.'

Towards evening on 6 September, Bonaparte dictated this proclamation; it was known to most of his troops only after the victory:

'Soldiers, here is the battle for which you have longed so ardently. Henceforth victory depends on you; we need it to bring us plenty and a speedy return home. Conduct yourselves as you did at Austerlitz, Friedland, Vitebsk, and Smolensk, and may the most remote posterity cite your conduct on this day. May men say of you: "He was at that great battle beneath the walls of Moscow."'

Bonaparte spent the night in a state of anxiety, now thinking that the enemy was withdrawing, now worrying about the destitution of his soldiers and the weariness of his officers. He knew what was being said all around him: 'Why have we been made to march two thousand miles to find nothing but marshy water, famine, and bivouacs in smoking ruins? Every year the war grows worse; fresh conquests force him to seek out fresh enemies. Soon Europe will not be enough for him; he will hanker after Asia.' And indeed Bonaparte had not looked with an indifferent eye at the waters which flowed into the Volga; born for Babylon, he had already been tempted by another route. Halted at Jaffa at the western entrance to Asia, and halted at Moscow at the northern gateway to the same continent, he was to go and die among the seas bordering that part of the world where mankind and the sun were born.

In the middle of the night, Napoleon sent for one of his aides-de-camp, who found him with his head buried in his hands.

'What is war?' he asked. 'A barbaric profession whose only secret consists in being the stronger at a given point.'

He complained of the inconstancy of fortune; he asked for reports on the enemy positions; he was told that there were the same number of fires burning, and just as brightly; he calmed down. At five o'clock in the morning, Ney sent a messenger to ask for the attack formation; Bonaparte went out and exclaimed:

'Let us open the gates of Moscow!'

Dawn broke; Napoleon pointed to the sky in the east which was beginning to redden.

'The sun of Austerlitz!' he cried.

Anathema to the victories which are not won in defence of the motherland, but which serve only to feed the vanity of a conqueror!

The Guard, composed of twenty-five thousand crack troops, played no part in the Battle of Borodino; Bonaparte refused to throw it in on various pretexts. Contrary to his custom, he stayed away from the fighting and could not follow the manoeuvres with his own eyes. He would sit down or pace to and fro beside a redoubt taken the day before; when he was told of the death of some of his generals, he made a gesture of resignation. This impassibility on his part caused considerable surprise. Ney asked:

'What is he doing behind the army? There, only reverses can reach him, not successes. Since he has stopped fighting for himself, since he is no longer a true general, and since he wants to play the emperor everywhere, let him go back to the Tuileries and leave us to be generals in his place.'

Murat admitted that on that great day he had been unable to distinguish any sign of Napoleon's genius.

Uncritical admirers have attributed Napoleon's torpor to the worsening of the ailments from which, so they tell us, he was suffering; they maintain that he was frequently obliged to dismount and that often he would stand still with his forehead pressed against the barrel of a cannon. This may be true: a temporary indisposition could have contributed at that moment to the diminution of his energy; but in view of the fact that he recovered that energy in the campaign in Saxony and in his famous French campaign, one must look for another explanation of his inaction at Borodino. He confesses in his bulletin that *it would have been easy to manoeuvre in such a way as to force the enemy to abandon his good position, but that would have postponed the issue*; yet although he has enough *mental agility* to condemn thousands of our soldiers to death, he has not enough *physical strength* to order his Guard so much as to go to their aid. There can be no other explanation of this than the very nature of the man: adversity had come upon the scene; its first touch froze his blood. Napoleon's greatness was not of the sort which thrives on calamity; only success left him in full possession of his faculties: he was not made for misfortune.

Between the Moskva and Moscow, Murat joined battle outside Moshaisk. The French entered the town to find ten thousand dead and dying; the dead were thrown out of the windows to make room for the living. The Russians fell back in good order towards Moscow.

During the evening of 13 September, Kutusoff had summoned a council of war: all the generals declared that 'Moscow was not the motherland'. Buturlin, the same officer that Alexander sent to join the Duc d'Angoulême in Spain, writing in his *History of the Russian Campaign*, and Barclay, in his *Justificatory Memoir*, give the reasons for the council's opinion. Kutusoff proposed a cease-fire to the King of Naples while the Russian troops passed through the ancient capital of the Tsars. The cease-fire was agreed to, for the French wanted to keep the city intact; only Murat pressed the enemy rearguard hard, and our grenadiers followed on the heels of the retreating Russian grenadiers. But Napoleon was a long way from achieving the success which he believed to be within reach: hiding behind Kutusoff was Rostopchin.

Count Rostopchin was the Governor of Moscow. He had laid plans for vengeance to drop from Heaven: a huge balloon, constructed at considerable expense, was to float above the French army, pick out the Emperor among his thousands of troops, and fall upon him in a shower of fire and steel. When it was tried out, the wings of the airship broke, and the idea of a bombshell falling from the clouds had to be abandoned; but Rostopchin kept the flares. The news of the Borodino disaster had reached Moscow while the rest of the Empire was still rejoicing over what Kutusoff's bulletin called a victory. Rostopchin had issued various proclamations in rhyming prose, in which he said:

'Come, my friends the Muscovites, let us march into battle too! We will gather together one hundred thousand men, we will take a picture of the Holy Virgin and one hundred and fifty guns, and we will put an end to everything.'

He advised the inhabitants to arm themselves with nothing but a pitchfork, a Frenchman weighing no more than a sheaf of corn.

It is known that Rostopchin later denied that he had played any part in the burning of Moscow; it is known too that Alexander never made any statement on the subject. Did Rostopchin wish to avoid the reproaches of the nobles and merchants who had been ruined by the fire? Was Alexander afraid of being called a Barbarian by the Institut? This is such a contemptible age, and Napoleon had monopolized its splendours to such a degree, that when something praiseworthy happened, everyone repudiated it and disclaimed all responsibility for it.

The burning of Moscow will go down in history as a heroic deed which saved the freedom of one nation and contributed to the liberation of several others. Numantia* has not lost its right to the admiration of mankind. What does it matter that Moscow was burnt; had it not been burnt seven times already? Has it not been splendidly restored, in spite of Napoleon's prophecy that 'the burning of this capital would put the clock back a hundred years in Russia'? 'The very misfortune of Moscow,' says Mme de Staël in an admirable judgement, 'regenerated the empire: that holy city died like a martyr whose blood when it is shed gives new strength to his surviving brothers.'

Where would the nations be if Bonaparte, enthroned in the Kremlin, had covered the world with his tyranny as with a pall? The rights of the human race are paramount. Speaking for myself, if the world were an explosive globe, I would not hesitate to set fire to it if it were a question of setting my country free. All the same, it needs nothing less than the superior interests of human liberty to induce a Frenchman, his head

---

* A town in Spain which was destroyed by the Romans in 133 BC.

bowed in mourning and his eyes full of tears, to speak of a decision which was to prove fatal to so many of his fellow
countrymen.

The evacuation of Moscow had begun; the roads to Kazan
were covered with fugitives on foot or in carriages, alone or
accompanied by their servants. An omen had been observed
which had raised everyone's spirits for a moment: a vulture had
got caught in the chains supporting the cross on the principal
church; Rome, like Moscow, would have seen in this omen
Napoleon's captivity.

At the approach of the long convoys of wounded Russian
soldiers arriving at the gates of the city, all hope vanished.
Kutusoff had promised Rostopchin to defend the city with the
ninety-one thousand men that remained to him: you have just
seen how the council of war compelled him to withdraw. Rostopchin was left alone.

Night fell: messengers went knocking mysteriously at every
door, announcing that all must leave and that Nineveh was
doomed. Inflammable matter was introduced into public buildings and bazaars, into private houses and shops; the city's
fire-brigade apparatus was taken away.

Then Rostopchin ordered the prisons to be opened: from the
midst of a filthy horde of prisoners a Russian and a Frenchman
were brought forward; the Russian, a member of a sect of
German illuminati, was accused of having tried to deliver his
country to the enemy and of having translated the French proclamation; his father ran up; the Governor granted him a few
moments to bless his son. 'Me bless a traitor!' cried the old
Muscovite, and he cursed him. The prisoner was handed over
to the populace and killed.

'As for you,' said Rostopchin to the Frenchman, 'you were
bound to want your fellow countrymen to arrive: you are free.
Go and tell your people that Russia had only a single traitor
and that he has been punished.'

The other prisoners who were released were given, with
their freedom, instructions on setting fire to the city when the
time was ripe. Rostopchin was the last to leave Moscow, just as
a captain is the last to leave a sinking ship.

Napoleon had joined his vanguard on horseback. One height remained to be crossed; it overlooked Moscow as Montmartre overlooks Paris; it was called Salvation Hill, because the Russians used to pray there within sight of the holy city, like the pilgrims when they saw Jerusalem. Moscow of the gilded cupolas, as the Slav poets say, shone in the sunlight with its two hundred and ninety-five churches, its fifteen hundred castles, its wooden houses coloured yellow, green, and pink: nothing was missing but the cypresses and the Bosphorus. The Kremlin formed part of this mass of buildings roofed with polished or painted iron. In the midst of smart villas in brick and marble, the Moskva flowed through parks planted with firs, the palm-trees of that region: Venice in the days of its glory was not more splendid in the waves of the Adriatic. It was on 14 September, at two o'clock in the afternoon, that Bonaparte, by the light of a sun studded with the diamonds of the Pole, saw his new conquest for the first time. Moscow, like a European princess on the confines of his empire, decked out in all the riches of Asia, seemed to have been brought there to marry Napoleon.

A shout went up.

'Moscow! Moscow!' cried our soldiers; they clapped their hands again; in the days of our old glory, they used to shout, in victory or defeat: 'Long live the King!' 'It was a wonderful moment,' says Lieutenant-Colonel de Baudus, 'when the magnificent panorama presented by the whole of that huge city first opened up before my eyes. I shall always remember the emotion that was shown among the ranks of the Polish division; it struck me all the more in that it was revealed in an impulsive action marked by religious feeling. On seeing Moscow, whole regiments fell on their knees and thanked God for bringing them through victory to the capital of their bitterest foe.'

The acclamations died away; the army made its way quietly towards the city; no deputation came out through the gates to present the keys in a silver bowl. The movement of life had been suspended in the great city. Moscow fell in silence before the stranger: three days later she had disappeared; the Circassian of the North, the beautiful fiancée, had laid herself on her funeral pyre.

When the city was still standing, Napoleon exclaimed as he
went towards it: 'So this is the famous city!' and he gazed at it:
Moscow, abandoned to its fate, looked like the city mourned
over in the Lamentations. Already Eugène and Poniatowski
had climbed the walls; a few of our officers entered the city;
they came back and told Napoleon:

'Moscow is deserted!'

'Moscow deserted? I can't believe that. Bring me the boyars.'

But there were no boyars left, only a few poor beggars in
hiding. The streets were empty, the windows closed: no smoke
rose from the houses from which clouds would soon be escaping. There was not the slightest sound to be heard. Bonaparte
shrugged his shoulders.

Murat, pushing on as far as the Kremlin, was greeted with
howls of fury from the prisoners who had been released in
order to save their country: the French had to blast the gates
open with their guns.

Napoleon had gone to the Dorogomilow gate; he installed
himself in one of the first houses in the suburb, went riding
along the Moskva, and met no one. He returned to his quarters
and appointed Marshal Mortier governor of Moscow, General
Durosnel army commandant, and M. de Lesseps administrative
officer in his capacity as quartermaster-general. The Imperial
Guard and all the troops were in full-dress uniform to parade
before a populace that was absent. Bonaparte soon learnt for
certain that the city was threatened with some calamity. At two
o'clock in the morning he was told that fire had broken out.
The conqueror left the suburb of Dorogomilow and took refuge in the Kremlin; this was on the morning of the 15th. He
experienced a moment of joy on entering the palace of Peter the
Great; in his contented pride he wrote a few words to Alexander, by the light of the bazaar which had just started burning,
just as the defeated Alexander had written him a note from the
battlefield of Austerlitz.

In the bazaar long rows of shops were seen to be locked up.
The fire was contained at first, but during the second night it
broke out again all over the city; globes thrown into the air by
rocket devices burst and fell in sheaves of light on the palaces

and churches. A strong north wind drove the sparks before it and scattered the flakes of fire on the Kremlin: the imperial palace contained a powder magazine; an artillery-park had been left under Bonaparte's very windows. Our soldiers were driven from one district to another by the effluvia of the volcano. Gorgons and Medusas, torch in hand, ran across the livid crossroads of this inferno; others poked the fire with spears of tarred wood. Bonaparte, in the halls of the new Pergamos, rushed to the windows, crying:

'What extraordinary determination! What men! They are Scythians!'

The rumour spread that the Kremlin was mined: servants fainted and soldiers resigned themselves to their fate. The mouths of various fires outside grew wider, came nearer, and met; the tower of the Arsenal, like a tall taper, burnt in the midst of a blazing sanctuary. Soon the Kremlim was nothing but a black island washed by the waves of a sea of fire. The sky, reflecting the glow from the city beneath, looked as if it were dappled by the moving lights of an aurora borealis.

The third night fell; the French could scarcely breathe in the suffocating atmosphere; on two occasions fuses had been attached to the building occupied by Napoleon. How were they to make their escape? The flames had drawn together to block the gates of the citadel. After looking everywhere, some-one found a postern opening on to the Moskva. The conqueror and his guards slipped out through this gateway to safety. All around him in the city, archways were collapsing with a thunderous roar, and belfries, from which torrents of molten metal were pouring, were leaning over, breaking away, and falling. Beams, rafters, and roofs, cracking, sparkling, and crumbling, plunged into a Phlegethon whose burning waves they sent splashing up in a million golden spangles. Bonaparte made his escape over the cold embers of a district already reduced to ashes, and went to Petrovsky, the Tsar's villa.

From the shores of St Helena, Napoleon looked back in memory and saw the city of the Scythians burning once more.

'Never,' he said, 'for all their poetry, can any of the fictional accounts of the fire of Troy approach the reality of the burning of Moscow.'

Leaving Moscow during the night of 15 September, Napoleon returned to the city on the 18th. On his way back, he had come across camp-fires burning in the mud, fed with mahogany furniture and gilded panelling. Around these fires were filthy, mud-stained soldiers, dressed in rags, lying on silk sofas or sitting in velvet armchairs, using Kashmir shawls, Siberian furs or golden fabrics from Persia as carpets under their feet, and eating out of silver dishes a black paste or the bleeding flesh of grilled horse.

Irregular looting having begun, it was put on a regular basis; each regiment fell upon the quarry in turn. Peasants driven from their huts, Cossacks and deserters from the enemy army roamed around the French camps and fed on the leavings of our troops. Everything that could be carried was taken; often, overloaded with this booty, our soldiers threw it away, when they happened to remember that they were fifteen hundred miles from home.

The expeditions they went on to find provisions produced some pathetic incidents: one French patrol was bringing back a cow when a woman came up to them, accompanied by a man who was carrying in his arms a child a few months old; they pointed to the cow which had just been taken from them. The mother tore the wretched clothes covering her breasts, to show that she had no milk left; the father made a gesture as if to break the child's head on a stone. The officer made his men return the cow, and adds: 'The effect which this scene had on my soldiers was such that for a long time not a single word was spoken in the ranks.'

The Kremlin contained a double throne for two brothers: Napoleon did not share his. In one of the rooms there was the stretcher shattered by a cannon-ball on which the wounded Charles XII had had himself carried in the Battle of Pultava. Always eclipsed as he was by others when it was a question of

generous feelings, did Bonaparte, when he visited the tombs of
the Tsars, remember that on feast-days they were covered with
magnificent palls; that when a subject had some favour to
solicit, he laid his petition on one of the tombs, and that only
the Tsar had the right to remove it?

These petitions of misfortune, presented by death to power
and majesty, were not to Napoleon's taste. He was preoccupied
with other matters: partly out of a desire to deceive, and partly
because it was in his nature, he planned, as he had done on leaving Egypt, to send for actors to come to Moscow, and he declared
that an Italian singer was going to arrive. He pillaged the churches
of the Kremlin, and filled his wagons with sacred ornaments and
icons next to the crescents and horse-tails captured from the
Mohammedans. He had the huge cross on the tower of Ivan the
Great taken down: he intended to put it on the dome of the Invalides: it would have complemented the masterpieces from the
Vatican with which he had decorated the Louvre. While this cross
was being removed, crows fluttered around, cawing loudly.

'What do those birds want with me?' asked Bonaparte.

The moment of decision drew near: Daru raised objections
to various plans outlined by Bonaparte.

'What should we do then?' asked the Emperor.

'Stay here, turn Moscow into a huge fortified camp, spend
the winter here, salt the horses that can't be fed, and wait for
spring. Our reinforcements and the Lithuanians will come to
relieve us and complete the conquest of Russia.'

'That's a lion's advice,' replied Napoleon. 'But what would
Paris say? France would not suffer my absence.'

'What are they saying about me in Athens?' Alexander used
to say.

He gave himself up once more to uncertainty; to stay or to
go? He could not make up his mind. There followed countless
deliberations. Finally an engagement that took place at Vinkovo on 18 October persuaded him to leave the ruins of Moscow
with his army: that same day, without any fuss, without any
noise, without even looking back, wishing to avoid the direct
route to Smolensk, he took one of the two roads to Kaluga.

For thirty-five days, like those fearsome African monsters

which go to sleep when they have eaten their fill, he had forgotten himself: this was apparently the time it took to change the lot of a man such as Napoleon. During that period the star of his destiny sank in the heavens. At last he awoke, pressed between the winter and a burnt-out capital; he hurried away from the ruins; it was too late; a hundred thousand men were doomed to die.

Going through Gjatsk, Napoleon pressed forward to Viasma; he went on, not having met the enemy whom he had been afraid of encountering in that town. On 3 November he reached Slavskovo; there he learnt that a battle had been fought behind him at Viasma; this battle with Miloradovich's troops was fatal to the French: our wounded soldiers and officers, their arms in slings and their heads bandaged, threw themselves with superhuman courage upon the enemy's guns.

This succession of engagements in the same places, these layers of dead added to other layers, these battles echoed by other battles, would have immortalized these fatal fields twice over, if oblivion did not spread rapidly over our dust. Who gives a thought to those peasants left behind in Russia? Are those rustics happy to have been 'at the great battle beneath the walls of Moscow'? I am perhaps the only person who, on autumn evenings, watching the birds from the north flying high up in the sky, remembers that they have seen the graves of our fellow countrymen. Industrial companies have gone out into the wilderness with their furnaces and their cauldrons; the bones have been turned into animal-black: whether it comes from dog or man, varnish is the same price, and it does not shine any more brightly for being taken from obscurity or glory. There you have the respect which we show the dead today. There you have the sacred rites of the new religion. *Diis Manibus.** Fortunate companions of Charles XII, you were not visited by these sacrilegious hyenas! During the winter the ermine frequents the virginal snows, and during the summer the flowering mosses of Pultava.

* 'To the Gods of the Shades': the traditional Roman epitaph.

On 6 November the thermometer dropped to zero: everything disappeared under a blanket of snow. The bootless soldiers felt their feet dying; their stiff, purple fingers dropped their muskets whose very touch burnt; their hair bristled with hoarfrost, their beards with their frozen breath; their pitiful rags turned into frosty cassocks. They fell, and the snow covered them; they formed little furrows of tombs on the ground. It was impossible to tell which way the rivers flowed; they had to break the ice to find out which direction to take. Lost in the wilderness, the various army corps lit fires to call one another and recognize one another, just as ships in peril fire a distress signal. Fir-trees transformed into motionless crystals stood here and there, serving as candelabra for these obsequies. Crows and packs of white dogs followed this procession of corpses at a distance.

It was galling, after a long march, to be obliged, at a deserted halting-place, to take the precautions of a strong, well-equipped army, to post sentries, to occupy positions, to station outpost pickets. During nights lasting sixteen hours, battered by squalls from the north, our troops did not know where to sit or where to lie; trees chopped down with all their alabaster trimmings refused to catch fire; it was as much as they could do to melt a little snow in order to mix a spoonful of rye flour with it. They had no sooner stretched themselves out on the bare ground than the howling of Cossacks echoed through the woods; the light artillery of the enemy rumbled; our soldiers' fast was saluted like a royal banquet, when kings sit down to dinner; cannon-balls rolled like iron loaves among the famished guests. At dawn, which was never followed by daybreak, the beating of a drum draped in frost or the hoarse sound of a trumpet could be heard: there could be nothing sadder than this mournful reveille, calling to arms warriors whom it roused no more. The growing light revealed circles of infantrymen sitting stiff and dead around extinguished fires.

Smolensk was finally reached on 9 November. An order from Bonaparte had forbidden anyone to be allowed to enter before the sentry-posts had been handed over to the Imperial Guard.

The soldiers outside gathered together at the foot of the walls; the soldiers inside kept the gates shut. The air was rent with the curses of the desperate outcasts, who were dressed in patched greatcoats, ragged cloaks and uniforms, blankets and horse-cloths, with their heads covered with caps, twisted kerchiefs, battered shakos, warped and dented helmets; all this spattered with blood or snow, riddled with bullets or scarred with sword-cuts. Haggard and drawn, they gazed up at the ramparts with dark, flashing eyes, gnashing their teeth and looking like those mutilated prisoners who, under Louis the Fat, carried their amputated left hand in their right: one might have taken them for mourners in a frenzy or for demented patients who had escaped from a madhouse. The Guards arrived, and entered the town which had been burnt down when we had passed through it for the first time. There were shouts of anger directed at the privileged band: 'Will the army never have anything but their leavings?' The famished cohorts ran pell-mell to the shops like an insurrection of ghosts; they were repulsed and started fighting: the dead were left in the streets, the women, the children, and the dying in carts. The air reeked of the corruption of a host of old corpses; some soldiers were stricken with imbecility or madness; some whose hair was tangled or standing on end, blaspheming or shaking with crazy laughter, dropped dead. Bonaparte vented his anger on a poor, incompetent contractor, none of whose orders had been carried out.

The army of a hundred thousand men, now reduced to thirty thousand, was accompanied by a mob of fifty thousand camp-followers. There were only eighteen hundred cavalry who still had their horses; Napoleon placed them under the orders of M. de Latour-Maubourg. This officer, who led the cuirassiers in the attack on the great redoubt at Borodino, had his head split open by sword-thrusts; later he lost a leg at Dresden. Seeing his orderly weeping he said to him: 'What are you complaining about? You will only have one boot to polish now.' This general, remaining faithful to misfortune, has become Henri V's tutor for the first years of the young prince's exile: I raise my hat when I pass him, for it is as if I were passing honour incarnate.

*

At Malodeczno, on 3 December, the French found all the couriers who had been halted there for the past three weeks. It was there that Napoleon thought of abandoning the flag.

'Can I remain,' he asked, 'at the head of a rout?'

At Smorgoni, the King of Naples and Prince Eugène urged him to return to France. The Duc d'Istrie acted as spokesman; at his very first words Napoleon flew into a fury, shouting:

'Only my worst enemy could suggest that I should leave the army in its present situation.'

He made as if to hurl himself at the marshal, sword in hand. In the evening he sent for the Duc d'Istrie and said to him:

'Since you all wish it, I shall have to go.'

The scene was carefully arranged; the decision to go had already been taken when it was acted. M. Fain tells us in fact that the Emperor had resolved to leave the army in the course of the march 'which took him from Malodeczno to Biclitza'. Such was the comedy with which the great actor brought his tragic drama to a close.

At Smorgoni the Emperor wrote his twenty-ninth bulletin. On 5 December he got on to a sledge with M. de Caulaincourt: it was ten o'clock in the evening. He crossed Germany hidden under the name of his companion in flight. With his disappearance everything collapsed: in a storm, when a granite colossus buries itself in the sands of the Thebaid, not a single shadow remains in the desert. A few soldiers in whom nothing was left alive but their heads, ended up by eating one another in shelters made of pine-branches. Misfortunes which had seemed incapable of becoming any worse reached fruition: winter, which so far had been only the autumn of those regions, descended. The Russians no longer had the heart to fire, in the icy wastes, at the frozen shadows which Bonaparte had left to wander after him.

SIX

The Fall of Napoleon

It needed nothing less than the calamities weighing upon France to maintain the aversion which Napoleon inspired and at the same time to resist the admiration which he aroused once he bestirred himself again. He was the greatest genius of action that ever existed; his first Italian campaign and his last French campaign (I am not speaking of Waterloo) are his two finest campaigns: he was Condé in the first, Turenne in the second, a great soldier in the former, a great man in the latter; but they differed in their results: by the one he won the Empire, by the other he lost it. His last hours of power, chaotic and destitute though they were, could not be drawn from him, like a lion's teeth, save by the combined efforts of the arms of Europe. The name of Napoleon was still so awe-inspiring that the enemy armies crossed the Rhine in terror; they kept looking over their shoulders to make sure that they had a line of retreat open; masters of Paris, they trembled for all that. Alexander, casting his eyes towards Russia as he entered France, congratulated those who were able to return, and communicated his anxieties and regrets to his mother.

On 20 March an engagement took place near Arcis-sur-Aube. During an artillery barrage, a shell fell in front of a square of the Guards and the square appeared to make a slight movement. Bonaparte dashed up to the projectile, whose fuse was smoking, and made his horse sniff at it; the shell exploded, and the Emperor came safe and sound from the midst of the shattered thunderbolt.

The battle was to begin again the following day, but Bonaparte, yielding to the inspiration of genius, an inspiration which was nonetheless fatal to him, withdrew in order to bear upon the rear of the allied troops, separate them from their stores, and swell his own army with the garrison of the frontier forts. The foreigners were preparing to fall back upon the Rhine when Alexander, by one of those heaven-sent impulses which change a whole world, made up his mind to march on Paris, the road to which was opening up. Napoleon thought he was drawing the bulk of the enemy force after him, and he was followed by only ten thousand cavalry, whom he took to be the vanguard of the main body of troops, when in fact they masked the real movement of the Prussians and Muscovites. He scattered those ten thousand horse at Saint-Dizier and Vitry, and then perceived that the main allied army was not behind them; that army, which was rushing towards the capital, had nothing before it but Marshal Marmont and Marshal Mortier with some twelve thousand conscripts.

Men's minds were greatly agitated. The hope of seeing the end, whatever it might cost, of a cruel war which for twenty years had been weighing down upon a France sated with misfortune and glory, carried the day, among the masses, over the feeling of national pride. Everyone began thinking about the decisions he would have to make in the approaching catastrophe. Every evening my friends came to talk at Mme de Chateaubriand's, where they recounted and discussed the day's happenings. MM. de Fontanes, de Clausel, and Joubert came along with a host of those transient friends which events bring and events take away. Mme la Duchesse de Lévis, beautiful, tranquil, and devoted, kept Mme de Chateaubriand faithful company. Mme la Duchesse de Duras was also in Paris, and I often went to see Mme la Marquise de Montcalm, the Duc de Richelieu's sister.

I continued to be convinced, in spite of the approach of the fighting, that the Allies would not enter Paris and that a national uprising would put an end to our fears. This conviction prevented me from feeling the presence of the foreign armies as keenly as I might have done; but I could not help thinking about the calamities which we had inflicted upon Europe, as I saw Europe bringing them back home to us.

I went on working on my pamphlet *De Bonaparte et des*

Bourbons; I was preparing it as a remedy for the time when anarchy was going to burst upon us. We no longer write like that nowadays, living as we do with easy minds and nothing to fear but newspaper skirmishes: at night I locked myself in my room; I put my papers under my pillow, and a pair of loaded pistols on my table. I slept between these two muses.

I had nonetheless been obliged to entrust a printer with my secret; he had agreed to take on this dangerous commission; according to the news of the hour, he would return the half-composed proofs to me or come to take them back, as the sound of gunfire drew nearer to or farther away from Paris: I played pitch and toss with my life in this way for a fortnight.

The circle was tightening around the capital: every moment we heard of some progress made by the enemy. Russian prisoners and French wounded were carried pell-mell through the gates in carts; some of them, half-dead, fell under the wheels, which they stained with blood. Conscripts called up from the interior crossed the capital in a long file on their way to join the armies. At night, artillery trains could be heard passing along the outer boulevards, and it was impossible to tell whether the distant detonations announced decisive victory or final defeat.

The war finally came and installed itself outside the gates of Paris. From the towers of Notre-Dame, one could see the heads of the Russian columns appearing, like the first waves of the tide on a beach. I felt what a Roman must have experienced when, from the top of the Capitol, he saw Alaric's soldiers* and the ancient city of the Latins at his feet, just as I could see the Russian soldiers and, at my feet, the ancient city of the Gauls. Farewell, then, paternal gods, hearths which preserved the country's traditions, roofs beneath which had breathed both Virginia,† sacrificed by her father to modesty and liberty, and Héloïse, consecrated by love to letters and religion.

Paris had not seen the smoke of an enemy's camp-fires for

* Alaric, King of the Visigoths, laid siege to Rome in 409 and took the city in 410.
† Virginia was killed by her father, Virginius, in 449 BC to save her from Appius Claudius, one of the Decemvirs of Rome.

centuries, and it was Bonaparte who, going from triumph to triumph, had brought the Thebans within sight of the women of Sparta. Paris was the point from which he had started to conquer the world: he returned to it leaving behind him the immense conflagration of his useless conquests.

People rushed to the Jardin des Plantes, which in olden times the fortified Abbey of Saint-Victor might have been able to protect: the little world of swans and plantain-trees, to which our power had promised eternal peace, was rudely disturbed. From the top of the maze, looking over the great cedar, over the granaries which Bonaparte had not had time to finish building, beyond the site of the Bastille and the keep of Vincennes (spots which told the tale of our historical development), the crowd watched the infantry-fire in the fighting at Belleville. Montmartre was taken by assault: the cannon-balls fell as far as the Boulevard du Temple. A few companies of the National Guard made a sortie and lost three hundred men in the fields around the tomb of the 'martyrs'. Never did military France shine with brighter glory in the midst of her reverses: the last heroes were the one hundred and fifty boys of the Polytechnic School, transformed into gunners in the redoubts along the Vincennes road. Surrounded by the enemy, they refused to surrender; they had to be torn from their guns: the Russian grenadier seized them, blackened with gunpowder and covered with wounds; while they struggled in his arms, he lifted those young French palm-branches in the air with cries of triumph and admiration, and restored them, bleeding as they were, to their mothers.

God had pronounced one of those words which at rare intervals interrupt the silence of eternity. Then, in the midst of the present generation, the hammer rose to strike the hour which Paris had heard sound only once before: on 25 December 496 Reims announced the baptism of Clovis, and the gates of Lutetia opened to the Franks; on 30 March 1814, after the baptism of blood of Louis XVI, the old hammer which had remained motionless for so long rose once more in the belfry of the ancient monarchy: a second stroke rang out, and the Tartars entered Paris.

Bonaparte had waged an unjust war against Alexander, his

admirer, who had gone down on his knees to beg for peace; Bonaparte had ordered the slaughter of Borodino; he had forced the Russians themselves to burn Moscow; Bonaparte had plundered Berlin, humiliated its King, insulted its Queen: what reprisals were we, then, to expect? You shall see.

I had wandered in the Floridas around nameless monuments, devastated in olden days by conquerors of whom no trace remains, and I had lived to see the Caucasian hordes encamped in the courtyard of the Louvre. In those historic events, which, according to Montaigne, 'are feeble testimonies of our worth and capacity', my tongue cleaves to my palate: *adhaeret lingua mea faucibus meis.**

The Allied Army entered Paris at midday on 31 March 1814, only ten days after the anniversary of the death of the Duc d'Enghien, 21 March 1804. Was it worth Bonaparte's while to commit a deed of such long remembrance for the sake of a reign which was to last so short a time? The Emperor of Russia and the King of Prussia rode at the head of their troops, whom I watched marching along the boulevards. Stupefied and amazed within myself, as if my name as a Frenchman had been torn from me to be replaced by the number by which I was henceforth to be known in the mines of Siberia, I felt at the same time my exasperation increase against the man whose glory had reduced us to this shame.

However, this first invasion of the Allies has remained unparalleled in the annals of the world: peace, order, and moderation reigned on every hand; the shops opened again; Russian guardsmen, six foot tall, were piloted through the streets by little French urchins who made fun of them, calling them jumping-jacks and carnival mummers. The vanquished might have been taken for the victors; the latter, trembling at their success, looked as if they were apologizing for it. The National Guard alone garrisoned the interior of Paris, except for the houses in which the foreign kings and princes were lodged. On 31 March 1814 countless armies were occupying France; a few months later, all these troops went back across our frontiers,

* Psalms, xxi, 16.

without firing a musket-shot and without shedding a drop of blood after the return of the Bourbons. The France of old found herself enlarged on some of her frontiers; the ships and stores of Antwerp were shared with her; three hundred thousand prisoners, scattered over the countries where victory or defeat had left them, were restored to her. After twenty-five years of fighting, the sound of arms ceased from one end of Europe to the other. Alexander departed, leaving us the masterpieces which we had conquered and the liberty lodged in the Charter, a liberty which we owed as much to his enlightenment as to his influence. The head of the two supreme authorities, an autocrat by the sword and by religion, he alone of all the sovereigns of Europe had understood that, at the age of civilization which France had attained, she could be governed only by virtue of a free constitution.

In our very natural hostility to foreigners, we have tended to confuse the invasions of 1814 and 1815, which were in no sense alike.

Alexander regarded himself simply as an instrument of Providence and took no credit to himself. When Mme de Staël complimented him on the good fortune which his subjects, lacking a constitution, enjoyed of being ruled by him, he made his well-known reply:

'I am only a happy incident.'

A young man in a Paris street expressed to him his admiration at the affability with which he greeted the humblest citizens; he replied:

'Are not sovereigns made for that?'

He refused to occupy the Tuileries, remembering that Bonaparte had taken his pleasure in the palaces of Vienna, Berlin, and Moscow.

Looking at the statue of Napoleon on the column in the Place Vendôme, he said:

'If I were as high up as that, I should be afraid of becoming giddy.'

When he was going over the Palace of the Tuileries, he was shown the Salon de la Paix.

'What use,' he asked laughingly, 'was this room to Bona-parte?'

On the day of Louis XVIII's entry into Paris, Alexander hid behind a window, wearing no mark of distinction, to watch the procession go by.

He sometimes revealed considerable elegance and charm of manner. Visiting a madhouse, he asked a woman if there were many women there who had gone mad with love.

'Not at present,' she replied, 'but it is to be feared that the number will increase as from the time of Your Majesty's entry into Paris.'

One of Napoleon's grand dignitaries said to the Tsar:

'We have been waiting and hoping for your arrival for a long time, Sire.'

'I would have come sooner,' he replied; 'you must blame only French valour for the delay.'

It is known that when crossing the Rhine he had regretted not being able to return in peace to his family.

At the Hôtel des Invalides, he found the maimed soldiers who had defeated him at Austerlitz: they were silent and gloomy; nothing could be heard but the sound of their wooden legs in their deserted courtyards and their denuded church. Alexander was touched by this noise of brave men: he gave orders that twelve Russians guns should be given back to them.

A proposal to change the name of the Pont d'Austerlitz was put to him.

'No,' he said, 'it is enough for me to have crossed that bridge with my army.'

Alexander had something calm and sad about him. He went about Paris, on horseback or on foot, without a suite and with-out affectation. He seemed surprised at his victory; his almost tender gaze wandered over a population whom he appeared to consider superior to himself: one gained the impression that he thought himself a Barbarian among us, just as a Roman felt ashamed of himself in Athens. Perhaps too he reflected that these same Frenchmen had been in his burnt-out capital; that his sol-diers in their turn were masters of Paris, where he might have found some of the now extinguished torches by which Moscow was liberated and consumed. This fickle destiny, these changing fortunes, this common distress of peoples and of kings were bound to make a profound impression on a mind as religious as his.

But what was the victor of Borodino doing? As soon as he had heard of Alexander's decision, he had sent orders to Major Maillard de Lescourt of the artillery to blow up the Grenelle powder-magazine: Rostopchin had set fire to Moscow, but he had evacuated the inhabitants first. From Fontainebleau, to which he had returned, Napoleon advanced as far as Villejuif: there he looked down at Paris; foreign soldiers were guarding the city gates; the conqueror remembered the days when his grenadiers had kept watch on the ramparts of Berlin, Moscow, and Vienna.

Events efface other events; how paltry today seems the grief of Henri IV learning of the death of Gabrielle at Villejuif, and returning to Fontainebleau! Bonaparte too returned to that solitude; there nothing awaited him but the memory of his august prisoner*: the captive of peace had just departed from the palace in order to leave it free for the captive of war, 'so swiftly does misfortune fill its places'.

The Regency had retired to Blois. Bonaparte had given orders for the Empress and the King of Rome to leave Paris, saying that he would rather see them at the bottom of the Seine than taken to Vienna in triumph; but at the same time he had urged Joseph to stay in the capital. His brother's flight made him furious, and he accused the King of Spain of ruining everything. The ministers, the members of the Regency, Napoleon's brothers, his wife, and his son arrived in disorder at Blois, swept away by the débâcle; wagons, baggage-vans, carriages, everything was there; even the King's coaches had been brought along and were dragged through the mud of the Beauce to Chambord, the only morsel of France left to the heir of Louis

* Pope Pius VII, who had been released from his captivity at Fontainebleau on 23 January 1814.

XIV. Some of the ministers did not stop there, but went on to hide in Brittany, while Cambacérès was carried in state in a sedan-chair through the steep streets of Blois. Various rumours were current: there was talk of two camps and of a general requisition. For several days they knew nothing of what was happening in Paris; the uncertainty ceased only with the arrival of a wagoner whose pass was signed 'Sacken'.* Soon the Russian General Schouvaloff arrived at the Auberge de la Galère: he was promptly besieged by the grandees, who were desperate to obtain visas for their stampede. However, before leaving Blois, they all drew upon the funds of the Regency for their travelling expenses and their arrears of salary; they held their passports in one hand and their money in the other, taking care at the same time to assure the Provisional Government of their support, for they did not lose their heads. Madame Mère and her brother, Cardinal Fesch, left for Rome. Prince Esterhazy came on behalf of Francis II to fetch Marie-Louise and her son. Joseph and Jerome withdrew to Switzerland, after vainly trying to compel the Empress to accompany them. Marie-Louise hastened to join her father: indifferently attached to Bonaparte, she found the opportunity to console herself and rejoiced at being freed from the double tyranny of a husband and a master. When, the following year, Bonaparte inflicted the same confusion of flight upon the Bourbons, the latter, only recently rescued from their long tribulations, had not enjoyed fourteen years of unexampled prosperity in which to accustom themselves to the comfort of a throne.

However, Napoleon was not yet dethroned; more than forty thousand of the best soldiers in the world were still around him; he was in a position to retire behind the Loire; the French armies which had arrived from Spain were growling in the south; the volcanic military population might start spreading its lava; even among the foreign leaders, there was still talk of Napoleon or his son reigning over France: for two days

* Fabian Wilhelm, Prince von der Osten-Sacken, had been appointed Governor of Paris by Alexander.

Alexander hesitated. M. de Talleyrand secretly inclined towards the policy which favoured crowning the King of Rome, for he was afraid of the Bourbons; if he did not unreservedly accept the plan for the Regency of Marie-Louise, it was because, Napoleon not having died, he, the Prince de Bénévent, feared that he would be unable to retain the control of affairs during a minority threatened by the existence of a restless, unpredictable, enterprising man still in the prime of life.

It was during these critical days that I published my pamphlet *De Bonaparte et des Bourbons* in order to turn the scale; the effect it had is well known. I threw myself headlong into the fray to serve as a shield to renascent liberty against a tyranny which was still alive and whose strength was increased threefold by despair. I spoke in the name of the Legitimacy, in order to lend my words the authority of positive politics. I taught France what the old royal family was; I told her how many members of that family were alive, what their names were, and their characters; it was as if I had drawn up a list of the children of the Emperor of China, to so great an extent had the Republic and the Empire invaded the present and relegated the Bourbons to the past. Louis XVIII declared that my pamphlet had been of greater use to him than an army of one hundred thousand men; he might have added that it had been a certificate of existence to him. I helped to give him the crown a second time through the favourable issue of the Spanish War.

From the very beginning of my political career, I became unpopular with the people, but from that time too I failed to win the favour of the mighty. All who had been slaves under Bonaparte detested me; on the other hand, I was an object of suspicion to all who wished to place France in a state of vassalage. At first, of all the sovereigns, the only one whom I had on my side was Bonaparte himself. He read my pamphlet at Fontainebleau; the Duc de Bassano had brought it to him: he discussed it impartially, saying:

'This is true; that is not true. I have nothing to reproach Chateaubriand with: he opposed me when I was in power, but those swine, so-and-so . . .' and he named them.

My admiration for Bonaparte has always been great and sincere, even when I attacked Napoleon with the greatest ferocity.

Posterity is not as fair in its judgements as is usually maintained: there are passions, infatuations, and errors born of distance just as there are passions and errors born of proximity. When posterity admires unreservedly, it is shocked that the contemporaries of the man it admires should not have had the same opinion of that man as itself. This is easy to explain, however: the things which caused offence in that person are past; his infirmities have died with him; all that remains of him is his imperishable life; but the evil which he caused is nonetheless real for all that; evil in itself and in its essence, and evil above all for those who endured it.

It is fashionable today to magnify Bonaparte's victories: those who suffered by them have disappeared; we no longer hear the curses of the victims and their cries of pain and distress; we no longer see France exhausted, with only women to till her soil; we no longer see parents arrested as hostages for their sons, or the inhabitants of a village punished jointly and severally with the penalties applicable to a single deserter; we no longer see the conscription notices pasted up at street corners, and the passers-by gathering in a crowd in front of those huge death-warrants, looking in consternation for the names of their children, their brothers, their friends, their neighbours. We forget that everybody bewailed the news of a victory; we forget that in the theatre, the slightest remark directed against Bonaparte which had escaped the censors' notice was hailed with rapture; we forget that the people, the Court, the generals, the ministers, and Napoleon's relatives were weary of his tyranny and his conquests, weary of that game which was always being won yet went on being played, of that existence which was brought into question again every morning because of the impossibility of peace.

The reality of our sufferings is demonstrated by the catastrophe itself: if France had been devoted to Bonaparte, would she have abandoned him twice, abruptly and completely, without making a last effort to keep him? If France owed everything to Bonaparte: glory, liberty, order, prosperity, industry, commerce, factories, monuments, literature, and fine arts; if, before his time, the nation had done nothing itself; if the Republic, devoid of genius and courage, had neither defended nor enlarged its territory, then France must have been very ungrateful, very cowardly, to let Napoleon fall into the hands of his enemies, or, at least, not to protest against the imprisonment of so great a benefactor.

This reproach, which might justly be made against us, is not made against us; and why? Because it is evident that, at the moment of his fall, France did not wish to defend Napoleon, and on the contrary deliberately abandoned him: in our bitter mortification, we no longer saw in him anything but the author and contemner of our woes. The Allies did not defeat us: we ourselves, choosing between two scourges, gave up shedding our blood, which had ceased to flow for our freedom.

On 12 April, the Comte d'Artois arrived in the capacity of Lieutenant-General of the Kingdom. The day before his arrival, Napoleon, after fruitless negotiations with Alexander through M. de Caulaincourt, had published his act of abdication:

'The Allied Powers having proclaimed that the Emperor Napoleon was the only obstacle to the restoration of peace in Europe, the Emperor Napoleon, faithful to his oath, declares that he renounces for himself and his heirs the thrones of France and Italy, because there is no personal sacrifice, even that of life itself, which he is not ready to make in the interest of the French people.'

To these resounding words the Emperor did not delay, by his return, to give a no less resounding contradiction: he needed only the time to go to the island of Elba. He remained at Fontainebleau until 20 April.

The 20th of April having arrived, Napoleon went down the double flight of steps leading to the peristyle of the deserted palace of the Capets. A few grenadiers, the remnants of the soldiers who had conquered Europe, formed up in line in the great courtyard, as if on their last battlefield; they were surrounded by the old trees, the mutilated companions of François

I and Henri IV. Bonaparte addressed the last witnesses of his battles in these words:

'Generals, officers, non-commissioned officers, and men of my Old Guard, I bid you farewell; for twenty years I have been well content with you; I have always found you on the road to glory.

'The Allied Powers have armed the whole of Europe against me, part of the army has betrayed its duty, and France herself has chosen other destinies.

'With you and the brave men who have remained faithful to me, I could have carried on a civil war for three years, but France would have suffered and that was contrary to the aim which I had adopted.

'Be faithful to the new King whom France has chosen; do not abandon our beloved country, which has been unhappy for too long. Love her always, that dear country of ours, and love her well.

'Do not pity my lot; I shall always be happy if I know that you are happy.

'I could have died; nothing would have been easier for me; but I shall always follow the path of honour. I have yet to write the history of all that we have accomplished.

'I cannot embrace you all, but I will embrace your general.... Come here, general ...'

He clasped General Petit in his arms.

'Bring me the eagle!'

He kissed it.

'Dear eagle! May these kisses resound in the hearts of all my men! ... Farewell, my lads. ... My prayers will always accompany you; do not forget me.'

Having said this, Napoleon struck his tent, which covered the world.

SEVEN
The Hundred Days

While Bonaparte, who was known to the whole world, was slipping out of France to an accompaniment of curses, Louis XVIII, whom everyone had forgotten, was leaving London under a canopy of white banners and garlands. Napoleon, landing on the island of Elba, found his old strength there. Louis XVIII, landing at Calais, might have come face to face with Louvel;* he met General Maison, who, sixteen years later, was entrusted with the task of putting Charles X on board ship at Cherbourg. Charles X, apparently to render him worthy of his future mission, had given M. Maison the baton of a marshal of France, just as a knight, before fighting, would confer knighthood on the man of lesser rank with whom he deigned to cross swords.

I have present in my memory, as if I could see it still, the sight which I witnessed when Louis XVIII, entering Paris on 3 May, went to visit Notre-Dame: in order to spare the King the sight of the foreign troops, it was a regiment of the old Foot-guards who lined the route from the Pont-Neuf to Notre-Dame, along the Quai des Orfèvres. I do not believe that human faces ever wore so threatening and terrible an expression. Those battle-scarred grenadiers, the conquerors of Europe, who had seen so many thousands of cannon-balls pass over their heads, who smelt of fire and powder; those same men, robbed of their captain, were forced to salute an old king,

---

* Louis-Pierre Louvel, who assassinated the Duc de Berry in February 1820. He then told the police that he had sworn to kill all the Bourbons, and that he had gone to Calais in April 1814 with the intention of stabbing Louis XVIII.

disabled by time, not war, watched as they were by an army of Russians, Austrians, and Prussians, in Napoleon's occupied capital. Some, moving the skin of their foreheads, brought their great busbies down over their eyes, as if to avoid seeing anything; others turned down the corners of their mouths in angry contempt; others again showed their teeth through their moustaches, like tigers. When they presented arms, it was with a furious movement, and the sound of those arms made one tremble. Never, it must be admitted, have men been put to so great a test and suffered such agonizing torment. If at that moment they had been called upon to exact vengeance, it would have been necessary to exterminate every one of them, or they would have devoured the earth.

At the end of the line there was a young hussar on horseback; he held a drawn sword, and made it leap and as it were dance with a convulsive movement of anger. His face was pale; his eyes rolled in their sockets; he kept opening and shutting his mouth, clashing his teeth together, and stifling cries of which one heard only the first sound. He caught sight of a Russian officer: the look he gave him cannot be described. When the King's carriage passed before him, he made his horse rear into the air, and there can be no doubt that he was tempted to hurl himself at the King.

During the first year of the Restoration, I witnessed the third transformation of society within my lifetime: I had seen the old monarchy turn into the constitutional monarchy, and the latter into the Republic; I had seen the Republic change into military despotism; and now I was seeing military despotism turning back into a free monarchy, the new ideas and the new generations returning to the old principles and the old men. The marshals of the Empire became marshals of France; with the uniforms of Napoleon's Guard there mingled the uniforms of the Lifeguards and the Maison-Rouge, cut exactly after the old styles; the old Duc d'Havré, with his powdered wig and his black cane, ambled along, nodding his head, as Captain of the Lifeguards, beside Marshal Victor, who limped in the Bonaparte manner; the Duc de Mouchy, who had never seen a shot fired in anger, went to Mass beside Marshal Oudinot, who was riddled with wounds; the Palace of the Tuileries, so clean and soldierly under Napoleon, began to reek, instead of the smell of powder, with the breakfast odours which rose on every side: under the gentlemen of the Bedchamber, and with the officers of the Mouth and the Wardrobe, everything resumed an air of domesticity. In the streets, one could see decrepit emigrants wearing the airs and clothes of former times, highly respectable men no doubt, but looking as outlandish in the modern crowd as did the Republican captains among Napoleon's soldiers. The ladies of the Imperial Court brought along the dowagers of the Faubourg Saint-Germain and taught them 'their way around' the palace. Deputations arrived from Bordeaux sporting armlets, and parish captains from the Vendée wearing La Rochejacquelein hats. All these people retained the expression of the feelings, thoughts, habits, and manners which were familiar to them. Liberty, which lay at the root of this period, made things exist together which at first sight looked as if they should not exist at all; but it was difficult to recognize that liberty, because it wore the colours of the ancient monarchy and the imperial tyranny. Moreover nobody was familiar with the language of the constitution: the Royalists made glaring errors when talking Charter; the Imperialists were even less well informed; while the Conventionals, who had become in turn counts, barons, and senators under Napoleon and peers under Louis XVIII, would lapse now into the republican jargon which they had almost forgotten, now into the absolutist idiom which they had learnt by heart. Lieutenant-colonels were promoted to the status of royal gamekeepers. Aides-de-camp of the last military tyrant were heard talking about the inviolable liberty of the people, and regicides upholding the sacred dogma of the Legitimacy.

These metamorphoses would be hateful if they did not belong in part to the flexibility of the French genius. The people of Athens governed itself; orators appealed to its passions in public; the sovereign crowd was composed of sculptors, painters, and artisans, 'who are accustomed to looking at speeches and listening to deeds', as Thucydides says. But when, good or bad, a decree was delivered, who came forward to execute it from that incoherent and inexpert mass? Socrates, Phocion, Pericles, Alcibiades.

Is it the Royalists who are 'to blame' for the Restoration, as is suggested today? Not in the least: this would imply that thirty million men stood by in consternation while a handful of Legitimists accomplished a hated restoration, against everyone's wishes, by waving a few handkerchiefs and tying a ribbon of their wives' round their hats! The vast majority of Frenchmen was, it is true, delighted; but that majority was not *Legitimist* in the narrow sense of the word, applicable only to the rigid supporters of the old monarchy. The majority was a mass of people comprising every shade of opinion, happy at being delivered from tyranny, and violently incensed against the man whom it held responsible for all its misfortunes: hence the success of my pamphlet. How many avowed aristocrats were there among those who proclaimed the King's name? MM. Matthieu and Adrien de Montmorency; MM. de Polignac, who had escaped from their gaol; M. Alexis de Noailles; M. Sosthène de la Rochefoucauld. Did these seven or eight men, whom the people neither knew nor followed, lay down the law to a whole nation?

Mme de Montcalm had sent me a purse containing twelve hundred francs to be distributed among thoroughbred Legitimists: I sent it back to her, having been unable to place a single crown-piece. An ignoble cord was fastened round the neck of the statue which surmounted the column in the Place Vendôme; there were so few Royalists to be found to cock a snook at glory and pull the rope that it was the authorities, Bonapartists to a man, who had to lower their master's effigy with the aid of a derrick: the colossus was forced to bow his head; he fell at the feet of the sovereigns of Europe, who had so often prostrated themselves before him. It was the men of the Republic and the Empire who greeted the Restoration with the greatest enthusiasm. The people who owed their elevation to the Revolution behaved with abominable ingratitude to him whom they pretend today to regret and admire.

Imperialists and Liberals, it is you into whose hands power

fell, you who knelt down before the sons of Henri IV. It was
perfectly natural that the Royalists should be happy to recover
their princes and to see the end of the reign of a man they
regarded as a usurper; but you, the creatures of that usurper,
surpassed the Royalists in the exaggeration of your feelings.
The ministers and grand dignitaries vied with one another in
their eagerness to swear loyalty to the Legitimacy; all the civil
and judicial authorities queued up to protest their hatred for
the newly proscribed dynasty and their love for the ancient
family whom they had condemned a thousand times. Who
drew up those proclamations and addresses accusing and
insulting Napoleon with which France was flooded? Royalists?
No: the ministers, the generals, and the authorities chosen and
maintained in office by Bonaparte. Where was all the jobbery
of the Restoration done? At the homes of the Royalists? No:
at M. de Talleyrand's. With whom? With M. de Pradt, chaplain
to 'the god Mars' and mitred mountebank. Where and with
whom did the Lieutenant-General of the Kingdom dine on his
arrival? At a Royalist's house with Royalist guests? No: at the
Bishop of Autun's, with M. de Caulaincourt. Where were
receptions given to 'the infamous foreign princes'? At the châ-
teaux of the Royalists? No: at Malmaison, at the Empress
Josephine's. To whom did Napoleon's dearest friends, Berthier,
for instance, offer their ardent devotion? To the Legitimacy.
Who spent all their time with the autocratic Alexander, that
brutal Tartar? The members of the Institut, the scholars, the
men of letters, the philosophers of philanthropy, theophilan-
thropy, and so forth; they returned utterly enchanted, laden
with praise and snuff-boxes. As for us poor devils of Legitimists, we were admitted nowhere; we counted for nothing.
Now we were told in the streets to go home to bed; now we
were recommended not to shout 'God save the King' too loudly,
others having taken on that responsibility. So far from forcing
people to be Legitimists, those in power declared that nobody
would be obliged to change his functions or his language, that
the Bishop of Autun would be no more compelled to say Mass
under the monarchy than he had been compelled to go to Mass
under the Empire. I saw no lady of the manor, no Joan of Arc

proclaim the rightful sovereign with a falcon on her wrist or a lance in her hand; but I saw Mme de Talleyrand, whom Bonaparte had fastened to her husband like a signboard, driving through the streets in a barouche, singing hymns about the pious family of the Bourbons. A few sheets hanging from the windows of the familiars of the Imperial Court made the simple Cossacks believe that there were as many fleurs-de-lis in the hearts of the converted Bonapartists as white rags at their casements. Contagion is a wonderful thing in France, and a man would cry: 'Off with my head!' if he heard his neighbour cry the same. The Imperialists went so far as to enter our houses and make us Bourbonists put out, by way of spotless flags, such scraps of white as our linen-rooms contained. This happened at my house; but Mme de Chateaubriand would have none of it, and valiantly defended her muslins.

Bonaparte had refused to embark in a French ship, setting store at that time only by the English Navy, because it was victorious; he had forgotten his former hatred, and the calumnies and insults which he had heaped upon perfidious Albion; he saw no one now who was worthy of his admiration save the triumphant party, and it was the *Undaunted* which took him to the place of his first exile. He was not without anxiety as to the way he would be received. Would the French garrison hand over to him the territory which it was guarding? Of the Italian islanders, some wanted to call in the English and others to remain free of all masters: the tricolour and the white flag waved on nearby headlands. Everything was arranged nevertheless. When it became known that Bonaparte was bringing millions of francs with him, public opinion generously decided to receive 'the august victim'. The civil and religious authorities were brought round to the same conviction. Joseph Philippe Arrighi, the Vicar-General, issued a pastoral letter:

'Divine Providence,' said the pious injunction, 'has decreed that in the future we shall be the subjects of Napoleon the Great. The island of Elba, raised to so sublime an honour, receives the Lord's Anointed in its bosom. We order a solemn *Te Deum* to be sung by way of thanksgiving, etc.'

The Emperor had written to General Dalesme, the commander of the French garrison, that he should tell the people of Elba that he had 'chosen' their island as his place of residence on account of the mildness of their manners and their climate. He landed at Porto-Ferrajo, to the sound of a double salute from the English frigate which had brought him and the batteries on shore. From there he was taken under the parish canopy to the church, where the *Te Deum* was sung. The beadle, who acted as master of ceremonies, was a short, fat man, who was unable to join his hands across his body. Napoleon was then taken to the town hall, where an apartment had been prepared for him. The new Imperial Standard was unfurled: a white ground intersected by a red stripe powdered with three gold bees. Three violins and two basses followed him with joyful scraping sounds. The throne, hastily erected in the public ballroom, was decorated with gilt paper and scarlet rags. This pomp appealed to the theatrical side of the prisoner's nature: Napoleon played his part in all seriousness, just as he used to amuse his Court with old-fashioned games in his palace at the Tuileries, before going to kill men by way of a pastime. He formed his household: it consisted of four chamberlains, three orderly officers, and two stewards. He stated that ladies would be received twice a week, at eight o'clock in the evening. He gave a ball. For his own residence, he took possession of a building intended for the engineer corps. Bonaparte was for ever meeting in his life the two sources from which it had sprung: democracy and royal authority; his strength was derived from the masses, his rank from his genius; this is why he passed effortlessly from the market-place to the throne, from the kings and queens who crowded round him at Erfurt to the bakers and grocers who danced in his barn at Porto-Ferrajo. He had something of the people among princes, and of a prince among the people. At five o'clock in the morning, in silk stockings and buckled shoes, he presided over his masons on the island of Elba.

Installed in his empire, which had been producing an inexhaustible supply of iron ever since the days of Virgil – *Insula*

inexhaustis Chalybum generosa metallis * – Bonaparte had not
forgotten the outrages to which he had recently been subjected;
he had not abandoned his intention of tearing off his shroud;
but it suited him to give the impression of being safely buried,
making only a few phantom movements around his tomb. That
is why he lost no time in visiting his iron quarries, as if he
thought of nothing else; one might have taken him for the former Inspector of Mines of his sometime states. He regretted
having once allocated the revenue of the Elban forges to the
Legion of Honour: five hundred thousand francs now seemed
to him worth more than a bloodstained cross on the breast of
his grenadiers.

'What was I thinking of?' he said. 'But I have issued several
stupid decrees of that sort.'

He concluded a commercial treaty with Leghorn and proposed to conclude another with Genoa. He began building,
somewhat haphazardly, five or six furlongs of highroad, and
planned the sites of four big towns, just as Dido marked out the
boundaries of Carthage. A philosopher who had had his fill of
human grandeur, he declared that he intended henceforth to
live like a justice of the peace in an English county; yet when he
climbed a hill overlooking Porto-Ferrajo and saw the sea lapping against the foot of the cliffs on every side, these words
escaped his lips:

'The devil take it! It must be admitted that my island is terribly small!'

He had inspected the whole of his domain within a few
hours; he wished to join to it a rock called Pianosa.

'Europe,' he said with a laugh, 'will accuse me of starting a
new career of conquest.'

The Allied Powers made merry over the fact that they had
contemptuously left him four hundred soldiers; he needed no
more to bring them all back to the flag.

Napoleon's presence off the coast of Italy, which had seen

---

* Island generous in those inexhaustible metals which the Chalybes forge
(Virgil, *Æneid*).

the dawn of his glory and which retains his memory, caused considerable agitation. Murat was his neighbour; his friends and complete strangers came secretly or openly to his retreat; his mother and his sister, the Princess Pauline, visited him; Marie-Louise and her son were expected to arrive soon after. A woman did in fact appear with a child;* she was received with great secrecy and went to live in a secluded villa in the most remote corner of the island: on the shores of Ogygia, Calypso spoke of her love to Ulysses, who, instead of listening to her, thought of how to defend himself against the suitors. After two days' rest, the Swan of the North put out to sea again, to land among the myrtles of Baiae, taking her little one away in her white yawl.

If we had been less trustful, it would have been easy for us to see a catastrophe approaching. Bonaparte was too close to his cradle and his conquests; his funeral island was to be farther away and surrounded by a greater expanse of sea. It is difficult to understand what possessed the Allies to think of banishing Napoleon to the rocks where he was to serve his apprenticeship in exile; how could they possibly imagine that seeing the Apennines, smelling the powder of the battlefields of Montenotte, Arcola, and Marengo, and making out Venice, Rome, and Naples, his three beautiful slaves, his heart would not be seized with irresistible temptations? Had they forgotten that he had turned the whole world topsy-turvy and that he had admirers and debtors everywhere, all of whom were his accomplices? His ambition had been disappointed, not extinguished; misfortune and the thought of vengeance rekindled its flames: when the Prince of Darkness looked upon man and the world from the frontiers of the newly created universe, he resolved to destroy them.

All of a sudden the telegraph informed Napoleon's veterans and an incredulous world that the man had landed:† Mon-

---

* The Countess Walewska with her son by Napoleon, who later became the Duc de Walewski, Napoleon III's Foreign Minister and President of the Legislative Body.
† On 1 March 1815.

sieur* hurried to Lyons with the Duc d'Orléans and Marshal
Macdonald, and came straight back. Marshal Soult, denounced
in the Chamber of Deputies, surrendered his office on 11 March
to the Duc de Feltre. Bonaparte found facing him, as Minister
of War under Louis XVIII in 1815, the general who had been
his last Minister of War in 1814.

The boldness of the enterprise was quite incredible. From
the political point of view, this enterprise might be regarded as
Napoleon's irremissible crime and capital error. He knew that
the princes, who were still gathered together at the Congress,
and Europe, which was still under arms, would not allow him
to return to power; his judgement must have warned him that
a success, if he obtained it, would be only for a day: he was
sacrificing to his longing to return to the stage of world events
the peace of a people which had lavished its blood and its treasures upon him; he was exposing to dismemberment the country
from which he derived everything he had been in the past and
everything he would be in the future. In this fantastic undertaking there lay a ferocious egoism and a terrible lack of gratitude
and generosity towards France.

All this is true in the light of practical reason, for a man with
a heart rather than a brain; but for people of Napoleon's temperament there exists a reason of another sort; those creatures
of high fame have a way of their own: the comets describe
curves which defy calculation; they are tied to nothing and
seem good for nothing; if a globe happens to be in their way,
they shatter it and disappear into the abysses of the sky; their
laws are known to God alone. Extraordinary individuals are
the monuments of the human mind; they are not its rule.

Bonaparte was therefore persuaded into this enterprise less
by the false reports of his friends than by the necessity of his
genius: he took up the cross by virtue of the faith that was in
him. For a great man, being born is not everything: he must die
as well. Was the island of Elba a fitting end for Napoleon?
Could he accept the sovereignty of a cabbage-patch, like Dio-
cletian at Salona? If he had waited till later, would he have had

* The Comte d'Artois, Louis XVIII's brother.

a greater chance of success, at a time when the memory of him would have aroused less emotion, when his old soldiers would have left the army, and when new social attitudes would have been adopted?

He accordingly pitted himself against the world; and at the beginning, he must have believed that he had not deceived himself as to the prestige of his power.

One night, that of 25–26 February, at the end of a ball of which the Princess Borghese was doing the honours, he escaped with success, which had long been his comrade and accomplice; he crossed a sea covered with our fleets, met two frigates, a ship of seventy-four guns, and the brig *Zephyr,* which stopped him and challenged him; he himself answered the captain's questions; the sea and the waves saluted him, and he pursued his course. The deck of the *Inconstant,* his little ship, served as a promenade and a study; he dictated in the midst of the winds and had copies made, on that tossing table, of three proclamations to the army and to France; some feluccas, carrying his companions in adventure, accompanied his guard-ship, flying a white flag strewn with stars. On 1 March, at three o'clock in the morning, he reached the French coast between Cannes and Antibes, at Golfe-Juan; he landed, strolled along the shore, picked some violets, and bivouacked in an olive-grove. The astonished population kept out of the way. He avoided Antibes and plunged into the mountains of Grasse, passing through Sernon, Barrême, Digne, and Gap. At Sisteron, twenty men could have stopped him, and he found nobody. He went on without meeting any opposition from those inhabitants who, a few months earlier, had tried to cut his throat. If a few soldiers happened to enter the void which formed around his gigantic shadow, they were irresistibly captivated by the attraction of his eagles. His spellbound enemies searched for him and did not see him; he hid himself in his glory, just as the lion of the Sahara hides himself in the rays of the sun to avoid being seen by the dazzled hunters. Enveloped in a fiery whirlwind, the bloody ghosts of Arcola, Marengo, Austerlitz, Jena, Friedland, Eylau, Borodino, Lützen, and Bautzen escorted him together with a million dead. From the midst of this column of fire and smoke, there issued, at the entrance to every town, a few trumpet-blasts accompanied by the waving of the tricolour standard: and the gates of the town fell. When Napoleon crossed the Niemen at the head of four hundred thousand foot and a hundred thousand horse, to blow up the palace of the Tsars in Moscow, he was less astonishing than when, breaking his ban and flinging his chains in the faces of the kings, he came alone from Cannes to Paris, to sleep peacefully at the Tuileries.

Yet could the Emperor trust his former supporters and his self-styled friends? Had they not shamefully deserted him at the time of his fall? That Senate which used to crawl at his feet and which was now ensconced in the peerage, had it not decreed its benefactor's deposition? Could he believe those men when they came and said to him:

'The interests of France are inseparable from your own. If Fortune betrayed your efforts, Sire, reverses would not weaken our perseverance and would double our attachment to your person.'

Your perseverance! Your attachment doubled by misfortune! You said this on 11 June 1815. What had you said on 2 April 1814? What would you say a few weeks later, on 19 July 1815?

The Minister of the Imperial Police was in correspondence with Ghent, Vienna, and Basle; the marshals to whom Bonaparte was obliged to entrust the command of his troops had only recently taken an oath of loyalty to Louis XVIII; they had published the most violent proclamations against Bonaparte: since then, it is true, they had wedded their sultan once more; but if he had been arrested at Grenoble, what would they have done with him? Is it enough to break an oath to restore its entire strength to another oath which has been violated? Do two perjuries add up to loyalty?

A few more days, and those men who had sworn obedience to Bonaparte on the Champ de Mai would take their devotion back to Louis XVIII at the Tuileries; they would approach the sacred table of the God of Peace, in order to have themselves appointed ministers at the banquets of war; heralds-at-arms and bearers of the royal insignia at Bonaparte's coronation, they would fulfil the same functions at the coronation of Charles X; then, as the agents of another power, they would lead that King a prisoner to Cherbourg, trying hard to find a little empty space in their consciences where they might hang the badge of their new oath. It is not an easy thing to be born in times of improbity, when two men talking together have to be careful to keep back certain words from their tongue, for fear of offending each other or making each other blush.

Those who had not been able to bind themselves to Napoleon by his glory, who had not been able to adhere out of gratitude to the benefactor from whom they had received their riches, their honours, and their very names, were they going to sacrifice themselves now to his scanty hopes? Were they going to tie themselves to a precarious fortune making a fresh start, these ingrates whom a fortune consolidated by unexampled successes and by the spoils of sixteen years of victories had failed to attach? So many chrysalises which, between two springtimes, had put off and put on, shed and resumed the skin of the Legitimist and the revolutionary, of the Napoleonist and Bourbonist; so many promises made and broken; so many crosses moved from the knight's breast to the horse's tail, and from the horse's tail to the knight's breast; so many valiant warriors changing their banners and strewing the lists with their pledges of perjured loyalty; so many noble ladies waiting on Marie-Louise and Marie-Caroline in turn, were calculated to leave in the depths of Napoleon's heart nothing but distrust, horror, and contempt; that great man, grown old before his time, stood alone among all those traitors, men and fortune, on a tottering earth, under a hostile sky, face to face with his accomplished destiny and the judgement of God.

Napoleon had found no faithful friends but the phantoms of his past glory; these escorted him, as I have told you, from the place where he landed to the capital of France. But the eagles which had 'flown from steeple to steeple' from Cannes to Paris settled wearily on the chimneys of the Tuileries, unable to go any farther.

Napoleon did not hurl himself upon Belgium, at the head of an enthusiastic populace, before an Anglo-Prussian army could

have time to assemble there; he stopped; he tried to negotiate
with Europe and humbly to maintain the treaties of the Legitimacy. The Congress of Vienna drew the Duc de Vicence's
attention to the abdication of 11 April 1814; by that abdication, Bonaparte 'recognized that he was the only obstacle to the
restoration of peace in Europe' and consequently 'renounced,
for himself and his heirs, the thrones of France and Italy'. Now,
since he had returned to re-establish his power, he was mani-
festly violating the Treaty of Paris and placing himself once
more in the political situation which existed before 31 March
1814: thus it was he, Bonaparte, who was declaring war on
Europe, and not Europe on Bonaparte. These logical quibbles
of diplomatic attorneys were worth as much as they could be
before the battle.

The news of Bonaparte's landing at Cannes had reached
Vienna on 6 March, in the middle of an entertainment purport-
ing to represent an assembly of the divinities of Olympus and
Parnassus. Alexander had just received the proposal for an alliance between France, Austria, and England; he hesitated for a
moment between the two pieces of news, and then said:

'It is not a question of myself, but of the safety of the world.'

And a courier was sent off to St Petersburg with orders to
despatch the Guards. The armies which were returning home
halted; their long line faced about, and eight hundred thousand
enemies turned their eyes towards France.

On 18 June 1815, I left Ghent* about noon by the Brussels
gate; I was going to finish my walk alone on the highroad. I had
taken Caesar's *Commentaries* with me and I strolled along,
immersed in my reading. I was over two miles from the town
when I thought I heard a dull rumbling: I stopped and looked
up at the sky, which was fairly cloudy, wondering whether I
should walk on or turn back towards Ghent for fear of a storm.
I listened; I heard nothing more but the cry of a moorhen in the
rushes and the sound of a village clock. I continued on my way:

* Chateaubriand had followed Louis XVIII into exile in Belgium, where he
had been appointed interim Minister of the Interior.

I had not taken thirty steps before the rumbling began again, now short, now drawn out, and at irregular intervals; sometimes it was perceptible only through a trembling of the air, which was so far away that it communicated itself to the ground as it passed over those vast plains. The detonations, less prolonged, less undulating, less interrelated than those of thunder, gave rise in my mind to the idea of a battle. I found myself opposite a poplar planted at the corner of a hop-field. I crossed the road and leant against the trunk of the tree, with my face turned in the direction of Brussels. A southerly wind sprang up and brought me more distinctly the sound of artillery. That great battle, nameless as yet, whose echoes I was listening to at the foot of a poplar, and for whose unknown obsequies a village clock had just struck, was the Battle of Waterloo!

A silent and solitary hearer of the solemn judgement of the fates, I would have been less moved if I had found myself in the fray: the danger, the firing, the press of death would have left me no time for meditation; but, alone under a tree, in the countryside near Ghent, like the shepherd of the flocks grazing around me, I was overwhelmed by the weight of my reflections. What was this battle? Was it going to be decisive? Was Napoleon there in person? Were lots being cast for the world, as for Christ's garments? In the event of victory or defeat for one side or the other, what would be the consequence for the nations: liberty or slavery? But what blood must be flowing! Was not every sound that reached my ears the last sigh of a Frenchman? Was this a new Crécy, a new Poitiers, a new Agincourt, which France's bitterest enemies were going to enjoy? If they triumphed, was not our glory lost? If Napoleon won the day, what was to become of our liberty? Although victory for Napoleon meant eternal exile for myself, my country was foremost in my heart at that moment; my prayers were for France's oppressor if, while saving our honour, he was to rescue us from foreign domination.

But what if Wellington triumphed? Then the Legitimacy would re-enter Paris behind those red uniforms which had just renewed their dye in the blood of the French! Then the monarchy would have as state coaches at its coronation the ambulance-wagons filled with our maimed grenadiers! What sort of restoration would it be, carried out under such auspices? ... These are just a few of the ideas that tormented me. Every cannon-shot gave me a shock and made my heart beat twice as quickly. A few miles from an immense catastrophe, I did not see it; I could not touch the huge funeral monument growing minute by minute at Waterloo, just as from the shores of Bulak, on the banks of the Nile, I had stretched out my hands in vain towards the Pyramids.

No traveller appeared; some women in the fields, peacefully hoeing rows of vegetables, did not seem to have heard the noise to which I was listening. But then I saw a courier approaching: I left the foot of my tree and stood in the middle of the road; I stopped the courier and questioned him. He was in the Duc de Berry's service and came from Alost. He told me:

'Bonaparte entered Brussels yesterday (17 June), after a bloody fight. The battle was due to begin again today (18 June). The Allies are thought to have suffered a decisive defeat, and the order has been given to retreat.'

The courier continued on his way.

I followed him as fast as I could: I was passed by the carriage of a merchant who was fleeing with his family; he confirmed the courier's story.

Everything was in confusion when I got back to Ghent: the gates of the city were being closed; only the wickets remained half-open; some ill-armed civilians and a few soldiers from the regimental depot were standing guard. I went to the King's house.

Monsieur had just arrived by a circuitous route: he had left Brussels on hearing the false report that Bonaparte was about to enter the city, and that after losing a first battle there was no hope of winning a second. It was rumoured that, as the Prussians had not formed their lines, the English had been crushed.

At these reports, the stampede became general: those who possessed some resources left; I, who am accustomed never to have anything, was ready as usual. I wanted Mme de Chateaubriand

to move out before me, since although she was a great Bona-
partist, she hated gunfire; but she refused to leave me.

In the evening there was a council at His Majesty's: we heard
Monsieur's reports all over again, as well as the rumours picked
up at the military commandant's or at the Baron d'Eckstein's.
The wagon which contained the Crown diamonds was put to:
I had no need of a wagon to remove my treasure. I put the
black silk handkerchief in which I wrap my head at night into
my limp ministerial portfolio, and placed myself at His
Majesty's disposal, with that important document on the
affairs of the Legitimacy. I was richer on my first emigration,
when my haversack did duty as my pillow and served as a
swaddling band for *Atala*; but in 1815 *Atala* was a big, gawky
girl of thirteen or fourteen, who went round the world by herself and who, to her father's honour, had got herself talked
about too much.

On 19 June, at one o'clock in the morning, a letter from M.
Pozzo, brought to the King by a courier, re-established the truth
of the situation. Bonaparte had never entered Brussels; he had
most certainly lost the Battle of Waterloo. Leaving Paris on
12 June, he had joined his army on the 14th. On the 15th, he
broke the enemy's lines on the Sambre. On the 16th, he beat
the Prussians on those fields of Fleurus where victory always
seems to be faithful to the French. The villages of Ligny and
Saint-Amand were taken. At Quatre-Bras, a further success:
the Duke of Brunswick remained among the dead. Blücher, in
full retreat, fell back upon a reserve of thirty thousand men
under the command of General Bülow; the Duke of Wellington, with the English and the Dutch, stood with his back to
Brussels.

On the morning of the 18th, before the first shot had been
fired, the Duke of Wellington declared that he would be able to
hold out until three o'clock; but that at that time, if the Prussians had not appeared, he would necessarily be destroyed:
forced back on Planchenois and Brussels, he was cut off from
all retreat. Napoleon had taken him by surprise, and his strategic position was deplorable; he had accepted it and had not
chosen it.

First of all, the French, advancing on the enemy's left flank, took the heights commanding the Château of Hougoumont as far as the farms of La Haye-Sainte and Papelotte; on the right flank, they attacked the village of Mont Saint-Jean; the farm of La Haye-Sainte was taken in the centre by Prince Jerome. But the Prussian reserves came into sight near Saint-Lambert at six in the evening: another new furious onslaught was made on the village of La Haye-Sainte; Blücher arrived with fresh troops and cut off the squares of the Imperial Guard from the rest of our forces. Around that immortal phalanx, the torrent of fugitives carried everything with it among clouds of dust, fiery smoke, and grape-shot, in darkness streaked with Congreve rockets, and amid the roar of three hundred guns and the headlong gallop of twenty-five thousand horses: it was as it were the epitome of all the battles of the Empire. Twice the French cried: 'Victory!' and twice their shouts were stifled under the pressure of the enemy's columns. The fire from our lines died out; the cartridges were exhausted; a few wounded grenadiers, in the midst of the thirty thousand dead and a hundred thousand bloodstained cannon-balls, lying cold and conglobated at their feet, remained erect, leaning on their muskets, their bayonets broken, their barrels empty. Not far from them, the man of battles, his eyes fixed in a stare, listened to the last cannon-shot he was to hear in all his life. In that field of slaughter, his brother Jerome was still fighting with his outnumbered and expiring battalions; but his courage was powerless to retrieve the victory.

A great many falsehoods and a few rather curious truths have been retailed about this catastrophe. The phrase 'The Guard dies but does not surrender' is an invention which no one dares to defend any longer. It seems to be certain that at the beginning of the action Soult made some strategic observations to the Emperor, and that Napoleon dryly replied:

'Just because Wellington has defeated you, you persist in considering him a great general.'

At the end of the battle, M. de Turenne urged Bonaparte to withdraw, to avoid falling into the enemy's hands. Bonaparte, emerging from his thoughts as from a dream, flew into a passion at first; then, all of a sudden, in the midst of his anger, he threw himself upon his horse and fled.

On 23 June the Cambrai Declaration was published. In it the King stated:

'I intend to banish from my presence only those men whose reputation is a subject of pain to France and of fear to Europe.'

Now it happened that Monsieur kept pronouncing the name of Fouché with expressions of gratitude. The King laughed at his brother's new passion and remarked:

'It has certainly not come to him from divine inspiration.'

At Roye, a council was held. M. de Talleyrand had two old horses put to his carriage and drove to His Majesty's. His coach and horses occupied the whole breadth of the square, from the Minister's inn to the King's door. He alighted from his chariot with a memoir which he read out to us: he considered the policy which would have to be adopted on arrival; he ventured few words on the need to admit everyone indiscriminately to the distribution of appointments; he insinuated that even Louis XVI's judges might generously be included. His Majesty flushed, and striking both arms of his chair, he cried:

'Never!'

A never of twenty-four hours' duration.

The Duke of Wellington arrived. I saw him going by in a barouche, the feathers in his hat waving in the air; he had come to bestow upon France M. Fouché and M. de Talleyrand, a twofold gift which the victor of Waterloo was making to our country. When it was suggested to him that the Duc d'Otrante's regicide might be a drawback, he replied:

'Why, that's of no importance!'

An Irish Protestant, a British general with no understanding of our history or our way of life, a man who saw nothing in the French year of 1793 but the English antecedent of 1649, was given the task of deciding our fate! Bonaparte's ambition had brought us to this sorry pass.

We travelled on to Saint-Denis: along both sides of the road there stretched the bivouacs of the Prussian and English troops; in the distance we could see the spires of the abbey: into its foundations Dagobert threw his jewels, and in its vaults successive dynasties buried their kings and their great men; four months earlier, we had laid the bones of Louis XVI there to replace the dust of his predecessors. When I returned from my first exile in 1800, I had crossed this same plain of Saint-Denis; then only Napoleon's soldiers were encamped there; Frenchmen still replaced the old bands of the Constable de Montmorency.

A baker gave us lodgings. At nine o'clock in the evening I went to pay my court to the King. His Majesty was lodged in the abbey buildings: his staff were hard put to it to prevent the little girls of the Legion of Honour* from shouting: 'Long live Napoleon!' I went into the church first: a piece of wall next to the cloister had fallen; the old abbey church was lit only by a single lamp. I said my prayers at the entrance to the vault into which I had seen Louis XVI lowered: full of fear as to the future, I do not know that I have ever felt my heart drowned in a more profound or more religious melancholy. Next I went to His Majesty's: shown into one of the rooms which led to the King's, I found no one there; I sat down in a corner and waited. Suddenly a door opened: silently Vice entered leaning on the arm of Crime, M. de Talleyrand walking in supported by M. Fouché; the infernal vision passed slowly before me, penetrated into the King's room, and vanished. Fouché had come to swear fealty and homage to his lord; the trusty regicide, going down on his knees, laid the hands which caused Louis XVI's head to fall between the hands of the royal martyr's brother; the apostate bishop went surety for the oath.

Before leaving Saint-Denis, I was received by the King, and had the following conversation with him:

'Well?' said Louis XVIII, opening the conversation with this exclamation.

'Well, Sire, so you are taking the Duc d'Otrante?'

'I have had to: from my brother down to the Bailli de Crussol (and the latter is above suspicion), everyone said that we could not do otherwise. What do you think?'

* A school for daughters of members of the Legion of Honour had been installed in the buildings of the Abbey of Saint-Denis in 1809.

'Sire, the thing is done: I beg Your Majesty's permission to say nothing.'

'No, no, speak: you know how I have resisted since leaving Ghent.'

'Sire, I am only obeying your orders; pardon my loyalty: I think the monarchy is finished.'

The King kept silence; I was beginning to tremble at my boldness when His Majesty remarked:

'Well, Monsieur de Chateaubriand, I am of your opinion.'

This conversation concludes my account of the Hundred Days.

EIGHT
St Helena

If a man were unexpectedly transferred from life's most clamorous scenes to the silent shores of the Arctic Ocean, he would feel what I feel beside Napoleon's tomb, for suddenly we find ourselves standing by that tomb.

Having left Paris on 25 June, Napoleon waited at Malmaison for the moment of his departure from France. I return to him there: going back over past days and anticipating the future, I shall not leave him again until after his death.

Malmaison, where the Emperor rested, was empty. Josephine was dead;* Bonaparte found himself alone in that retreat. There he had begun his triumphant career; there he had been happy; there he had become intoxicated with the incense of the world; there, from the heart of his tomb, he had issued orders that had shaken the world. In those gardens where once the feet of the mob raked up the sandy paths, grass and brambles grew green: I had discovered this when walking there. Already, for want of attention, the exotic trees were pining away; the black Australian swans no longer glided along the canals; the cage no longer held the tropical birds prisoners: they had flown away to await their host in their native land.

At the sight of those neglected gardens, of those unoccupied apartments, of those galleries faded by entertainments, of those rooms in which song and music had fallen silent, Napoleon was able to look back over his career: he was able to ask himself whether with a little more moderation he might not have preserved his happiness. It was not foreigners and enemies that

* The Empress Josephine had died at Malmaison on 29 May 1814.

were banishing him now; he was not going off as a quasi victor, leaving the nations lost in admiration of his prodigious campaign of 1814: he was retiring beaten, Frenchmen and friends were demanding his immediate abdication, urging his departure, refusing even to have him as a general, sending him one courier after another to force him to leave the soil over which he had shed as much glory as suffering.

Added to this harsh lesson came other warnings: the Prussians were prowling around Malmaison: Blücher, reeling about in his cups, ordered them to seize and hang the conqueror who had 'put his foot upon the neck of kings'. The rapidity of the fortunes, the vulgarity of the manners, the promptness of the elevation and degradation of modern men will, I fear, rob our times of some of the nobility of history: Rome and Greece did not talk of hanging Alexander and Caesar.

The scenes which had taken place in 1814 were repeated in 1815, but with something more offensive about them, because the ingrates were stimulated by fear: they had to get rid of Napoleon quickly: the Allies were arriving; Alexander was not there at the beginning to temper the triumph and curb the insolence of victory; Paris was no longer adorned with its lustral inviolability; a first invasion had profaned the sanctuary; it was no longer God's wrath that was falling upon us, it was the contempt of Heaven: the thunderbolt had spent itself.

There never was such a complete desertion; Bonaparte was responsible for it: he was insensible to other people's troubles, and the world repaid him with indifference for indifference. Like most despots, he was on good terms with his servants; but at bottom he cared for no one: a solitary man, he was sufficient unto himself; misfortune did nothing but restore him to the desert that was his life.

When I collect my memories, when I recall seeing Washington in his little house in Philadelphia and Bonaparte in his palaces, it seems to me that Washington, living in retirement on his plot of land in Virginia, cannot have experienced the regrets of Bonaparte awaiting exile in his gardens at Malmaison. Nothing was changed in the life of the first; he relapsed into his modest habits; he had not raised himself above the happiness of the husbandmen whom he had freed; but everything was altered in the life of the second.

Napoleon left Malmaison* accompanied by Generals Bertrand, Rovigo, and Beker, the latter acting in the capacity of warder or commissary. On the way, he was seized with a desire to stop at Rambouillet. He left that palace to take ship at Rochefort, as did Charles X to take ship at Cherbourg; Rambouillet, the inglorious retreat where all that was greatest in men or dynasties was eclipsed: the fatal spot where François I died; where Henri III, escaping from the barricades, slept booted and spurred; where Louis XVI left his shadow! How fortunate Louis, Napoleon, and Charles would have been, if they had been merely the humble keepers of the herds of Rambouillet!

Arriving at Rochefort,† Napoleon hesitated: the Executive Commission sent off peremptory orders:

'The garrisons of Rochefort and La Rochelle,' said the despatches, 'must use main force to make Napoleon take ship. . . . Employ force . . . make him go . . . his services cannot be accepted.'

Napoleon's services could not be accepted! And had you not accepted his gifts and his chains? Napoleon did not go away; he was expelled: and by whom?

Bonaparte had believed in nothing but good fortune; he gave no thought to misfortune; he had acquitted the ungrateful in advance: a just retribution submitted him to his own system. When success ceased to animate his person and became incarnate in another individual, the disciples abandoned the master for the school. I who believe in the legitimacy of gifts and the sovereignty of misfortune, if I had served Bonaparte, I would not have left him; I would have proved to him, by my loyalty, the falsity of his political principles; sharing his disgrace, I would have remained at his side as a living contradiction of his barren doctrines and of the worthlessness of the right of prosperity.

* On 29 June 1815.
† On 3 July 1815.

Since the first of July, there had been frigates waiting for him
in the Rochefort roadstead: hopes which never die, memories
inseparable from a final farewell detained him. How he must
have regretted his childhood days, when his serene eyes had not
yet seen the first raindrops! He gave the English fleet time to
approach. It was still possible for him to embark on two lug-
gers which were due to join a Danish ship at sea (this was the
course adopted by his brother Joseph), but his resolution failed
him when he looked at the coast of France. He had an aversion
for a republic; the liberty and equality of the United States were
repugnant to him. He felt inclined to ask the English for
asylum.

'What disadvantage do you see in that course?' he asked
those he consulted.

'That of dishonouring you,' answered a naval officer. 'You
must not fall into the hands of the English, dead or alive. They
will have you stuffed and put you on show at a shilling a head.'

In spite of these observations, the Emperor decided to give himself up to his conquerors. On 13 July, when Louis XVIII had
already been in Paris for five days, Napoleon sent the captain
of the English ship *Bellerophon* the following letter for the
Prince Regent:

Your Royal Highness,

A prey to the factions which are dividing my country and to
the enmity of the greatest powers in Europe, I have brought my
political career to a close, and I come, like Themistocles,* to
throw myself upon the hospitality of the British people. I place
myself under the protection of their laws, which I ask of Your
Royal Highness as of the most powerful, the most constant and
the most generous of my enemies.

Rochefort, 13 July 1815.

If Bonaparte had not heaped insults for twenty years upon

* The Athenian general Themistocles was forced to take refuge with his former
enemy Admetes, King of the Molossians.

the English people, its government, its King, and the heir to
that King, one might have found a certain propriety of tone in
this letter; but how had this 'Royal Highness', despised and
insulted for so long by Napoleon, suddenly become 'the most
powerful, the most constant and the most generous' of enemies
by the mere fact of being victorious? Napoleon could not be
convinced of what he was saying; and that which is not true is
not eloquent. The phrase setting out the situation of a fallen
greatness addressing itself to an enemy is very fine; the banal
example of Themistocles is superfluous.

In this step taken by Bonaparte there is something worse than
a lack of sincerity; there is a want of consideration for France: the
Emperor busied himself only with his individual catastrophe;
when the fall came, we no longer counted for anything in his eyes.
Without reflecting that, by preferring England to America, his
choice became an insult to the nation's grief, he begged asylum of
the government which, for twenty years, had paid Europe to fight
us, of the government whose commissary with the Russian army,
General Wilson, urged Kutusoff, in the retreat from Moscow, to
exterminate us completely: the English, victorious in the final
battle, were encamped in the Bois de Boulogne. Go then,
Themistocles, and sit quietly by the British hearth, while the soil
has not yet finished drinking the French blood shed for you at
Waterloo! What part would the fugitive have played if he had
been royally entertained on the banks of the Thames, with France
invaded and Wellington dictator at the Louvre? Napoleon's
noble destiny served him better: the English, allowing themselves
to be carried towards a shortsighted and spiteful policy, missed
their final triumph; instead of humiliating their supplicant by
admitting him to their fortresses or their banquets, they rendered more brilliant for posterity the crown which they
imagined they had taken from him. He grew greater in his captivity by virtue of the terrible apprehension of the Powers: the
ocean enchained him in vain: Europe in arms camped on the
shore, her eyes fixed upon the sea.

On 15 July the *Épervier* conveyed Bonaparte to the *Bellerophon*. The French boat was so small that, from the deck of the

English ship, they could not see the giant riding the waves. The
Emperor, accosting Captain Maitland, said to him:

'I come to place myself under the protection of the laws of
England.'

For once at least, the contemner of the laws admitted their
authority.

The fleet set sail for Torbay: a multitude of ships cruised
around the *Bellerophon*; the same excitement was shown at
Plymouth. On 30 July, Lord Keith handed the supplicant the
Act which confined him at St Helena.

'It is worse than Tamerlane's cage,' said Napoleon.*

This violation of the law of humanity and of the respect due
to hospitality was revolting. If you see the light of day on board
any ship, provided it is *under sail*, you are *English born*; by virtue of the age-old customs of London, the *waves* are considered
the *soil of Albion*. And an English ship was not an inviolable
altar for a supplicant; it did not place the great man who
embraced the poop of the *Bellerophon* under the protection of
the British trident! Bonaparte protested; he argued about laws,
talked of treachery and perfidy, and appealed to the future.
Did this become him? Had he not laughed at justice? Had he
not, in his might, trampled underfoot the sacred things whose
protection he now invoked? Had he not carried off Toussaint-
Louverture and the King of Spain? Had he not had English
travellers arrested who happened to be in France at the time of
the rupture of the Peace of Amiens, and kept them prisoners for
years? It was permissible therefore for mercantile England to
imitate what he had done himself, and to carry out ignoble
reprisals; but she could have acted differently.

With Napoleon, the heart did not match the head in greatness: his quarrels with the English are deplorable: they revolt
Lord Byron. How could he condescend to honour his gaolers
with so much as a word? It is painful to see him stooping to
wordy conflicts with Lord Keith at Torbay, with Sir Hudson
Lowe at St Helena, issuing statements because they break faith

* The cage in which Tamerlane imprisoned Bajazet I after defeating him at the
beginning of the fifteenth century.

with him, and quibbling about a title, about a little more, or a
little less, gold or honours. Bonaparte, reduced to himself, was
reduced to his glory, and that should have been sufficient for
him: he had nothing to ask of men; he did not treat adversity
despotically enough; one could have forgiven him for making
misfortune the last of his slaves. I find nothing remarkable in
his protest against the violation of hospitality except the place
and signature of that protest:

'On board the *Bellerophon*, at sea. Napoleon.'

There are immense harmonies to be seen here.

From the *Bellerophon* Bonaparte was transferred to the
Northumberland. Two frigates laden with the future garrison
of St Helena escorted him. Some of the officers of that garrison
had fought at Waterloo. The explorer of the globe was allowed
to keep with him M. and Mme Bertrand, and MM. de Montholon, Gourgaud, and de Las Cases, voluntary and generous
passengers on the submerged plank. According to one clause in
the captain's instructions, 'Bonaparte was to be disarmed':
Napoleon alone, a prisoner on board ship, in the middle of the
ocean, 'disarmed'! What magnificent proof of the terror of his
power! But what a lesson from Heaven to men who abuse the
sword! The stupid Admiralty treated the grand convict of the
human race as a Botany Bay felon: did the Black Prince 'dis-
arm' King John?

The squadron weighed anchor. Since the boat which carried
Caesar, no ship had been laden with so great a destiny. Bonaparte drew near to that sea of miracles over which the Arab
of Mount Sinai had seen him pass. The last French territory
that Napoleon saw was Cape la Hogue: another trophy of the
English.

The Emperor had misjudged the interest of his memory,
when he had wanted to stay in Europe; he would soon have
become nothing but an ordinary, insignificant prisoner: his old
role was finished. But beyond that role, a new situation revivi-
fied him with a new fame. No man of universal renown has had
an end similar to Napoleon's. He was not, as after his first fall,
proclaimed autocrat of a few quarries of iron and marble, the
first to furnish him with a sword, the second with a statue;

eagle that he was, he was given a rock on the point of which he remained in the sunlight until his death, in full view of the whole world.

At the moment when Bonaparte is leaving Europe, giving up his life to go in search of the destinies of his death, it is fitting to examine this man of two existences, to depict the false and the true Napoleon: they blend to form a whole from the mixture of their reality and their falsehood.

From the conjunction of our preceding observations, it can be seen that Bonaparte was a poet in action, an immense genius in war, an indefatigable, able, and intelligent mind in administration, a thorough and rational legislator. That is why he has so great a hold on the imagination of whole peoples, and so much authority over the judgement of practical men. But as a politician he will always appear deficient in the eyes of statesmen. This observation, which has been made inadvertently by most of his panegyrists, will, I feel convinced, become the definitive opinion concerning him; it will explain the contrast between his prodigious actions and their pitiful results. At St Helena, he himself severely condemned his political conduct on two points: the Spanish War and the Russian War; he might have extended his confession to embrace other sins. His admirers will surely not maintain that, when condemning himself, he was mistaken? Let us recapitulate:

Bonaparte acted in defiance of all prudence, not to speak again of the iniquity of the deed, in killing the Duc d'Enghien; he attached a weight to his life. Despite all that his puerile apologists may say, that death, as we have seen, was the hidden leaven of the conflicts which subsequently broke out between Alexander and Napoleon, as also between Prussia and France.

The attack on Spain was wholly improper: the Peninsula belonged to the Emperor; he could have turned it to the most profitable account: instead of that, he turned it into a school for the English soldiers and into the cause of his own destruction through the rising of a nation.

The detention of the Pope and the annexation of the States of the Church to France were the caprices of tyranny by which he lost the advantage of passing for the restorer of religion.

Bonaparte did not stop, as he should have done, when he had married the daughter of the Caesars: Russia and England were crying quarter to him.

He did not revive Poland, when the safety of Europe depended on the restoration of that kingdom.

Madness having set in, he went on beyond Smolensk; everything told him that he should not go any farther at his first attempt, that his first northern campaign was over, and that the second, as he himself felt, would make him master of the Empire of the Tsars.

He was incapable of either computing the days or of foreseeing the effect of the climate, which everyone in Moscow computed and foresaw. Consider too the Continental Blockade and the Confederation of the Rhine: the first was a gigantic conception but a dubious act; the second an important achievement, but spoilt in execution by the camp instinct and the fiscal mentality. Napoleon inherited the old French monarchy as the centuries and an uninterrupted succession of great men had made it, as the majesty of Louis XIV and the alliances of Louis XV had left it, and as the Republic had enlarged it. He seated himself on that magnificent throne, stretched out his arms, seized hold of the nations, and gathered them around him; but he lost Europe as speedily as he had won it, and twice he brought the Allies to Paris in spite of the marvels of his military intelligence. He had the world under his feet, and all he got out of it was a prison for himself, exile for his family, and the loss of all his conquests together with a portion of the old French territory.

That is history proved by facts and which none can dispute. Where did the faults which I have just indicated come from, faults followed by so speedy and so fatal a catastrophe? They came from Bonaparte's inadequacy as a politician.

In his alliances, he enchained the other governments only with concessions of territory, whose boundaries he would soon start altering, constantly showing a tendency to take back what he had given, and always making his supremacy felt; in his invasions, he reorganized nothing, Italy excepted. Instead of stopping at every step to raise up again behind him, in another form, what he had overthrown, he did not halt his progress through ruins: he went so fast that he scarcely had time to breathe as he passed by. If, by a sort of Treaty of Westphalia, he had settled and assured the existence of the States in Germany, Prussia, and Poland, then on his first retrograde march he could have fallen back on contented populations and found shelter among them. But his poetic edifice of victories, lacking a foundation and suspended in mid-air only by his genius, fell when his genius failed. The Macedonian built empires as he ran: Bonaparte, as he ran, knew only how to destroy; his sole aim was to be the master of the world, without troubling his head about ways of preserving it.

A monstrous pride and an incessant affectation spoil Napoleon's character. At the time of his supremacy, what need had he to exaggerate his stature, when the Lord of Hosts had furnished him with the chariot 'whose wheels are living'?

He took after his Italian ancestors: his nature was complex: great men, a very small family on earth, can unfortunately find nobody but themselves to imitate them. At once a model and a copy, a real person and an actor playing that person, Napoleon was his own mime; he would not have believed himself a hero if he had not dressed himself up in a hero's costume. This curious weakness imparts something false and equivocal to his astonishing realities: one is afraid of taking the King of Kings for Roscius* or Roscius for the King of Kings.

Napoleon's qualities are so greatly adulterated in the gazettes, the pamphlets, the poems, and even the popular songs impregnated with imperialism, that those qualities are completely unrecognizable. All the touching things attributed to Bonaparte in the *ana* about the 'prisoners', the 'dead', and the 'troops' are fabrications to which the actions of his life give the lie.

The *Grand'mère* of my illustrious friend Béranger is just an admirable ballad: Bonaparte had nothing good-natured about him. Tyranny personified, he was hard and cold: that coldness formed an antidote to his fiery imagination; he found in himself

* A Roman actor of the first century BC.

no word, he found only a deed, and a deed ready to grow angry at the slightest display of independence: a gnat that flew without his permission was a rebellious insect to his mind.

It was not enough to lie to the ears; it was necessary to lie to the eyes as well. Here, in an engraving, we see Bonaparte taking his hat off to the Austrian wounded; there, we have a little soldier-boy preventing the Emperor from passing; farther on, Napoleon touches the plague-stricken people of Jaffa, when in fact he never touched them, or he crosses the St Bernard Pass on a high-spirited horse in driving snow, when in fact the weather was as fine as it could be.

Are not people trying now to transform the Emperor into a Roman of the early days of the Aventine, into a missionary of liberty, into a citizen who instituted slavery only out of love of the opposite virtue? Draw your own conclusions from two characteristic acts of the great founder of equality: he ordered his brother Jerome's marriage to Miss Patterson to be annulled, because Napoleon's brother could ally himself only with the blood of princes; and later, on his return from the island of Elba, he invested the new 'democratic' constitution with a peerage and crowned it with the 'Additional Act'.

That Bonaparte, following up the Republic's triumphs, disseminated principles of independence everywhere; that his victories helped to loosen the bonds between the peoples and their kings, releasing those peoples from the power of the old customs and the ancient ideas; that, in this sense, he contributed to social emancipation – these are facts which I do not pretend to contest; but that, of his own free will, he deliberately worked for the political and civil deliverance of the nations; that he established the narrowest of tyrannies with the idea of giving Europe and France in particular the widest of constitutions; that he was simply a tribune disguised as a despot – these are suppositions which I cannot accept.

The Emperor took a hand in everything; his mind never rested; he had a sort of perpetual agitation of ideas. With his impulsive nature, instead of progressing steadily and continuously, he advanced by leaps and bounds, he threw himself upon the world and shook it; he did not want that world if he had to wait for it: an incomprehensible creature, who found the secret of debasing his loftiest actions in despising them, and who raised his least elevated actions to his own level. Impatient of will, patient of character, incomplete and as it were unfinished, Napoleon had gaps in his genius: his understanding resembled the sky of that other hemisphere under which he was to die, that sky whose stars are separated by empty spaces.

One may wonder by what magic spell Bonaparte, so aristocratic and so hostile to the mob, came to win the popularity which he enjoyed: for that forger of yokes has certainly remained popular with a nation whose pretension it was to raise altars to liberty and equality; this is the solution to the enigma:

Daily experience shows that the French are instinctively attracted by power; they have no love for liberty; equality alone is their idol. Now equality and tyranny have secret connexions. In those two respects, Napoleon had his fountain-head in the hearts of the French, militarily inclined towards power, democratically enamoured of a dead level. Mounting the throne, he seated the common people beside him; a proletarian king, he humiliated the kings and nobles in his ante-chambers; he levelled the ranks of society, not by lowering but by raising them: levelling down would have pleased plebeian envy more; levelling up was more flattering to its pride. French vanity was puffed up too by the superiority which Bonaparte gave us over the rest of Europe; another cause of Napoleon's popularity was the suffering of his last days. After his death, as people became better acquainted with what he had endured at St Helena, they were moved to pity; they forgot his tyranny and remembered only that after conquering our enemies, and after subsequently drawing them into France, he had defended us against them; we imagine that he might have saved us today from the disgrace into which we have sunk: we were reminded of his fame by his misfortune; his glory has profited by his adversity.

Finally, his wonderful feats of arms have fascinated the young and taught us all to worship brute force. His incredible good fortune has left to the conceit of every man of ambition the hope of reaching the point which he attained.

And yet this man, who passed an egalitarian roller over France, was the mortal enemy of equality and the greatest organizer of aristocracy within democracy.

I cannot join in the false praises with which others, trying to justify everything in Bonaparte's conduct, have insulted him; I cannot surrender my reason nor go into ecstasies before that which arouses my horror or my pity.

If I have succeeded in conveying what I have felt, there will remain of my portrait one of the leading figures in history; but I have taken over no part of the legendary being composed of lies: lies which I saw being born, and which, recognized at first for what they were, gradually assumed the appearance of truth through the infatuation and the imbecile credulity of mankind. I refuse to behave like a simpleton and fall into a fit of admiration. I strive to depict people conscientiously, without robbing them of what they have, and without giving them what they lack. If success were considered to be innocence; if, corrupting even posterity, it loaded it with its chains; if, a future slave, begotten by a slavish past, that suborned posterity became the accomplice of whoever had been victorious, where would be the right, where would be the reward of sacrifice? Good and evil becoming purely relative qualities, all morality would be banished from human actions.

Such is the difficulty which a great renown causes an impartial writer; he ignores it as far as he can, in order to lay bare the truth; but the glory returns like a golden haze and instantly covers his picture.

In order to avoid admitting the diminution of territory and power which we owe to Bonaparte, the present generation consoles itself with the thought that he has given back to us in glory what he has taken from us in strength. 'Are we not famous now,' it asks, 'in the four quarters of the earth? Is not a Frenchman feared, noticed, sought out, and recognized on every shore?'

But were we placed between those two conditions: either immortality without power, or power without immortality? Alexander made the name of the Greeks famous the world over; yet for all that he left them four empires in Asia, and the

language and civilization of the Hellenes extended from the
Nile to Babylon and from Babylon to the Indus. At his death,
his ancestral kingdom of Macedon, far from being diminished,
had increased a hundredfold in strength. Bonaparte spread our
fame to every shore; under his command, the French brought
Europe so low that France still prevails by her name, and the
Arc de l'Étoile can rise up without seeming a puerile trophy;
but before our reverses that monument would have stood as a
witness, instead of being only a record. And yet, had not
Dumouriez with his conscripts given the foreigner his first lessons, Jourdan won the Battle of Fleurus, Pichegru conquered
Belgium and Holland, Hoche crossed the Rhine, Masséna triumphed at Zürich, and Moreau at Hohenlinden: all exploits
which were difficult to perform and which prepared the way
for others? Bonaparte made a whole of these scattered successes; he continued these victories and made them shine forth:
but without those first wonders, could he have achieved the
last? He triumphed only when his reason was putting into execution the inspirations of the poet.

Our sovereign's fame cost us only two or three hundred
thousand men a year: we paid for it with only three million of
our soldiers; our fellow-citizens bought it only at the cost of
their sufferings and their liberties for fifteen years: can such
trifles count? Are not the generations that have come after us
resplendent in their glory? So much the worse for those who
have disappeared! The calamities which occurred under the
Republic served to ensure the safety of all; our misfortunes
under the Empire did much more: they deified Bonaparte! That
should be enough for us.

It is not enough for me: I will not stoop so low as to hide my
country behind Bonaparte; he did not make France: France
made him. No genius, no superiority will ever induce me to
support a power which, with one word, can deprive me of my
independence, my home, my friends: if I do not say of my fortune and my honour, it is because one's fortune does not seem
to me to be worth defending; as for honour, it is immune to
tyranny: it is the soul of martyrdom; bonds encompass it but

do not enchain it; it breaks through prison walls and carries the whole man away with it.

The wrong which true reason will never forgive Bonaparte is that of having accustomed society to passive obedience, thrust mankind back towards the times of moral degradation, and perhaps corrupted human nature to such a degree that it is impossible to say when men's hearts will begin to throb with noble feelings. The weakness of our situation as regards both ourselves and Europe, our present abasement, are the result of the Napoleonic slavery: it has left us nothing but the ability to bear the yoke. Bonaparte unsettled even the future: it would not surprise me if, in our sickly impotence, we were to grow even weaker, to barricade ourselves against Europe instead of going to seek it out, to give up our liberties within to deliver ourselves from an imaginary danger without, and to lose ourselves in ignoble precautions, contrary to our genius and to the fourteen centuries which have gone to the making of our way of life. The despotism which Bonaparte left in the air will close in upon us like a fortress.

The fashion nowadays is to greet liberty with a sardonic laugh, to look upon it as an outdated notion which, like honour, has fallen into disuse. I am not in the fashion: I believe that there can be nothing in this world without liberty; it makes life worth while; if I were to remain the last to defend it, I would never cease to proclaim its rights. To attack Napoleon in the name of things that are past, to assail him with ideas that are dead, is to provide him with fresh triumphs. He can be fought only with something greater than himself, and that is liberty: he offended against liberty and thus against the human race.

Bonaparte is no longer the real Bonaparte, but a legendary figure fashioned from the vagaries of the poet, the talk of the soldier, and the tales of the people; it is the Charlemagne and the Alexander of the medieval epics that we behold today. This fantastic hero will remain the real character: the other portraits will disappear. Bonaparte was such an absolute despot that, after enduring the tyranny of his person, we have to endure the tyranny of his memory. This latter tyranny is more overbearing than the former, for if men sometimes opposed Napoleon when he was on the throne, there is universal agreement that we should accept the chains which he throws to us now that he is dead. He is an obstacle to future events: how could a power issuing from the camps establish itself after him? Has he not killed all military glory by surpassing it? How could a free government come into being, when he has corrupted the principle of freedom in men's hearts? No legitimate power can now drive the usurping spectre from the mind of man: soldier and citizen, Republican and Monarchist, rich and poor alike place busts and portraits of Napoleon in their homes, in their palaces or cottages; the sometime vanquished are in agreement with the sometime victors; one cannot take a single step in Italy without coming across him: one cannot enter Germany without meeting him, for in that country the young generation which rejected him has gone. Generally, the centuries sit down before the portrait of a great man, and finish it by dint of long, successive labours. This time, the human race refused to wait: perhaps it was in too much of a hurry to stump a pastel drawing. It is time to place the finished part of the idol side by side with the defective part.

Bonaparte is not great by virtue of his words, his speeches, his writings, or by virtue of a love of liberty which he never possessed and which he never attempted to foster; he is great in that he created a solid and powerful government, a code of laws adopted in various countries, courts of law, schools, and a strong, active, intelligent administration on which we are still living; he is great in that he revived, enlightened, and governed Italy superlatively well; he is great in that, in France, he restored order from the midst of chaos, in that he rebuilt the altars, in that he pressed into his service wild demagogues, vain scholars, anarchical men of letters, Voltairean atheists, open-air orators, cut-throats from the prisons and the streets, starvelings from the tribune, the club, and the scaffold; he is great in that he curbed an anarchical mob; he is great in that he put an end to the familiarities of a common fortune, in that he forced soldiers, his equals, and captains, his superiors or his rivals, to bend before his will; he is great above all in that he was born of himself alone, in that he was able, with no other authority than

his genius, to compel the obedience of thirty-six million subjects, in an age which has no illusions about thrones; he is great
in that he overthrew all the kings who opposed him, in that he
defeated all the armies, however much they differed in discipline and valour, in that he taught his name to savage as well as
to civilized peoples, in that he surpassed all the conquerors
who preceded him, in that he filled ten years with prodigies so
great that today we find it difficult to comprehend them.

The famous offender in triumphal matters is no more; the
few men who still appreciate noble sentiments can do homage
to glory without fearing it, but also without repenting of having stigmatized all that was baleful in that glory, without
recognizing the destroyer of freedom as the father of emancipation: Napoleon has no need for merits to be ascribed to him; he
was sufficiently endowed at birth.

Now, therefore, that, severed from his time, his history has
ended and his epic is beginning, let us go to see him die: let us
leave Europe; let us follow him beneath the sky of his apothe-
osis! The trembling of the seas where his ships struck sail will
show us the spot where he disappeared: 'At the extremity of
our hemisphere,' says Tacitus, 'one can hear the sound made by
the sun sinking into the sea: *sonum insuper immergentis audiri.*'

On 15 August the wandering colony celebrated St Napoleon's
Day on board the vessel which was taking Napoleon to his last
resting-place. On 15 October the *Northumberland* was abreast
of St Helena. The passenger went up on deck; he had difficulty
in making out an imperceptible black speck in the bluish
immensity; he took a spyglass and surveyed that particle of
earth, as he might once have surveyed a fortress in the middle
of a lake. He saw the little town of St James set in sheer rocks;
there was not a wrinkle in that barren face but had a gun clinging to it: they seemed to wish to receive the captive in a manner
suited to his genius.

On 16 October 1815 Bonaparte landed on the rock, his
mausoleum, just as on 12 October 1492 Christopher Columbus landed in the New World, his monument: 'There,' says
Walter Scott, 'at the entrance to the Indian Ocean, Bonaparte

was deprived of the means of making a second *avatar* or incarnation on earth.'

Before being moved to the residence of Longwood, Bonaparte occupied a villa at Briars, near Balcomb's Cottage. On 9 December, Longwood, hurriedly enlarged by the carpenters of the English fleet, received its guest. The house, standing on a plateau in the mountains, consisted of a drawing-room, a dining-room, a study, and a bedroom. It was not much: those who occupied the Temple and the keep of Vincennes were given even worse accommodation; true, their hosts were considerate enough to cut short their stay. General Gourgaud, M. and Mme de Montholon with their children, M. de Las Cases and his son camped out for the time being in tents; M. and Mme Bertrand installed themselves in Hut's Gate, a cottage on the boundary of the grounds of Longwood.

Bonaparte had a stretch of sand twelve miles long in which to take exercise; sentries surrounded that space and look-outs were posted on the highest peaks. The lion could extend his walks farther, but in that case, he had to agree to allow himself to be watched by an English *bestiarius*. Two camps guarded the excommunicated enclosure: at night, the circle of sentries was drawn in around Longwood. After nine o'clock, Napoleon was not allowed out; the patrols went on their rounds; cavalry on vedette duty and infantry-men posted here and there kept watch in the creeks and in the ravines which ran down to the sea. Two armed brigs cruised around, one to leeward, the other to windward of the island. What precautions to guard one man in the middle of the ocean! After sunset, no boat could put out to sea; the fishing-boats were counted, and at night they remained in the harbour under the responsibility of a naval lieutenant. The sovereign generalissimo who had summoned the world to his stirrup was called upon to appear twice a day before a junior officer. Bonaparte refused to answer that summons; if it happened that he failed to escape the notice of the officer on duty, that officer did not dare say where and how he had seen him of whom it was more difficult to establish the absence than to prove the presence to the world.

Sir George Cockburn, the author of these severe regulations, was replaced by Sir Hudson Lowe. There then began the bickering of which all the memories have told us. If we are to believe these memoirs, the new Governor belonged to the family of the enormous St Helena spiders, and was the reptile of those woods where snakes are unknown. England showed a lack of generosity, Napoleon a lack of dignity. To put an end to the requirements of etiquette, Bonaparte sometimes seemed determined to hide behind a pseudonym, like a monarch travelling in a foreign country; he had the touching idea of taking the name of one of his aides-de-camp who had been killed at the Battle of Arcola. France, Austria, and Russia appointed commissaries to the St Helena residence: the captive was accustomed to receiving the ambassadors of the two latter Powers; the Legitimacy, which had not recognized Napoleon as Emperor, would have acted more nobly by not recognizing Napoleon as a prisoner.

A large wooden house, constructed in London, was sent to St Helena; but Napoleon did not feel well enough to live in it. His life at Longwood was arranged in this way: he rose at no special hour; M. Marchand, his valet, read to him when he was in bed; when he got up early, he dictated to Generals Montholon and Gourgaud and to the son of M. de Las Cases. He breakfasted at ten o'clock, went for a ride or a drive until about three, came indoors about six, and went to bed at eleven. He affected the costume in which he is depicted in the portrait by Isabey: in the morning he wrapped himself in a caftan and wound a Madras kerchief round his head.

St Helena lies between the two Poles. Navigators on their way from one to the other welcome the sight of this first station where the land gladdens eyes wearied by the spectacle of the ocean and offers fruit and the coolness of fresh water to mouths chafed by salt. Bonaparte's presence changed this promised land into a plague-stricken rock; foreign ships no longer called there; as soon as they were sighted fifty miles away, a cruiser went to challenge them and ordered them to keep off: none were allowed into port, except in stormy weather, but ships of the British Navy.

Some of the English travellers who had recently admired or

were going to see the marvels of the Ganges visited another marvel on their way: India, accustomed to conquerors, had one in chains at her gates.

Napoleon allowed these visits only with the greatest reluctance. He agreed to see Lord Amherst on the latter's return from his Chinese embassy. Admiral Sir Pulteney Malcolm he liked.

'Does your Government,' he asked him one day, 'intend to detain me on this rock until my dying day?'

The admiral replied that he feared so.

'Then my death will occur very soon.'

'I hope not, Monsieur; I hope you will live long enough to record your great feats; they are so numerous that the task will ensure you a long life.'

Napoleon did not take offence at that simple appellation of Monsieur; he revealed himself at that moment in his true greatness. Fortunately for himself, he never wrote the story of his life; he would have reduced its dimensions: men of that nature must leave their memoirs to be recounted by the unknown voice which belongs to nobody and which issues from the nations and the centuries. Only we humble folk may talk of ourselves, for otherwise nobody would talk of us.

Bonaparte was approaching his end; plagued by an internal wound poisoned by sorrow, he had borne that wound in the midst of prosperity: it was the only legacy which he had received from his father; the rest came to him from God's munificence.

Already he had been six years in exile; he had needed less time than that to conquer Europe. He stayed indoors nearly all the time, and read Ossian in Cesarotti's Italian translation. Everything saddened him under a sky beneath which life seemed shorter, the sun remaining three days less in that hemisphere than in ours. When Bonaparte went out, he passed along stony paths lined with aloes and scented broom. He walked among the flowering gum-trees which the prevailing winds bent the same way, or else he hid in the thick clouds which rolled along at ground level. He was seen sitting at the foot of Diana's Peak, Flag Staff, or Leader Hill, gazing at the sea through the gaps in the mountains. Before him stretched the

Ocean which on one side washes the coasts of Africa, on the other the American shores, and which goes, like a river without banks, to lose itself in the southern seas. There is no civilized land nearer than the Cape of Storms. Who shall tell the thoughts of that Prometheus torn alive by death, when, his hand pressed to his aching breast, he looked out over the waves? Christ was carried to a mountain peak from which He saw the kingdoms of the world; but in the case of Christ the tempter of mankind was told: 'Thou shalt not tempt the Lord thy God.'

Bonaparte, forgetting a thought of his which I have quoted ('Not having given myself life, I shall not deprive myself of it'), spoke of killing himself; he also forgot his order of the day on the suicide of one of his soldiers. He had sufficient confidence in the devotion of his companions in captivity to believe that they would agree to suffocate with him in the smoke from a brazier: the illusion was considerable. Such are the intoxications born of a long supremacy; but in the case of Napoleon's fits of impatience, we have to consider the degree of suffering to which he had attained. M. de Las Cases, having written to Lucien on a piece of white silk, in contravention of the regulations, was ordered to leave St Helena: his absence increased the void around the exile.

On 18 May 1817, Lord Holland, in the House of Lords, introduced a motion on the subject of the complaints transmitted to England by General Montholon.

'Posterity will not ask,' he said, 'whether Napoleon was justly punished for his crimes, but whether England showed the generosity befitting a great country.'

Lord Bathurst opposed the motion.

Cardinal Fesch sent two priests from Italy to see his nephew. The Princess Borghese begged the favour of being allowed to join her brother.

'No,' said Napoleon, 'I do not wish her to witness my humiliation and the insults to which I am subjected.'

That beloved sister of his, *germana Jovis*,* did not cross the seas: she died in the regions where Napoelon had left his fame.

* The sister of Jupiter.

Plans were made for his abduction: a certain Colonel Lata-pie, at the head of a band of American adventurers, plotted a landing on St Helena. Johnston, a bold smuggler, thought of carrying Bonaparte off by means of a submarine vessel. Some young lords entered into these plans; they schemed together to break the chains of the oppressor; they would have left the liberator of the human race to die in irons without giving him a thought. Bonaparte hoped that his liberation would come from the political movements of Europe. If he had lived till 1830, perhaps he would have returned to us; but what would he have done among us? He would have seemed decrepit and old-fashioned in the midst of the new ideas. In the past his tyranny looked like liberty to our slavery; now his greatness would look like despotism to our pettiness. At the present time, everything disintegrates in a day; whoever lives too long dies alive. As we advance through life, we leave behind three or four images of ourselves, different one from the other: we see them again in the haze of the past, like portraits of our different ages.

Bonaparte, stripped of his power, occupied his days with childish pastimes: he amused himself by making an ornamental pool in the garden; he put a few fish into it; the cement used in making the pool contained some copper, and the fish died. Bonaparte said:

'Everything I love is doomed.'

Towards the end of February 1821, Napoleon was obliged to take to his bed, and he did not get up again.

'How low I have fallen!' he murmured. 'I have stirred up the whole world, and I cannot lift my eyelids!'

He had no faith in medicine and objected to a consultation between Antomarchi and the Jamestown doctors. However, he allowed Dr Arnott to approach his death-bed. From 13 to 27 April, he dictated his will; on the 28th, he ordered his heart to be sent to Marie-Louise; he forbade any English surgeon to lay a hand upon him after his death. Convinced that he was succumbing to the disease with which his father had been afflicted, he asked for the report of his autopsy to be sent to the Duke of Reichstadt: this paternal precaution has become useless; Napoleon II has joined Napoleon I.

At this last hour, the religious feeling with which Bonaparte had always been imbued awoke. Thibaudeau, in his *Mémoires sur le Consulat*, tells us, with reference to the restoration of public worship, that the First Consul said to him:

'Last Sunday, in the midst of the silence of Nature, I was walking in these gardens (at Malmaison); the sound of the bell of Ruel suddenly struck my ear and renewed all the impressions of my youth; I was moved, so strong is the force of early habit, and I said to myself: "If this can happen to me, what effect must similar memories not produce on ordinary, credulous men?" Let your philosophers find an answer to that!'

And, raising his hands to the sky:

'Who is He that made all that?'

In 1797, by his Proclamation of Macerata, Bonaparte gave permission for the French priests who had taken refuge in the Papal States to remain there, forbade them to be molested, ordered the monastic orders to support them, and allotted them a stipend in money.

His vagaries in Egypt, his fits of anger against the Church of which he was the restorer, show that an instinct of spirituality predominated in the very midst of his errors, for his lapses and his rages are not of a philosophical nature and bear the impress of the religious temperament.

When he was giving Vignali details of the tapers with which he wished his remains to be surrounded in the mortuary chapel, Bonaparte thought he saw signs that his instructions were displeasing to Antomarchi; he explained his conduct to the doctor, saying:

'You are above these weaknesses: but I am not. I am neither a philosopher nor a doctor; I believe in God; I am of my father's religion. We cannot all be atheists. . . . How can you not believe in God? For, after all, everything proclaims His existence, and the greatest geniuses have believed in it. . . . But then, you are a doctor . . . Those people deal with nothing but matter: they never believe anything.'

You rationalists, abandon your admiration for Napoleon; you have nothing in common with that poor man: did he not imagine that a comet had come to fetch him, just as it had once carried off Caesar? Worse still, he *believed in God*; he was *of his father's religion*; he was not a *philosopher*; he was not an *atheist*; unlike you he had not joined battle with the Almighty, although he had defeated a good number of kings; he found that *everything proclaimed the existence* of the Supreme Being; he declared that *the greatest geniuses had believed in His existence*, and he wanted to believe as his forefathers did. And lastly, horrible to relate, this foremost man of modern times, this man of all the ages, was a Christian in the nineteenth century! His will begins with this statement:

I DIE IN THE APOSTOLIC AND ROMAN RELIGION, IN THE
BOSOM OF WHICH I WAS BORN OVER FIFTY YEARS AGO.

In the third paragraph of Louis XVI's will, we read:

I DIE IN THE UNION OF OUR HOLY MOTHER THE CATHOLIC,
APOSTOLIC, AND ROMAN CHURCH.

The Revolution has taught us many a lesson, but is there any one of them to be compared with this? Napoleon and Louis XVI making the same profession of faith! Do you wish to know the value of the Cross? Then search the whole world for what best suits virtue in distress or the man of genius in his death-agony.

On 3 May, Napoleon was given Extreme Unction and received the Blessed Viaticum. The silence of the bedroom was broken only by the irregular breathing of the dying man and the steady sound of a clock pendulum: the shadow, before stopping on the dial, did a few more rounds; the sun that made it was finding it difficult to die. On the 4th, the tempest of Cromwell's death-agony arose: nearly all the trees at Longwood were uprooted. Finally, on the 5th, at eleven minutes to six in the evening, in the midst of the wind and rain and the thunder of the waves, Bonaparte rendered up to God the mightiest breath of life that ever animated human clay. The last words heard upon the conqueror's lips were: 'Head . . . army' or 'Head of the army'. His thoughts were still of battle. When he closed his eyes for ever, his sword, which died with him, lay beside him, and a crucifix rested on his breast: the symbol of peace, applied to Napoleon's heart, calmed the throbbing of that heart just as a ray of sunlight makes the wave fall.

Bonaparte had first asked to be buried in the Cathedral of Ajaccio; then, by a codicil dated 16 April 1821, he bequeathed his bones to France: Heaven had served him better; his real mausoleum is the rock on which he expired: turn back to my account of the death of the Duc d'Enghien. Finally, foreseeing opposition to his last wishes from the British Government, Napoleon chose a burying-place at St Helena.

In a narrow valley known as Slane or Geranium Valley, and now as Tomb Valley, there is a spring at which Napoleon's Chinese servants, as faithful as Camoëns's Javanese, used to fill their pitchers: weeping willows hang over this spring; green grass, studded with tchampas, grows all around. 'The tchampas,' say the Sanskrit poems, 'for all its colour and perfume, is not a sought-after flower, because it grows on graves.'

Napoleon liked the willows by the spring; he asked Slane Valley for peace, just as the exiled Dante asked for peace from the convent of Corvo. Out of gratitude for the transient rest which he enjoyed there in the last days of his life, he chose this valley to shelter him during his eternal rest. Speaking of the spring, he said: 'If God granted me recovery, I should erect a monument in the place where it rises.' That monument was his tomb. In Plutarch's time, in a spot consecrated to the nymphs on the banks of the Strymon, one could still see a stone seat on which Alexander had sat.

Napoleon, booted and spurred, dressed in the uniform of a colonel of the Guard and decorated with the Legion of Honour, was laid in state on his little iron bedstead; upon the face which had never shown surprise, the soul, as it fled, had left a sublime stupor. The planishers and joiners soldered and nailed Bonaparte into a fourfold coffin of mahogany, lead, mahogany again, and tin: it was as if they were afraid that he would never be sufficiently imprisoned. The cloak which the conqueror of old had worn at the vast funeral of Marengo served as a pall for the coffin.

The obsequies were held on 28 May. The weather was fine; four horses, led by grooms on foot, drew the hearse; twenty-four English grenadiers, carrying no arms, surrounded it; Napoleon's horse followed after. The garrison of the island lined the slopes along the road. Three squadrons of dragoons preceded the procession; the 20th Regiment of Infantry, the Marines, the St Helena Volunteers, and the Royal Artillery with fifteen guns, brought up the rear. Bands of musicians, stationed at intervals on the rocks, exchanged mournful tunes. Coming to a narrow pass, the hearse stopped; the twenty-four unarmed grenadiers picked up the body and had the honour of carrying it on their shoulders to the burying-place. Three artillery salvoes saluted Napoleon's remains at the moment when he sank into the earth: all the noise which he had made on that earth did not penetrate six feet beneath it.

A stone, which was to have been used in the building of a new house for the exile, was lowered on to his coffin, like a trap-door on his last dungeon.

The verses from Psalm lxxxviii were recited:

'I am poor, and in labours from my youth: and being exalted have been humbled and troubled. Thy wrath hath come upon me. . . .'

Every minute the flag-ship fired its guns. This warlike harmony, lost in the immensity of the ocean, sounded a response to the *Requiescat in pace*. The Emperor, buried by his victors of Waterloo, had heard the last cannon-shot of that battle; he did not hear the last detonation with which England disturbed and honoured his sleep at St Helena. All withdrew, each holding a willow-branch in his hand, as if returning from the Feast of Palms.

Lord Byron thought that the dictator of kings had abdicated his fame with his sword, and that he was going to die forgotten. The poet ought to have known that Napoleon's destiny was a muse, like all lofty destinies. That muse was able to change an abortive issue into a tragedy which revived its hero. The solitude of Napoleon's exile and tomb has spread over an illustrious memory a spell of a different kind. Alexander did not die under the eyes of Greece; he disappeared in the far reaches of Babylon. Bonaparte did not die under the eyes of France; he vanished beyond the sumptuous horizons of the torrid zone. He sleeps like a hermit or a pariah in a valley, at the end of a deserted pathway. The magnitude of the silence which weighs upon him matches the immensity of the noise which surrounded him. The nations are absent, their multitudes have withdrawn; the tropical bird, harnessed, as Buffon says, to the chariot of the sun, plunges earthward from the orb of light; where does it rest today? It rests upon ashes whose weight tilted the globe.

Since it is my own life which I am writing even while dealing with the lives of others, great or small, I am obliged to mix this life with men and things when it happens to be recalled. Did I revive straight off, without ever stopping, the memory of the exile who, in his ocean prison, awaited the execution of God's decree? No.

The peace which Napoleon had not concluded with the kings his gaolers he had made with me: I was a son of the sea like himself; my birthplace was a rock like his. I flatter myself that I knew Napoleon better than they who saw him more often and approached him more closely.

Napoleon at St Helena, no longer having any need to maintain his anger against me, had abandoned his hostility; I, becoming more just in my turn, wrote this article in the *Conservateur*:

The nations have called Bonaparte a scourge; but God's scourges retain something of the eternity and grandeur of the divine wrath from which they emanate: 'Ye dry bones . . . I will send spirit into you, and you shall live.'* Born on an island to go and die on an island, on the boundaries of three continents, cast in the midst of seas where Camoëns seemed to prophesy his presence by placing there the genius of the tempests, Bonaparte cannot stir on his rock but we are apprised of it by a shock; a single step taken by

* Ezek., xxxvii, 4–5.

the new Adamastor* at the other Pole can be felt at this. If Napoleon, escaping from the clutches of his gaolers, were to retire to the United States, his gaze fixed upon the Ocean would be enough to disturb the nations of the Old World; his mere presence on the American shore of the Atlantic would oblige Europe to set up camp on the opposite shore.

This article reached Bonaparte at St Helena; a hand which he thought hostile poured the last balm on his wounds; he said to M. de Montholon:

'If, in 1814 and 1815, the royal trust had not been placed in men whose souls were enervated by circumstances too strong for them, or who, traitors to their country, saw safety and glory for their master's throne only under the yoke of the Holy Alliance; if the Duc de Richelieu, whose ambition it was to deliver his country from the presence of the foreign bayonets, or Chateaubriand, who had just rendered eminent services at Ghent, had had the direction of affairs, then France would have emerged powerful and formidable from those two great national crises. Chateaubriand has been endowed by Nature with the Promethean fire: his works prove it. His style is not that of Racine, it is that of the prophet. If ever he comes to the helm of State, it is possible that Chateaubriand may go astray: so many others have come to grief there! But what is certain is that all that is great and national must befit his genius, and that he would have indignantly rejected the shameful acts of the administration of that time.'

Such were my last relations with Bonaparte. Why should I not admit that this judgement 'flatters my heart's proud weakness'?† Many little men to whom I have rendered great services have not judged me as favourably as the giant whose might I had dared to challenge.

While the Napoleonic world was disintegrating, I made inquiries about the place where Napoleon himself had died. The

* The giant of the tempests invented by Camoëns.
† Racine: *Iphigénie.*

tomb at St Helena has already worn out one of the willows that
were his contemporaries: the decrepit, fallen tree is daily mutilated by pilgrims. The burial-place is surrounded by a cast-iron
railing; three flagstones have been laid in the form of a cross
over the grave; a few irises are growing at the head and feet; the
spring of the valley still flows in the spot where a prodigious
life ran dry. Travellers brought here by the tempest consider
themselves obliged to record their obscurity on the illustrious
sepulchre. An old woman has established herself near by and
lives on the shadow of a memory; a pensioner mounts guard in
a sentry-box.

The old Longwood, two hundred paces from the new, has
been completely abandoned. Crossing a yard filled with
manure, you come to a stable; it used to be Bonaparte's bedroom. A Negro shows you a sort of passage occupied by a
hand-mill and says:

'Here he died.'

The room where Napoleon first saw the light of day was
probably neither larger nor more luxurious.

At the new Longwood, Plantation House, where the Governor lives, you can see a portrait of the Duke of Wellington and
pictures of his battles. A glass-fronted cupboard contains a piece
of the tree beside which the English general stood at Waterloo;
this relic has been placed between an olive-branch gathered in
the Garden of Olives and some ornaments worn by South Sea
savages: a curious association on the part of the abusers of the
waves. It is useless for the victor to try to substitute himself here
for the vanquished, under the protection of a branch from the
Holy Land and the memory of Cook; it is enough that, at
St Helena, one finds solitude, the ocean, and Napoleon.

If one were to investigate the history of the transformation
of shores made famous by tombs, cradles, and palaces, what a
variety of things and destinies one would see, since such strange
metamorphoses occur even in the obscure dwellings to which
our puny lives are attached! In what hut was Clovis born? In
what chariot did Attila first see the light? What torrent covers
Alaric's burial-place? What jackal stands upon the site of Alexander's gold or crystal coffin? How many times have all these

ashes changed their place? And all those mausoleums in Egypt and India: to whom do they belong? Only God knows the reason for those changes linked with the mystery of the future: for men there are truths hidden in the depths of time; they come forth only with the help of the ages, just as there are stars so far removed from the earth that their light has not yet reached us.

But while I was writing all this, time has marched on: it has produced an event which would have a certain grandeur if events nowadays did not fall into the mud. We have asked London for Bonaparte's remains to be returned; the request has been granted: what does England care about old bones? She will give us as many presents of that sort as we like. Napoleon's remains have come back to us at the moment of our humiliation; they could have been submitted to the right of search, but the foreigner was indulgent: he gave a pass to the ashes.

The translation of Napoleon's remains is an offence against fame. No sepulchre in Paris will ever be as good as Slane Valley: who would wish to see Pompey elsewhere than in the furrow of sand thrown up by a poor freedman, with the assistance of an old legionary? What shall we do with those magnificent relics in the midst of our woes? Can even the hardest granite represent the perpetuity of Bonaparte's achievements? It is not as if we had a Michelangelo to carve the memorial statue. What sort of monument will he be given? To little men mausoleums, to great men a stone and a name. They might at least have suspended the coffin on the coping of the Arc de Triomphe, so that the nations could see their master from afar, borne on the shoulders of his victories. Was not Trajan's urn set at the top of his column in Rome? Napoleon, among us, will be lost in the mob of those tatterdemalions who steal away in silence. God grant that he is not exposed to the vicissitudes of our political changes, protected though he may be by Louis XIV, Vauban, and Turenne! Beware of those violations of tombs which are so common in our country! Let one side of the Revolution triumph, and the conqueror's dust may go to join the dust which our passions have already scattered: men will forget the vanquisher of nations to remember only the oppressor of liberties. Napoleon's bones will not reproduce his genius: they will only teach his despotism to second-rate soldiers.

Be that as it may, a frigate was supplied to one of Louis-Philippe's sons: a name dear to our former naval victories protected it on the waves.* Sailing from Toulon, where Bonaparte had embarked in all his might for the conquest of Egypt, the new *Argo* came to St Helena to claim something that no longer existed. The sepulchre, wrapped in silence, still stood motionless in Slane or Geranium Valley. Of the two weeping willows, one had fallen; Lady Dallas, wife of a governor of the island, had planted, to replace the dead tree, eighteen young willows and thirty-four cypresses; the spring, which was still there, flowed as when Napoleon drank its water. During the whole of one night, under the supervision of an English captain called Alexander, the work of opening the monument was carried out. The four coffins fitted one inside the other, the mahogany coffin, the lead coffin, the second mahogany or West Indian wood coffin, and the tin coffin were found to be intact. The inspection of these mummy-moulds was performed inside a tent, in the centre of a circle of officers, some of whom had known Bonaparte.

When the last coffin was opened, everyone looked inside. 'We saw,' says the Abbé Coquereau, 'a whitish mass which covered the whole length of the body. Dr Gaillard, touching it, recognized it as a white satin cushion which lined the inside of the coffin lid: it had come undone and enveloped the remains like a shroud. . . . The whole body seemed to be covered with a light foam; it was as if we were looking at it through a diaphanous cloud. The head was unmistakable; a pillow raised it slightly; we could distinguish his broad forehead and his eyes, the sockets of which were outlined beneath the eyelids, still fringed with a few lashes; his cheeks were swollen; only his nose had suffered; his mouth, which was half-open, revealed three remarkably white teeth; on his chin the traces of his beard were perfectly clear; his two hands in particular seemed to

---

* Louis-Philippe's third son, the Prince de Joinville, was given the frigate *Belle-Poule* on which to bring home Napoleon's remains in 1840.

belong to someone who still breathed, they were so fresh in tone and colouring; one of them, the left hand, was raised a little higher than the right; his nails had grown after death; they were long and white; one of his boots had come unsewn and showed four dull-white toes.'

What was it that struck the disinterrers? The inanity of earthly things? Human vanity? No, the beauty of the dead man; only his nails had grown longer, to tear, I presume, at what remained of liberty in the world. His feet, restored to humility, no longer rested on a cushion of crowns; they lay bare in their dust. Condé's son too was laid fully dressed in the moat at Vincennes; yet Napoleon, for all that he was so well preserved, had been reduced to precisely those 'three teeth' which the bullets had left in the Duc d'Enghien's jaw.

The vanished star of St Helena has reappeared to the joy of the nations: the world has seen Napoleon again; Napoleon has not seen the world again. The conqueror's vagrant ashes have been looked upon by the same stars that guided him to his exile: Bonaparte passed through the tomb, as he passed through everything, without stopping. Landed at Le Havre, the corpse arrived at the Arc de Triomphe, a canopy beneath which the sun shows its face on certain days of the year. From that arch to the Invalides, one saw nothing but wooden columns, plaster busts, a statue of the Great Condé (a hideous mass of pulp which wept), and deal obelisks commemorating the victor's indestructible life. Bitterly cold weather made the generals drop around the hearse, as in the retreat from Moscow. Nothing was beautiful, except the funeral barge which had silently carried Napoleon and the crucifix along the Seine.

Robbed of his rocky catafalque, Napoleon had come to be buried in the grime of Paris. Instead of the ships which used to salute the new Hercules, consumed upon Mount Oeta, the washerwomen of Vaugirard will roam around him with pensioners unknown to the Grand Army. By way of a prelude to this pettiness, little men could think up nothing better than an open-air waxwork show. After a few days' rain, nothing remained of these decorations but mud-stained odds-and-ends. Whatever we may do, posterity will always see the conqueror's real sepulchre in the midst of the seas: the body is with us, the life immortal at St Helena.

Napoleon has closed the era of the past: he made war too great for it to return in a form capable of interesting mankind. He slammed the doors of the Temple of Janus behind him; and behind those doors he heaped up piles of corpses, to prevent them from ever opening again.

In Europe I have been to visit the place where Bonaparte landed after breaking his ban at Elba. I alighted at the inn at Cannes at the very moment when the guns were firing in commemoration of the 29th of July:* one of the results of the Emperor's incursion which he doubtless failed to foresee. Night had fallen when I arrived at Golfe-Juan; I stopped at a lonely house beside the highroad. Jacquemin, potter and innkeeper, the owner of the house, led me to the sea. We went by way of sunken roads between olive-trees under which Bonaparte had bivouacked: Jacquemin himself had put him up and guided me. To the left of the cross-path stood a sort of shed: Napoleon, invading France by himself, had deposited the luggage with which he had landed in that shed.

Reaching the beach, I saw a calm sea wrinkled by not the slightest breath; the swell, as thin as gauze, rolled over the sand without making any noise or foam. An astonishing sky, resplendent with constellations, hung above me. The crescent of the moon soon sank and hid behind a mountain. In the whole gulf, there was only one ship at anchor, and two boats; on the left could be seen the Antibes lighthouse, on the right the Lérin Isles; in front of me, the open sea stretched away to the south in the direction of that city of Rome to which Bonaparte had first sent me.

The Lérin Isles, now called the Sainte-Marguerite Isles, once sheltered a few Christians fleeing from the Barbarians. St Honoratus, coming from Hungary, landed on one of those rocks: he climbed a palm-tree, made the sign of the Cross, and all the

* The date of Charles X's abdication in 1830; Chateaubriand visited Cannes in 1838.

serpents died; that is to say, paganism disappeared, and the new civilization was born in the West.

Fourteen hundred years later, Bonaparte came to put an end to that civilization in the very spot where the saint had begun it. The last solitary to inhabit those cells was the Man in the Iron Mask, if in fact he ever existed. From the silence of Golfe-Juan, from the peace of those islands haunted by the anchorites of old, there issued the noise of Waterloo, which crossed the Atlantic to die away at St Helena.

One can imagine what I felt, between the memories of two societies, between a world that was extinct and a world that was about to become extinct, at night, on that deserted shore. I left the beach in a sort of religious consternation, leaving the waves to pass to and fro, without ever obliterating them, over the traces of Bonaparte's last step but one.

At the end of each great epoch, some voice, full of a melancholy nostalgia, can be heard sounding the curfew: thus they moaned who saw the disappearance of Charlemagne, St Louis, François I, Henri IV, and Louis XIV. What could I not say in my turn, eyewitness that I am of two or three vanished worlds? When one has met, as I have, Washington and Bonaparte, what does there remain to look at behind the plough of the American Cincinnatus and the tomb at St Helena? Why have I outlived the epoch and the men to whom I belonged by the date of my birth? Why did I not fall with my contemporaries, the last of an exhausted race? Why have I remained alone to search for their bones in the dust and darkness of a crowded catacomb? I am weary of my survival. Ah, if only I possessed the indifference of one of those old longshore Arabs that I met in Africa. Sitting cross-legged on a little rope mat, their heads wrapped in their burnous, they while away their last hours in following with their eyes, in the azure of the sky, the beautiful flamingo flying over the ruins of Carthage; lulled by the murmur of the waves, they half-forget their own existence and sing in a low voice a song of the sea: they are going to die.

PART THREE

RESTORATION AND REVOLUTION
1814–1841

ONE
Triumph and Disgrace

Man is as much deceived by the success of his wishes as by their disappointment: I had asked, contrary to my natural instinct, to go to the Congress of Verona; taking advantage of a prejudice of M. de Villèle's, I had induced him to force M. de Montmorency's hand. Well, the truth of the matter is that my real inclination was not for what I had obtained; I should doubtless have felt somewhat vexed if I had been compelled to stay in England; but soon the idea of going to see Lady Sutton, of making a tour of the three kingdoms, would have overcome the impulse of an artificial ambition which is not part of my nature. God ordained differently, and I left for Verona: hence the change in my life, hence my ministry, the Spanish War, my triumph, and my fall, soon followed by that of the Monarchy.

One of the two handsome children for whom Charlotte had asked me to do something in 1822 has just been to see me in Paris: he is now Captain Sutton; he is married to a charming young wife, and he tells me that his mother has been very ill and has recently spent a winter in London.

I embarked at Dover on 8 September 1822, at the same port from which, twenty-two years before, 'M. Lassagne' of Neuchâtel had set sail. Between that first departure and the moment of writing, thirty-nine years have elapsed. When a man looks at or listens to his past life, he seems to see on a deserted sea the wake of a vessel that has vanished; he seems to hear the tolling of a bell whose old tower is lost from sight.

Here, in the order of dates, comes *Le Congrès de Vérone*, which I have published in two separate volumes. Should anyone by

some chance feel a wish to read it again, he can find it everywhere. My Spanish War, the great political event of my life, was
a gigantic undertaking. For the first time the Legitimacy was
going to wage war under the White Flag, to fire its first gun-shot
after those gun-shots of the Empire which will be audible to the
remotest posterity. To bestride Spain with a single step, to suc-
ceed on the same soil where the conqueror's arms had met
defeat, to do in six months what he was unable to do in seven
years, who could have hoped to accomplish something so prodigious? Yet that is what I did; but how many curses fell upon
my head at the gaming-table at which the Restoration had
seated me! I had before me a France hostile to the Bourbons,
and two great foreign ministers, Prince von Metternich and
Mr Canning. Not a day went by but I received letters prophesy-
ing disaster, for the war with Spain was not at all popular,
either in France or in Europe. Indeed, it was not long after my
successes in the Peninsula that my fall occurred.

In our joy at the receipt of the telegraphic despatch announcing the liberation of the King of Spain, we ministers hurried to
the Palace. There I had a presentiment of my fall: I received a
bucketful of cold water over my head which restored me to my
customary humility. The King and Monsieur did not notice us.
Madame la Duchesse d'Angoulême, overjoyed by her husband's triumph, had eyes for nobody. That immortal victim
wrote a letter on Ferdinand's deliverance ending with this
exclamation, sublime in the mouth of Louis XVI's daughter:

'So it has been proved that one can save an unfortunate
king!'

On the Sunday, I returned, before the meeting of the council,
to pay my court to the Royal Family; the august princess spoke
graciously to each of my colleagues: to me she did not address
a single word. Not, of course, that I deserved such an honour.
The silence of the orphan of the Temple can never be ungrateful: Heaven has a right to the worship of the earth and owes
nothing to anyone.

After that, I lingered on until Whitsuntide; my friends, however, were not unanxious, and often said to me:

'You will be dismissed tomorrow.'

'This very moment, if you like,' I used to reply.

On Whit Sunday, 6 June 1824, I had made my way to the first drawing-rooms of Monsieur: an usher came to tell me that someone was asking to see me. It was Hyacinthe, my secretary. He told me, when he saw me, that I was out of office. I opened the packet which he handed to me; I found inside it a note from M. de Villèle:

> Monsieur le Vicomte,
>
> In obedience to the King's orders, I am at once communicating to Your Excellency an ordinance which His Majesty has issued.
>
> The Sieur Comte de Villèle, President of our Council of Ministers, is appointed *ad interim* Minister for Foreign Affairs, *vice* the Sieur Vicomte de Chateaubriand.

This ordinance was in the handwriting of M. de Rainneville, who is good enough still to be embarrassed about it in my presence. Heavens above! Do I know M. de Rainneville? Have I ever given him a thought? I meet him fairly often. Has he ever noticed that I knew that the ordinance by which I was struck off the list of ministers was written in his hand?

And yet, what had I done? Where was the proof of my intrigues and my ambition? Was it in order to obtain M. de Villèle's place that I went off for lonely, secret walks in the Bois de Boulogne? It was, in fact, that strange life of mine that ruined me. I was naïve enough to remain as Heaven had made me, and, because I longed for nothing, they thought that I wanted everything. Today I can see that my secluded life was a great mistake. What! You do not want to be anything? Away with you! We do not like a man to despise what we worship, and to think himself entitled to insult the mediocrity of our life.

The difficulties of wealth and the disadvantages of poverty followed me to my lodging in the Rue de l'Université: on the day of my dismissal, I was due to give a huge dinner-party at the Foreign Office; I had to send my apologies to the guests and to squeeze three great courses prepared for forty people into my little kitchen for two. Montmirel and his assistants set to work and, cramming saucepans, grease-pans, and preserving-pans into every corner, he put his warmed-up masterpiece under shelter. An old friend came to share the marooned sailor's first meal. Town and Court came hurrying along, for everyone was indignant at the iniquity of my dismissal after the service which I had just rendered; they were convinced that my disgrace would not last long; they gave themselves an air of independence in consoling a misfortune of a few days, at the end of which time they would profitably remind the unlucky man when he had returned to power that they had never forsaken him.

They were mistaken; they wasted their courage; they had counted on my lack of spirit, on my whining and whimpering, on my boot-licking ambition, on my eagerness to plead guilty, to wait on those who had driven me out: they showed that they did not know me. I retired without even claiming the salary which was due to me, without receiving a single favour or a single farthing from the Court; I closed my door to those who had betrayed me; I spurned the sympathetic crowd, and I took up arms. Thereupon all dispersed; universal condemnation burst forth, and my case, which had at first seemed admirable to the drawing-rooms and ante-chambers, suddenly appeared reprehensible.

After my dismissal, would I not have been better advised to keep silent? Had not the brutality of the deed brought public opinion back to my side? M. de Villèle has repeatedly said that the letter of dismissal was delayed; by this accident, it had unfortunately been handed to me only at the Palace. Perhaps this was so; but, when we play, we must calculate the chances of the game; we must, above all, take care not to write to a friend of some worth a letter which we would be ashamed to address to a thieving valet whom we would throw out of the house without ceremony or remorse. The irritation of the Villèle party against myself was all the greater in that they wanted to appropriate my work to themselves and that I had displayed considerable ability in matters of which I had been supposed to know nothing.

No doubt with silence and moderation, as they said at the time, I should have won the praises of those who live in perpetual adoration of the portfolio; by doing penance for my innocence, I should have prepared the way for my return to the

Council. It would have been better in the ordinary way of things; but that was taking me for the man I am not; that was suspecting me of a desire to return to the helm of the State, a wish to make my way in life: a desire and a wish which would not occur to me in a hundred thousand years.

I began fighting my new battle in the Opposition immediately after my fall, but it was interrupted by the death of Louis XVIII* and was not actively resumed until after the coronation of Charles X.† In July I joined Mme de Chateaubriand at Neuchâtel; she had gone there to wait for me, and had taken a cottage by the lake. The chain of the Alps stretched north and south in front of us; we had our backs to the Jura, whose slopes, black with pine-trees, rose steeply above our heads. The lake was deserted; I took my exercise in a wooden gallery. When I climbed to the top of the Jura, I saw the Lake of Bienne, to whose breezes and waters Jean-Jacques Rousseau owes one of his happiest inspirations. Mme de Chateaubriand went to visit Fribourg and a country house which we had been told was charming but which she found icy-cold, for all that it was called the *Petite Provence*. A lean black cat, which was half-wild and caught little fish by dipping its paw into a large bucket filled with water from the lake, was my only distraction. A quiet old woman, who was always knitting, prepared our banquet in an earthenware cooking-pot without stirring from her chair. I had not lost the habit of the country-mouse's meal.

The King's illness brought me back to Paris. The King died on 16 September, scarcely four months after my dismissal. My pamphlet entitled *Le Roi est mort: vive le Roi!*, in which I hailed the new sovereign, did for Charles X what my pamphlet *De Bonaparte et des Bourbons* had done for Louis XVIII. I went to fetch Mme de Chateaubriand at Neuchâtel, and we came to Paris to live in the Rue du Regard. Charles X made the beginning of his reign popular by abolishing the censorship; the coronation took place in the spring of 1825.

* 16 September 1824.
† 29 May 1825.

Among my papers I find the following notes written at Reims:

Reims, Saturday, eve of the Coronation

I have seen the King's entry; I have seen the gilded coaches of the monarch who not so long ago had not a horse to ride; I have seen those carriages roll by filled with courtiers who were unable to defend their master. This mob went to the Cathedral to sing the *Te Deum*, and I went to look at a Roman ruin and to walk by myself in a wood of elm-trees known as the Wood of Love. I heard from afar the jubilation of the bells, and I gazed at the towers of the Cathedral, age-old witnesses of that ceremony which is always the same and yet so different through history, circumstance, ideas, manners, practices and customs. The monarchy perished and for some years the Cathedral was turned into a stable. Does Charles X, seeing it again today, remember that he saw Louis XVI anointed in the same place where he is to be anointed in his turn? Will he believe that a coronation provides protection against misfortune? There is no longer any hand virtuous enough to heal the King's evil, no longer any holy phial salutary enough to make kings inviolable.

I hurriedly wrote the above on the half-blank pages of a pamphlet entitled *Le Sacre: par Barnage de Reims, avocat,* and on a printed letter from the Great Referendary, M. de Sémonville, saying:

'The Great Referendary has the honour to inform His Lordship, Monsieur le Vicomte de Chateaubriand, that places in the chancel of Reims Cathedral are intended and reserved for such of Messieurs the Peers who wish to be present, the day after His Majesty's coronation, at the ceremony of the reception of the Chief and Sovereign Grand Master of the Orders of the Holy Ghost and St Michael and of the reception of Messieurs the Knights and Commanders.'

However, Charles X had intended to make his peace with me. The Archbishop of Paris spoke to him at Reims of the men in the Opposition; the King said:

'Those who will have nothing to do with me, I leave alone.'

The Archbishop said:

'But, Sire, Monsieur de Chateaubriand?'

'Oh, he is a man I shall miss!'

The Archbishop asked the King if he might tell me so; the King hesitated, took two or three turns round the room, and replied:

'Well, all right, tell him.'

And the Archbishop forgot to speak to me about it.

At the ceremony of the Knights of the Orders, I found myself kneeling at the King's feet just as M. de Villèle was taking his oath. I exchanged a few polite words with my companion in knighthood with regard to a feather which had come loose from my hat. We left the Sovereign's knees, and it was all over. The King, having had some difficulty in removing his gloves to take my hands in his, had said to me with a laugh:

'A gloved cat catches no mice.'

It was thought that he had spoken to me at length, and the rumour spread that I had returned to favour. It is probable that Charles X, thinking that the Archbishop had told me of his goodwill towards me, expected some expression of gratitude from me and was offended by my silence.

Thus I have been present at the last coronation of the successors of Clovis; I had brought it about by the pages in which I had called for the coronation and described it in my pamphlet *Le Roi est mort: vive le Roi!* Not that I had the slightest faith in the ceremony; but since the Legitimacy lacked everything, it was necessary, in order to sustain it, to use every available argument for what it was worth. I recalled Adalbéron's definition: 'The coronation of a King of France is a public event, not a private matter: *publica sunt haec negotia, non privata.*' And I quoted the admirable prayer reserved for the coronation:

'O God, who by Thy virtues counsel Thy peoples, give to this Thy servant the spirit of Thy wisdom. May these days see equity and justice come to all men; to friends succour, to enemies hindrance, to the afflicted consolation, to the young correction, to the rich instruction, to the needy pity, to pilgrims hospitality, to poor subjects peace and safety in their homeland. Let him (the King) learn to control himself, and to govern each man moderately according to his condition, so that, O Lord, he may set all the people an example pleasing to Thee.'

Before reproducing in my pamphlet *Le Roi est mort: vive le Roi!* this prayer recorded by Du Tillet, I had exclaimed:

'Let us humbly beseech Charles X to imitate his ancestors: thirty-two sovereigns of the Third Dynasty have received the royal unction.'

All my duties having been fulfilled, I left Reims, and was able to say, like Joan of Arc:

'My mission is ended.'

TWO
Madame Récamier

We come now to the Roman Embassy, to Italy, the dream of my life. Before going on with my story, I must speak of a woman who will not be lost from sight until the end of these *Memoirs*. A correspondence is about to be opened from Rome to Paris between her and myself: the reader will therefore need to know to whom I am writing, and how and when I came to know Mme Récamier.

She met in the various ranks of society more or less famous people playing their parts on the stage of the world; one and all worshipped her. Her beauty mingles its ideal existence with the material facts of our history: a serene light illuminating a stormy picture.

Let us turn back once more into the past; let us try, by the light of my setting sun, to sketch out a portrait on the sky over which my approaching night will soon spread its shadows.

A letter published in the *Mercure* after my return to France in 1800 had caught the attention of Mme de Staël. I had not yet been struck off the list of emigrants; *Atala* drew me out of my obscurity. At M. de Fontanes's request, Mme Bacciochi (Elisa Bonaparte) asked for and obtained the erasure of my name. Mme de Staël had worked to achieve the same object; I went to thank her. I can no longer remember whether it was Christian de Lamoignon or the author of *Corinne* who introduced me to her friend, Mme Récamier; the latter was then living in her house in the Rue du Mont-Blanc. Coming from my woods and the obscurity of my life, I was still extremely shy; I scarcely dared to raise my eyes to a woman surrounded by admirers.

One morning, about a month later, I was at Mme de Staël's;

she had received me at her toilet; while Mlle Olive was dressing her, she talked to me, at the same time toying with a little green twig in her hand. Suddenly Mme Récamier came in, wearing a white dress; she sat down in the middle of a blue silk sofa. Mme de Staël remained standing and continued her animated conversation, speaking with considerable eloquence; I scarcely replied, my gaze fixed upon Mme Récamier. I had never invented anything so beautiful, and I felt more discouraged than ever: my admiration turned into annoyance with myself. Mme Récamier left, and I did not see her again until twelve years later.

Twelve years! What hostile power cuts and wastes our days in this fashion, ironically lavishing them on all the indifferent relationships called attachments, on all the paltry pleasures known as joys? Then, as a further mockery, when it has blighted and spent the most precious part of your life, it brings you back to your point of departure. And how does it bring you back? With your mind filled with strange ideas, importunate ghosts, and disappointed or incomplete notions of a world which has given you no lasting happiness. These ideas, these ghosts, these notions come between you and what happiness you might still enjoy. You return with your heart ravaged by regrets and grieved by these youthful errors which are so painful to the memory in mature and modest years. That is how I returned after being in Rome and Syria, after seeing the passing of the Empire, after becoming the man of noise, after ceasing to be the man of silence. What had Mme Récamier been doing? What had her life been like?

I have not known the greater part of the at once brilliant and secluded existence of which I am about to tell you: I am therefore obliged to have recourse to authorities other than mine, but they are unimpeachable. First of all, Mme Récamier has described to me such events as she has witnessed and has communicated certain precious letters to me. She has written notes about what she has seen, the text of which she has allowed me to consult and all too rarely to quote. Then Mme de Staël in her correspondence, Benjamin Constant in his memoirs, some in print and some in manuscript, M. Ballanche in an essay on our common friend, Mme la Duchesse d'Abrantès in her sketches, and Mme de Genlis in hers, have provided me with abundant material for my story: all I have done is to string these splendid names together, filling the gaps with my own account when some links in the chain of events were missing or broken.

Montaigne says that men go gaping at future things: I have a mania for gaping at things of the past. Everything is sheer delight, especially when one turns one's gaze upon the first years of those one loves: one prolongs a cherished life; one extends the affection which one feels to embrace days which one has not known and which one resuscitates; one embellishes what was with what is; one re-creates youth.

During the short Peace of Amiens,* Mme Récamier paid a visit to London with her mother. She had letters of introduction from the old Duc de Guignes, who had been Ambassador to England thirty years before. He had kept up a correspondence with the most notable women of the time: the Duchess of Devonshire, Lady Melbourne, the Marchioness of Salisbury, and the Margravine of Anspach, with whom he had been in love. His embassy was still famous, his memory green among these distinguished ladies.

Such is the power of novelty in England that, on the morning after her arrival, the newspapers were full of the foreign beauty. Mme Récamier received visits from nearly all the people to whom she had sent her letters. Among these persons, the most remarkable was the Duchess of Devonshire, who was then between forty-five and fifty years of age. She was still in vogue and beautiful, although she had lost one eye, which she covered with a lock of her hair. The first time that Mme Récamier appeared in public, it was in her company. The duchess took her to her box at the Opera, where she met the Prince of Wales, the Duc d'Orléans, and the latter's brothers the Duc de Montpensier and the Comte de Beaujolais: the first two were to become kings; one was almost on the throne, the other still separated from it by an abyss.

Eyes and opera-glasses were turned towards the duchess's

* The Peace of Amiens lasted from 27 March 1802 till 18 May 1803.

box. The Prince of Wales said to Mme Récamier that if she did not want to be suffocated she would have to leave before the end of the performance. She had scarcely got to her feet than the doors of all the boxes were flung open; she could not escape, and was swept along by the tide of the crowd to her carriage.

The next day, Mme Récamier went to Kensington Gardens, accompanied by the Marquess of Douglas, later the Duke of Hamilton, who has since received Charles X at Holyrood, and by his sister the Duchess of Somerset. The crowd followed hard on the fair foreigner's heels. This phenomenon was repeated every time she showed herself in public; the newspapers resounded with her name; her portrait, engraved by Bartolozzi, was distributed all over England. The author of *Antigone*, M. Ballanche, adds that ships carried it as far as the isles of Greece: beauty returned to the place where its image had been invented. We have a sketch of Mme Récamier by David, a full-length portrait by Gérard, and a bust by Canova. The portrait is Gérard's masterpiece, but I do not care for it, because although I can recognize the model's features in it, I cannot recognize her expression.

On the eve of Mme Récamier's departure, the Prince of Wales and the Duchess of Devonshire asked leave to call on her and to bring with them some of their acquaintances. Some music was played. Together with the Chevalier Marin, the first harpist of the time, she performed some variations on a theme by Mozart. This evening was mentioned in the press as a farewell concert which the beautiful foreigner had given to the Prince of Wales.

The next day she set sail for The Hague, taking three days to make a crossing of sixteen hours. She has told me that, during those stormy days, she read the whole of *Le Génie du Christianisme*; I was 'revealed' to her, to quote her gracious expression: I recognize there the kindness which the winds and the sea have always shown me.

In Naples, where Mme Récamier went in the autumn, the occupations of solitude ceased for her. She had scarcely lighted at her inn than King Joachim's ministers came hurrying to see her.

Murat, forgetting the hand which had changed his whip into a
sceptre, was ready to join the Coalition. Bonaparte had planted
his sword in the middle of Europe, just as the Gauls planted
their swords in the middle of the *mallus*; around Napoleon's
sword there was a ring of kingdoms which he distributed to his
family. Caroline had been given that of Naples. Mme Murat
was not as elegant an antique cameo as the Princess Borghese,
but she had more expression and more wit than her sister. In
the firmness of her character one could recognize Napoleon's
blood. If the diadem had not been for her an ornament for a
woman's head, it would still have been the emblem of a queen's
power.

On 11 January 1814, Murat, obliged to make a rapid choice,
signed a treaty with the Court of Vienna: he undertook to provide the Allies with a corps of thirty thousand men. In return
for this defection he was guaranteed his Neapolitan kingdom
and his right of conquest on the Papal Marches. Mme Murat
had told Mme Récamier about this important agreement. Just
as he was on the point of making his decision public, Murat,
deeply moved, met Mme Récamier in Caroline's apartments
and asked her what policy she thought he ought to adopt; he
begged her to give due consideration to the interests of the
people whose sovereign he had become. Mme Récamier said
to him:

'You are a Frenchman and you must remain loyal to the
French.'

Murat's face became distorted, and he replied:

'So I am a traitor? How can I help it? It is too late!'

He threw open a window and pointed to an English fleet
entering the port under full sail.

Vesuvius was in a state of eruption and throwing out flames.
Two hours later, Murat was on horseback at the head of his
guards; the crowd surrounded him shouting: 'Long live King
Joachim!' He had forgotten everything; he seemed drunk with
joy. The next day, there was a gala performance at the Teatro
di San-Carlo; the King and Queen were greeted with frantic
acclamations unknown to people this side of the Alps. Francis
II's envoy was also applauded; the box of Napoleon's minister

was empty; Murat seemed to be troubled about this, as if he had seen the ghost of France at the back of that box.

Murat's army, set in motion on 16 February 1814, forced Prince Eugène to fall back upon the Adige. But Murat did not follow the Viceroy to the Adige; he hesitated between the Allies and the French, according to the chances which Bonaparte seemed to be winning or losing.

In the fields of Brienne, where Napoleon was educated by the old monarchy, he gave, in the latter's honour, the last and most admirable of his bloody tourneys. Favoured by the *carbonari*, Joachim now thought of declaring himself the liberator of Italy, now hoped to divide her between himself and a victorious Bonaparte.

One morning the courier brought to Naples the news of the entry of the Russians into Paris. Mme Murat was still in bed, and Mme Récamier, sitting at her bedside, was talking with her: an enormous pile of letters and newspapers was laid upon the bed. Among the latter was my pamphlet *De Bonaparte et des Bourbons*. The Queen exclaimed:

'Ah, here is a work by Monsieur de Chateaubriand; we will read it together.'

And she went on opening her letters.

Mme Récamier picked up the pamphlet and, after glancing through it, put it back on the bed and said to the Queen:

'Madame, you shall read it alone, I have to go home.'

Napoleon was relegated to the Isle of Elba; the Allies, with rare intelligence, had placed him on the coast of Italy. Murat learnt that they were trying at the Congress of Vienna to rob him of the States for which he had paid so high a price; he therefore came to a secret understanding with his brother-in-law, who had lately become his neighbour. One is always surprised that Napoleon should have relations: who knows the name of Arrhidaeus, Alexander's brother? In the course of the year 1814, the King and Queen of Naples gave a reception at Pompeii; an excavation was carried out to the sound of music: the ruins which Caroline and Joachim had dug up did not warn them of their own ruin; on the last borders of prosperity one

hears nothing but the final strains of the dream which is passing away.

At the time of the Peace of Paris, Murat was a member of the
Alliance: the Milanese having been handed back to Austria, the
Neapolitans withdrew into the Roman Legations. Having
changed sides, Murat left the Legations and marched with forty
thousand men towards Upper Italy to create a diversion in
favour of Napoleon. At Parma, he rejected the conditions
which the frightened Austrians offered him once more: to each
of us there comes a critical moment; well chosen or ill, it decides
our future. The Baron de Firmont forced back Murat's troops,
took the offensive, and drove them before him as far as Macerata. The Neapolitans broke ranks and fled; their King and
general returned to Naples accompanied by four lancers. He
went to his wife and said:

'Madame, I have not succeeded in dying.'

The next day, a boat took him in the direction of the island
of Ischia; out at sea he joined a smack carrying some of his staff
officers, and set sail with them for France.

Mme Murat, left by herself, displayed admirable presence of
mind. The Austrians were about to appear: in the change from
one authority to another, an interval of anarchy might have
been filled with disturbances. The Regent did not hurry her
departure; she allowed the German troops to occupy the town
and had her galleries lit up during the night. The people, seeing
the lights from outside, and thinking that the Queen was still
there, remained quiet. Meanwhile Caroline left by a secret
staircase and went on board her ship. Sitting on the poop, she
saw gleaming on the bank the illuminated but empty palace
which she was leaving behind, a symbol of the dazzling dream
which she had had during her sleep in fairyland.

Caroline met the frigate which was bringing Ferdinand*
back. The ship of the fugitive Queen fired a salute: the ship of
the reinstated King did not return it: Prosperity does not recognize her sister Adversity. Thus do illusions, shattered for one,

---

* Ferdinand I of the Two Sicilies and IV of Naples reigned in Naples from
1759 to 1806 and from 1815 to 1825.

begin again for another; thus do the fickle destinies of human life pass each other on the windswept waves: happy or baleful, the same abyss carries them and engulfs them.

Murat was finishing his course elsewhere. On 25 May 1815, at ten o'clock at night, he landed at Golfe-Juan, where his brother-in-law had landed. Fate made Joachim parody Napoleon. The latter did not believe in the strength of misfortune, or in the succour which it gives to great minds: he forbade the dethroned King to come to Paris; he banished to the lazaret this man stricken with the plague of defeat; he relegated him to a country house called *Plaisance*, near Toulon. He would have been better advised to show less fear of a contagion with which he himself had been affected: who knows what difference a soldier like Murat might have made to the Battle of Waterloo?

Bonaparte lost the Empire a second time; Murat was a vagrant on the same beaches which have since seen the wanderings of the Duchesse de Berry. Some smugglers agreed, on 22 August 1815, to take him and three others across to Corsica. A storm greeted him: the felucca which plied between Bastia and Toulon took him on board. He had scarcely left his rowing boat than she split open. Landing at Bastia on 25 August, he went and hid in the village of Vescovato, at old Colonna-Ceccaldi's. Two hundred officers joined him with General Franceschetti. He marched on Ajaccio: Bonaparte's native town alone still supported her son; of the whole of his Empire, Napoleon now possessed only his cradle. The garrison of the citadel saluted Murat and wanted to proclaim him King of Corsica: he refused; he considered only the sceptre of the Two Sicilies equal to his greatness. His aide-de-camp Macirone arrived from Paris with the Austrian decree according to which he was to relinquish the title of King and retire to either Bohema or Moldavia.

'It is too late,' replied Joachim; 'my dear Macirone, the die is cast.'

On 28 September, Murat sailed for Italy; seven boats were laden with his two hundred and fifty followers: he had scorned to have for his kingdom the narrow motherland of the great man; full of hope, and carried away by the example of a fate loftier than his own, he set out from the island which Napoleon had left to take possession of the world: it is not the same places, but similar geniuses, that produce the same destinies.

A storm scattered the flotilla; Murat was cast ashore, on 8 October, in the Gulf of Santa Eufemia, almost at the same time that Bonaparte landed on the rock of St Helena.

Of his seven praams, only two were left, including his own. Landing with some thirty men, he tried to stir up the population of the coast; the local inhabitants fired on his band. The two praams put out to sea; Murat had been betrayed. He ran to a stranded boat and tried to float it; the boat would not move. Surrounded and captured, Murat, insulted by the same mob that used to shout itself hoarse with cries of 'Long live King Joachim!' was taken to Pizzo Castle. Mad proclamations were found on him and his companions: they showed with what dreams men delude themselves until their last hour.

Calm and unworried in prison, Murat said:

'I shall keep only my Kingdom of Naples, my cousin Ferdinand can keep the second Sicily.'

And at that moment a military tribunal was condemning Murat to death. When he heard his sentence, his courage deserted him for a few instants; he wept a little and cried:

'I am Joachim, King of the Two Sicilies!'

He forgot that Louis XVI had been King of France, the Duc d'Enghien grandson of the Great Condé, and Napoleon arbiter of Europe: Death takes no account of what we may have been.

A priest is always a priest, whatever he may say or do; he comes and restores a brave heart's failing strength. On 13 October 1815, Murat, after writing to his wife, was taken to a room in Pizzo Castle, reviving in his romantic person the brilliant or tragic adventures of the Middle Ages. Twelve soldiers, who perhaps had once served under him, were waiting for him, drawn up in two lines. Murat saw them load their muskets, refused to be blindfolded, and, experienced captain that he was, chose himself the position where the bullets could best hit him.

When the soldiers had taken aim and were on the point of opening fire, he said:

'Men, spare the face; aim at the heart!'

He fell, holding in his hands the portraits of his wife and children which had previously adorned the hilt of his sword. This was just one more affair for the gallant soldier which he had settled this time with his life.

The different manners of death of Napoleon and Murat preserve the characters of their lives.

Murat, so fond of pomp, was buried without any ceremony at Pizzo, in one of those Christian churches into whose charitable bosom all ashes are mercifully received.

It was at a sad time for the glory of France that I met Mme Récamier again: at the time of Mme de Staël's death. Returning to Paris after the Hundred Days, the author of *Delphine* had fallen ill on the way; I had seen her since at her house and at Mme la Duchesse de Duras's. As her condition gradually worsened, she was obliged to keep to her bed. One morning I went to see her in the Rue Royale. The shutters of her windows were two-thirds closed; the bed, which had been pushed up towards the wall at the far end of the room, left only a narrow space on the left; the curtains, drawn back on their rods, formed two columns at the head of the bed. Mme de Staël was propped up by pillows in a half-sitting position. I approached and, once my eyes had grown a little accustomed to the darkness, I was able to make out the patient's features. A feverish flush coloured her cheeks. Her splendid eyes met mine in the shadows, and she said to me, in English:

'Good morning, my dear Francis. I am ailing, but that does not prevent me from loving you.'

She held out her hand, which I pressed and kissed. As I raised my head I saw on the other side of the bed, in the space by the wall, something white and thin rising up: it was M. de Rocca,* haggard and hollow-cheeked, with bleary eyes and a sallow complexion; he was dying; I had never seen him before and I never saw him again. He did not open his mouth; he

* Mme de Staël's lover, whom she married secretly in 1816 and who died in 1818 at the age of thirty.

bowed as he passed me; the sound of his footsteps was inaudible: he went away like a shadow. Stopping for a moment at the door, he turned round towards the bed to wave good-bye to Mme de Staël. Those two ghosts looking at one another in silence, the one erect and pale, the other seated and flushed with blood that was ready to flow down again and congeal at the heart, made one shudder.

A few days later, Mme de Staël changed her lodging. She invited me to dine with her in the Rue Neuve-des-Mathurins: I went there; she was not in the drawing-room and was unable even to come in to dinner; but she did not know that the fatal hour was so close. We sat down to table. I found myself sitting next to Mme Récamier. It was twelve years since I had seen her for only a moment. I did not look at her; she did not look at me; we did not exchange a single word. When, towards the end of the dinner, she timidly addressed a few words to me about Mme de Staël's illness, I turned my head a little and raised my eyes. I should be afraid to profane today with my aged lips a feeling which preserves all its youth in my memory and whose charm increases as life withdraws. I separate my younger days to discover behind those days celestial visions, to hear from the depths of the abyss the harmonies of a happier region.

Mme de Staël died.* The last note which she wrote to Mme de Duras was traced in big, straggling letters like a child's. It contained an affectionate word for 'Francis'. The talent which expires impresses one more than the individual who dies: it is a general grief that afflicts society; everyone suffers the same loss at the same time.

With Mme de Staël there disappeared a considerable portion of the age in which I had lived: some such gaps which the fall of a superior intelligence creates in a century are never filled. Her death made a deep impression on me, with which was mingled a sort of mysterious astonishment: it was at that illustrious woman's house that I had first met Mme Récamier, and after a long separation, it was Mme de Staël who brought together again two travellers who had almost become strangers to one

* On 14 July 1817.

another: at her funeral banquet she left them her memory and the example of her immortal attachment.

I went to see Mme Récamier in the Rue Basse-du-Rempart, and later in the Rue d'Anjou. When a man has been reunited with his destiny, he imagines that he has never left it: life, according to Pythagoras, is nothing but a reminiscence. Who, in the course of his existence, does not recall certain minor circumstances indifferent to all except to him who remembers them? The house in the Rue d'Anjou had a garden; and in that garden there was a bower of lime-trees between whose leaves I used to see a moonbeam when I was waiting for Mme Récamier: it seems to me now that that beam was mine, and that if I went to look for it in the same place I should find it. Yet I can scarcely remember the sun which I have seen shine on so many foreheads.

It was at that time that I was obliged to sell the Vallée-aux-Loups, which Mme Récamier had rented, going halves with M. de Montmorency.

Increasingly tried by fate, Mme Récamier soon retired to the Abbaye-aux-Bois. There she had two small rooms separated by a dark corridor. I maintained that this vestibule was lit by a gentle light. The bedroom was furnished with a bookcase, a harp, a piano, a portrait of Mme de Staël, and a view of Coppet by moonlight; on the window-sills there were some pots of flowers. When, quite breathless from climbing three flights of stairs, I entered this cell as dusk was falling, I was entranced. The windows overlooked the Abbaye garden, in whose green enclosure nuns walked round and round and schoolgirls ran hither and thither. The top of an acacia-tree reached up to eye-level. Pointed steeples pierced the sky and on the horizon one could see the hills of Sèvres. The dying sun gilded the picture and entered through the open windows. Mme Récamier was sitting at her piano; the Angelus was tolling; the sound of the bell, which seemed 'to mourn the dying day', *il giorno pianger che si muore*,* mingled with the final notes of the Invocation of the Night from Steibelt's *Romeo and Juliet*. A few

---

* Dante, *Purgatorio*, VIII.

birds came and settled in the blinds; I was united with the silence and solitude in the distance, across the noise and tumult of a great city.

God, by giving me those hours of peace, compensated me for my hours of trouble; I caught a glimpse of the future rest which my faith believes in and my hope invokes. Worried as I was elsewhere with political preoccupations, or disgusted by the ingratitude of Courts, peace of heart awaited me in that retreat, like the coolness of the woods when one leaves a scorching plain. I recovered my calm beside a woman who spread serenity around her, though not a serenity that was too even, for it passed through deep affection. Alas, the men whom I used to meet at Mme Récamier's, Matthieu de Montmorency, Camille Jordan, Benjamin Constant, and the Duc de Laval, have gone to join Hingant, Joubert, and Fontanes, other absentees from another absent company. Among those successive friendships have risen young friends, the vernal offshoots of an old forest in which the felling never stops. I beg them, I beg M. Ampère, who will read this when I have gone, I ask them all to keep me in their memory: I hand on to them the thread of life, the end of which Lachesis is spinning out on my distaff. My inseparable companion on the road of life, M. Ballanche, has found himself alone at the beginning and at the end of my career: he has seen my friendship broken by time just as I have seen his swept away by the Rhône;* rivers always undermine their banks.

The unhappiness of my friends has often weighed upon me, and I have never shrunk from the sacred burden: the moment of reward has arrived; a serious attachment deigns to help me to bear all that the number of my bad days add to their weight. As I draw near my end, it seems to me that everything that I have loved I have loved in Mme Récamier, and that she was the hidden source of my affections. My memories of various ages, those of my dreams as well as those of my realities, have become moulded, mingled, and blended into a compound of joys and sweet sufferings of which she has become the visible

* Ballanche's early friendships were connected with Lyons.

embodiment. She rules over my feelings, in the same way as Heaven has brought happiness, order, and peace to my duties.

I have followed the fair traveller along the path which she has trodden so lightly; soon I shall go before her to a new country. As she passes through these *Memoirs*, through this basilica which I am hurrying to complete, she may come across the chapel which I here dedicate to her; it will perhaps please her to rest in it: I have placed her image there.

THREE

Rome

I had given balls and receptions in London and Paris, and though a child of a different desert, I had not passed too badly through those new solitudes; but I had had no inkling of what Roman entertainments could be like: they have something about them akin to ancient poetry, which places death by the side of pleasure. At the Villa Medicis, where I received the Grand Duchess Helen, the gardens themselves are beautiful and the frame of the picture is magnificent: on one side, the Villa Borghese, with Raphael's house; on the other the Villa Monte-Mario and the slopes bordering the Tiber; below the spectator, the whole of Rome, like an old, abandoned eagle's nest. Among the groves there thronged, together with the descendants of the Paulas and the Cornelias, beauties from Naples, Florence, and Milan: the Princess Helen seemed to be their queen. Boreas, descending suddenly from the mountain, ripped open the banqueting-tent and fled with shreds of canvas and garlands, as though to provide us with a symbol of all that time has swept away on this shore. The embassy staff were appalled; I felt an indescribable ironical gaiety at seeing a breath from heaven carry off my gold of a day and my joys of an hour. The damage was promptly repaired. Instead of lunching on the terrace, we lunched in the graceful palace: the music of the horns and oboes, scattered by the wind, had something of the murmur of my American forests. The groups of guests disporting themselves in the squalls, the women whose tortured veils beat against their hair and faces, the *sartarello* which continued during the storm, the extempore performer declaiming to the clouds, the balloon bearing the arms of the Daughter

of the North* flying off at a tangent: all this gave a new character to these sports in which the habitual tempests of my life
seemed to be taking part.

How fascinating this would have been for any man who had
not nearly run his course and who asked the world and the
storm for illusions! I find it difficult indeed to remember my
autumn when, at my receptions, I see passing before me those
women of the spring who disappear among the flowers, the
music, and the lights of my successive galleries, like swans
swimming towards radiant climes. To what pastime are they
going? Some are seeking what they have already loved, others
what they do not yet love. At the end of the road, they will fall
into those sepulchres which are always open here, into those
ancient sarcophaguses which serve as basins to fountains hanging from porticoes; they will go to join so many other light and
charming ashes. These waves of beauties, diamonds, flowers,
and feathers roll by to the sound of Rossini's music, which is
re-echoed and grows feebler from orchestra to orchestra. Is that
melody the sigh of the breeze which I heard in the savannahs of
the Floridas or the moaning which I heard in the Temple of
Erectheus at Athens? Is it the distant wail of the north winds
which rocked me on the ocean? Could my sylph be hidden
beneath the form of some of these dazzling Italian women? No:
my wood-nymph has remained faithful to the willows of the
meadows where I used to talk with her on the other side of the
grove at Combourg. I have very little in common with these
frolics of the society which has attached itself to my footsteps
towards the end of my race; and yet there is a certain intoxication in this enchanted scene which goes to my head; I get rid of
it only by going to cool my brow in the solitary square
of St Peter's or in the deserted Colosseum. Then the petty sights
of the earth disappear, and I can find nothing to match the sudden change of scene but the old melancholy of my early days.

I shall soon be leaving Rome, but I hope to return. I have fallen
in love again with this sad and beautiful city: I shall have a view

* Russia.

from the Capitol, where the Prussian Minister is going to let me have the little Caffarelli Palace; at Sant' Onofrio I have set up another retreat. Pending my departure and my return, I keep going for walks in the Campagna; there is not a single little road between two hedges that I do not know better than the Combourg lanes. From the top of the Monte Mario and the surrounding hills, I can see the horizon of the sea beyond Ostia; I rest beneath the graceful, crumbling porticoes of the Villa Madama. In these noble buildings which have been turned into farms I often find no one but a shy girl, as timid and agile as her goats. When I go out by the Porte Pia, I walk to the Ponte Lamentano over the Teverone; I admire, as I pass St Agnes's, a head of Christ by Michelangelo, which keeps watch over the practically deserted convent. The masterpieces of the great artists scattered in this way across the desert fill the soul with a profound melancholy. It grieves me that they should have gathered together the Roman pictures in a museum; I should have preferred to go along the slopes of the Janiculum, under the fall of the Aqua Paola and across the solitary Via delle Fornaci to look for the *Transfiguration* in the Recollect Monastery of San Pietro in Montorio. When one looks at the place on the high altar of the church once occupied by the ornament of Raphael's funeral, one's heart is saddened and distressed.

Beyond the Ponte Lamentano, yellow pasture-lands stretch to the left as far as the Tiber; the river which washed Horace's gardens here flows unknown. Following the highroad, you will come across the pavement of the ancient Via Tiburtina. There I saw the first swallow arrive this year.

I go herborizing at the tomb of Caecilia Metella: the wavy reseda and the Apennine anemone look delightful against the whiteness of the ruin and the ground. Taking the Ostia road, I go to St Paul's, which has lately fallen victim to a fire; I sit down on some calcined porphyry and watch the workmen silently building a new church; someone had pointed out to me a half-finished column as I came down the Simplon: the whole history of Christianity in the West begins at St Paul's Without the Walls.

In France, when we put up the smallest shanty, we make

a tremendous din, with scores of machines and men and shouts; in Italy, immense operations are undertaken almost without a murmur. The Pope, at this very moment, is having the fallen portion of the Colosseum rebuilt; half a dozen mason's labourers, without any scaffolding, are lifting up the colossus upon whose shoulders there died a nation changed into workmen slaves.* Near Verona, I often used to stop and watch a village priest who was building a huge steeple by himself, with his farmer acting as mason under him.

I often go round the walls of Rome on foot; as I follow this circular road, I read the history of the queen of the pagan and Christian world written in the various forms, styles, and ages of these walls.

I also go looking for some dilapidated villa within the walls of Rome. I visit Santa Maria Maggiore, St John Lateran with its obelisk, Santa Croce di Girusalemme with its flowers; I listen to the singing; I pray. I love to pray on my knees; like that my heart is nearer to the dust and to the peace of eternity; I draw closer to the grave.

My excavations are only a variation on the same pleasures. From the plateau of some hill one can see the dome of St Peter's. What does one pay the owner of the place where treasures lie buried? The value of the grass destroyed by the excavation. Perhaps I shall give my clay to the earth in exchange for the statue it will give me: we shall only be bartering one image of man for another.

He has not seen Rome who has not walked through the streets of its suburbs, streets interspersed with empty spaces, with gardens full of ruins, with enclosures planted with trees and vines, and with cloisters where palm-trees and cypresses stand, the former looking like women of the East, the latter like nuns in mourning. Coming out of these ruins, one sees tall Roman women, poor and beautiful, on their way to buy fruit or to fetch water from the cascades flowing from the aqueducts of the emperors and popes. To see Roman life in all its simplicity, I pretend to be looking for an apartment to let; I knock at

* The Jewish prisoners whom Titus set to work in Rome in 79.

the door of a secluded house; someone replies: '*Favorisca.*' I go in and find, in a bare room; either a workman pursuing his trade or a proud *zitellla* knitting with a cat in her lap, who watches me walking about without rising from her seat.

When the weather is bad, I take shelter in St Peter's, or else lose myself in the museums of the Vatican, with its eleven thousand rooms and its eighteen thousand windows. What oases of masterpieces! You reach them by way of a gallery whose walls are encrusted with epitaphs and ancient inscriptions: Death seems to have been born in Rome.

There are more tombs than dead in this city. I imagine that the deceased, when they feel too warm in their marble resting-place, slip into another which has remained empty, just as a sick man is moved from one bed to another. One can almost hear the skeletons passing during the night from coffin to coffin.

The first time I saw Rome, it was the end of June: the hot season makes the city more deserted than ever; the visitors take flight, the citizens stay indoors; you meet no one in the streets during the day. The sun darts its rays upon the Colosseum, where weeds hang motionless and nothing stirs but the lizards. The earth is bare; the cloudless sky appears emptier than the earth. But soon the night brings the inhabitants out of their palaces and the stars out of the firmament; earth and the heavens are repopulated; Rome revives; and this life silently beginning again in the darkness, around the tombs, resembles the life and movement of the shades which go down to Erebus again at the approach of day.

Yesterday I wandered by moonlight in the Campagna, between the Porta Angelica and the Monte Mario. A nightingale was singing in a narrow valley railed in with weeds. There, for the first time, I discovered that tuneful melancholy of which the ancient poets speak with regard to the bird of spring. The long whistle which everyone knows, and which precedes the brilliant flourishes of the winged musician, was not piercing like that of our nightingales; it had a muffled sound like the whistle of the bullfinch of our woods. All its notes were a semitone lower; its song was transposed from the major to the minor key; it sang softly, as if it wished to charm the sleep of the dead and not to wake them. Over this untilled land had passed Horace's Lydia, Tibullus's Delia, and Ovid's Corinna; only Virgil's Philomela remained. That hymn of love had a potent effect in that place and at that hour; it gave one an ineffable longing for a second life: according to Socrates, love is the desire to be born again through the agency of beauty; it was this desire which a Greek girl inspired in a youth when she said to him:

'If I had nothing left but the thread of my pearl necklace, I would share it with you.'

If I have the good fortune to end my days here, I have arranged to have a retreat at Sant' Onofrio adjoining the room where Tasso died. In the leisure moments which my embassy may leave me, I shall continue my *Memoirs* at the window of my cell. In one of the most beautiful spots on earth, among the orange-trees and the holly oaks, with all Rome under my eyes every morning, as I sit down to work, between the deathbed and the tomb of the poet, I shall invoke the genius of glory and misfortune.

In the early days after my arrival in Rome, when I was wandering at random in this way, I met a school of young boys between the Baths of Titus and the Colosseum. They were in the care of a master in a slouch hat and a torn, trailing gown, who looked like a poor Brother of Christian Doctrine. As I passed him, I looked at him and thought he bore a vague resemblance to my nephew Christian de Chateaubriand, but I did not dare believe my eyes. He looked at me in his turn, and without showing any surprise said:

'Uncle!'

I rushed up to him, deeply moved, and clasped him in my arms. With a wave of the hand he stopped his obedient and silent flock behind him. Christian was at once pale and brown, sapped by fever and burnt by the sun. He told me that he was prefect of studies at the Jesuit College, which was then on holiday at Tivoli. He had almost forgotten his native tongue and found it difficult to express himself in French, since he talked and taught only in Italian. My eyes filled with tears as

I looked at my brother's son, a Frenchman turned foreigner, a schoolmaster in Rome, dressed in a shabby, dusty black coat, and covering with a cenobite's hat the noble brow which the helmet became so well.

I had seen Christian born; a few days before my emigration I attended his baptism. His father, his grandfather, the Président de Rosanbo, and his great-grandfather, M. de Malesherbes, were present. The last stood sponsor to him and gave him his own name, Christian. The Church of Saint-Laurent was empty and already half-devastated. The nurse and I took the child from the priest's hands.

> *Io piangendo ti presi, e in breve cesta*
> *Fuor ti portai.**

The newborn child was taken back to its mother and laid upon her bed, where she and its grandmother, Mme de Rosanbo, greeted it with tears of joy. Two years later, father, grandfather, great-grandfather, mother, and grandmother had perished on the scaffold and I, a witness at the christening, was wandering in exile. Such were the recollections which the sudden appearance of my nephew revived in my memory in the midst of the ruins of Rome. Christian has already passed half his life as an orphan; he has dedicated the other half to the altar, the ever-open home of the common Father of mankind.

Christian had an ardent and jealous affection for Louis, his worthy brother: when Louis married, Christian left for Italy; he met the Duc de Rohan-Chabot there, and Mme Récamier: like his uncle, he has come back to live in Rome, he in a cloister, I in a palace. He entered religion to restore to his brother a fortune to which he did not consider himself entitled under the new laws; and so Malesherbes and Combourg now both belong to Louis.

After our unexpected meeting at the foot of the Colosseum, Christian came to see me at the Embassy, accompanied by a Jesuit brother: his bearing was sad, his expression serious: in

---

* Weeping, I took you and, in a little basket, carried you away (Tasso).

the old days he was always laughing. I asked him if he was happy; he answered:

'I suffered for a long time; now my sacrifice is made and I am content.'

Christian has inherited the iron character of his paternal grandfather, M. de Chateaubriand, my father, and the moral qualities of his maternal great-grandfather, M. de Malesherbes. His feelings are locked up inside him, although he displays them, without considering the prejudices of the mob, when his duties are concerned: as a dragoon in the Guards, he would dismount to go straight to communion; no one laughed at him, for his courage and kindliness were the admiration of his mess-mates. After he left the service, it was discovered that he secretly used to help a considerable number of officers and soldiers; he still has some pensioners in the garrets of Paris, and Louis discharges his brother's debts. One day, in France, I asked Christian if he ever intended to get married.

'If I were to marry,' he replied, 'I should take one of my little cousins, the poorest of them all.'

Christian spends his nights in prayer; he practises mortifica-tions which alarm his superiors: a sore which appeared on one of his legs was the result of his persistence in remaining on his knees for hours on end; never did innocence repent so fervently.

Christian is not a man of this century: he reminds me of those dukes and counts of Charlemagne's Court who, after fighting the Saracens, founded monasteries on the lonely sites of Gellone or Malavalle and became monks there. I regard him as a saint and would willingly invoke his name. I am convinced that his good works, added to those of my mother and my sis-ter Julie, would obtain grace for me before the sovereign Judge. I too have a leaning towards the cloister; but, if my hour were to come, I would go and ask for a cell at the Portioncula, under the protection of my patron saint, who is called François because he spoke French.

Rumours of ministerial changes reached our fir-groves. Well-informed people went so far as to mention the Prince de Polignac, but I was quite incredulous. At last the newspapers

arrived: I opened them, and my eyes fell upon the official ordinance confirming the rumours which had been current. I had
experienced a good many changes of fortune since I had come
into the world, but I had never received so great a surprise. My
destiny had once more extinguished my dreams; this breath of
fate not only put out my illusions, but also carried away the
monarchy. This blow hurt me dreadfully; I felt a momentary
despair, for my mind was made up immediately: I felt that I
must retire. The post brought me a host of letters: all urged me
to send in my resignation. Even people whom I scarcely knew
thought themselves obliged to prescribe my retirement.

I was shocked by this officious interest in my reputation.
Thank Heaven, I have never needed any advice on affairs in
which my honour was involved; my life has been a series of
sacrifices, which have never been exacted from me by anyone;
in matters of duty, I act spontaneously. A fall from office spells
ruin for me, for I possess nothing but debts, debts which I con-
tract in places where I do not stay long enough to pay them; so
that every time I retire from public life, I am forced to hire
myself out to a bookseller. Some of those proud, obliging
people who preached honour and liberty to me through the
post, and preached it even more loudly when I arrived in Paris,
resigned from the Council of State; but some were rich and the
others took care not to resign the secondary offices which they
held and which left them the means of existence. They behaved
like the Protestants, who reject some of the dogmas of the
Catholics and keep others just as difficult to believe in. There
was nothing complete about these sacrifices, no real sincerity;
men surrendered an income of ten or fifteen thousand francs, it
is true, but returned home rich in their patrimonies, or at least
provided with the daily bread which they had prudently
retained. In my case, there was no quibbling; others were full of
self-abnegation on my behalf, and could not strip themselves
sufficiently of all that I possessed:

'Come now, Georges Dandin, pluck up your courage; dam-
mit, son-in-law, don't let us down; off with your coat! Throw
out of the window two hundred thousand livres a year, a post
to your liking, an exalted and dignified post, the empire of the

arts in Rome, the happiness of at last receiving the reward of your long laborious struggle. Such is our pleasure. At that price you will enjoy our esteem. Just as we have taken off our cloaks, leaving a good flannel waistcoat underneath, you must throw off your velvet cloak and remain stark naked. There you have perfect equality, absolute parity of altar and sacrifice.'

And, strange to relate, in this generous eagerness to turn me out, the men who informed me of their wishes were neither my real friends nor the fellow supporters of my political opinions. I was expected to sacrifice myself on the spot to Liberalism, to the doctrine which had constantly attacked me; I was expected to run the risk of shaking the legitimate throne in order to win the praises of a few cowardly enemies who had not the whole-hearted courage to starve.

I was to find myself swamped by the costs of a long embassy; the receptions which I had given had ruined me; I had not paid the expenses of my initial establishment. But what broke my heart was the loss of what I had promised myself in the way of happiness for the rest of my life.

I spent several days rending my heart in my Utica; I wrote letters to demolish the edifice which I had raised so lovingly. Just as, in a man's death, it is the little details, the familiar, homely actions that move us, so, in the death of a dream, it is the little realities which destroy it that hurt most. Eternal exile among the ruins of Rome had been my dearest dream. Like Dante, I had arranged never to return to my native land. These testamentary elucidations will not possess for the readers of these *Memoirs* the same interest that they have for me. The old bird falls from the branch where it has taken refuge; it leaves life for death. Carried away by the current, it has only changed one stream for another.

FOUR

The July Revolution

The 27th began badly. The King invested the Duc de Raguse with the command of Paris, which was relying on ill fortune. The marshal moved into the headquarters of the Guard in the Place du Carrousel at one o'clock. M. Mangin sent some men to seize the *National*'s presses; M. Carrel resisted; MM. Mignet and Thiers, thinking the game was up, disappeared for a couple of days; M. Thiers went into hiding in the Montmorency Valley, at the house of a certain Mme de Courchamp, a relative of the two MM. Bequet, one of whom worked for the *National* and the other for the *Journal des Débats*.

An argument on constitutionalism took place at the *Temps* offices between M. Baude and a police commissioner.

The Attorney-General issued forty-four warrants against the signatories to the journalists' protest.

About two o'clock, the monarchical party of the revolution met at M. Périer's, as had been agreed the day before: they failed to come to any decision. The deputies adjourned till the next day, the 28th, at M. Audry de Puyraveau's. M. Casimir Périer, a man of order and wealth, did not wish to fall into the hands of the people; he still cherished the hope of coming to an arrangement with the legitimate monarchy; he said sharply to M. de Schonen:

'You are ruining your chances by going against the law; you are forcing us out of a superb position.'

This spirit of legality prevailed everywhere: it appeared at two entirely opposite meetings, one at M. Cadet-Gassicourt's, the other at General Gourgaud's. M. Périer belonged to that middle class which had appointed itself the heir of the common people and the army. He had courage and fixity of purpose: he flung himself bravely across the revolutionary torrent to dam it; but he was too preoccupied with his health and too careful of his fortune.

'What can you do with a man,' M. Decazes asked me, 'who is always inspecting his tongue in a looking-glass?'

The mob increased in size and began to appear under arms. The commanding officer of the Gendarmerie came to warn the Duc de Raguse that he had not enough men and that he was afraid he might be overwhelmed. The marshal then made his military dispositions.

It was half past four in the afternoon of the 27th before orders reached the barracks to take up arms. The Paris Gendarmerie, supported by a few detachments of the Guard, tried to open up the Rue de Richelieu and the Rue Saint-Honoré to traffic. One of these detachments was attacked in the Rue du Duc de Bordeaux with a shower of stones. The leader of this detachment was taking care not to fire when a shot from the Hôtel Royal, in the Rue des Pyramides, decided the question: it seems that a certain Mr Folks, who was living at this hotel, had taken his fowling-piece and fired at the Guards from his window. The soldiers replied with a volley aimed at the house, and Mr Folks and a couple of servants fell dead. This is the way in which the English, who live a sheltered life on their island, take revolution to other nations; you find them in the four corners of the world mixed up in quarrels which are no concern of theirs: provided they can sell a piece of calico, what do they care if they plunge a nation into calamity? What right had this Mr Folks to shoot at French soldiers? Was it the British Constitution that Charles X had violated? If anything could bring discredit on the July fighting, it would be that it was started by an English bullet.

This first fighting, which on the 27th did not begin until about five o'clock in the afternoon, stopped at dusk. The gunsmiths handed over their arms to the mob; the street-lamps were either broken or remained unlighted; the tricolour flag was hoisted in the darkness on the towers of Notre-Dame: the storming of the guard-houses, the seizure of the arsenal and the powder-magazines, and the disarming of the militiamen, all this was done without opposition at daybreak on the 28th, and everything was over by eight o'clock.

The democratic and proletarian party of the revolution, in smocks and half-naked, was under arms; it did not spare its poverty or its rags. The mob, represented by electors whom it had chosen from different bands, had managed to have a meeting called at M. Cadet-Gassicourt's.

The usurping party did not show itself yet: its leader,* hiding outside Paris, did not know whether to go to Saint-Cloud or the Palais-Royal. The middle-class or monarchical party, the deputies, decided after due deliberation not to be drawn into the movement.

M. de Polignac went to Saint-Cloud and, at five o'clock in the morning of the 28th, persuaded the King to sign the ordinance placing Paris under martial law.

On the 28th, the groups formed up again in greater numbers; the cry of 'The Charter for ever!' could still be heard, but already the cry of 'Liberty for ever! Down with the Bourbons!' was being raised. People were also shouting: 'Long live the Emperor! Long live the Black Prince!' – the mysterious Prince of Darkness who appears to the popular imagination in all revolutions. Memories and passions were discarded; the mob pulled down and burnt the French arms; they hung them from the ropes of the shattered street-lamps; they tore the fleur-de-lis badges from the uniforms of the diligence guards and the postmen; the notaries removed their escutcheons, the bailiffs their badges, the carriers their official signs, the Court purveyors their warrants. Those who had once covered their Napoleonic eagles painted in oils with Bourbon lilies in distemper needed only a sponge to wipe away their loyalty: nowadays people efface gratitude and empires with a few drops of water.

The Duc de Raguse wrote to the King that it was essential that steps should be taken to pacify the mob and that the next day, the 29th, would be too late. A messenger from the Prefect

* Louis-Philippe, the Duc d'Orléans.

of Police came to ask the marshal if it was true that Paris had been placed under martial law: the marshal, who knew nothing about it, looked surprised; he hurried to the President of the Council's house; there he found the ministers gathered together, and M. de Polignac handed him the ordinance. Because the man who had trodden the world underfoot had placed cities and provinces under martial law, Charles X had imagined that he could imitate him. The ministers told the marshal that they were coming to install themselves at the headquarters of the Guard.

No orders having arrived from Saint-Cloud, at nine o'clock in the morning of the 28th, when it was too late to hold everything but it was time to recapture everything, the marshal ordered the troops, some of whom had already shown themselves the day before, to leave barracks. No arrangements had been made to lay in provisions at the headquarters in the Carrousel. The bake-house, on which they had forgotten to set an adequate guard, was carried by the mob. M. le Duc de Raguse, a man of intelligence and merit, a brave soldier and a clever but unlucky general, proved for the thousandth time that military genius is not enough to deal with civil disturbances; any police officer would have known better than the marshal what had to be done. Perhaps too his mind was paralysed by his memories; he remained as it were stifled under the weight of the fatality of his name.

The marshal, who had only a handful of men under his command, devised a plan which he would have needed thirty thousand soldiers to put into execution. Various columns were detailed for considerable distances, while another was ordered to occupy the Hôtel de Ville. After completing their operations to restore order everywhere, the troops were to converge on the municipal buildings.

The column sent to occupy the Hôtel de Ville followed the Quais des Tuileries, du Louvre, and de l'École, crossed half the Pont-Neuf, took the Quai de l'Horloge and the Marché-aux-Fleurs, and reached the Place de Grève by the Pont Notre-Dame. Two platoons of Guards created a diversion by making for the new suspension bridge. A battalion of the 15th

Light Infantry was supporting the Guards, and was to leave two platoons on the Marché-aux-Fleurs.

There was some fighting as the troops crossed the Seine on the Pont Notre-Dame. The mob, with drums beating, faced the Guards bravely. The officer in command of the Royal Artillery pointed out to the mass of people that they were risking their lives to no purpose, and that, since they had no guns, they would be shot down without the slightest chance of success. The mob stood firm; the guns were fired. The soldiers streamed on to the embankments and the Place de Grève, where they were joined by two other platoons of Guards coming from the Pont d'Arcole. They had been obliged to force their way through crowds of students from the Faubourg Saint-Jacques. The Hôtel de Ville was duly occupied.

A barricade went up at the entrance to the Rue du Mouton; a brigade of Swiss Guards carried it; the mob, rushing up from the adjacent streets, recaptured its position with loud shouts. The barricade finally remained in the hands of the Guards.

In all those poor, lower-class districts, the people fought spontaneously, without any ulterior motives: French recklessness, cynical, gay, and intrepid, had gone to everyone's head; glory, for our nation, has the intoxicating quality of champagne. The women at the windows encouraged the men in the streets; notes were written promising a marshal's baton to the first colonel who should go over to the people; bands of men marched along to the sound of a violin. There was a medley of tragic and comic scenes, circus antics, and triumphal displays; oaths and shouts of laughter could be heard in the midst of musket-shots and the dull roar of the crowd, through clouds of smoke. Bare-footed and with forage-caps on their heads, improvised carriers with permits signed by unknown leaders drove convoys of wounded through the combatants, who separated to let them pass.

In the wealthy districts a different spirit prevailed. The National Guards had resumed the uniforms of which they had been stripped, and gathered in considerable numbers at the Mairie of the First Arrondissement to maintain order. In all these encounters, the Guards suffered more than the people, because they were exposed to the fire of invisible enemies in the houses. Others will give the names of the drawing-room heroes who, safely ensconced behind a shutter or a chimney-stack, amused themselves by shooting down Guards officers whom they recognized. In the streets, the animosity of the labourer and the soldier did not go beyond striking the blow: once one of them had been wounded, the other went to his aid. The mob saved several of its victims. Two officers, M. de Goyon and M. Rivaux, who put up an heroic defence, owed their lives to the generosity of the victors. Captain Kaumann of the Guard was struck on the head with an iron bar: dazed and with his eyes filled with blood, he struck up with his sword the bayonets of his soldiers who were taking aim at the workman responsible.

The Guard was full of Bonaparte's grenadiers. Several officers lost their lives, among them Lieutenant Noirot, a man of exceptional courage, who in 1813 had received the cross of the Legion of Honour from Prince Eugène for a feat of arms performed in one of the redoubts at Caldiera. Colonel de Pleinselve, mortally wounded at the Porte Saint-Martin, had fought in the wars of the Empire in Holland and Spain, with the Grand Army and in the Imperial Guard. At the Battle of Leipzig, he captured the Austrian General Merfeld. Carried by his soldiers to the Hôpital du Gros-Caillou, he refused to have his wounds dressed until all the other people wounded in the July Revolution had been treated. Dr Larrey, whom he had met on other battlefields, amputated his leg at the thigh; it was too late to save him. They were indeed fortunate, those noble adversaries who had seen so many cannon-balls pass over their heads, if they did not fall to a bullet fired by one of those liberated convicts whom justice has found again, since the day of victory, in the ranks of the victors! Those criminals were unable to defile the national triumph of the Republicans; they have been prejudicial only to Louis-Philippe's monarchy. Thus there perished obscurely, in the streets of Paris, the last of those famous soldiers, who had escaped from the cannon at Borodino, Lützen, and Leipzig: we massacred under Charles X those heroes whom we had so greatly admired under Napoleon. Only one man was missing: that man had disappeared at St Helena.

*

On the morning of the 30th, having received a note from the
Great Referendary summoning me to the meeting of the Peers
at the Luxembourg, I decided first of all to find out the latest
news. I went down the Rue d'Enfer, across the Place Saint-
Michel, and along the Rue Dauphine. There was still a little
excitement around the battered barricades. I compared what I
saw with the great revolutionary movement of 1789 and it
struck me as quiet and orderly; the change was obvious.

On the Pont-Neuf, the statue of Henri IV, like a standard-
bearer in the League, held a tricolour flag in its hand. Some
men of the people, looking at the bronze King, said:

'You would never have been such a fool, you old rascal.'

Groups of people had gathered on the Quai de l'École. I
made out from a distance a general and two aides-de-camp, all
on horseback. I went in their direction. As I pushed my way
through the crowd, I looked at the general; he had a tricolour
sash across his coat and his hat was the wrong way round and
cocked to one side. He in his turn caught sight of me and
exclaimed:

'Heavens, it's the viscount!'

And I, surprised, recognized Colonel or Captain Dubourg,
my companion at Ghent, who on our way back to Paris had
taken a succession of open towns in the name of Louis XVIII,
and who brought us half a sheep for dinner in a filthy lodging-
house at Arnouville. This was the officer whom the newspapers
had depicted as a grim Republican soldier with grey moustaches, who had refused to serve under the imperial tyranny
and who was so poor that they had been obliged to buy him a
shabby uniform from the days of Larevellière-Lépeaux at an
old-clothes shop.

'Why, it's you!' I cried. 'How . . .'

He held out his arms to me, and shook hands with me over
Flanquine's neck; a circle was formed around us.

'My dear fellow,' said the Provisional Government's military
leader, pointing to the Louvre, 'there were twelve hundred of
them in there. We peppered their behinds, and they ran, oh,
how they ran!'

M. Dubourg's aides-de-camp burst into roars of laughter,

the mob laughed in unison, and the general spurred his nag, which caracoled like a worn-out animal, followed by two other Rosinantes slipping on the paving-stones and looking as if they were ready to collapse between their riders' legs.

Thus, proudly carried away, the Diomedes of the Hôtel de Ville, a man of courage too and wit, parted company with me I have seen men who, treating all the events of 1830 seriously, blushed at this story, because it conflicted somewhat with their heroic credulity. I myself was ashamed to see the comic side of the most solemn revolutions and how easy it is to trifle with the good faith of the common people.

M. Louis Blanc, in the first volume of his excellent *Histoire de dix ans*, published after what I have just written here, confirms my story:

> A man [he says] of medium height, with an expressive face, and dressed in a general's uniform, was crossing the Marché des Innocents, followed by a considerable number of armed men. It was M. Évariste Dumoulin of the *Constitutionnel* who had supplied this man with his uniform, which had been obtained at an old-clothes shop; and the epaulets which he wore had been given to him by Perlet the actor: they came from the property-room of the Opéra-Comique.
>
> 'Who is that general?' everybody was asking.
>
> And when those around him answered: 'It is General Dubourg,' 'Long live General Dubourg!' cried the people, who had never heard the name before.

Another sight met my eyes a little farther on: a ditch had been dug in front of the colonnade of the Louvre; a priest in surplice and stole was praying beside the ditch: the dead were being laid to rest in it. I took off my hat and made the sign of the Cross. The silent crowd stood respectfully watching this ceremony, which would have been nothing if religion had not appeared in it. So many memories and thoughts occurred to my mind that I remained perfectly motionless. Suddenly I felt people crowding round me; a shout went up:

'Long live the defender of the freedom of the press!'

I had been recognized by my hair. Some young men promptly laid hold of me and said:

'Where are you going? We'll carry you.'

I did not know what to answer; I begged to be excused; I struggled; I implored them to let me go. The time fixed for the meeting in the House of Peers had not yet come. The young men kept shouting:

'Where are you going? Where are you going?'

I replied at random:

'All right then, to the Palais-Royal!'

I was immediately escorted there to the accompaniment of shouts of 'The Charter for ever! The freedom of the press for ever! Long live Chateaubriand!' In the Cour des Fontaines, M. Barba, the bookseller, came out of his house to embrace me.

We arrived at the Palais-Royal; I was bundled into a café under the wooden arcade. I was dying from the heat. With clasped hands I repeated my request for remission of my glory: it was no use; the young people refused to let me go. In the crowd there was a man wearing a jacket with the sleeves turned up, a man with black hands, a sinister face, and burning eyes, such as I had seen so often at the beginning of the Revolution. He kept trying to come up to me and the young men kept pushing him back. I never learnt either his name or what he wanted with me.

I had to make up my mind in the end to say that I was going to the House of Peers. We left the café; the cheering started again. In the courtyard of the Louvre, various shouts were raised. Some cried: 'To the Tuileries! To the Tuileries!' and others 'Long live the First Consul!' – apparently wishing to make me the heir of Bonaparte the Republican. Hyacinthe, who was with me all this time, received his share of handshakes and embraces. We crossed the Pont des Arts and went down the Rue de Seine. People ran to see us and crowded the windows. I found all these honours painful, for my arms were being torn from their sockets. One of the young men pushing me from behind suddenly put his head between my legs and lifted me up on his shoulders. There was more cheering; they shouted to the spectators in the street and at the windows:

'Hats off! The Charter for ever!'

To which I replied:

'Yes, gentlemen, the Charter for ever! But long live the King!'

This cry was not taken up, but it provoked no anger. And that is how the game was lost. Everything could still have been patched up, but it was necessary to present only popular men to the people: in a revolution, a name does more than an army.

I implored my young friends so feelingly that they finally put me down. In the Rue de Seine, opposite M. Le Normant's, my bookseller's, an upholsterer offered me an armchair to be carried in; I refused, and eventually made a triumphant entry into the main courtyard of the Luxembourg. My generous escort then left me, after giving voice to fresh cries of 'The Charter for ever! Long live Chateaubriand!' I was touched by the sentiments of these fine young men: I had shouted: 'Long live the King!' in their midst, as safely as if I had been in my own house; they knew my opinions; they carried me themselves to the House of Peers, where they knew that I was going to speak and stand firm in support of my King; and yet it was 30 July, and we had just passed close by the ditch where they were burying the citizens killed by Charles X's bullets!

FIVE
The Plague in Paris

The cholera, starting from the Ganges delta in 1817, has spread
over an area measuring 5,500 miles from north to south and
8,750 miles from east to west; it has plunged fourteen hundred
towns into mourning and reaped a harvest of forty million
people. There is a map that traces the conqueror's march. It has
taken fifteen years to come from India to Paris, travelling as
fast as Bonaparte: the latter took almost the same number of
years to go from Cadiz to Moscow, and he caused the deaths of
only two or three million men.*

What is the cholera? Is it a deadly wind? Is it insects which
we swallow and which devour us? What is this great black
death armed with its scythe which, crossing mountains and
seas, has come like one of those awe-inspiring pagodas worshipped on the shores of the Ganges to crush us under its
chariot-wheels on the banks of the Seine? If this scourge had
fallen upon us in a religious age, if it had spread in the midst of
poetic manners and popular beliefs, it would have created a
striking picture. Imagine a pall flying by way of a flag from
the towers of Notre-Dame; the cannon firing single shots at
intervals to warn the imprudent traveller to turn back; a cor-
don of troops surrounding the city and allowing no one to
enter or leave it; the churches filled with a groaning multitude;
the priests chanting day and night the prayers of a perpetual

* After ravaging Asia and Western Europe, the cholera reached England on
12 February 1832 and remained until May. It crossed the Channel to Calais
on 15 March and struck down its first victim in Paris on 26 March. It did not
disappear from the French capital until 30 September, by which time it had
killed 18,406 people. Chateaubriand wrote this chapter in May 1832.

death-agony; the Viaticum carried from house to house with
bell and candle; the church bells constantly tolling the funeral
knell; the monks at the crossroads, crucifix in hand, summoning the people to repentance and preaching the wrath and
judgement of God, made manifest in the corpses already blackened by hellfire.

Then the closed shops; the pontiff, surrounded by his clergy,
going, with every curé at the head of his parish, to fetch the
shrine of St Geneviève; the sacred relics carried round the city,
preceded by the long procession of the different religious
orders, guilds, corporations, congregations of penitents, groups
of veiled women, scholars of the university, ministers of the
alms-houses, and soldiers marching along without arms or
with pikes reversed; the *Miserere* chanted by the priests min-
gling with the hymns of the girls and children; and all, at certain
signals, prostrating themselves in silence and rising to utter
fresh complaints.

There is nothing of this today; the cholera has come to us in
an age of philanthropy, incredulity, newspapers, and material
administration. This unimaginative scourge found no old cloisters awaiting it, no monks, no vaults, no Gothic tombs; like the
Terror of 1793, it wandered about with a mocking air, in broad
daylight, in a new and unfamiliar world, accompanied by its
bulletin, which recited the remedies which had been used
against it, the number of victims it had claimed, the progress it
had made, the hopes which were entertained of seeing it come
to an end, the precautions which had to be taken to guard
against it, what one should eat, how one should dress. And
everyone continued to attend to his business, and the theatres
were full. I have seen drunkards at the city gates, sitting drinking at a little wooden table outside a pot-house, saying as they
raised their glasses:

'Here's to your health, Morbus!'

Morbus, out of gratitude, came running up, and they fell dead
under the table. The children played at cholera, calling it 'Nicholas Morbus' and 'Morbus the Rascal'. And yet the cholera had
its terrifying side: the bright sunshine, the indifference of the
crowd, the ordinary course of life, which went on everywhere,

invested these days of pestilence with a new character and a different sort of horror. You felt aches and pains in every limb; your mouth was parched by a cold, dry north wind; the air had a certain metallic quality which took you by the throat. In the Rue du Cherche-Midi, wagons from the artillery depot were used to cart away the dead bodies. In the Rue de Sèvres, which was particularly affected, especially on one side, the hearses came and went from door to door; there were not enough of them to satisfy the demand and people shouted from the windows:

'Over here, hearse!'

The driver answered that he was full up and could not attend to everybody. One of my friends, M. Pouqueville, on his way to dine at my house on Easter Sunday, was stopped when he got to the Boulevard du Mont-Parnasse by a succession of biers, nearly all of which were being carried along. He noticed, in this procession, the coffin of a young girl, on which a wreath of white roses had been laid. A smell of chlorine left a sickly atmosphere in the wake of this floral cortège.

In the Place de la Bourse, where processions of workmen used to meet, singing the *Parisienne*, one often saw funerals making their way towards the Montmartre Cemetery as late as eleven o'clock at night, by the light of pitch torches. The Pont-Neuf was crowded with litters laden with patients for the hospitals or dead who had expired during the journey. The exaction of the toll was dropped for a few days on the Pont des Arts. The booths disappeared and, since a north-east wind was blowing, all the stall-holders and all the shopkeepers on the embankments closed their doors. One met carts covered with tarpaulins and preceded by mutes, with a registrar dressed in black walking in front, carrying a list in his hand. There were not enough of these registrars to go round; they had to send for more from Saint-Germain, La Villette, and Saint-Cloud. Other hearses would be laden with five or six coffins roped together. Omnibuses and hackney-carriages were used for the same purpose; it was not unusual to see a cab adorned with a corpse laid across the apron. A few of the dead were taken to church: a priest sprinkled holy water over these faithful Christians gathered together for the journey to eternity.

In Athens, the people believed that the wells near the Pire-aeus had been poisoned; in Paris, the tradesmen were accused of poisoning their wine, spirits, sweets, and foodstuffs. Several individuals were man-handled, dragged in the gutter, and thrown into the Seine. The authorities were to blame for hav-ing issued stupid or criminal proclamations.

How did the scourge pass like an electric spark from Lon-don to Paris? No one knows. This whimsical death often picks on a patch of ground or a house, and leaves the neighbourhood of that infested spot untouched; then it retraces its steps and takes what it had forgotten. One night I felt myself attacked. I was seized with a fit of shivering together with cramp in my legs; I did not want to ring, for fear of frightening Mme de Chateaubriand. I got up; I heaped everything I could find in my room on the bed; I got back under the blankets; and a copious perspiration pulled me through. But I was left weak and ach-ing, and it was in this sorry condition that I was obliged to write my pamphlet on Mme la Duchesse de Berry's gift to the poor of 12,000 francs.

I should not have been sorry to go, carried off under the arm of the eldest son of Vishnu, whose distant glance killed Bona-parte on his rock at the gateway to the Indian Ocean. If all mankind, stricken with a universal contagion, were to die, what would happen? Nothing: the depopulated world would continue its solitary course without need of any other astron-omer to plot its passage than Him who has measured it through all eternity; it would present no sign of change to the eyes of the inhabitants of the other planets; they would see it performing its accustomed functions; on its surface, our little works, our cities, our monuments would be replaced by forests restored to the sovereignty of the lions; no void would appear in the uni-verse. And yet there would be lacking that human intelligence which knows the stars and which has even attained an aware-ness of their Creator. How immense, then, are the works of God, in which, if the genius of man, which is equal to the whole of Nature, were to disappear, it would be no more missed than the smallest atom withdrawn from Creation!

Conclusion

I began writing these *Memoirs* at the Vallée-aux-Loups on 4 October 1811; I have just finished re-reading them and correcting them in Paris today, 25 September 1841: I have therefore, for thirty years, eleven months, and twenty-one days,* been secretly holding my pen while writing my public books, in the midst of all the revolutions and all the vicissitudes of my existence. My hand is weary: may it not have weighed upon my ideas, which have never wavered and which I feel to be as lively now as when I embarked on my career. I had planned to add a general conclusion to my thirty years' work: I meant to say, as I have often mentioned, what the world was like when I entered it and what it is like now that I am leaving it. But the hour-glass is before me; I see the hand which sailors used to believe they saw coming out of the waves at the moment of shipwreck: that hand bids me to be brief; I will therefore reduce the scale of the picture without omitting anything essential.

Two new empires, Prussia and Russia, preceded me by scarcely half a century on this earth; Corsica became French at the moment I appeared; I arrived in the world twenty days after Bonaparte. He brought me with him. I was about to enter the Navy, in 1783, when Louis XVI's fleet put in to Brest; it carried the birth certificate of a nation which had been hatched under the wings of France. My birth is connected with the birth of a man and a people, pale reflection that I was of an immense light.

* Chateaubriand is, of course, a year out in his calculations.

If we fix our gaze upon the present-day world, we see it, as the result of the movement initiated by a great revolution, shaken from the Middle East as far as China, which seemed to be closed for ever; so that our past upheavals may soon be as nothing, and the noise of Napoleon's fame be scarcely audible in the convulsion of the nations, just as he, Napoleon, drowned all the noises of our old world.

When will society disappear? What accidents will suspend its movements? In Rome, the reign of man was substituted for the reign of law: the Romans passed from republic to empire; our revolution is being carried out in the opposite direction: we are inclined to pass from monarchy to republic, or, not to specify any particular form, to democracy; this is something which will not be done easily.

To mention only one point in a thousand: will property, for instance, remain distributed as it is? The monarchy born at Reims was able to keep that system of property going by tempering its severity by the diffusion of moral laws, just as it changed humanity into charity. Is it possible for a political system to subsist, in which some individuals have so many millions a year while other individuals are dying of hunger, when religion is no longer there with its other-worldly hopes to explain the sacrifice? There are children whom their mothers feed at their withered breasts for want of a mouthful of bread to give their dying babies; there are families whose members are reduced to huddling together at night for want of blankets to warm them. That man sees his countless furrows ripen; this one will never possess anything but the six feet of earth lent to his grave by his native land. Now how many ears of corn can six feet of earth give a dead man?

As education reaches down to the lower classes, the latter gradually discover the secret canker which gnaws away at the irreligious social order. The excessive disproportion of conditions and fortunes was endurable as long as it remained concealed; but as soon as this disproportion was generally perceived, the old order received its death-blow. Recompose the aristocratic fictions, if you can; try to convince the poor man, once he has learnt to read and ceased to believe, once he has become as well informed as yourself, try to convince him that he must submit to every sort of privation, while his neighbour possesses a thousand times what he needs: as a last resource you will have to kill him.

When steam has been perfected and when, linked with the telegraph and the railways, it has destroyed distances, we shall see not only merchandise travel but also ideas, restored to the use of their wings. When fiscal and commercial barriers between the various States have been abolished, as they have already been abolished between the provinces of a single State, and when different countries, in daily contact with one another, seek to promote the unity of all nations, how can you hope to resuscitate the old type of separation?

Society, on the other hand, is no less threatened by the spread of intelligence than it is by the development of brute nature: imagine labour condemned to idleness by reason of the multiplication and variety of new machines; picture to yourselves a single, universal mercenary matter replacing the mercenaries of farm and household: what will you do with the unemployed human race? What will you do with the passions which have fallen idle at the same time as the intellect? The strength of the body is maintained by physical exercise; once labour is lacking, strength disappears; we shall become like those Asiatic nations which fall a prey to the first invader and which are unable to defend themselves against a hand that bears the sword. Thus freedom is preserved only by work, because work produces strength; remove the curse pronounced against the sons of Adam: 'In the sweat of thy face thou shalt eat bread', and they will die in slavery. The divine curse therefore enters into the mystery of our lot; man is less the slave of his sweat than of his thought: that is why, after studying every side of society, after living through the various types of civilization, after imagining new forms of progress, one finds oneself back where one started, in the presence of the Scriptural truths.

Will this work inspired by my ashes and destined for my ashes survive me? It may be that my work is bad; it may be that these *Memoirs* will fade into nothingness on seeing the light of day: at least the things which I have told myself will have served to beguile the tedium of these last hours which no one wants and which one does not know how to employ. The end of a lifetime is a bitter age: nothing pleases because one is worthy of nothing; useful to no one, a burden to everyone, close to our last resting-place, we have only a step to take to reach it: what would be the good of daydreaming on a deserted shore? What pleasing shadows could one hope to see in the future? Fie upon the clouds that hover now over my head!

One idea returns to trouble me: my conscience is uneasy about the innocence of my nightly labours; I fear the effects of my blindness and man's complacency towards his faults. Is what I write in keeping with justice? Are morality and charity rigorously observed? Have I had the right to speak of others? What would it avail me to repent if these *Memoirs* did any harm? You who are hidden and obscure, you whose lives are pleasing to God and work miracles, all hail to your secret virtues!

There are poor men, destitute of knowledge, about whom no one will ever trouble, who, by the mere doctrine of their way of life, have exerted upon their companions in suffering the divine influence which emanated from the virtues of Christ. The finest book on earth is not worth as much as a single unknown act of those nameless martyrs 'whose blood Herod had mingled with their sacrifices'.

You have seen me born; you have seen my childhood, the idolatry of my strange creation in the Château of Combourg, my presentation at Versailles, my participation in the initial phases of the Revolution. In the New World I met Washington; I plunged into the forests; shipwreck brought me back to the coast of my native Brittany. Then came my sufferings as a soldier, my poverty as an emigrant. Returning to France, I became the author of *Le Génie du christianisme*. In a changed society, I made and lost friends. Bonaparte stopped me and threw himself, with the bloodstained body of the Duc d'Enghien, across my path; I stopped in my turn and led the great man from his cradle in Corsica to his grave at St Helena. I shared in the Restoration and I saw its end.

Thus I have known public and private life. I have crossed the seas four times; I have followed the sun in the East; I have touched the ruins of Memphis, Carthage, Sparta, and Athens; I have prayed at St Peter's tomb and worshipped on Golgotha. Poor and rich, powerful and weak, happy and miserable, a man of action and a man of thought, I have given my hand to the century and my mind to the desert; real life has shown itself to me in the midst of illusions, just as the land appears to sailors among the clouds. If those facts spread across my dreams, like the varnish which preserves fragile paintings, do not disappear, they will mark the places through which my life has passed.

Thanks to the exorbitance of my years, my monument is finished. This is a great relief to me; I could feel someone urging me on: the captain of the boat on which my seat is reserved was warning me that I had only a moment left to go on board. If I had been the master of Rome, I should say, like Sulla, that I am finishing my *Memoirs* on the very eve of my death; but I should not conclude my story with those words with which he concludes his: 'I have seen in a dream one of my children who showed me Metella, his mother, and exhorted me to come and rest in the bosom of eternal happiness.' If I had been Sulla, glory could never have given me rest and happiness.

New storms will arise; the future seems to promise calamities which will surpass the afflictions with which we have been burdened in the past; already, men are thinking of binding up their old wounds in order to return to the field of battle. However, I do not believe in the imminent outbreak of fresh misfortunes; peoples and kings alike are weary: what comes after me will be only the effect of the general transformation. No doubt there will be painful moments; the world cannot change its appearance without causing suffering. But, once again, there will be no separate revolutions: just the great revolution approaching its end. The scenes of tomorrow do not concern me; they call for other painters: it is your turn, gentlemen!

As I write these last words, on 16 November 1841, my window, which looks west over the gardens of the Foreign Missions, is open: it is six o'clock in the morning; I can see the pale and swollen moon; it is sinking over the spire of the Invalides scarcely touched by the first golden ray from the east: one might imagine that the old world was ending and the new beginning. I behold the light of a dawn whose sunrise I shall never see. It only remains for me to sit down at the edge of my grave: then I shall descend boldly, crucifix in hand, into eternity.

Index

Aaron, St, 27

Abbeville, Comtesse d', 23

Abencerages, les
(Chateaubriand), 6

Abercromby, Sir Ralph,
1734–1801, English general
defeated by Montcalm, 142

Abrantès, Laure de Saint-Martin-
Permon, Duchesse d',
1784–1838, 336

Achard de Villerai, Comte,
officer in the Navarre
Regiment, 82, 165

Achilles, 58

Acropolis, Corinth, 152

Adamastor* (Camoëns), 318

Admetus, King of the
Molosses, 142

Aeneid (Virgil), 276–7

Aeschylus, 525–456 BC, Greek
tragedian, 63–4

Agamemnon (Aeschylus), 63–4

Agincourt, Battle of, 1415, 284

Agincourt, Seroux d', 1730–1814,
art historian, 212

Agrippina, mother of Nero, 220

Aguesseau, Marie-Catherine
Lamoignon, Marquise d',
1759–1849, returned from
Emigration with FC, 199

Ajaccio, 315, 342

Alabama, 148

Alain III, Count of Brittany, 7

Alaric, King of the Visigoths,
259, 319

Albani, 1578–1660, painter, 58

Alcibiades, 450–404 BC, 273

Alcinous, King of the
Phaeacians, 142

Alderney, 158, 177

Alexander, English captain at
St Helena, 321

Alexander I, 1777–1825,
Emperor of Russia, 1801–25,
236, 238, 246, 249, 257,
258, 260–61, 262, 263,
266, 268, 274, 298

Alexander the Great, 356–323
BC, 176

Alexandra, Fedorowna, 1798–
1860, daughter of Frederick
William III of Prussia,
Grand Duchess Nicholas
1821, Empress Alexandra
of Russia, 1825, 76

Algiers, 122

Almack's, London, 117, 185

Almanach des Muses, 93

Alost, 285

Amherst, William Pitt,
Earl Amherst of Arrakan,
1773–1857, 310

Amiens, 296, 337

Amour de la Compagne, L'
(FC), 93

Ampère, Jean-Jacques, 1800–
1864, literary historian,
friend of Mme Récamier, 347

Andrezel, Christophe-François-
Thérèse Picon, Comte d',
officer in the Navarre
Regiment, 82, 83, 85

Angoulême, Louis-Antoine de
Bourbon, Duc d', 1775–
1844, elder son of Charles
X, 245, 328

Angoulême, Marie-Thérèse,
Duchesse d', 1778–1851,
wife of above, daughter of
Louis XVI, 101, 328

Anselme, Père (Père de
Guibourg), d. 1694,
historian, 6

Anspach, Elizabeth Craven,
Margravine of,
1750–1828, 337

Antibes, 280, 323

Antigone (Ballanche), 338

Antomarchi, François,
1780–1838, Corsican
doctor, attended Napoleon at
St Helena, 1820–21, 312, 313

Aquitaine, Grand Priory of, 8

Arcis-sur-Aube, 257

Arcola, Battle of, 1796, 278,
280, 309

Arenenberg, 234

Arete, 142

Argentière, Chapter of L, 7, 55,
97, 208

Argentré, Bertrand d', 1519–90,
jurist, 6

Argos, 63–4

Arlon, 177

Armida* (Tasso), 68, 87, 155

Arnott, Dr, military surgeon at
St Helena, 312

Arnouville, 365

Arrhidaeus, d. 317 BC, King
of Macedonia 323–317
BC, 340

Arrighi, Joseph-Philippe,
Vicar-General of the island
of Elba, 275

Artois, Comte d', *see* Charles X

Asgill, Sir Charles, English
general sentenced to death
during American War of
Independence, reprieved
after intervention by Louis
XVI and Marie Antoinette

Atala* (FC), 118, 147, 149, 153,
159, 176

Atala (FC), 119, 147, 172, 198,
206, 286, 335

Athenaeus, Alexandrian writer
of third century, 156

Athens, 75, 99, 155, 272,
372, 377

Audry de Puyraveau, Deputy
1830, 359

Augustus, Caesar Octavianus,
63 BC–AD 14, Emperor
27 BC–AD 14, 51

Aulnay, 5

Aulnay, Comtesse Lepelletier
d', daughter of President
de Rosanbo, granddaughter
of Malesherbes who had
no daughter of that
name, 95

Aumale, Henri d'Orléans, Duc d',
1822–97, fifth son of
Louis-Philippe, 222

Austerlitz, Battle of, 1805, 240,
241, 243, 249, 280

Babylon, 47, 243, 304, 317

Bacciochi, Marie-Anne (Elisa) Bonaparte, Madame, d. 1820, 335

Baden, 217

Baghdad, 67

Baiae, 278

Baily, Jean-Sylvain, 1736–93, President of Constituent Assembly, Mayor of Paris, 103, 105

Bajazet, Sultan, 296

Balaschoff, Russian Minister of Police, 238

Ballanche, Pierre-Simon, 1776–1847, philosopher, friend of FC and Mme Récamier, 211, 336, 338, 347

Baltimore, Maryland, 112, 120, 128, 129

Barba, Gustave, bookseller, 367

Barclay de Tolly, Michael, Prince, 1761–1818, Russian general of Scottish ancestry, 238, 241

Barentin, Charles-Louis-François de, d. 1819, Keeper of the Seals 1789, 184

Barrême, 280

Basil, St, c. 329–379, 79

Basle, 281

Bassano, Duc de, see Maret

Bastia, 342

Bastille, Prison of the, Paris, 8, 102, 103, 133, 260

Bathurst, Lord, 311

Baude, Baron, 1792–1862, Minister of the Interior, 1830, journalist, 359

Baudus, Lieutenant-Colonel, 243, 248, 250

Bautzen, Battle of, 1813, 280

Baylie, London printer who lodged FC and printed the Essai, 181, 182, 184, 186

Bayonne, 186

Bazouches-la-Pérouse, 70

Beaufort, Seigneury of, 16

Beaujolais, Comte de, 1779–1808, youngest brother of Louis-Philippe, 337

Beaumarchais, Pierre Augustin Caron de, 1732–99, author of Le Mariage de Figaro, 107

Beaumont, Pauline-Marie-Michelle-Frédérique-Ulrique de Montmorin-Saint-Hérem, Comtesse de, 1768–1803, mistress of FC, d. 4 Nov. 1803, 108, 205, 206, 208, 211, 212, 213, 214, 215, 216, 218, 223, 225, 230

Beauvau, Charles-Juste, Duc de, 1720–93, Marshal of France, Minister of Louis XVI, 1789, 90

Beccles, 185, 186, 190

Bécherel, 34

Bedée, Ange-Annibal de, 1696–1761, maternal grandfather of FC, m. 1720 Marie-Anne de Ravenel du Boisteilleul, 13, 20, 21

Bedée, Apolline-Jeanne-Suzanne de, see Chateaubriand, Apolline-Jeanne-Suzanne de

Bedée, Caroline de, 1762–1849, daughter of Marie-Antoine-Bénigne de Bedée and cousin of FC, 21

Bedée, Claude-Marie-Jeanne de, 1765–1815, sister of above and cousin of FC, 21

Bedée, Flore de, sister of above and cousin of FC, 21

Bedée, Marie-Angélique-Fortunée-Cecile-Renée Ginguené de Lévenière, Mme de, 1729–1823, wife of Marie-Antoine-Bénigne de Bedée and aunt of FC, 21

Bedée, Marie-Anne de Ravenel du Boisteilleul, Mme de, 1698–1795, maternal grandmother of FC, m. 1720 Ange-Annibal de Bedée, 13, 19–20

Bedée, Marie-Annibal-Joseph de, Comte de la Bouetardais, 1758–1809, son of Marie-Antoine-Bénigne de Bédee and cousin of FC, 21

Bedée, Marie-Antoine-Bénigne de, 1727–1807, son of Ange-Annibal de Bedée and maternal uncle of FC, emigrant in Jersey 1792–1804, 16, 21, 160, 164, 177, 178–9, 179, 184, 187

Beker, Nicholas-Léonard, 1770–1840, general, 293

Bellerophon, English ship, 294, 295–6, 297

Belleville, 260

Belliard, Comte, 1769–1832, cavalry general, 240

Benedict Labre, St, 1748–83, 164

Bennigsen, Théophile, Comte de, 1745–1826, 238

Bequet, Etienne, 1800–38, journalist, 359

Béranger, Pierre-Jean, 1780–1857, song-writer, 300

Bérée, Priory of, 7

Berlin, 75, 84, 94, 118, 261, 262, 264

Berry, Charles-Ferdinand, Duc de, 1778–1820, son of Charles X, assassinated by Louvel 13 Feb. 1820, 75, 285

Berry, Marie-Caroline-Ferdinande de Naples, Duchesse de, 1798–1870, wife of above, m. 1816, widowed 1820, tried to stir up La Vendée against Louis-Philippe 1832, imprisoned 1832–33, m. Count Hector de Lucchesi-Palli, 1833, championed by FC, 282, 342, 372

Berthier, Louis-Alexandre, 1753–1815, Prince of Wagram and Neuchâtel, Marshal of France, 274

Bertier de Sauvigny, Louis-Bénigne-François, 1742–89, lynched with father-in-law Foullon 12 July 1780, 103

Bertin, Louis, 1766–1841, founder of the *Journal des Débats*, 211

Bertrand, Captain, 233

Bertrand, Comte Gratien, 1773–1844, 293, 297, 308

Bertrand, Madame, wife of above, 297, 308

Besançon, 98

Bessières, Marshal, Duc d'Istrie, 1766–1813, 256

Biclitza, 256

Billing, Baron, diplomat, 114

Blackheath, 115

Black Prince *see* Edward, Prince
    of Wales

Blanc, Louis, 1811–82, writer
    and politician, 366

Blois, 264

Blücher, Gebhard Leberecht von,
    1742–1819, Prussian
    general, 286, 287, 292

Boguet, Didier, 1755–1839,
    painter, 212

Boisé-Lucas the elder *or*
    Delaunay-Boisé-Lucas, host
    to Armand de Chateaubri-
    and in 1809, 231

Boisé-Lucas the younger, son of
    above, implicated in
    Armand de Chateaubriand
    case in 1809, 231, 233, 234

Boisteilleul, Hyacinthe-Eugène-
    Pierre de Ravenel du,
    1784–1867, cousin
    and nephew by marriage
    of FC, 50

Boisteilleul, Jean-Baptiste-
    Joseph-Eugène de Ravenel
    du, cousin of FC, 50, 52

Boisteilleul, Marie-Anne de
    Ravenel du, *see* Bedée,
    Marie-Anne de Ravenel du

Boisteilleul, Pauline-Zoé-Marie
    de Farcy de Montavallon,
    Mme de Ravenel du, 1784–
    1814, wife of Hyacinthe-
    Eugène-Pierre de Ravenel du
    Boisteilleul, daughter of Julie
    de Farcy, niece of FC, 70

Boisteilleul, Suzanne-Apolline de
    Ravenel du, 1704–90, sister
    of Marie-Anne de Bedée,

great-aunt of FC, 16,
    20, 21

Bombay, 194

Bonald, Louis, Vicomte de,
    1754–1840, 206

Bonaparte, Elisabeth, *née*
    Patterson, 1785–1879,
    m. Jerome Bonaparte in
    Baltimore 1803, later
    deserted by him, 301

Bonaparte et des Bourbons, De
    (FC), 266, 331, 340

Bonaparte, Hortense, *née*
    Beauharnais, 1783–1837,
    Queen of Holland,
    Duchesse de Saint-Leu, 234

Bonaparte, Jerome, 1784–1860,
    King of Westphalia, 264–5,
    287, 301

Bonaparte, Joseph, 1768–1844,
    King of Naples 1806,
    King of Spain 1808–13,
    264–5, 294

Bonaparte, Lucien, 1775–1840,
    209, 217

Bonaparte, Maria-Letizia
    (Madame Mère),
    1750–1836, 265, 278

Bonaparte, Napoleon, *see*
    Napoleon I

Bonnevie, Abbé Pierre-Étienne
    de, 1761–1849, 214

Bordeaux, Duc de, *see* Henri V

Bordier, actor, hanged for
    causing riot at Rouen Aug.
    1789, 109

Borghese, Pauline Bonaparte,
    Princess, 1780–1825, 216,
    278, 280, 311, 339

Borodino, Battle of, 1812, 240,
    241, 242, 245, 255, 261,
    264, 280, 364

Bosphorus, 155, 248

Bossuet, Jacques-Bénigne,
    1627–1704, prelate, writer,
    and orator, 222, 238

Boston, Massachusetts, 131

Bouëtiez, Chevalier du, 8

Bouillon, Philippe
    d'Auvergne, Prince de,
    1754–1816, 179

Bourienne, Fauvelet de,
    1769–1834, Napoleon's
    secretary, 218

Bourqueney, François-Adolphe,
    Comte de, 1799–1869,
    diplomat, 115

Boutin, Charlotte-Magdeleine,
    m. Charles de Montboissier,
    not Malesherbes, 167

Boutin, financier, 167

Brest, 11, 50, 51, 55, 61, 373

Breteuil, Louis-Auguste Le
    Tonnelier, Baron de,
    1730–1807, Minister of
    State under Louis XVI, 101

Bretteville-sur-Ay, 232

Briars, 308

Brien, Jean, sailor, 232

Bristol, 132

Broglie, Victor-François, Duc de,
    1718–1804, Minister under
    Louis XVI 1789, 101

Brougham, Henry, Lord
    Brougham and Vaux,
    1778–1868, lawyer, writer,
    and politician, 117

Brunswick, Charles-William,
    Duke of, 169, 286

Brussels, 169, 283, 285, 286

Brutus, 97

Buffon, Georges-Louis Leclerc,
    Comte de, 1707–88,
    naturalist, 317

Buffon, Marguerite-Françoise de
    Bouvier de Cépoy, Comtesse
    de, 1767–1808, 108

Bülow, Friedrich-Wilhelm von,
    1755–1816, Prussian
    general, 286

Bungay, 188, 192

Buturlin, Russian officer and
    historian, 245

Byron, George Gordon, Lord,
    1788–1824, author of
    Childe Harold, 192,
    296, 317

Cadet-Gassicourt, 1789–1861,
    chemist, 359, 361

Cadiz, 369

Cadoudal, Georges, 1771–1804,
    member of conspiracy
    against Bonaparte, 217, 219

Caesar, Julius, 101–44 BC, 16,
    97, 292, 297, 314

Caffarelli, Palace, Rome, 351

Calais, 114, 200, 201, 270, 369

Calypso, 278

Cambracérès, Prince Jean-Jacques-
    Régis, 1753–1824, Duc de
    Parme, Arch-Chancellor of
    the Empire, 265

Cambrai, 72, 81, 82, 83, 282

Cambrai, Declaration of, 288

Camden Collection, 185, 197

Camoens, Luis de, 1525–80,
    Portuguese poet, author of
    The Lusiads recounting
    voyages of Vasco da Gama,
    315, 318

Cannes, 280, 281, 283, 323

Canning, George, 1770–1827,
    English Foreign Secretary,
    1822, 117, 194, 328

Canning, Lady, 185

Canova, Antonio, 1757–1821, Italian sculptor, 338

Canterbury, 115

Cape la Hogue, 297

Caraman, Georges, Comte de, diplomat, 115

Carline (Marie-Gabrielle Malagrida), actress at Théâtre-Italien, 108

Carrel, Armand, 1800–36, historian and journalist, 359

Carron, Abbé Guy-Toussaint-Joseph, 1760–1821, biographer, 79

Carthage, 377

Cartier, Jacques, 1491–1557, French sailor born at Saint-Malo, 24

Castlereagh see Londonderry

Caud, Jacques-Louis-René de, 1727–97, brother-in-law of FC, Captain of Guard at Rennes, retired 1791, m. Lucile de Chateaubriand, 3 Aug. 1796, d. at Rennes 15 March 1797, 63, 200, 208

Caud, Lucile-Angélique de Chateaubriand, Mme de, 1764–1804, wife of above and sister of FC, admitted with title of Comtesse to Chapter of L'Argentière 1783, imprisoned 1793–4, m. Jacques de Caud 1796, widowed 1797, spent last weeks of life in Augustine convent, d. 10 Nov. 1804, 7, 11, 14, 18, 48, 53, 54, 55, 56, 58, 59, 62, 63, 64, 65, 69, 74, 79, 83, 85, 86, 93, 95, 97, 111, 160, 161, 162, 164, 187, 200, 206, 208, 223, 225, 226, 227

Caulaincourt, Louis, Marquis de, Duc de Vicence, 1772–1827, aide-de-camp to Bonaparte at time of execution of Duc d'Enghien, Ambassador to St Petersburg and French Foreign Minister under Empire, 238, 256, 268, 274, 283

Causans, Jacques de Mauléon, Marquis de, 1751–1826, 38

Céluta* (FC), 153

Cesarotti, 1730–1808, translator of Homer and Ossian, 310

Cézembre, 19

Chactas* (FC), 159

Chalmel, Abbé, chaplain at Combourg, 37

Chambord, 264

Chamfort (Nicolas-Sébastien Roch), 1741–94, moralist, 64, 110

Chantilly, 22, 219, 222

Charenton, 133

Charlemagne, 742–814, King of the Franks, 305, 324, 356

Charles I, 1600–49, King of England 1625–49, beheaded 30 Jan. 1649, 49, 116, 173–4, 182

Charles II, 1630–85, King of England 1660–85, 116

Charles IX, 1550–74, King of France, 1560–74, 29

Charles VII, 1403–61, King of France 1422–61, 332

Charles X, 1757–1836, King of France 1824–30, Comte

d'Artois, emigrated 1789,
    succeeded brother Louis
    XVIII 1824, dethroned
    by July Revolution 1830,
    29, 161, 268, 270, 279,
    282, 293, 323, 328, 329,
    331, 332, 333, 334,
    338, 360, 361, 362,
    364, 368
Charles XII, 1682–1718, King
    of Sweden 1697–1718, 241,
    251, 253
Chastenay, Mme de, friend of
    Annibal Moreau, 79, 80,
    81, 87
Chateaubourg, Bénigne-Jeanne
    de Chateaubriand, Comtesse
    de Québriac, *then* de la Celle
    de, 1761–1848, m. Jean-
    François-Xavier, Comte de
    Québriac 1780, widowed
    1783, m. Paul-Marie-
    François de la Celle, Comte
    de Chateaubourg 1786,
    widowed 1816, d. 16 May
    1848, 14, 40, 49, 81, 85
Chateaubourg, Paul-Marie-
    François, de la Celle, Comte
    de, 1752–1816, m. Bénigne-
    Jeanne de Chateaubriand
    24 April 1786, 81
CHATEAUBRIAND FAMILY
    (chronologically)
Chateaubriand, Brient I, Baron
    de, first recorded ancestor
    of FC, probably fought in
    Battle of Hastings 1066, 7
Chateaubriand, Geoffrey IV,
    second Baron de, d. 126,
    7, 22
Chateaubriand, Sybille de, wife
    of above, 7

Chateaubriand de Beaufort,
    Guillaume de, founded stall
    in Dol Cathedral 1529, 34
Chateaubriand de la Guerrande,
    Christophe de, paternal
    great-great-great-grand-
    father of FC, 9
Chateaubriand de la Guerrande,
    Michel de, elder son of Jean
    de Chateaubriand de la
    Guerrande, grandson of
    above, 10
Chateaubriand de la Guerrande,
    Alexis de, elder son of
    above, 9–10
Chateaubriand, Amaury de,
    younger son of Jean de
    Chateaubriand de la
    Guerrande, grandson of
    Christophe de Chateaubri-
    and de la Guerrande,
    paternal greatgrandfather of
    FC, 10
Chateaubriand de la Villeneuve,
    Jacques-François de,
    1683–1729, paternal
    grandfather of FC, m.
    Pétronille-Claude Lamour
    de Lanjégu, 27 Aug. 1713,
    d. 28 March 1729, 10
Chateaubriand, Pétronille-
    Claude Lamour de Lanjégu,
    Mme de, 1692–1781,
    paternal grandmother of
    FC, m. above 1713,
    widowed 1729, d. 22 Oct.
    1781, 10
Chateaubriand, François-Henri,
    Abbé de, 1717–76, eldest
    son of above, uncle of FC,
    Rector of Saint-Leuc and
    Merdrignac, 10

Chateaubriand du Parc, Joseph-
Urbain de, 1728–72,
youngest son of Jacques-
François de Chateaubriand
de la Villeneuve, uncle of
FC, 10

Chateaubriand du Plessis,
Pierre-Anne-Marie de,
1727–94, third son of
Jacques- François de
Chateaubriand de la
Villeneuve, uncle of FC,
sailor, m. Marie-Jeanne-
Thérèse Brignon de Lehen
12 Feb. 1760, imprisoned
during Terror, d. 20 Aug.
1794, 10, 11, 25–6

Chateaubriand du Plessis,
Stanislas-Pierre: Jean-Marie
de, 1767–?, elder son of
above, cousin of FC, page
to the Queen, then sailor,
drowned off Africa, 25–6

Chateaubriand du Plessis,
Armand-Louis-Marie de,
1768–1809, younger son of
Pierre-Anne-Marie de
Chateaubriand du Plessis,
cousin of FC, fought with
FC in Army of Princes,
emigrated to Jersey, m.
Jeanne Le Brun 1795,
shipwrecked and captured
1809, shot 31 March 1809,
12, 25, 174, 230–31,
233, 234

Chateaubriand, René-Auguste,
de, 1718–86, father of FC,
m. Apolline-Jeanne-Suzanne
de Bedée 3 July 1753, d. 6
Sept. 1786, disinterred and
burnt by villagers of

Combourg at beginning of
Revolution, 10, 11, 12–13,
13–14, 18, 29, 31, 36, 38,
41–2, 47, 55, 56, 57, 58,
59, 60, 61, 69, 72, 73, 74,
83, 84, 84–5, 356

Chateaubriand, Apolline-Jeanne-
Suzanne de Bedée, Mme de,
1726–98, wife of above,
daughter of Ange-Annibal
de Bedée, mother of FC, m.
1753, widowed 1786,
imprisoned 1794, d. 31 July
1798, 13, 13–14, 14–15,
18, 19, 22–3, 24, 29, 31–2,
44, 53, 54, 55, 58, 59, 69,
73, 84, 85, 98, 112, 160,
187, 188, 195–6, 196,
200, 227

Chateaubriand, Geoffrey-
René-Marie de, b. 1758,
eldest brother of FC, d. in
infancy, 14

Chateaubriand, Jean-Baptiste-
Auguste, Comte de,
1759–94, elder brother of
FC, counsellor at High
Court of Brittany 1779, m.
Aline-Thérèse Le Pelletier
de Rosanbo 1787, guillo-
tined with her, Mme de
Rosanbo and Malesherbes
22 April 1794, 14, 39, 54,
64, 73, 78, 81, 85, 85–6,
86–7, 88, 92, 95, 97, 111,
112, 160, 167, 168, 169,
179, 186, 200

Chateaubriand, Aline-Thérèse Le
Pelletier de Rosanbo,
Comtesse de, wife of above,
sister-in-law of FC, m.
1787, guillotined with

husband 22 April 1794, 86,
    95, 96, 186, 355
Chateaubriand, Marie-Anne
    de, *see* Chateaubourg,
    Comtesse de
Chateaubriand, Julie-Marie-
    Agathe de, *see* Farcy de
    Montavallon, Comtesse de
Chateaubriand, Lucile, *see*
    Caud, Lucile-Angélique de
Chateaubriand, François-René,
    Chevalier, then Vicomte
    de, 1768–1848, author of
    the *Mémoires d'ontre-
    tombe, passim*
Chateaubriand, Céleste Buisson
    de la Vigne, Vicomtesse de,
    1774–1847, wife of above,
    161, 162, 163, 165, 215,
    218, 219, 226, 227, 229,
    258, 275, 285, 331, 372
Chateaubriand, Geoffroy-Louis,
    Comte de, 1790–1873, son
    of Jean-Baptiste-Auguste de
    Chateaubriand, nephew of
    the author, 187, 355, 356
Chateaubriand, Christian-
    Antoine, de, 1791–1843,
    brother of above, nephew
    of FC, 354–5, 356
Chateaubriand de la Guerrande,
    Charles-Hilaire, Abbé de,
    1708–1802, cousin of FC,
    last member of this branch
    of the family, 43
Châtenay, 5
Châtillon, Pauline de
    Lannoy, Duchesse de,
    1774–1826, 230
Cheftel, doctor at Bazouches, 70
Chênedollé, Charles-Julian Lioult
    de, 1769–1833, 206, 209

Chénier, André, 1762–94,
    poet, 54
Cherbourg, 270, 282, 293
Chérin, Bernard, 1718–85,
    genealogist, 6–7
Chesapeake Bay, 128
Chillicothe, 153–4
Chilpéric, King of the Franks,
    90, 141
Christina, 1626–89, Queen of
    Sweden, 1632–54, 56
Cicero, Marcus Tullius, 106–43
    BC, 186
Cimarosa, Domenico, d. 1801,
    composer, 144
Cithaeron, Mount, 152
Clarke, Henri-Jacques Guillaume,
    Marshal of France, Duc de
    Feltre, Minister of War
    under Napoleon and Louis
    XVIII, 279
Clausel de Coussergues,
    Jean-Claude, 1759–1846,
    friend and adviser of FC,
    219, 258
Clement, St, 79
Clisson, Oliver de, 1336–1407,
    Constable of France, 11
Clodion, Frank chieftain, 90
Clovis, King of the Franks, d.
    511, 260, 319
Coblentz, 169
Cockburn, Sir George, 1772–
    1853, 309
Coëtquen *see* Duras, Louise-
    Françoise-Maclovie-Céleste
    de
Coigny, Marie-Henry-François
    Franquetot, Duc de,
    1737–1821, Master of the
    Horse under Louis XVI,
    90, 91

Coislin, Marie-Anne de Mailly-
    Nesle, Marquise de,
    1732–1817, 229
Collinet, flautist, 185, 199
Colonna-Ceccaldi, 342
Columbus, Christopher,
    1451–1506, 128, 143,
    307–8
Combourg, 13, 16, 17, 31, 33,
    34, 36, 37–8, 38, 40, 41,
    43, 45, 49, 52, 54, 55, 56,
    57, 58, 61, 64, 65, 66, 70,
    73, 74, 75, 76, 85, 94, 111,
    131, 186, 187, 231, 350,
    351, 355, 376
Commentaries (Julius
    Caesar), 283
Condé, Louis-Henri-Joseph, Duc
    de Bourbon, Prince de,
    1756–1830, father of Duc
    d'Enghien, found hanged at
    Saint-Leu-Taverny, 222
Condé, Louis II, Prince de, the
    Great Condé, 1621–86,
    222, 257, 322, 343
Condé, Louis-Joseph de Bour-
    bon, Prince de, 1736–1818,
    emigrated with son Duc de
    Bourbon and grandson Duc
    d'Enghien, commanded
    Army of Princes, 43, 58, 222
Condorcet, Antoine Caritat,
    Marquis de, 1743–94,
    mathematician, 96
Congrés de Vérone, Le (FC),
    327–8
Consalvi, Cardinal, 212
Conservateur, 75, 317–18
Constant de Rebecque,
    Benjamin, 1767–1830, writer
    and politician, 336, 347
Constantinople, 54, 84

Constitutionnel, 366
Contades de Plouër, Françoise-
    Marie-Gertrude, Comtesse
    de, d. 1776, daughter of
    Louis- Georges-Érasme,
    Marquis de Contades,
    godmother of FC, 15
Contades, Louis-Georges-
    Érasme, Marquis de,
    Marshal of France,
    1704–95, 14, 15
Contat, Louise, actress at
    Théâtre-Français, 108
Cook, Captain James, 1728–79,
    sailor, 135, 319
Coppet, 346
Coquereau, Abbé, 321
Corinna* (Ovid), 354
Corinne (Mme de Staël), 335
Corinth, 152
Corseul, 16
Cortois de Pressigny, Gabriel,
    Comte, 1745–1823, Bishop
    of Saint-Malo, 46, 98
Corvo, Convent of, 315
Couëdic, Chevalier du,
    1739–80, naval officer,
    distinguished himself
    in American War of
    Independence, 51
Courchamp, Mme de, 359
Coutances, 359
Crécy, Battle of, 1346, 284
Cromwell, Oliver, 1599–1658,
    'Protector' of England, 48,
    182, 314
Cymbeline (Shakespeare), 198
Cyropaedia (Xenophon), 87
Cyrus (Mme de Scudéry), 13

Dagobert, c. 600–639 King of
    the Franks 632–639, 56, 90

Dalesme, General, 1763–1832,
    Commander of the French
    garrison on Elba, 1814, 276
Dallas, Lady, 321
Dandin, Georges* (Molière), 357
Dante, Alighieri, 1265–1321,
    author of *La Divina
    Commedia*, 188, 315, 358
Danton, Georges-Jacques,
    1759–94, statesman and
    orator, guillotined, 165
Danzig, 12, 84
Daru, Pierre-Antoine, Comte,
    1726–1829, Quartermaster
    general of Grand Army,
    239, 252
David, Louis, 1748–1825,
    painter, 338
Davoust, Marshal, Duc
    d'Anerstädt, Prince
    d'Eckmühl, 1770–1823,
    240, 242
Deboffe, London bookseller who
    published FC's *Essai* 1797,
    182, 186
Decazes, Édouard, Baron,
    nephew of the Duc Decazes,
    diplomat, 115
Decazes, Élie, Duc, 1780–1860,
    French Ambassador in
    London 1820–22, 116, 360
Delattre, Dr, Jersey doctor, 179
De Launay, Bernard-René
    Jourdan, Marquis, 1740–89,
    Governor of the
    Bastille, 102
Delaunay-Boisé-Lucas *see*
    Boisé-Lucas
Delia* (Tibullus), 354
Delisle de Sales (Jean-Baptiste
    Isoard), 1743–1816,
    philosopher, 95

Delos, 152
Delphine (Mme de Staël), 344
Depagne, companion of
    Armand de Chateaubriand
    in 1809, 232
Desmarets, Charles, 1763–1830,
    Chief of the Imperial
    Police, 233
Desmarets, Jean, *c.* 1312–83,
    Advocate-general at High
    Court of Paris, beheaded
    1383, 47
Desmoulins, Camille, 1760–94,
    orator, 100
Detroit, Michigan, 140
Devonshire, Georgina Spencer,
    Duchess of, 1746–1806,
    patroness of letters,
    337, 338
Diderot, Denis, 1713–84,
    philosopher, editor of the
    Encyclopédie, 39
Dieppe, 95
Digne, 280
Dinan, 10, 12, 16, 55, 99
Dinan, College of, 55
Dino, Dorothée, Duchesse de,
    1795–1862, 76
Dnieper, River, 240
Dol, 32, 34–5, 38, 41
Dol, College of, 31, 44, 45,
    47, 50
Dorogobouj, 241
Dorogomilow, 249
Doudeauville, Sosthène, Vicomte
    de La Rochefoucauld, Duc
    de 1785–1864, 273
Dover, 114, 200, 201, 327
Dresden, 255
Dubourg-Butler, Frédéric,
    Comte, 1778–1850,
    365, 366

Dugazon, Louise-Rosalie
Lefèvre, Mme, 1755–1821,
actress at Théâtre-Italien,
108

Duguay-Trouin, René,
1673–1736, sailor, 24

Duhamel, Abbé, master at Dinan
College, 55

Duhamel-Dumonceau, Henri-
Louis, 1700–82,
agriculturist, 111

Dujardin, Captain, master of the
Saint-Pierre, 112

Dulau, A., former Benedictine,
bookseller in London,
began printing the first
Génie du christianisme
1799, 197, 200

Dumoulin, Évariste,
journalist, 366

Dumouriez, Charles-François,
1739–1824, general, 304

Du Paz, Père, genealogist, 6

Duquesne, 171

Duras, Claire-Louise-Rose-
Bonne de Coët-Nempren de
Kersaint, Duchess de,
1778–1828, daughter-in-
law of above, mistress of
FC, 258

Duras, Emmanuel-Félicité de
Durfort, Duc de, Marshal
of France, 1715–89,
presented FC and his
brother to Louis XVI in
1787, 17, 88

Duras, Louise-Françoise-Maclovie
Céleste de Coëtquen,
Duchesse de, d. 1802, wife of
above, in 1736, bringing her
husband Château of Com-
bourg, sold Combourg to

FC's father 1761, widowed
1789, 17, 344, 345

Durosnel, General, 1771–1849,
249

Du Tillet, Jean, d. 1570, 334

Du Touchet, tutor of Louis
XVII, 101

Eckstein, Baron d', 1790–1861,
Governor of Ghent 1815, 286

Écreho, 232

Edda (ed. Soemond), 99

Edith, the swan-necked, 80

Edward III, 1312–77, King of
England 1327–77, 238

Edward, Prince of Wales, the
Black Prince, 1330–76, 297

Égault, Abbé Julian-Jean-Marie,
1752–1821, master of Dol
College, 36, 45

Elba, island of, 268, 270, 276,
277, 280, 301, 340

Enghien, Louis-Antoine-Henri
de Bourbon, Duc d',
1772–1804, b. at Chantilly,
shot at Vincennes, 217,
219, 221, 261, 298, 322,
343, 376

Épervier, ship, 295

Erie, 155

Erythia, 156

Escotais, Louis-Joseph des,
Grand Prior of Aquitaine, 8

Essai historique, politique et
moral sur les Révolutions
anciennes et modernes
(FC), 118, 136, 147, 181,
182, 186, 196, 197

Estaing, Charles-Hector, Comte
d', 1729–94, sailor, 51, 119

Esterhazy, Prince Paul,
diplomat, 265

Estrées, Gabrielle d', 1573–99,
    mistress of Henri IV, 264
Eugène de Beauharnais, Prince,
    1781–1824, 249, 256, 364
Eve* (Milton), 194
Eylau, Battle of, 280
Fain, Baron, 1778–1837,
    240, 256
Falkland, Lucius Carey, Viscount,
    1610–43, Secretary of State
    to Charles I, d. in Battle of
    Newbury, 173–4
Farcy de Montvallon, Annibal-
    Pierre-François, b. 1749,
    brother-in-law of FC, m.
    Julie-Marie-Agathe de
    Chateaubriand 23 April
    1782, separated 1792, 49
Farcy de Montvallon, Julie-
    Marie-Agathe de
    Chateaubriand, Comtesse
    de, 1763–99, wife of above,
    sister of FC, m. 1782,
    separated 1792, imprisoned
    1793–4, d. 25 July 1799,
    11, 14, 49, 50, 64, 64–5,
    74, 79, 80, 85, 86, 93, 94,
    95, 100, 164, 195–6, 200,
    208, 223, 356
Favras, Thomas Mahy, Marquis
    de, 1744–90, hanged for
    plotting against La Fayette
    and Necker, 108
Feltre, Duc de, see Clarke
Fénelon, François de Salignac de
    la Mothe, 1651–1715,
    Archbishop of Cambrai,
    author of Télémaque,
    13, 83
Ferdinand I, 1751–1825, King
    of Naples as Ferdinand IV
    1759–1806, King of the

Two Sicilies 1816–25,
    341, 343
Ferdinand VII, 1784–1833,
    King of Spain 1808 and
    1813–33, 328
Ferron de la Sigonière, François-
    Prudent-Malo, 1768–1815,
    classmate of FC at Dinan,
    comrade-in-arms in Army
    of Princes, 177
Feryd-Eddyn, Persian poet, 157
Fesch, Cardinal Joseph,
    1763–1839, uncle of
    Napoleon, 212, 216,
    265, 311
Firmont, Baron de, 341
Flesselles, Jacques de, 1721–89,
    provost of merchants of
    Paris, 102
Fleurus, Battle of, 1794, 286, 304
Fleury, actor at Théâtre-
    Français, 108
Fleury, André-Hercule, Cardinal
    de, 1653–1743, Minister of
    Louis XV, 12
Florence, 211, 234, 349
Folks, English student killed
    1830, 360
Fontainebleau, 264, 266, 268
Fontanes, Louis, Marquis de,
    1757–1821, friend of FC,
    Grand Master of Imperial
    University under Napoleon,
    63, 195, 199, 206, 219,
    258, 335, 347
Fontenoy, Battle of, 1745, 20
Fort Royal, Saint-Malo, 19, 22
Fouché, Joseph, 1759–1820,
    Duc d'Otrante and Minister
    of Police under Napoleon,
    233, 234, 288, 289,
    289–90

Fougères, 40, 49, 54, 73,
    85, 94, 95, 111,
    209, 225
Foullon, François-Joseph,
    1715–89, Treasury official,
    lynched 12 July 1789,
    101, 103
Francheschetti, Dominique-
    César, 1776–1835,
    general, 342
Francis II, 1768–1835, Emperor
    of Germany 1792–1806,
    Emperor of Austria as
    Francis I 1804–35,
    164, 265
François I, 1494–1547, King of
    France 1515–47, 58, 66–7,
    90, 107, 293, 324
Frederick II, the Great, 1712–86,
    King of Prussia, 1740–86,
    76, 83
Frederick William II, 1744–97,
    King of Prussia 1786–97,
    169, 170, 177
Frederick William III, 1770–
    1840, King of Prussia
    1797–1840, 261
Freiburg, 222
Fribourg, 331
Friedland, Battle of, 1807, 280
Froissart, Jean, c. 1337–1404,
    historian, 16

Gaillard, doctor at St Helena, 321
Ganges, River, 149, 310, 369
Gazette de France, 89
Gazette de Leyde, 84
Genesee, 143
Génie du christianisme, Le
    (FC), 6, 46, 83, 115, 196,
    197, 199, 206, 209,
    338, 376

Genlis, Comtesse de,
    1746–1830, 337
George IV, 1762–1830, King of
    England 1820–30, 116,
    184, 192, 294, 337, 338
Georgia, 148
Gérard, Baron François,
    1770–1832, painter, 338
Germanicus, Roman general, d.
    AD 19, 221
Gesbert, Jean-Baptiste, Seneschal
    at Combourg, 37
Gesril du Papeu, Joseph-
    François-Anne, 1767–95,
    childhood friend of FC,
    captured after Quiberon
    landing, shot 27 Aug. 1795,
    25–6, 26–7, 28, 29, 30,
    48, 49, 51, 52, 112, 180, 231
Ghent, 281, 283, 284, 285, 290,
    318, 365
Ginguené, Pierre-Louis,
    1748–1816, literary
    critic, 110
Gjatsk, 253
Golfe-Juan, 323–4, 342
Gourgaud, General, 1783–1852,
    240, 297, 308, 309, 359
Gouvion Saint-Cyr, Laurent,
    Marquis de, 1764–1830,
    Marshal of France, actor in
    his youth, 107
Gouyon-Miniac, Pierre-Louis-
    Alexandre de, d. 1818,
    Captain of 7th Breton
    Company in Army of
    Princes, 170, 177
Goyon, Armand de, 1769–1809,
    cousin by marriage of FC,
    shot with Armand de
    Chateaubriand, 233,
    234, 235

Goyon-Beaufort, Comte de,
    1725–94, 56
Goyon, Julie-Renée Potier de la
    Savarière, d. 1847, wife of
    above, 234
Goyon, Officer of the Guard in
    1830, 364
Graciosa, island in the Azores,
    121, 122, 127
Granada, 67, 109
Grand-Bé, Saint-Malo, 19
Grande-Force, Prison of La,
    Paris, 233
Grand' mère (Béranger), 300
Granville, 159
Grasse, 280
Grenoble, 281
Grétry, André-Ernest-Modeste,
    1741–1813, composer, 108
Grew, Nehemiah, 1628–1711,
    botanist, 111
Guénan, Chevalier de, officer in
    the Navarre Regiment,
    81–2
Guer, Julien-Hyacinthe de
    Marnière, Chevalier de,
    1748–1816, 80
Guernsey, 158, 178
Guiche, Duc de, 199
Guignes, Duc de, 337
Guillaume le Breton, 1165–
    1227, historian and poet, 7
Guillaumy, fisherman, 126, 127
Gwydir, Lady, London hostess, 117

Hague, The, 338
Hallay-Coëtquen, Marquis du,
    1799–1867, 17
Hamilton, Sir William, 1730–
    1803, British ambassador at
    Naples 1764–1800, 338
Hampstead, 117

Harold II, c. 1022–66, King of
    the Angles, 80
Hastings, Battle of, 1066, 80
Hautefeuille, Charles-Louis-
    Texier, Comte d',
    1770–1865, debutant at
    Versailles with FC, 90
Havré, Duc d', 1744–1839, 271
Hearne, Samuel, 1745–92,
    English explorer, 96
Hector, 58
Hector, Charles Jean, Comte d',
    1722–1808, commander of
    port of Brest, 1780–91, 50
Helen, Grand Duchess,
    1806–73, wife of Grand
    Duke Michael Paulovitch,
    sister-in-law of Nicholas
    I, 349
Helen of Troy, 156
Héloïse, 1101–64, wife of
    Abélard, 259
Hénin, Laure-Auguste de
    Fitz-James, Mme d',
    1744–1814, lady-in-waiting
    to Marie Antoinette, 108
Henri III, 1551–89, King of
    France 1574–89, 293
Henri IV, 1553–1610, King of
    France 1589–1610, 67, 90,
    264, 269, 274, 324, 365
Henri V of France, Duc de
    Bordeaux, Comte de
    Chambord, 1820–83,
    posthumous son of Duc de
    Berry, grandson of Charles
    X, 94, 255
Henry-Larivière, P.-E.-J.,
    1761–1838, deputy
    outlawed in 1797, 231, 233
Hercé, Mgr Urbain-René de,
    1726–95, Bishop of Dol,

shot after Quiberon
    landing, 34, 35
Hercules, 156
Herodotus, Greek historian, 156
Hingant de la Tiemblais,
    François-Marie, 1761–1827,
    counsellor at High Court of
    Brittany emigrated to
    England with F.C, 180,
    181, 182, 183, 184,
    192, 347
Histoire de dix ans (Blanc), 366
*Histoire des grands officers de
    la Couxonne* (Père
    Anselme), 6
*Histoire généalogique de
    plusieurs maisons illustres
    de Bretagne* (Père du Paz), 6
*Histoire philosophique des deux
    Indes (Raynal)*, 84
Hoche, General Lazare,
    1768–97, 304
Hohenlinden, Battle of,
    1800, 304
Holland, Henry Richard Fox,
    Lord, 1773–1840, 311
Holyrood, 338
Homer, 124, 188, 230
Horace, Quintus Horatius
    Flaccus, 65–8 BC, poet, 40,
    147, 354
Horatius Cocles, Roman of sixth
    century BC, who lost an eye
    while defending a bridge
    single-handed against an
    Etruscan army, 28
Hôtel de Ville, Paris, 102,
    103, 105
Hougoumont, Château of, 287
Hulin, General, 1759–1841, 233
Hyde Park, 181
Hymettus, Mount, 152

Île aux Chiens, 124–5
Inconstant, ship, 280
Iphigénie (Racine), 318
Istrie, Duc d', *see* Bessières
Itinéraire de Paris à Jerusalem
    (FC), 6, 228
Ives, Charlotte, *see* Sutton, Lady
Ives, Rev. John, d. 1812, Vicar
    of Bungay, 188, 189, 190
Ives, Sarah, d. 1822, wife of
    above, 189, 190

Jacquemin, innkeeper, 323
Jacquin, botanist, 111
Jaffa, 301
Jamestown, 312
Janus, 323
Jean II, le Bon, 1319–64, King
    of France 1350–64, 297
Jean V, 1338–99, Duke of
    Brittany from 1354, 21
Jena, Battle of, 1806, 280
Jersey, 38, 123, 164, 178, 180,
    181, 232
Jersey, Lady, 1787–1867,
    117, 185
Jerusalem, 6, 22, 68, 146
Joan of Arc, 1412–31, 334
Job, 64, 210
Jogues, Père Isaac, 1607–46,
    French Jesuit martyred in
    Canada, 148
Johannisberg, 222
Johnston, smuggler, 312
Joinville, François d'Orléans,
    Prince de, 1818–1900, third
    son of Louis-Philippe, 321
Jordan, Camille, 1771–1821,
    politician, friend of Mme
    Récamier, 347
Josephine, Empress, 1754–1824,
    234, 274, 291

Joubert, Adélaïde-Victorine-
    Thérèse, wife of Joseph
    Joubert, 206
Joubert, Joseph, 1754–1824,
    philosopher, friend of FC,
    205, 206, 208, 215, 225,
    258, 347
Joubert, Victor, 1794–1838, son
    of above, 206
Jourdan, Jean-Baptiste, 1762–
    1833, Marshal of France, 304
Journal de Francfort, 84
Journal des Débats, 359
Julian, Roman Emperor 361–3, 75
Junken, Bishop of Dol, early
    eleventh century, 17
Jussieu, Bernard de, 1699–1777,
    naturalist, 111
Juvisy, 206

Kaumann, Captain of the Guard
    in 1830, 364
Keith, Elphinstone George,
    Lord, 1746–1823, 296
Kensington, 118, 181, 338
Kolodrina, 241
Kutusoff, Michael Ilarionovich,
    Prince of Smolensk,
    1745–1813, Russian
    general, fought Napoleon at
    Borodino, defeated Davoust
    and Ney at Smolensk, 238,
    241, 242, 245, 247, 295

La Belinaye, Renée de, 1728–
    1816, aunt of Comtesse de
    Trojolif, 95
Laborde, Alexandre-Louis-
    Joseph de, 1773–1842, 228
La Bourdonnaye-Montlue,
    Chevalier de, of the Order
    of Malta, 8

La Conchée, Saint-Malo, 19
La Fayette, Gilbert de
    Motier, Marquis de,
    1757–1834, general and
    politician, 111
La Fontaine, Jean de, 1621–95,
    fabulist, 156
La Galaisière, Minister under
    Louis XVI 1789, 101
La Harpe, Jean-François de,
    1739–1803, literary critic,
    friend of Mme Récamier,
    110, 235
La Haye-Sainte, 287
La Hougue, 159
La Laurencie, Chevalier de, of
    the Order of Malta, 8
Lallemand, Père Jérôme,
    1593–1673, 148
Lally-Tolendal, Trophime-
    Gérard, Marquis de,
    1751–1830, 103
La Luzerne, Anne-César, Comte
    de, 1741–91, diplomat,
    confused by FC with his
    uncle César-Guillaume,
    54, 101
La Martinière, officer in the
    Navarre Regiment, 82,
    83, 170
Lamballe, 16, 167
Lambesc, Charles-Eugène
    de Lorraine, Prince de,
    1751–1825, Colonel of
    the Royal-Allemand
    Regiment, 102
Lamoignon, Auguste, Marquis
    de, 1765–1845, emigrated
    to England in French
    Revolution, 199
Lamoignon, Christian, Vicomte
    de, 1770–1827, brother of

above, likewise emigrated to England, 199, 335

La Morandais, François-Placide Maillard de, Steward of Combourg, 38, 39

La Motte-Picquet, Toussaint-Guillaume, 1720–91, sailor, 51

Lanjamet, Chevalier de, of the Order of Malta, 8

La Pérouse, Jean-François de Galaup, Comte de, 1741–88, sailor, killed by savages of Vanikoro, 52, 171

La Porte, Minister under Louis XVI, 101

Larevellière-Lépeaux, 1753–1824, Member of the Directory, 365

Lariboisière, Comte, 1759–1812, general, 240

La Rochefoucauld see Doudeauville

La Rochefoucauld see Liancourt

La Rochejaquelein, Henri du Vergier, Comte de, 1772–94, Royalist general killed at Nouaillé, 111, 272

La Rochelle, 293

La Rouërie, Charles-Armand Tuffin, Marquis de, 1751–93, fought in American War of Independence as 'Colonel Armand', started Royalist conspiracy in Brittany 1792, 49, 70, 111, 133

Larrey, Baron Dominique, 1766–1842, Chief Surgeon of the Grand Army, 364

Las Cases, Emmanuel, Comte de, 1766–1842, 297, 308, 309

Lassagne, name of a Swiss clockmaker in Neuchâtel assumed by FC to return to France in 1800, 200, 201, 206, 229

Latapie, Colonel, 312

Latour-Maubourg, Marquis de, 1768–1850, general and minister, 255

Launay de la Bliardière, David-Joseph-Marie, b. 1766, son of Gilles de Launay de la Bliardière, 37

Launay de la Bliardière, Gilles-Marie de, tobacco-bonder at Combourg, 37

Lautrec de Saint-Simon, friend of Mirabeau the Younger, 106

Lauzun, Armand-Louis de Gontaut-Biron, Duc de, guillotined 1793, 111, 199

Laval, Duc de, see Montmorency, Anne-Pierre

Lavalette, Hôtel de, Paris, 229

Lavalette, hotel-keeper, 229

Lavandier, chemist at Combourg, 42

La Vauguyon, Paul-François, Duc de, 1746–1818, Minister under Louis XVI, 1789, 101

Lavigne, Alexis-Jacques Buisson de, father-in-law of FC, 161

Lavigne, Céleste de, see Chateaubriand, Céleste Buisson de Lavigne, Contesse de

Lavigne, Céleste Rapion de la Placelière, Mme Buisson de, wife of Alexis-Jacques Buisson de Lavigne, mother-in-law of FC, 161, 162

Lavigne, François-André Buisson de, son of Jacques-Pierre-Guillaume Buisson de Lavigne, uncle by marriage of FC, 161

Lavigne, Jacques-Pierre-Guillaume Buisson de, 1713–93, 161

Laya, Jean-Louis, 1761–1833, Academician, 233

Le Borgne, Guy, seventeenth-century genealogist, 6

Lebrun, Élisabeth Vigée, Mme, 1755–1842, painter, 205

Le Corvaisier, Julien, tax collector at Combourg, 37

Leghorn, 277

Le Havre, 95, 156, 159, 160, 321

Leipzig, Battle of, 1813, 364

Le Normant, furniture-dealer, 368

Lens, 222

Leopold II, 1747–92, Emperor of Germany 1799–92, 164

Le Plessis, see Plessis

Leprince, Abbé René-Jacques-Joseph, d. 1782, master at Dol College, 35, 36, 41, 46

Lérin Isles, 323

Lesseps, Jean-Baptiste Barthélemy, Baron de, 1766–1834, 249

Le Val, 90, 92

Lewis, footman, 119

Liancourt, François-Alexandre-Frédéric de la Rochefoucauld, Duc de, 1747–1827, 108, 111

Libba, deaf-mute mistress of Armand de Chateaubriand in 1792, 175, 230

Ligny, 286

Lille, 166, 168

Limoëlan de Cloriviëre, Joseph-Pierre Picot de, 1768–1826, fellow pupil of FC at Rennes and Dinan, involved in Rue Saint-Nicaise conspiracy 1799, escaped to America, became priest, d. at Georgetown, 47–8, 49

Lindsay, Anne Suzanne O'Dwyer, known as Mrs, 1764–1826, daughter of Irish innkeeper, mistress of Auguste de Lamoignon and Benjamin Constant, 199

Liverpool, Robert Banks Jenkinson, Lord, 1770–1827, English Prime Minister, 116

Liverpool (the City), 132

Livy, 59 BC–AD 17, historian, 26

Lobineau, Dom, 1666–1727, historian, 6

Lombard, Charles, pilgrim to Holy Land in 1669, 146

London, 54, 142, 270, 296, 309, 320, 337, 372
    FC emigrant in
    FC ambassador in, 114, 115, 116, 117, 118, 119, 129, 192, 327, 349
    FC emigrant in, 115, 116, 117, 118, 119, 136, 184, 190, 191, 192, 198, 200

Londonderry, Robert Stewart, Viscount Castlereagh, Marquis of, 1769–1822, English Foreign Secretary, committed suicide during FC's embassy, 117, 185, 194

Longwood, 308, 314, 319

Longwy, 177
Loudon, Lord, English general
    defeated in Canada by
    Montcalm, 142
Louis II, Prince de Condé, see
    Condé, Louis II
Louis-Philippe I, 1773–1850,
    Duc d'Orléans, King of the
    French, 1830–48, 222, 279,
    321, 337, 361, 364
Louis-Philippe-Joseph, 1747–93,
    Duc d'Orléans, 'Philippe
    Egalité', father of Louis-
    Philippe, voted for death of
    Louis XVI, guillotined,
    101, 102, 108
Louis XI, or St Louis, 1215–70,
    King of France 1226–70,
    7, 22, 89, 105, 161, 173, 324
Louis XII, 1462–1515, King of
    France 1498–1515, 107
Louis XIV, 1638–1715, King of
    France 1643–1715, 13, 58,
    67, 77, 80, 88, 90, 237,
    299, 320, 324
Louis XV, 1710–74, King of
    France, 1715–74, 87, 102,
    142, 160, 218, 299
Louis XVI, 1754–93, King of
    France 1774–93, guillotined
    21 Jan. 1793, 102, 117,
    159, 171, 187, 234, 293,
    328, 343, 373
  FC with, 7, 17, 89, 90, 91–2
  at Hôtel de Ville, 103, 105
  flight to Varennes, 154
  execution, 179, 182, 198,
    260, 288, 289
  will, 314
Louis XVII, 1785–95, recog-
    nized by emigrants as King
    of France 1793–5, 102, 294

Louis XVIII, 1755–1824, King of
    France 1814–24, 115, 184,
    272, 279, 281, 288, 365
  FC with, 83, 283, 285, 286,
    289, 289–90
  return to France in 1814,
    263, 270
  FC on, 264–5, 270, 331
  death, 331
Louvel, Louis-Pierre, 1783–1820,
    saddler, assassinated Duc de
    Berry, executed, 270
Lowe, Sir Hudson, 1769–1844,
    296, 309
Lucretius, c. 98–55 BC, poet, 64
Lützen, Battle of, 1813, 280, 364
Luxembourg, Palais du, Paris,
    187, 365
Lydia* (Horace), 354
Lyons, 211, 347

Macdonald, Alexandre,
    1765–1840, Marshal of
    France, 279
Macerata, Proclamation of,
    1797, 313, 341
Macirone, aide-de-camp to
    Murat, 342
Mackenzie, Sir Alexander,
    1755–1820, Scottish
    fur-trader, discovered
    Mackenzie River in Canada
    1789, crossed Rockies to
    Pacific 1792–3, 96, 135, 136
Madame Mère, see Bonaparte,
    Maria Letizia
Magon, Hervine, 27–8
Maillard de Lescourt, Major, of
    the Artillery, 264
Maillis, Théodore Berbis de,
    officer in the Navarre
    Regiment, 82

Maintenon, Françoise
    d'Aubigné, Marquise de,
    founder of Saint-Cyr, 13
Maison, Nicolas-Joseph,
    1771–1840, General under
    Napoleon, Peer of France
    under Louis XVIII,
    Marshal of France under
    Charles X, Ambassador
    under Louis- Philippe, 270
Malcolm, Sir Pulteney, 310
Malesherbes, Chrétien- Guil-
    laume de Lamoignon,
    1721–94, Minister of State
    under Louis XVI, defended
    King before Convention,
    guillotined 22 April 1794,
    14, 64, 95, 96, 97, 110,
    136, 146, 174, 179, 186,
    187–8, 238, 355, 356
Malfilâtre, Alexandre-Henri de,
    1757–1803, counsellor at
    High Court of Brittany,
    64, 208
Malmaison, 274, 291, 292,
    293, 313
Malodeczno, 256
Mandini, singer at
    Opera-Buffa, 108
Mangin, Jean-Henri-Claude,
    1786–1835, magistrate
    and orator, Prefect of
    Police during 1830
    Revolution, 359
Mansfield, Lady, 117
Marais, Théâtre du, Paris, 107
Marat, Jean-Paul, 1743–93,
    revolutionary, 103
Marcellus, Marie-Louis-Jean-
    André Demartin du Tyrac,
    Comte de, 1795–1865,
    diplomat, 115

Marchand, valet of
    Napoleon, 309
Marengo, Battle of, 1800, 278,
    280, 316
Maret, Bernard-Hughes, Duc de
    Bassano, 1763–1839, 266
Maria, maidservant, 119
Marie Antoinette, 1755–93,
    Queen of France 1774–93,
    guillotined 16 Oct. 1793,
    25, 89, 90, 98, 101, 117
Marie-Caroline, see Berry
Marie-Louise, 1791–1847,
    Empress of the French,
    Duchess of Parma, 265,
    278, 280, 312
Marie-Thérèse Infirmary, Paris,
    163, 230
Marigny, 95
Marigny, François-Jean-Joseph
    Geffelot, Comte de, d.
    1793, brother-in-law of FC,
    m. Marie-Anne-Françoise
    de Chateaubriand 11
    Jan. 1780, 40
Marigny, Marie-Anne-Françoise
    de Chateaubriand,
    Comtesse de, 1760–1860,
    wife of above, sister of FC,
    m. 1780, widowed 1793, d.
    aged over 100 on 17 July
    1860, 14, 40, 49, 85, 111,
    206, 208
Marin, Chevalier, harpist, 338
Marmont Auguste-Frédéric-
    Louis-Viesse de, Marshal of
    France, Duc de Raguse,
    1774–1852, concluded
    truce with Russians 1814,
    regarded by Bonapartists as
    traitor, tried to suppress
    1830 Revolution, escorted

Charles X to Cherbourg 1830, 258, 359, 360, 361, 362

Marolles, Abbé Michel de, 1600–81, author of *Mémoires*, 56

Martyrs, Les (FC), 6, 230

Masséna, André, 1756–1817, Duc de Rivoli, Prince d'Essling, Marshal of France, 304

Massillon, Jean-Baptiste, 1663–1742, Bishop of Clermont, 66

Massorah, Battle of, 1250, 7

Mauritius, 149

Megara, 142

Melbourne, Lady, 337

Mémoires sur de Consulat (Thibaudeau), 313

Menelaus, 156

Mercure de France, 84, 220, 228, 229, 335

Mercy, François de, 177

Merdrignac, 10

Mère coupable, La (Beaumarchais), 107

Merfeld, General, 364

Messina, 67

Metella, wife of Sulla, 377

Metternich, Klemens Lothar Wenzel, Prince von, 1773–1859, 328

Metz, 175

Michelangelo Buonarroti, 1475–1654, 320, 351

Mignet, Auguste, 1796–1884, historian and politician, 359

Milan, 211, 349

Milton, John, 1608–74, author of *Paradise Lost*, 73, 194

Miquelon, island in Saint-Pierre-et-Miquelon archipelago, 124

Mirabeau, André-Boniface-Louis Riqueti, Vicomte de, 1754–92, soldier and orator, 105, 106

Mirabeau, Honoré-Gabriel, Comte de, 1749–91, orator and statesman, 54, 100, 105, 112

Moise (FC), 6

Molé, actor at Théâtre-Français, 108

Molé, Matthieu-Louis, Comte, 1781–1855, Foreign Minister and Prime Minister under Louis-Philippe, 206

Molière (Jean-Baptiste-Poquelin) 1622–73, 40

Monchoix, Château of, 16, 21

Monica, St, *c.* 322–87, 25

Monsieur *see* Charles X

Montaigne, Michel Eyquem de, 1533–92, essayist, 60, 182, 261

Montboissier, Charles-Philippe-Simon, Baron de, 1750–1802, 169, 174

Montboissier, Françoise-Pauline de Lamoignon de Malesherbes, Baronne de, 1758–1827, 95, 174

Montcalm, Armande de Richelieu Marquise de, friend of FC, 258, 273

Montcalm, Louis, Marquis de, 1712–59, French general killed before Quebec, 142, 143

Montenotte, Battle of,
    1796, 278
Montespan, Françoise-Anthénaïs
    de Rochechouart, Marquise
    de, 1641–1707, 80
Montholon, Charles-Tristan,
    Comte de, 1783–1853, 297,
    308, 311
Montholon, Comtesse de, wife
    of above, 308
Montlouet, François-Jean-
    Raphaël de Brunes,
    Marquis de, 1728–87, 56, 83
Montmorency, Anne de,
    1492–1567, 289
Montmorency, Anne-Pierre-
    Adrien de, Duc de Laval,
    1767–1837, 273, 327, 347
Montmorency, Matthieu-Jean-
    Félicité, Vicomte,
    1767–1826, 273, 346, 347
Montmorin, Auguste de, 216
Montmorin-Saint-Hérem,
    Armand-Marc, Comte de,
    1746–92, Foreign Minister
    under Louis XVI, 101, 108,
    171, 205, 212, 216, 218
Montpensier, Duc de,
    1775–1807, younger brother
    of Louis-Philippe, 337
Montreal, 140
Moreau, Annibal, d. 1808, son of
    Julie de Bedée, Mme
    Moreau, cousin of FC,
    78–9, 79, 87
Moreau de Saint-Méry,
    Médéric-Louis-Élie,
    1750–1819, President of
    Paris electors, 103
Moreau, General Jean-Victor,
    1763–1813, implicated in
    Cadoudal conspiracy 1804,

exiled to United States,
    killed fighting against
    France at Battle of Dresden,
    47–8, 219, 304
Morellet, Abbé André, 1727–
    1819, encyclopaedist, 176
Moréri, Louis, 1643–80, author
    of a Grand dictionnaire
    historique, 6
Morice, Dom, eighteenthcentury
    historian, 6
Mortemart, the name of the
    three daughters of Gabriel
    de Rochechouart, Duc de
    Mortemart: Gabrielle,
    Marquise de Thiange;
    Françoise-Athénaïs,
    Marquise de Montespan;
    Marie- Gabrielle, Abbess of
    Fontevrault, 80
Mortemart, Victurnien-
    Bonaventure-Victor de
    Rochechouart, Marquis de,
    1753–1823, Colonel of the
    Navarre Regiment, 82,
    109, 170
Mortier, Édouard-Joseph,
    Marshal of France, Duc de
    Trévise, 1768–1835, 258
Moscow, 236, 239, 240, 241,
    242, 243, 245, 246, 247,
    248, 249, 250, 252, 253,
    261, 262, 264, 281, 299,
    322, 369
Moselle, River, 174, 175
Moshaisk, 245
Moskva, River, 245, 248, 250
Mouchy, Duc de, see Noailles
Mozart, Wolfgang Amadeus, 338
Munich, Christopher, Count of,
    1687–1777, German
    general in Russian army, 12

Murat, Caroline Bonaparte,
    Mme, 1782–1839, wife of
    above, Queen of Naples,
    339, 340, 341, 342
Murat, Chevalier de, of the
    Order of Malta, 8
Murat, Joachim, 1767–1815,
    King of Naples, 1808–14,
    217, 240, 245, 249, 256,
    278, 338, 339, 340, 341,
    342, 343, 344

Nagot, Abbé François-Charles,
    1734–1816, Superior of the
    Saint-Sulpice Seminary in
    Paris, sent to America to
    found seminary at Balti-
    more, 112, 120, 124
Nantes, Edict of, 1685, 133
Naples, 67, 212, 245, 278,
    340, 343
Naples, King of, see Murat,
    Joachim
Napoleon I, 1769–1821, First
    Consul of France 1799–
    1804, Emperor of France
    1804–14, 48, 50, 80, 199,
    234, 235, 260, 261, 262,
    263, 270, 271, 272,
    274, 275, 339, 344,
    364, 372
  compared with FC, 110,
    367, 373
  meets FC, 209, 210, 211
  and the Enghien affair,
    217–22, 261, 298, 376
  judged by FC, 221, 233, 234,
    240, 245, 251, 253, 257,
    266, 267, 268, 278, 279,
    280, 291, 292, 294, 295,
    296, 297, 298–307,
    317–18, 318, 319, 339, 374

  on FC, 228, 229, 266, 267,
    318, 319
  and Russia, 236–56
  and 1814 campaign, 257,
    258, 264, 339
  takes leave of his troops, 269
  at Elba, 276, 277, 278, 340
  and the Hundred Days, 279–90
  leaves France, 293–6
  at St Helena, 307–24
  death, 314–15
  burial, 315–17
  brought back to France, 321–3
Napoleon II, 1811–32, Emperor
    of the French, King of
    Rome, Prince of Parma,
    Duke of Reichstadt, 264,
    265, 278, 312
Natchez, Les (FC), 118, 119,
    197, 200
National, 359
Navarre, Mme de, Mother
    Superior of the Dames
    Saint-Michel, 223, 225
Necker, Jacques, 1732–1804,
    banker, Finance Minister
    under Louis XVI, father of
    Mme de Staël, 108
Nero, Roman Emperor,
    78–92, 220
Neuchâtel, 200
Newfoundland, 124
Newton, Sir Isaac, 1642–1727,
    mathematician, 188
New York, 131, 137, 138,
    139, 159
Ney, Marshal, Duke of Elchingen,
    Prince of the Moskva,
    1769–1815, 244
Niagara, 140, 144, 145, 147,
    148, 155
Niagara Falls, 144, 145, 147

Nicholas, Grand Duchess, *see* Alexandra

Nicholas, Grand Duke, *see* Nicholas I

Nicholas I, 1796–1855, Emperor of Russia 1825–55, 76

Niemen, River, 236, 237, 281

Nile, River, 304

Noailles, Anne-Louise-Marie de Beauvau, Duchess de Mouchy, Princesse de Poix, Comtesse de, 108

Noailles, Louis-Adolphe-Alexis, Comte de, 1783–1835, 273

Noailles, Louis-Philippe-Marc-Antoine, Comte de, 1752–1819, Duc de Mouchy, 271

Noirot, Lieutenant, killed in 1830, 364

Nördlingen, 222

Northumberland, ship, 297, 307

Notre-Dame-d'Alloue, 233

Nouail, Abbé Pierre-Henri, Vicar General at Saint-Malo, 14

Nouvelle Héloïse, La (Rousseau), 153

Numantia, 246

Odyssey (Homer), 87

Oeta, Mount, 322

Ogygia, 278

Ohio, Nebraska, 109

Olive, Mlle, Mme de Staël's chambermaid, 335

Olivier, Mlle, actress at Théâtre-Français, 108

Ontario, 155

Opéra, Paris, 87

Orge, River, 206

Orlando Furioso (Ariosto), 241

Orléans, Duc de, *see* Louis-Philippe-Joseph *and* Louis-Philippe I

Ossian, heroic poet whose work James Macpherson claimed have collected and translated, 310

Ostend, 178

Osten-Sacken, Prince Fabian Wilhelm von der, 265

Ostia, 351

Otho, Marcus Salvius, Roman Emperor, 102

Otrante, Duc d', *see* Fouché

Oudinot, Charles, 1767–1847, Duc de Reggio, Marshal of France, 272

Ovid (Publius Ovidius Naso), 43–17 BC, 354

Oxford, 199

Paisiello, Giovanni, 1741–1815, composer,, 144

Palais-Royal, Paris, 80, 107, 165, 361, 367

Papelotte, 287

Parma, 341

Parthenon, 152

Pasquier, Étienne-Denis, Duc, Prefect of Police 1810, 206

Passy, Château de, 205

Pasta, Giuditta, 1789–1865, singer, 188

Patterson, Elisabeth, *see* Bonaparte, Elisabeth

Peltier, Jean-Gabriel, 1765–1825, French journalist, emigrated to London 1792, 182, 185, 186

Penn, William, 1644–1718, Governor of Pennsylvania, 128

Père de famille, Le (Diderot), 39

Pericles, 499–429 BC, 273

Périer, Casimir, 1777–1832, Minister of the Interior, 1831, 359

Peters, footman, 119

Peter the Great, 1672–1725, Emperor of Russia 1721–25, 241, 249

Petit, General Jean-Martin, 1772–56, 269

Petit, René, fiscal attorney at Combourg, 37

Philadelphia, Pennsylvania, 131–2, 136, 156, 292

Philomela* (Virgil), 354

Phocion, d. 317 BC, 273

Pierre de Langres, 29

Pierre, servant of Mme de Bedée, 20

Pilwisky, Forest of, 237

Pitt, William, 1759–1806, second son of Earl of Chatham, English Prime Minister for twenty years, leading adversary of French Revolution and Napoleon, 115

Pittsburgh, Pennsylvania, 138

Pius VII (Chiaramonti), 1740–1823, Pope 1800–23, 212, 298

Pius VIII (Saverio), 1761–1830, Pope 1829–30, 352

Placelière, Céleste Rapion de la, *see* Lavigne

Planchenois, 286

Plancoët, 16, 19, 21

Pleinselve, Colonel de, officer of the Empire killed in 1830, 364

Plélo, Louis-Robert-Hippolyte Bréhan, Comte de, 1699–1734, French diplomat killed in Siege of Danzig, 12

Plessis, Le, 10

Plessix de Parscau, Anne Buisson de Lavigne, Comtesse du, 1772–1813, 161, 165

Plessix de Parscau, Hervé-Louis-Joseph-Marie, Comte du, 1762–1831, 161

Plouër, Comtesse de, *see* Contades

Plutarch, c. 46–c. 120, historian, 315

Plymouth, 296

Poitiers, 8

Poitiers, Battle of, 1356, 284

Poix, Mme de, *see* Noailles

Polignac, Auguste-Jules-Armand-Marie, Prince de, 1780–1847, Prime Minister under Charles X, 1829–30, 273, 356, 361, 362

Pommereul, François-René-Jean, Baron de, 1745–1823, Director of Censorship under Empire, 80–1

Pompeii, 340

Pompey, Sextus, d. 35 BC, 51, 320

Pondicherry, 71

Poniatowski, Prince Joseph, 1762–1813, Marshal of France, 249

Portier, Abbé Joseph-François, 1739–91, Principal of Dol College, 34, 46

Porto-Ferrajo, 276, 277

Potelet, Jean-Baptiste, retired officer of the India Company, 37

Potsdam, 75, 76

Pouqueville, François,
    1770–1838, historian and
    friend of FC, 371
Pradt, Abbé Dufour de, 1759–
    1837, Archbishop of
    Malines, 274
Pultava, Battle of, 1709, 242,
    251, 253
Purgatorio (Dante), 346
Pythagoras, *c.* 580–*c.* 500 BC,
    Greek philosopher and
    mathematician, 346

Quatre-Bras, 286
Quebec, 140, 142, 143, 148
Québriac, Bénigne-Jeanne de
    Chateaubriand, Comtesse
    de, *see* Chateaubourg,
    Comtesse de la Celle de
Québriac, Jean-François-Xavier,
    Comte de, 1742–83,
    brother-in-law of FC, m.
    Bénigne-Jeanne de
    Chateaubriand II Jan.
    1780, 40
Quiberon, 27, 35
Quintel, Michael, sailor, shot
    with Armand de Chateau-
    briand in 1809, aged
    thirty-five, 231, 233

Rabelais, François, *c.*
    1494–1553, 10
Racine, Jean, 1639–99, 13, 318
Raguse, Duc de, *see* Marmont
Rainneville, Alphonse-Valentin,
    Vicomte de, 1798–1864, 329
Rambouillet, 293
Raphael (Raffaello Santi),
    1483–1520, 25
Raymond VI, 1156–1222,
    Comte de Toulouse, 221

Raynal, Abbé Guillaume,
    1713–96, philosopher, 84
Récamier, Jeanne-Françoise- Julie-
    Adélaïde Bernard (Juliette),
    Mme, 1777–1849, 335, 336,
    337, 338, 339, 340, 344,
    345, 346, 347, 355
Reims, 260, 332, 374
Remiremont, Chapter of, 7, 55,
    97, 208
Rémusat, Claire-Élisabeth- Jeanne
    Gravier de Vergennes,
    Comtesse de, 1780–1821,
    wife of Antoine-Laurent de
    Rémusat, First Chamberlain
    to Napoleon, 234
René* (FC), 118, 181
René (FC), 198, 200
Rennes, 13, 34, 46, 47, 54, 56,
    72, 76, 78, 111, 188
Rennes, College of, 47, 48, 49, 50
Revolution, French, 14, 37, 84,
    94, 96, 106–7, 125, 133,
    163, 171, 218, 229, 320
Rhexenor, 142
Rhine, River, 237, 257, 258,
    299, 304
Richelieu, Armand-Emmanuel du
    Plessis, Duc de, 1766–1822,
    Foreign Minister and
    President of the Council
    under Louis XVIII, 318
Richmond, Surrey, 117
Rinaldo* (Tasso), 155
Rivallon, Lord of Combourg, 34
Rivaux, Officer of the Guard in
    1830, 364
Robert d'Artois, banished by
    Philippe de Valois, 182
Rocca, Jean-Albert-Michel (John),
    1788–1818, secretly married
    Mme de Staël 1816, 344

Rochambeau, Donatien de
    Vimeur, Comte de,
    1725–1807, general in
    American rebel army, 139
Rochefort, 171, 293, 294
Rocroi, Battle of, 1643, 222
Rohan, Renée de, d. 1616, 57
Rohan-Chabot, Louis-
    François-Auguste, Duc de,
    1788–1833, 355
Roi est mort: vive le Roi! (FC),
    331, 333, 334
Romanzoff, Nicolas, Count of,
    1750–1826, 238
Rome, 27, 102, 164, 247, 259,
    278, 320, 374, 377
  Mme de Beaumont in, 206,
    211–16
  FC in, 211–16, 323, 335,
    336, 349–58
Rome, King of, see Napoleon II
Romeo and Juliet (Steibelt), 346
Rosanbo, Aline-Thérèse Le
    Pelletier de, see Chateaubri-
    and, Aline-Thérèse Le
    Pelletier de Rosanbo,
    Comtesse de
Rosanbo, Louis Le Pelletier
    Marquis de, Président at High
    Court of Paris, m. Marie-
    Thérèse-Marguerite de
    Lamoignon de Malesherbes
    1769, 95, 96, 109, 355
Rosanbo, Marie-Thérèse-
    Marguerite de Lamoignon
    de Malesherbes, Mme le
    Pelletier de, 1756–94, wife
    of above, guillotined 22
    April 1794, 95, 96, 186
Roscius, 126–62 BC, Roman
    actor, 300
Rose, maidservant, 119

Rose, Mme (Mme Thodon),
    travelling-companion of FC
    on first journey to Paris,
    77, 78
Rossini, Gioacchino, 1792–1868,
    Italian composer, 350
Rostopchin, Count Fedor,
    1765–1826, Governor of
    Moscow, 245, 246, 247,
    248, 264
Rouen, 46, 109
Rouërie, Marquise de la, 111
Rouillac, Abbé René de,
    Principal of Dinan
    College, 55
Rousseau, Jean-Jacques,
    1712–78, author of La
    Nouvelle Héloïse, Les
    Confessions, etc., 64, 93,
    139, 153, 208, 331
Roussel or Rouxel, sailor, 231
Rovedino, singer at Opera-
    Buffa, 108
Rovigo, General, see Savary
Roye, 288
Ruel, 313

Sacre, Le (Barnage), 332
Saint-Aaron, Chapter of, 24
Saint-Amand, 286
Saint-Aubin, Jeanne-Charlotte
    Schroeder, Mme,
    1764–1850, actress at
    Théâtre-Italien, 108
Saint-Brieuc, 17
Saint-Cast, 231
Saint-Cloud, 361, 362
Saint-Cyr, Seine-et-Oise, 77
Saint-Cyr, College of, 13
Saint-Denis, 133, 288, 289
Saint-Dizier, 258
Saint-Germain, Forest of, 90

Saint-Germain, Mme, wife of
    above, servant of Mme de
    Beaumont, 215, 216
Saint-Germain, servant of Mme
    de Beaumont and later of
    Lucile, 225, 225–6
St Helena, 222, 250, 291,
    296, 297, 298, 307–24,
    343, 364, 376
St Helier, Jersey, 178
Saint-Huberti, Marie-Antoinette
    Clavel, Mme, 1756–1812,
    singer, 87
St James, 307
Saint-Lambert, 287
Saint-Launeuc, 10
Saint-Leu, Duchesse de, see
    Bonaparte, Hortense
Saint-Leu-Taverny, 222
Saint-Lô, 233
Saint-Louis (Louis Poullain),
    valet of Jean-Baptiste-
    Auguste de Chateaubriand,
    166–8
Saint-Malo, 10, 12–19, 22–3,
    29, 31, 38–9, 42, 47,
    55, 71, 72, 73, 85, 87,
    99, 111–12, 112, 119,
    160, 161, 162,
    179, 232
Saint-Malo, Bishop of, see
    Cortois de Pressigny
Saint-Marsault, Baron de,
    debutant at Versailles with
    brother and FC, 90
Saint-Marsault-Chatelaillon,
    Baron de, debutant at
    Versailles with FC, 90
Saint-Michel, Paris convent,
    223, 225, 226
Saint-Michel, Mont, 18
St Petersburg, 283

Saint-Pierre, island in Saint-
    Pierre-et-Miquelon
    archipelago, 127
Saint-Priest, François-Emmanuel
    Guignard, Comte de,
    1735–1821, Minister of
    Louis XVI 1789, 101
Saint-Riveul, André-François-
    Jean du Rocher de,
    1772–89, killed at Rennes
    27 Jan. 1789, 47, 48
Saint-Servan, 19, 28, 195
Saint-Simon, Claude-Anne,
    Duc de, 1743–1819,
    Colonel of the Conti
    Regiment, 38
Saint-Victor, Abbey of,
    Paris, 260
Salamis, 152
Salisbury, Marchioness of, 337
San Domingo, 149
San Luigi dei Francesi, 216
Sanson, Charles, 1740–93,
    executioner, guillotined
    Louis XVI, 101
Sans-Souci, Palace of,
    Potsdam, 75
Santa Cruz, 121, 122
Santa Eufemia, Gulf of, 343
Savary, Duc de Rovigo,
    1774–1833, 293
Savigny, 206, 208
Sceaux, 5
Schonen, Auguste-Jean-Marie,
    Baron de, 1782–1849,
    deputy, 359
Schouvaloff, General, 265
Scipio, Publius Cornelius,
    Africanus Major, 237–183
    BC, consul and general, 237
Scott, Walter, 1771–1832,
    novelist, 307–8

Ségur, Louis-Philippe, Comte de, 1753–1830, 237

Sémonville, Charles-Louis Huguet, Marquis de, 1759–1839, 332

Seneca, c. 2–66, philosopher, Nero's tutor, 220

Senef, 222

Sérilly, Anne-Louise, Thomas, Mme de, cousin of Pauline de Beaumont, 108

Sernon, 280

Sévigné, Marie, de Rabutin-Chantal, Marquise de, 1626–96, letter-writer, 13, 34

Sévin, Abbé René-Malo, d. 1817, Rector of Combourg, 83

Sèvres, 93, 105, 346

Shakespeare, William, 1564–1616, 198

Sicard, Abbé, 1742–1822, 233

Simiane, Comtesse de, Paris hostess, 108

Simon, Antoine, cobbler, appointed tutor to Louis XVII, guillotined 1794, 101

Sisteron, 280

Smith, William, Mayor of Southampton in 1793, 115

Smolensk, 239, 240, 241, 242, 243, 253, 299

Smorgoni, 256

Socrates, 470–399 BC, Athenian philosopher, 354

Sombreuil, Vicomte de, 1769–95, shot after the Quiberon landing, 27

Sophocles, c. 496–c. 405 BC, Athenian tragedian, 40

Soult, Duc de Dalmatie, 1769–1851, Marshal of France, 279, 287

Southampton, 115, 180

Sparta, 137, 260, 377

Staël, Anne-Louise-Germaine Necker, Baronne de, 1766–1817, essayist and novelist, 108, 238, 246, 262, 335, 336, 344, 345, 346

Stanislas Leszczinski, 1677–1766, King of Poland 1704–36, 12

Steibelt, Daniel, 1765–1823, German composer, 346

Suffren de Saint-Tropez, Pierre-André de, 1726–88, sailor, 51, 119

Sutton, Charlotte Ives, Lady, 1780–1852, m. Captain (later Admiral) Samuel Sutton 1806, 188, 189, 190, 191, 192, 193, 194, 194–5, 197, 327

Sutton, Captain Samuel, 1807–50, elder son of above, 327

Sutton, Admiral Samuel, d. 1832, 193, 194

Suvuroff, Alexander Vasilievitch, 1729–1800, Russian general, 241

Swedenborg, Emmanuel, 1688–1772, Swedish philosopher and mystic, 183

Swift, trader at Albany, 137, 138

Tacitus, Cornelius, c. 55–120, historian, 221, 307

Talleyrand, Mme de, 275

Talleyrand-Périgord, Charles-
    Maurice de, 1754–1838,
    Prince de Bénévent,
    sometime Bishop of Autun,
    266, 274, 288, 289
Talma, François-Joseph,
    1763–1826, tragic actor at
    Théâtre-Français, 108
Tamerlane, 1336–1405, Mongol
    chieftain, 296
Tasso, Torquato, 1544–95, poet,
    155, 188, 355
Télémaque (Fénelon), 83
Temps, 359
Thames, River, 295
Théatre-Français, Paris, 87
Thebes, 147, 240
Themistocles, c. 525 BC–c. 460
    BC, Greek general and
    statesman, 142, 294, 295
Thibaudeau, Antoine, 1765–
    1854, Prefect under
    Napoleon, 313
Thiers, Adolphe, 1797–1877,
    lawyer, historian,
    politician, 359
Thionville, 172, 174, 175, 176,
    177, 235
Tiber, River, 206
Tibullus, c. 50 BC–c. 18 BC,
    poet, 66, 354
Tilleul, du, companion of FC on
    journey to Jersey 1792, 178
Titus, 40–81, Roman Emperor
    79–81, 352
Tivoli Gardens, Paris, 354
Tocqueville, Louise-Madeleine
    Le Palletier de Rosanbo,
    Comtesse de, d. 1836, 95
Torbay, 296
Toulon, 171, 321, 342
Tournay, 169

Tournefort, Joseph de, 1656–
    1708, botanist, 111
Tourville, 171
Toussaint-Louverture, 1743–
    1803, Negro politician and
    general, who proclaimed
    independence of San
    Domingo in 1800, was
    captured by French and d.
    prisoner in France, 296
Toussaint, Saint-Luc, 6
Trémignon, Comte de, 20
Treves, 169, 171
Trianon, 77
Trojolif, Thérèse-Joséphine de
    Moëlien, Comtesse de,
    1759–93, daughter of
    counsellor at High Court
    of Brittany, involved in
    La Rouërie conspiracy,
    guillotined 18 June 1793,
    49, 95
Tulloch, Francis, FC's companion
    on crossing to America,
    120, 122, 129–30
Tunis, 122
Turenne, Henri-Amélie-
    Mercure, Comte de,
    1776–1852, First Chamber-
    lain to Napoleon, 287
Turenne, Henri de la Tour
    d'Auvergne, Vicomte de,
    Marshal of France, 1611–75,
    41, 58, 257, 320

Ulysses, 142, 278

Valentine, footman, 119
Vallée-aux-Loups, 5, 9,
    54, 65, 229, 230,
    346, 373
Valognes, 233

Vancouver, George, c. 1758–98,
    English sailor, 135
Varennes, 154
Vatican, 353
Vauban, Sébastien Le Prestre de,
    1633–1707, military
    engineer and Marshal of
    France, 320
Vaudreuil, Mme de, 108
Vaugirard, 322
Vauvert, Michel Bossinot de,
    1724–1809, uncle by
    marriage of FC, 162
Velléda* (FC), 56
Velly, Abbé Paul-François,
    1709–59, Jesuit
    historian, 141
Venice, 278
Verdun, 177
Verona, Congress of, 1822, 327
Versailles, 77, 88, 90, 93, 100,
    101, 173, 208
Vescovato, 342
Viasma, 242, 253
Vibicki, Senator, of the Diet of
    Warsaw, 238
Vicence, Duc de, see
    Caulaincourt
Vichy, 225
Victor (Victor Perrin), 1766–1841,
    Duc de Bellone, Marshal of
    France, 271
Vienna, 54, 262, 264,
    281, 283
Vienna, Congress of, 1814–15,
    279, 283, 340
Viganoni, Italian singer at the
    Opera-Buffa, Paris, 108
Vignali, Abbé, chaplain at
    St Helena, 313
Villedeneu, Demoiselles, 20
Villejuif, 264

Villèle, Joseph, Comte de,
    1773–1854, 75, 94, 327,
    329, 330, 333
Villeneuve, La, 10, 11
Villeneuve, La (Claude-Modeste-
    Thérèse Leux), 17, 18, 24,
    25, 28, 71, 72, 119
Villeneuve, Pierre, sailor, 119, 120
Villeneuve-sur-Yonne, 205, 223,
    225, 226
Vilna, 238
Vincennes, 217, 219, 221, 260,
    308, 322
Vinkovo, 253
Violet, scullion and dancing-
    master, 139, 140
Vire, 209
Virgil, 71–19 BC, poet, 12, 66,
    125, 276–7, 354
Virginia, 259
Virginie, servant of Lucile, 225
Vitebsk, 243
Vitellius, Aulus, 15–69, Roman
    Emperor, 102
Vitry, 258
Volga, River, 243
Voltaire (François-Marie-
    Arouet), 1694–1778, poet,
    dramatist, philosopher,
    75, 210

Waldeck, Christian-August,
    Prince of, 1744–99,
    commander of the Austrian
    corps in the Army of the
    Princes, 174, 176, 176–7
Wales, Caroline of Brunswick-
    Wolfenbüttel, Princess of,
    1768–1821, 199
Wales, Prince of, see George IV
Walewska, Countess Marie,
    1789–1817, 278

Walewski, Alexandre, Comte de, 1810–68, illegitimate son of above and Napoleon I, Foreign Minister under Napoleon III, 278

Washington, George, 1732–99, President of the American Re public 1789–97, 111, 128, 132, 133, 133–4, 210, 292, 324, 376

Waterloo, Battle of, 1815, 257, 284, 286, 288, 295, 297, 316, 324, 342

Wellington, Arthur Wellesley, Duke of, 1769–1852, 117, 185, 284, 286, 287, 288, 295, 319

Westminster Abbey, London, 181, 182

Westphalia, Treaty of, 1648, 300

Wignacourt, Antoine-Louis, Marquis de, Lieutenant-

Colonel of the Conti Regiment, 38

Wilkowiski, 236

William I, the Conqueror, 1027–87, King of England 1066–87, 237–8

Wilson, General Robert, 1779–1849, 295

Wolfe, James, 1727–59, the conqueror of Quebec, killed in the victorious battle with Montcalm for that city, 143

Ximena, character in the Spanish *Romanceros*, 150

Yarmouth, 185

York, Frederick, Duke of, 1763–1827, 184

Zephyr, brig, 280

Zürich, Battle of, 1799, 304

THE STORY OF PENGUIN CLASSICS

Before 1946 ... 'Classics' are mainly the domain of academics and students; readable editions for everyone else are almost unheard of. This all changes when a little-known classicist, E. V. Rieu, presents Penguin founder Allen Lane with the translation of Homer's *Odyssey* that he has been working on in his spare time.

1946 Penguin Classics debuts with *The Odyssey*, which promptly sells three million copies. Suddenly, classics are no longer for the privileged few.

1950s Rieu, now series editor, turns to professional writers for the best modern, readable translations, including Dorothy L. Sayers's *Inferno* and Robert Graves's unexpurgated *Twelve Caesars*.

1960s The Classics are given the distinctive black covers that have remained a constant throughout the life of the series. Rieu retires in 1964, hailing the Penguin Classics list as 'the greatest educative force of the twentieth century.'

1970s A new generation of translators swells the Penguin Classics ranks, introducing readers of English to classics of world literature from more than twenty languages. The list grows to encompass more history, philosophy, science, religion and politics.

1980s The Penguin American Library launches with titles such as *Uncle Tom's Cabin*, and joins forces with Penguin Classics to provide the most comprehensive library of world literature available from any paperback publisher.

1990s The launch of Penguin Audiobooks brings the classics to a listening audience for the first time, and in 1999 the worldwide launch of the Penguin Classics website extends their reach to the global online community.

The 21st Century Penguin Classics are completely redesigned for the first time in nearly twenty years. This world-famous series now consists of more than 1300 titles, making the widest range of the best books ever written available to millions – and constantly redefining what makes a 'classic'.

The Odyssey continues ...

The best books ever written

PENGUIN 🐧 CLASSICS

SINCE 1946

Find out more at www.penguinclassics.com